WASHED IN THE SPIRIT
TOWARD A PENTECOSTAL THEOLOGY OF WATER BAPTISM

Washed in the Spirit

Toward a Pentecostal Theology of Water Baptism

Andrew Ray Williams

CPT Press
Cleveland, Tennessee

Washed in the Spirit
Toward A Pentecostal Theology of Water Baptism

Published by CPT Press
900 Walker ST NE
Cleveland, TN 37311
USA
email: cptpress@pentecostaltheology.org
website: www.cptpress.com

Library of Congress Control Number: 2021942405

ISBN-13: 9781953358059

Copyright © 2021 CPT Press

All rights reserved. No part of this book may be reproduced or translated in any form, by print, photoprint, microfilm, microfiche, electronic database, internet database, or any other means without written permission from the publisher.

DEDICATION
To Anna, for your incredible love and support

Contents

Preface xii
Abbreviations xiii

Chapter 1
Introduction 1
  Research Context and Focus 1
  Limits of the Investigation 5
  Methodology 5
  Structure and Flow of the Argument 5

Chapter 2
Approaching Methodology: Surveying and Integrating the Methodological Strands 8
  Introduction 8
  Contemporary Pentecostal Theological Methods 9
  Major Scholarly Voices 9
    Simon Chan: The Ecumenical Approach 11
    John Christopher Thomas: The Revisioning Approach 15
    Mark Cartledge: The Empirical Approach 20
    Chris Green: The Integrative Approach 24
  A Pentecostal Programmatic Approach 27

Chapter 3
Classical Pentecostal Denominations and Water Baptism: The Foursquare Church 31
  Introduction 31
  Hearing Early Pentecostal Ordinary Theology 32
    The Bridal Call (1917-1923) 33
    The Bridal Call Foursquare (1923-1934) 43
    Hearing Early Pentecostal Ordinary Theology: Conclusions ... 50
  Hearing Official Denominational Statements 52
    The Foursquare Declaration of Faith 52
    Foursquare Licensing Process Guide 52
    Hearing Official Denominational Statements: Conclusions .. 55
  Hearing Foursquare Scholarly Voices 55
    Guy Duffield and N.M. Van Cleave 56
    Kyle W. Bauer 57
    Hearing Foursquare Scholarly Voices: Conclusions 60

viii *Washed in the Spirit*

Empiricizing Pentecostalism: Contemporary Foursquare
Ordinary Theology.. 61
   Fieldwork Technique 62
   New Life Church 66
   Participant Observation: The Baptismal Service 66
   Interviews... 71
   Secondary Literature.. 80
   Empiricizing Pentecostalism: Conclusions............................... 81
Water Baptism in the Foursquare Church: Conclusions 82

Chapter 4
Classical Pentecostal Denominations and Water Baptism: International Pentecostal Holiness Church................................. 84
   Introduction 84
   Hearing Early IPHC Ordinary Theology 85
      The Pentecostal Holiness Advocate (1917-1926)................ 85
      Hearing Early IPHC Ordinary Theology: Conclusions....... 99
   Hearing Official Denominational Statements 100
      IPHC Constitution Disciplines and Manuals..................... 100
      Hearing Official Denominational Statements:
      Conclusions 104
   Hearing IPHC Scholarly Voices 104
      J.H. King.. 104
      Noel Brooks 107
      Paul Beacham 109
      Harold D. Hunter... 111
      Terry Tramel.. 112
      Frank G. Tunstall.. 112
      A.D. Beacham, Jr... 113
      Hearing IPHC Scholarly Voices: Conclusions.................... 113
   Empiricizing Pentecostalism: Contemporary IPHC
   Ordinary Theology... 114
      Faith Assembly.. 115
      Participant Observation: The Baptismal Service 115
      Interviews... 119
      Secondary Literature... 127
      Empiricizing Pentecostalism: Conclusions......................... 127
   Water Baptism in The International Pentecostal Holiness
   Church: Conclusions 129

Chapter 5
Classical Pentecostal Denominations and Water Baptism: Pentecostal Assemblies of the World 131
Introduction..........131
Hearing Early PAW Ordinary Theology..........132
The Christian Outlook (1923-1932)..........132
Hearing Early PAW Ordinary Theology: Conclusions..........147
Hearing Official Denominational Statements and
Scholarly Voices..........149
PAW Statement of Faith..........149
G.T. Haywood..........150
Francis Leonard Smith..........152
Hearing Official Denominational Statements and Scholarly
Voices: Conclusions..........153
Empiricizing Pentecostalism: Contemporary PAW
Ordinary Theology..........153
New Horizons Fellowship..........155
Participant Observation..........155
Interviews..........158
Secondary Literature..........166
Empiricizing Pentecostalism: Conclusions..........167
Water Baptism in the Pentecostal Assemblies of the World:
Conclusions..........168

Chapter 6
Water Baptism in the Church's Scripture 170
Introduction..........170
A Distinctly Pentecostal Reading..........174
Reading Strategy..........175
'Buried in Baptism': Romans 6.1-11..........176
Introduction: Romans 6.1-11..........176
The Interpretive Framework: Literary Context and
Outline..........177
History of Interpretation..........178
Introduction..........178
The Period of Formulation (1917-1929)..........180
The Period of Entrenchment and Adaption
(1929-1967)..........181
The Period of Challenge (1967-1984)..........183
The Period of Reformulation (1984-Present)..........185

    Conclusions 189
    The Contemporary Dialogue 189
  'United with Him' 190
    Baptism as Crucifixion and Death 190
    Baptism as Burial 192
    Baptism as Resurrection 195
    Conclusions 197
Repentance, Water Baptism, and the Spirit: Acts 2.37-40 198
  Introduction: Acts 2.37-40 199
  The Interpretive Framework: Literary Context and
  Outline 199
  History of Interpretation 200
    Introduction 200
    The Period of Formulation (1917-1929) 201
    The Period of Entrenchment and Adaption
    (1929-1967) 203
    The Period of Challenge (1967-1984) 204
    The Period of Reformulation (1984-Present) 206
    Conclusions 211
    The Contemporary Dialogue 212
  'Brothers, What Should We Do?' 213
    Baptism and Repentance 213
    Baptized in the Name of Jesus 217
    Baptism and the Forgiveness of Sin 219
    Baptism and the Reception of the Spirit 222
    Conclusions 224
Water Baptism in the Church's Scripture: Conclusions 225

Chapter 7
Washed in the Spirit: Toward a Pentecostal Theology of Water Baptism 226
  Research Context and Focus 226
  The Role of Pentecostal Theology and the Responsibility
  of the Pentecostal Theologian 229
  The Spirit of Baptism 232
    Pentecostalism, Baptism(s), and Acts 232
    Re-reading the Evidence: Dialoguing with Sarah Hinlicky
    Wilson 234
    A Forgotten Paradigm: Jesus' Baptism as Archetype 237
  Spirit Baptism as the Release of the Spirit of Baptism 244

    Spirit Baptism: The Conception/Experience Distinction ...244
    Spirit Baptism: Exploring Terminology 250
    Subsequent Experiences: Loosing the Spirit 253
  The Baptizing God (Theology Proper) 256
  The Baptized Church (Ecclesiology) 262
  The Baptized Cosmos (Eschatology) 268
  Conclusion 271

Chapter 8
Conclusion 273
  Contributions 273
  Practical and Ecclesiological Implications 275
    Baptismal Practice 275
    Baptismal Liturgy 278
    Baptismal Context 281
  Suggestions for Further Research 282

Bibliography 284
Index of Biblical (and Other Ancient) References 295
Index of Authors 298

Preface

This monograph is a slightly revised edition of my PhD thesis completed at Bangor University, Wales, UK. I want to thank CPT Press for their hard work on this publication. It is truly a privilege to have my monograph listed alongside many groundbreaking works. I want to also thank Dr. Chris E.W. Green, my *doktorvater*, for his outstanding guidance and mentoring throughout the process.

There are many others who have offered support and encouragement in the writing of this monograph. First and foremost, I must thank Anna, my wife, for her patience, encouragement, and love. I want also to thank my two incredible daughters, Adelaide and Audrey. Over the past few years, my family has made sacrifices to enable me to devote myself to this work, and they did so lovingly, cheering me on along the way. I would also like to thank the rest of my family members who, in many ways, expressed confidence, support, and reassurance throughout the last few years.

I would like to acknowledge my church, Family Worship Center, for their loyalty and love. I want to express my thanks to Linda Henshaw for her assistance in reading through various early periodical sources, ensuring that I did not miss any vital material. Thank you to my friends and colleagues at the Centre for Pentecostal Theology for their inspiration and perceptive feedback on early drafts. I would like to thank Dr. David Bradnick for his friendship and encouragement throughout the writing of this monograph. Finally, I would like to recognize my friend, Dr. Rick Wadholm, Jr., for his editorial feedback in the final stages of this project.

ABBREVIATIONS

Early Pentecostal Periodicals
BC	*The Bridal Call*
BCF	*The Bridal Call Foursquare*
PHA	*The Pentecostal Holiness Advocate*
TCO	*The Christian Outlook*

Other
AJPS	*Asian Journal of Pentecostal Studies*
CHP	Robeck, C.M. Jr. and Amos Yong (eds.), *The Cambridge Handbook to Pentecostalism* (New York: Cambridge University Press, 2014).
CJPCR	*Cyberjournal for Pentecostal-Charismatic Research*
Dialog	*Dialog: A Journal of Theology*
DPCM	Burgess, S.M., *et al.* (eds.), *Dictionary of Pentecostal and Charismatic Movements* (Grand Rapids: Zondervan, 1988).
DTIB	Vanhoozer, K.J. (ed.), *Dictionary for Theological Interpretation of the Bible* (Grand Rapids: Baker Academic, 2005).
ER	*The Ecumenical Review*
HTR	*The Harvard Theological Review*
IJST	*International Journal of Systematic Theology*
JB&V	*Journal of Beliefs & Values*
JEPTA	*Journal of European Pentecostal Theological Association*
JES	*Journal of Ecumenical Studies*
JET	*Journal of Empirical Theology*
JPT	*Journal of Pentecostal Theology*
JPTSup	Journal of Pentecostal Theology Supplement
OHST	Boersma, H. and Matthew Levering, *The Oxford Handbook of Sacramental Theology* (Oxford: Oxford University Press, 2015).
PE	*Pro Ecclesia: A Journal of Catholic and Evangelical Theology*
Pneuma	*Pneuma: The Journal of the Society for Pentecostal Studies*
RHPT	Vondey, W. (ed.), *The Routledge Handbook of Pentecostal Theology* (London/New York: Routledge, 2020).
SJT	*Scottish Journal of Theology*
SVS	St Vladimir's Seminary Press

1

INTRODUCTION

A. Research Context and Focus

As Pentecostal theology comes of age, Pentecostal sacramentality calls for fuller and more discerning treatment. As Frank Macchia has noted, 'much theological work is still needed in the area of sacraments'.[1] In response, this project will seek to construct a distinctly Pentecostal theology of water baptism explicitly concerned with renewing Pentecostal teaching and practice, as well as ecumenical engagement.[2] To support this aim, this section will provide a foundation upon which to build. This research explores the relationship between the experience of Spirit baptism, the practice of footwashing, and the ministry of the church in relation to the event of water baptism, making clear the need for a robust Pentecostal theology of water baptism, and one that works outside the limits of the abbreviated or unstated theologies of water baptism that have shaped so much Pentecostal teaching and practice, as well as ecumenical engagement.

---

[1] Frank D. Macchia, 'Is Footwashing the Neglected Sacrament? A Theological Response to John Christopher Thomas' *Pneuma* 19.2 (1997), pp. 239-49 (249).

[2] A central conviction of this project is the inseparable relationship between Pentecostal theology and spirituality. Building on Steven Land's work, this project presupposes the 'integration of narrative beliefs and practices in the affections'. Steven Jack Land, *Pentecostal Spirituality: A Passion for the Kingdom* (Cleveland, TN: CPT Press, 2010), p. 14. Further, agreeing with K.M. Ranaghan, for Pentecostals 'worship has provided the vehicle for theology. One can say further and maintain that the theology has served basically as a commentary on the worship which has always been the central reality'. K.M. Ranaghan, 'Rites of Initiation in Representative Pentecostal Churches in the United States, 1901-1972' (PhD dissertation, University of Notre Dame, 1974).

Perhaps one of the reasons Pentecostalism has struggled to develop an adequate theology of water baptism is its complicated and often perplexing relationship with the 'crown jewel'[3] of Pentecostal theology – Spirit baptism. Traditionally articulated, water baptism and Spirit baptism have been understood as two unrelated events.[4] Nonetheless, the recent re-examination of the Pentecostal doctrine of Spirit baptism carries a new opportunity to bring clarity to the relationship between these two baptisms. As Shane Clifton has said, 'The traditional Pentecostal doctrine of baptism in the Spirit ... is coming under increasing pressure'.[5] This pressure has led Pentecostal scholars such as Andrew Gabriel, Frank Macchia, Simon Chan, and others to respond with various proposals.[6] This ongoing revisioning

---

[3] Frank D. Macchia, 'The Kingdom and the Power: Spirit Baptism in Ecumenical and Pentecostal Perspective' in Michael Welker (ed.), *The Work of the Spirit*, (Grand Rapids, MI: Eerdmans, 2006), p. 110.

[4] As 'renewal' theologian J. Rodman Williams put it, 'They (Spirit baptism and water baptism) are not two sides of the same event; nor does the former (water baptism) bring about the latter (Spirit baptism). The water baptism with all it represents was preparation and background but not the cause of the descent of the Spirit.' See Williams, *Renewal Theology: Salvation, the Holy Spirit and Christian Living*, (Grand Rapids, MI: Academic, 1990), p. 169. Howard Ervin argues for the classical Pentecostal position when stating that 'regeneration' is 'a prior condition to their baptism in water. After water-baptism ... baptism in the Spirit follows'. See Howard Ervin, *Spirit Baptism: A Biblical Investigation* (Peabody, MA: Hendrickson, 1987), p. 80. Conversely, Frank Macchia admits to 'a special relationship exist(ing) between water and Spirit baptism'. Nevertheless, he states that it is his 'conviction that that Spirit baptism as the eschatological gift of the Spirit transcends the water rite'. See Frank Macchia, *Baptized in the Spirit: A Global Pentecostal Theology* (Grand Rapids, MI: Zondervan, 2006), pp. 248-49.

[5] Shane Clifton, 'The Spirit and Doctrinal Development: A Functional Analysis of the Traditional Pentecostal Doctrine of the Baptism in the Holy Spirit', *Pneuma* 29.1 (2007), pp. 5-23 (5).

[6] Gabriel has suggested that any experience of Spirit-filling is subsequent to previous experiences of the reception of the Holy Spirit since we live in a Spirit-filled world. Therefore, these experiences of being filled by the Spirit (and Spirit baptism in particular) may be expressed with the metaphor of the intensity of the Spirit. See Andrew K. Gabriel, 'The Intensity of the Spirit in a Spirit-Filled World: Spirit Baptism, Subsequence, and the Spirit of Creation', *Pneuma* 34.3 (2012), pp. 365-82 (366). In another proposal, Macchia attempts to expand the boundaries of Spirit baptism to include applications to the whole of the Christian life, looking forward to God's eventual cosmic presence. See Macchia, *Baptized in the Spirit*, pp. 61-85. Simon Chan has suggested 'a sacramental view of Spirit-baptism may be more useful in clarifying the nature of the Pentecostal reality'. See Simon Chan, *Pentecostal Theology and the Christian Spiritual Tradition* (Eugene, OR: Wipf and Stock, 2011), p. 54. Though none of these scholars spend a considerable time discussing what this revisioning of Spirit baptism means for water baptism, the implications are apparent.

of Spirit baptism gives greater opportunity for Pentecostals to respond to Cecil Robeck's and Jerry Sandidge's lament that Pentecostals have 'done little serious theological reflection on baptism' by investigating the meaning of water baptism as a sacrament.[7]

Further, it is also significant for this study that Pentecostalism has historically placed a heavy emphasis on footwashing. Within contemporary scholarship, John Christopher Thomas has led the way in his work on footwashing.[8] Drawing on Thomas' research, both Frank Macchia and Lisa Stephenson have followed with significant contributions.[9] Most notably for this project, Macchia has suggested that the sacrament of footwashing can serve as a link between baptism and eucharist.[10] While water baptism establishes one in the church and sends one out from it missionally, believers return to have their feet washed in preparation of partaking in the eucharist. In this way, footwashing serves as a purgative act. Of course, this connection between footwashing and water baptism has yet to be fully developed, but the proposal has obvious promise both for Pentecostals and for the larger Christian tradition.[11]

Lastly, any theology of water baptism must be understood within the larger context of the study of the church and her ministry, for as Simon Chan has expressed, the way that the church becomes 'the people of God, the body of Christ and the temple of the Spirit' is through 'the church's worship'.[12] In other words, 'the church's most

---

[7] Cecil M. Robeck, Jr. and Jerry L. Sandidge, 'The Ecclesiology of *Koinonia* and Baptism: A Pentecostal Perspective', *JES* 27.3 (1990), pp. 504-34

[8] See John Christopher Thomas, 'Footwashing Within the Context of the Lord's Supper' in Dale R. Staffer (ed.), *The Lord's Supper: Believers' Church Perspectives* (Scottsdale, PA: Herald Press, 1997), pp. 169-84 (171-74); John Christopher Thomas, *Footwashing in John 13 and the Johannine Community* (Cleveland, TN: CPT Press, 2nd edn, 2014).

[9] See Macchia, 'Is Footwashing the Neglected Sacrament?', pp. 239-49; Lisa Stephenson, 'Getting Our Feet Wet: The Politics of Footwashing', *JPT* 23.2 (2014), pp. 154-70.

[10] Macchia, 'Is Footwashing the Neglected Sacrament?', p. 248.

[11] Kenneth Archer and Andrew Hamilton have noted footwashing's ecumenical potentials by stating that it is 'able to be shared among the various traditions of Christianity bringing them together in the ministry of our Lord Jesus'. See Kenneth J. Archer and Andrew S. Hamilton, 'Anabaptism-Pietism and Pentecostalism: Scandalous Partners in Protest', *SJT* 63.2 (2010), pp. 185-202 (202).

[12] Simon Chan, *Liturgical Theology: The Church as Worshiping Community* (IVP Academic: Downers Grove, IL, 2006), p. 40. Thus, while this project will have ecclesiological concerns, it will *also* be concerned with the doctrine of God and eschatology, speaking to God's agency, the church's vocation, and the eschatological

basic identity is to be found in its act of worship', and when we participate in the sacraments, we 'become the Body of Christ'.[13] Significantly for this project, Mark Cartledge has asserted that within Pentecostal ecclesiology 'where there is a problem it is often over the subject of baptism, or paedobaptism (infant baptism), to be precise'.[14] One might consider that this problem has less to do with a debate over who should be the recipient of baptism and more to do with the ambiguity surrounding the location of water baptism within the church and her ministry. In a discussion on Pentecostal ecclesiology, John Christopher Thomas has noted Pentecostalism's uncertainty surrounding the place the sacraments have 'in the community's worship'.[15] According to Chris E.W. Green, Pentecostals must address the present ecclesiological underdevelopment within Pentecostalism, 'not only for the sake of the movement's integrity but also to remain faithful to the call of the gospel'.[16] This call gives greater opportunity to explore the contributions a theology of water baptism might make to Pentecostal ecclesiology.

Thus, a cursory glance at a few emerging issues within Pentecostal theology exposes the great need for a revisioning of water baptism. As Steve Studebaker has pointed out, 'Pentecostals generally have not given a theology of water baptism sustained attention'.[17] Thus, in general, this project will respond to John Christopher Thomas' call for Pentecostal scholars to 'reclaim and appropriate the sacraments for a tradition that has been a bit uncertain about them and their place in the community's worship'.[18] More specifically, this project responds to Chris E.W. Green's invitation for scholars to 'develop a

---

nature of baptism. Rather than esteeming one over the other, this project seeks to allow these concerns to have corresponding consideration.

[13] Chan, Liturgical Theology, p. 42. See also Chan, Pentecostal Ecclesiology, p. 43.

[14] Mark J. Cartledge, 'Renewal Ecclesiology in Empirical Perspective', Pneuma 36.1 (2014), pp. 5-24 (22).

[15] John Christopher Thomas, 'Pentecostal Theology in the Twenty-First Century' Pneuma 20.1 (1998), pp. 3-19 (17).

[16] Chris E. Green, 'The Body of Christ, the Spirit of Communion': Re-Visioning Pentecostal Ecclesiology in Conversation with Robert Jenson', JPT 20 (2011), pp. 15-26 (16).

[17] Steve Studebaker, 'Baptism among Pentecostals' Praxis', in Gordon L. Heath and James D. Dvorak (eds.), Baptism: Historical, Theological, and Pastoral Perspectives (Eugene, OR: Pickwick, 2011), p. 205.

[18] Thomas, 'Pentecostal Theology in the Twenty-First Century', p. 18.

Pentecostal theology of these practices/rites',[19] that is, water baptism, footwashing, and the laying on of hands by anointing oil.

B. Limits of the Investigation

This investigation will be limited to the discussion of water baptism within the framework of North American Pentecostalism, excluding sources that fall outside the applicable linguistic and geographical context. It will also be restricted to classical Pentecostalism in its various forms,[20] thus excluding the wider charismatic movement. I am cognizant that such a division is in some cases impossible to uphold given the 'cross-pollination' that has taken place.[21] Nonetheless, this investigation will be limited to classical English-speaking Pentecostalism as far as it is possible to maintain.

C. Methodology

For this project, laying the methodological groundwork is essential at the onset. Broadly, this project is a work in constructive theology whereby I will converge the contributions of early Pentecostal periodicals, contemporary Pentecostal 'field study' perspectives, scholarly ecumenical and Pentecostal voices, and engagement with key biblical texts to construct a Pentecostal theology of water baptism that is intended to be a foundation for further interaction within the larger ecumenical conversation. Chapter 2 seeks to tease out the specific methodological framework in which this project is grounded.

D. Structure and Flow of the Argument

The argument begins (Chapter 2) by giving the rationale for a fresh, integrative Pentecostal methodology that brings together ecumenical, revisionist, and empirical ways of doing theology.[22] After proposing

---

[19] Chris E.W. Green, *Toward a Pentecostal Theology of the Lord's Supper* (Cleveland, TN: CPT Press, 2012), p. 328.

[20] This includes 'Oneness' (non-trinitarian) Pentecostals.

[21] I have borrowed this term 'cross-pollination' from Chris E.W. Green. See Green, *Toward a Pentecostal Theology of the Lord's Supper*, p. 5 n. 1.

[22] Empirical theology refers to the use of empirical research methods in practical theology developed in Europe and should not be confused with the American version of this designation associated with process theology. Cartledge notes that,

this explorative methodology, I will seek to survey and analyze the chief methodological voices within these three major strands of scholarship. This chapter seeks to give the necessary foundation and groundwork from which to move forward.

In the body of the study (Chapters 3-5), the proposed methodology will engage three classical Pentecostal denominations: one primarily white Finished-Work Pentecostal denomination (The Foursquare Church: Chapter 3), one primarily white Wesleyan-Holiness Pentecostal denomination (International Pentecostal Holiness Church: Chapter 4), and one primarily black Oneness Pentecostal denomination (Pentecostal Assemblies of the World: Chapter 5). These three denominations have been chosen because they characterize a cross-section of English-speaking North American Pentecostalism and are the most prominent denominations in terms of numbers for these cross-sections that have yet to have been sufficiently engaged via a revisionist (reception history) methodology (described in detail in Chapter 2).

In each of these three chapters, I will (1) include a careful reading of the denomination's earliest periodicals looking specifically for references to water baptism;[23] (2) summarize each denominational statement's section on water baptism and engage the denomination's scholarly voices that speak to the subject of water baptism; and (3) include original qualitative studies of present-day Pentecostal water baptisms and lay reflections on water baptism to provide a 'field study' perspective. This 'field study' research strategy will include conducting interviews of Pentecostal believers who have been water baptized and listening for these believer's *implicit* theology of water baptism in addition to their *explicit* statements on the rite and its meaning, while also providing reflections as a 'participant observer'

'it was first categorized as an approach by the practical theology department at Nijmegen University, under the influence of Johannes A. van der Ven. Since the founding of the *Journal of Empirical Theology* in 1988, it has become a well-established approach within practical theology'. See Mark J. Cartledge, 'Practical Theology: Attending to Pneumatologically-Driven Praxis' in Wolfgang Vondey (ed.), *RHPT* (London/New York: Routledge, 2020), p. 166.

[23] A narrower range of material is covered compared to others who have used this model such as Kimberly Ervin Alexander, Larry McQueen, and Chris E.W. Green. See Kimberly E. Alexander, *Pentecostal Healing: Models in Theology and Practice* (JPTSup 29; Blandford Forum, Dorset, UK; Deo, 2006); Larry McQueen, *Toward a Pentecostal Eschatology: Discerning the Way Forward* (JPTSup 39; Blandford Forum, Dorset, UK; Deo, 2012); Green, *Toward a Pentecostal Theology of the Lord's Supper*.

at water baptismal services. Each chapter will conclude by summarizing what each denomination can contribute to the construction of a Pentecostal theology of water baptism.

In Chapter 6, I will include a constructive engagement with select scriptural texts by contributing relevant theological readings of scripture. In Chapter 7, I will move to construct an innovative, ecumenically-sensitive Pentecostal theology of water baptism in dialogue with the previous chapters and in critical conversation with dialogue partners selected from the wider Christian tradition – Protestant, Catholic and Orthodox, historical, and contemporary. Thus, this chapter will aim to offer an original contribution to a Pentecostal theology of water baptism that is intended to be a foundation for further interaction within the larger ecumenical conversation. This study concludes (Chapter 8) with a summary of the general flow of the project while also outlining some contributions and practical implications that have arisen from the study, as well as points of entry into areas for further research.

2

Approaching Methodology: Surveying and Integrating the Methodological Strands

> There is a need for empirical theology as well as speculative and theoretical theology ... My own wish would be to find an honourable place for empirical theology alongside systematic and dogmatic theology so that each could interact with the other. – William Kay.[1]

A. Introduction

To construct a Pentecostal theology of water baptism, this study seeks to approach the subject in a way that is representative of the broader Pentecostal tradition. To that end, this chapter (1) surveys the contemporary methodological approaches to Pentecostal ecclesiology, in general, and the sacraments, in particular,[2] (2) examines the major scholarly voices within those approaches, and (3) articulates an interdisciplinary programmatic approach to the study that integrates and then builds upon the best aspects of the various approaches.[3]

---

[1] William K. Kay, 'Concluding Reflections' in John Christopher Thomas (ed.), *Toward a Pentecostal Ecclesiology: The Church and the Fivefold Gospel*, pp. 283-90 (287-88) (Cleveland, TN: CPT Press, 2010).

[2] As articulated in Chapter 1, this study is situated within the larger dialogue surrounding Pentecostal ecclesiology.

[3] Throughout, I will be using the terms 'method' and 'approach' synonymously.

B. Contemporary Pentecostal Theological Methods

Significantly, in his survey of Pentecostal ecclesiology, Mark Cartledge has identified two existing 'strands' of research – 'ecumenical' and 'retrieval' – while proposing a third which he calls 'empirical'.[4] First, Cartledge defines the ecumenical strand of Pentecostal scholarship as the works that have 'utilized resources beyond their own tradition, sometimes in dialogue with specific bilateral Pentecostal conversations'.[5] The second strand of scholarship, what Cartledge calls the 'retrieval strand' is the work of those Pentecostal scholars who have utilized resources 'within their own tradition'.[6] After surveying the ecclesiological scholarship within these various strands, Cartledge proposes that insights from congregational studies have been absent from the conversation which presents a weakness in Pentecostal ecclesiology.[7] In proposing this third strand of scholarship – the 'empirical strand' – he seeks to move from the abstract to the concrete through empirical data gathering.

For our purposes, Cartledge draws out three distinct methods (ecumenical, retrievalist, and empirical) that Pentecostal scholars have used in constructing Pentecostal ecclesiology. It is significant, then, for my project since water baptism is considered an ecclesiological matter. Cartledge even states 'where there is a problem' in Pentecostal ecclesiology 'it is often over the subject of baptism'.[8] Therefore, Cartledge's categories of ecclesiological method are particularly important and useful for my project yet used *constructively* instead of *descriptively*.

While using these methodological categories can be beneficial in constructing theology, using them descriptively of others' work may prove to be wanting. For instance, while Cartledge designates John Christopher Thomas' work to fit within the 'retrieval strand' of Pentecostal scholarship, Thomas' overall work has not ignored relevant outside resources. Additionally, while Cartledge rightly finds three

---

[4] Cartledge, 'Renewal Ecclesiology in Empirical Perspective', p. 5. As mentioned previously, empirical theology refers to the use of empirical research methods in practical theology developed in Europe and should not be confused with the American version of this designation associated with process theology.
[5] Cartledge, 'Renewal Ecclesiology in Empirical Perspective', p. 7.
[6] Cartledge, 'Renewal Ecclesiology in Empirical Perspective', p. 7.
[7] Cartledge, 'Renewal Ecclesiology in Empirical Perspective', p. 15.
[8] Cartledge, 'Renewal Ecclesiology in Empirical Perspective', p. 22.

broad categories of ecclesiological method among Pentecostal scholars, he does not note that some scholars have utilized more than one method in a single project. For example, in Chris Green's monograph, *Toward a Pentecostal Theology of the Lord's Supper*, he uses the 'retrieval' method by engaging early Pentecostal periodicals, while also making use of the 'ecumenical' method by dialoguing with outside voices within the greater church tradition. Thus, Cartledge's taxonomy is too tight at times accurately to describe every individual's work, even if the categories can make a helpful point about general approaches from which to build upon. It is for this reason that I will be using these categories *constructively* instead of *descriptively*. Thus, I will not be using these categories in an airtight way. In fact, these categories will be used in quite different ways than they have been used previously.

Another limitation of Cartledge's taxonomies is the language of 'retrieval'. I wonder whether the language of 'retrieval' accurately captures the essence of this broad methodology. Since this approach to Pentecostal scholarship seeks to hear *and* discern early Pentecostal voices in the service of 'revisioning' Pentecostal theology, I consider 'revisioning' language to better describe the movement than 'retrieval' language. To say the same thing another way, because this comprehensive approach seeks not only to retrieve early Pentecostal thought, but rather intentionally to *hear* early Pentecostal testimony and *discern* its potential contributions towards the revisioning of Pentecostal theology, 'revisioning' language will be used in lieu of 'retrieval' language.[9]

I contend that putting these three methods into dialogue with one another, alongside serious engagement with the biblical text, can help forge a fresh and integrative approach to Pentecostal theology. And while it may seem to some at first glance that this integrative proposal is merely a piecemealing of various present approaches, it will soon become clear that I am in fact offering a distinct methodological approach, because of the synthesis of these various methods effects a new configuration.[10] However, before moving into a proposal on

---

[9] Further, 'revisioning' language is original to the movement itself. See Land, *Pentecostal Spirituality*.

[10] I am aware that my approach might seem as if I am simply including multiple strategies instead of developing a new one. And while it is true that I am using

how to integrate these methodologies coherently and allow them to converge, we must first summarize and analyze some major voices who utilize such approaches in *some* of their work. Therefore, in the following section, I will move to engage through a summary and evaluation of the major voices utilizing the methodologies noted by Cartledge.

C. Major Scholarly Voices

To lay a framework for the methodology I will employ, I will dialogue with methodological voices that have worked within the same theological location. Since my project is situated within the broader topic of Pentecostal ecclesiology, I will exclude scholars working outside Pentecostal ecclesiological concerns. Thus, I will survey the major Pentecostal *ecclesiological* voices and address *how* they have formulated Pentecostal ecclesiology. While there are certainly many scholars worthy of engagement, I have limited my engagement to four scholars whose methodological and constructive work most resembles my intended project. Thus, I have chosen to engage (1) Simon Chan (ecumenical approach), (2) John Christopher Thomas (revisionist approach), and (3) Mark Cartledge (empirical approach) as the representatives of the major approaches. After engaging these three voices, which represent the major ways Pentecostal theologians have constructed ecclesiology, I will then propose that the logic for an integrative approach has already been laid in the work of Chris E.W. Green. This survey will aim to expose the strengths of the way Pentecostal scholars have approached ecclesiological concerns while also exposing the need for a holistic Pentecostal methodology that integrates all three approaches with the unique contributions of Green's work, all into one project. Following this survey, I will articulate *how* my project will utilize such an approach.

C.1 Simon Chan: The Ecumenical Approach

In Cartledge's assessment, Simon Chan serves as a major example of a Pentecostal scholar who engages in the 'wider conversation' of ecclesiology, but 'does not cut loose from the pentecostal tradition'.[11]

---

multiple methods, I am using these methods together in different ways than they have been used previously, thus creating a fresh approach.

[11] Cartledge, 'Renewal Ecclesiology in Empirical Perspective', p. 9.

Chan, then, is a model representative of those scholars whose work would fit within the 'ecumenical' strand. His work has also focused heavily upon Pentecostal ecclesiological matters. Overall, his work is broadly concerned with Pentecostals experiencing 'genuine traditioning' and an ecclesiology that supports such an effort.[12] Therefore, the following survey sets out to summarize one way of reading Chan's work on Pentecostal ecclesiology while also paying particular attention to how he engages such matters.

For Chan, Pentecostals ought to reexamine their ecclesiological framework by considering dialogue with sacramental traditions.[13] This engagement is especially fitting, since Pentecostalism's emphasis on experiences of Spirit baptism and glossolalia brings together both the ascetical and contemplative dimensions of the Christian community. Pentecostals, then, need to understand themselves as situated within the larger Christian spiritual tradition. His approach is thoroughly dialogical, and above all seeks to mine ecumenical resources that have enough affinity with Pentecostal spirituality to integrate without much difficulty, while also being divergent enough to bring about needed reform.

In his initial contribution to Pentecostal ecclesiology, Chan uses the metaphor of 'mother' for the church and understands the church as 'God's doing' and not merely a social construct as some Pentecostals might hold.[14] He moves then to discuss pneumatology in light of ecclesiology, calling for Pentecostals to adopt ecclesial pneumatology rather than one that is 'individualistic'.[15] In this work, Chan draws upon Catholic (Kilian McDonnell), Orthodox (John Zizioulas), and Protestant (Robert Jenson) sources to support his ecclesiological proposals. Therefore, from the start, Chan's ecclesiological method is largely dependent upon 'outside' dialogue partners.

In a later work, Chan calls for a 'radical re-visioning of the church' in hopes that it will 'help Pentecostals to recover a sense of genuine solidarity with all Christians that goes beyond the warm affinities with

---

[12] Simon Chan, *Pentecostal Ecclesiology: An Essay on the Development of Doctrine* (JPTSup 21; Blandford Forum, Deo Publishing, 2011), p. 7.

[13] Chan, *Pentecostal Theology and the Christian Spiritual Tradition*, pp. 37-38.

[14] Simon Chan, 'Mother Church: Toward a Pentecostal Ecclesiology', *Pneuma* 22.2 (2000), pp. 177-208 (178).

[15] Chan, 'Mother Church: Toward a Pentecostal Ecclesiology', p. 180.

fellow-charismatics and fellow-Evangelicals'.[16] In this effort, Chan is not seeking to 're-shape' Pentecostalism into his image, for he believes that theological interaction between Pentecostals and other traditions can aid in developing 'an ecclesiology which makes effective traditioning possible'.[17] For this to happen, Pentecostalism must reject individualistic tendencies and move toward a more robust ecclesiology where the Spirit is understood not just as 'my personal Comforter' but as foremost 'the Spirit for the *church*'.[18] In Chan's estimation, 'Pentecostals can learn much from Eastern Orthodoxy'.[19]

In an even more recent work, Chan commits more space to dialogue with 'older Christian traditions' because 'the evangelical and Protestant umbrellas are too small'.[20] Through these exchanges, he further integrates Pentecostal spirituality with Orthodoxy's ecclesial framework.[21] Chan finds Orthodoxy a useful dialogue partner largely because it shares deep affinity with Pentecostalism, while also being divergent enough for Pentecostals to 'learn from'.[22] Chan observes that both Orthodox and Pentecostal Christians emphasize experience, though Pentecostals articulate these experiences personally while Orthodox Christians articulate these experiences ecclesially. Therefore, Pentecostals can learn from Orthodoxy's 'theology of the church to sustain their practice'.[23]

Chan sees another area of affinity between Orthodoxy and Pentecostalism in the holding together of the Spirit and the church.[24] This pneumatological theme provides an opportunity for Pentecostals to develop their ecclesiology, for it is through the coming of the Spirit to the church 'that the full Trinitarian nature of God is revealed'.[25] In other words, Pentecost is necessary for understanding the 'true nature' of the *ecclesia* as well as the true nature of God. On

---

[16] Chan, *Pentecostal Theology and the Christian Spiritual Tradition*, p. 15. Chan's earlier work 'Mother Church: Toward a Pentecostal Ecclesiology' was reprinted as one of the chapters in this later work.
[17] Chan, *Pentecostal Theology and the Christian Spiritual Tradition*, p. 14.
[18] Chan, *Pentecostal Theology and the Christian Spiritual Tradition*, p. 14. Emphasis original.
[19] Chan, *Pentecostal Theology and the Christian Spiritual Tradition*, p. 14.
[20] Chan, *Pentecostal Ecclesiology*, p. ix.
[21] Chan, *Pentecostal Ecclesiology*, p. ix.
[22] Chan, *Pentecostal Ecclesiology*, p. 9.
[23] Chan, *Pentecostal Ecclesiology*, p. 8.
[24] Chan, *Pentecostal Ecclesiology*, p. 8.
[25] Chan, *Pentecostal Ecclesiology*, p. 8.

this point, he moves to argue for an inseparable link between the Spirit and the church using Orthodox resources and Pentecostal spirituality. He shows that through dialogue with Orthodoxy, one can affirm both creation-centered and church-centered pneumatologies. He concludes, however, that ultimately the Spirit is primarily the Spirit of Christ's body and 'through and in the church, creation finds its ultimate fulfillment'.[26]

Chan also believes that the 'supernaturalness' of Orthodox worship resonates with Pentecostal spirituality.[27] As he sees it, Pentecostalism is known for its emphasis on supernaturalism.[28] The issue that Pentecostals face, though, is the lack of a 'proper ecclesial framework' to support its rich spirituality. Chan believes that this is one way Orthodoxy can assist. While Catholicism emphasizes the church's institutional quality and Protestantism emphasizes the church as a 'sociological phenomenon', Orthodoxy imagines the church as 'the Body of Christ and the temple of the Spirit', which underscores both the institutional and spiritual character of the church.[29] Therefore, Orthodox Christianity not only resonates more with Pentecostal spiritual instincts but also contains elements that can accommodate and sustain Pentecostal spirituality for generations.

Chan also argues that Pentecostalism can learn the value of sacramental worship from Orthodoxy. While Pentecostalism has a strong 'implicit sacramental theology', Pentecostals need to re-think their explicit theology and praxis regarding the sacraments.[30] For Chan, liturgical worship is the most appropriate way of making the implicit sacramental theology explicit.[31] The use of trinitarian language within the liturgy can also help ground Pentecostal ecclesiology to the trinitarian relationship: '*to* the Father, *through* the Son, *in* the Spirit'.[32] While such features are a part of Orthodoxy, Chan admits that the move towards liturgical worship in particular 'cannot appeal to any historical precedent'.[33]

---

[26] Chan, *Pentecostal Ecclesiology*, p. 9.
[27] Chan, *Pentecostal Ecclesiology*, p. 31.
[28] Chan, *Pentecostal Ecclesiology*, p. 30.
[29] Chan, *Pentecostal Ecclesiology*, p. 30.
[30] Chan, *Pentecostal Ecclesiology*, p. 115.
[31] Chan, *Pentecostal Ecclesiology*, p. 120.
[32] Chan, *Pentecostal Ecclesiology*, p. 121.
[33] Chan, *Pentecostal Ecclesiology*, p. 120.

Chan's advocacy for Pentecostals to move towards liturgical worship without prior precedent sheds light on the major, underlying assumption of Chan's ecumenical/dialogical methodology: Pentecostal theology requires reform and outside, ecumenical voices must aid in this reform. This conviction is seen throughout all of Chan's work on ecclesiology. To illustrate this point further, a cursory glance of the footnotes of Chan's published works reveal his overall commitment to this ecumenical method. Chan's consistent use of outside dialogue partners such as (1) Robert Jenson, (2) John Zizioulas, and (3) Sergius Bulgakov further demonstrate this point.[34]

Therefore, in sum, Chan regularly employs an ecumenical methodology that gives outside Christian traditions and dialogue partners room to inform Pentecostal ecclesiology. Chan especially mines Orthodox Christianity in hopes that it can provide a framework for Pentecostals to both express and 'tradition' their spirituality. Quoting Orthodox theologian Nikos Nissiotis, Chan asserts that Orthodox theology has the structure 'to make things work', but it lacks the practitioners to 'put them to work'.[35] He suggests that Pentecostalism has the opposite problem. In the end, Chan submits that perhaps 'pattern makers and practical technicians could learn from one another'.[36] One might consider this proposal of mutual enrichment through ecumenical interchange serves as an explicit expression of Chan's core conviction surrounding theological method. Using Chan's own words, 'developing a Pentecostal ecclesiology does not mean that it has to be built from scratch' for 'much of what Pentecostals needs to recover in ecclesiology can be found within the larger Christian tradition'.[37]

C.2 John Christopher Thomas: The Revisioning Approach

No one working on Pentecostal ecclesiology stands more prominent within this strand of scholarship than John Christopher Thomas. In his 1998 presidential address given to the Society for Pentecostal Studies, Thomas proposed that the Wesleyan-Holiness Pentecostal

---

[34] See also Simon Chan, 'The Church and the Development of Doctrine', *JPT* 13.1 (2004), pp. 57-77 and Simon Chan, 'Jesus as Spirit-Baptizer: Its Significance for Pentecostal Ecclesiology' in John Christopher Thomas (ed.), *Toward a Pentecostal Ecclesiology: The Church and the Fivefold Gospel* (Cleveland, TN: CPT Press, 2010), pp. 139-156.

[35] Chan, *Pentecostal Ecclesiology*, p. 125.

[36] Chan, *Pentecostal Ecclesiology*, p. 125.

[37] Chan, *Pentecostal Ecclesiology*, pp. 7-8.

'five-fold gospel' – Jesus as Savior, Sanctifier, Spirit-Baptizer, Healer, and Coming King – provides a framework for Pentecostal theology in the twenty-first century.[38] He then develops this idea by suggesting that this programmatic could sketch possible Pentecostal ecclesiology utilizing the five-fold gospel themes. As Cartledge notes, years later this proposal was realized at a conference in Bangor, Wales, which papers were published together in an edited volume in 2010.[39]

Thomas' approach to Pentecostal theology is also leaving an imprint on emerging scholars because of his appointment as the Director for the Centre for Pentecostal and Charismatic Studies at Bangor University in Wales (2007-Present). His supervising of doctoral theses through this appointment has led to monographs employing distinctive ways of utilizing resources drawn from the Pentecostal tradition.[40]

Most notably, as mentioned previously, Thomas' major contribution to Pentecostal ecclesiology is his mapping out a proposed method for an area 'within the tradition where theological reflection arguably may be in its infancy'.[41] Thomas wishes Pentecostal ecclesiology to be 'written from the ground up', rather than built upon already-existing Evangelical foundations. Structuring a Pentecostal ecclesiology around the Wesleyan Pentecostal five-fold gospel 'seems like such a natural place to begin' and carries the strong possibility to construct a theology that is 'distinctively Pentecostal' and not just a repetition of Evangelical doctrines.[42] He notes that this paradigm reveals how the Pentecostal tradition is both similar and dissimilar to other traditions. For instance, while the fivefold paradigm finds resonance with the Holiness tradition, it also shows how Pentecostalism is something distinct from Evangelicalism.[43] This proposed framework can help provide a construction 'that is not only *conscious* but

---

[38] Thomas, 'Pentecostal Theology in the Twenty-First Century', pp. 3-19.

[39] John Christopher Thomas (ed.), *Toward a Pentecostal Ecclesiology: The Church and the Fivefold Gospel* (Cleveland, TN: CPT Press, 2010). See Thomas' introduction to the volume on pp. 3-6.

[40] For two examples, see Alexander, *Pentecostal Healing*, pp. 1-260, and McQueen, *Toward a Pentecostal Eschatology*, pp. 1-326. Most notably, under Thomas' supervision, Kimberly Alexander's use of early Pentecostal periodical literature spearheaded a new methodology for Pentecostal scholars that has been gaining much traction, especially among Bangor PhD researchers writing under Thomas' supervision.

[41] Thomas, 'Pentecostal Theology in the Twenty-First Century', p. 17.

[42] Thomas, 'Pentecostal Theology in the Twenty-First Century', p. 17.

[43] Thomas, 'Pentecostal Theology in the Twenty-First Century', p. 17.

intentional about its connection with the movement'.⁴⁴ Therefore, for Thomas, Pentecostal method must mine its own resources to remain distinctly Pentecostal.

Thomas moves to highlight prominent features of his proposal that could be particularly useful for developing Pentecostal ecclesiology. Construction using the fivefold approach would naturally include discussion on the 'nature, mission, and identity of the church' on each of the five elements.⁴⁵ Particularly, Thomas envisions discussions focusing on: 'the church and salvation (or the Church as Redeemed Community), the church and sanctification (or the Church as Holy Community), the church and Spirit baptism (or the Church as Empowered Missionary Community), the church and healing (or the Church as Healing Community), and the church and the return of Christ (or the Church as Eschatological Community)'.⁴⁶ For Thomas, such a method would clarify the relationship between the fivefold gospel and the community life of Pentecostal churches.

Arguably, the most creative component within Thomas' proposal and certainly the most significant for this project is his suggestion that Pentecostals need to rediscover the link between the sacraments and the church in Pentecostal theology. His proposal implores Pentecostals to reconsider the number and nature of the sacraments in Pentecostal worship by linking a 'sign' with an element of the fivefold gospel. Following this line of reasoning, Thomas connects water baptism to salvation, footwashing to sanctification, glossolalia to Spirit baptism, anointing oil to healing, and the Lord's Supper to Soon Coming King.⁴⁷ Notably, Thomas seeks the renewal of Pentecostal theology by beginning within and privileging Pentecostalism's tradition, rather than solely or preeminently looking for resources in other traditions such as those who utilize the ecumenical methodology. For Thomas, this is the way that theological reflection is 'wholly Pentecostal'.⁴⁸

---

⁴⁴ Thomas, 'Pentecostal Theology in the Twenty-First Century', pp. 17-18. My emphasis.
⁴⁵ Thomas, 'Pentecostal Theology in the Twenty-First Century', p. 18.
⁴⁶ Thomas, 'Pentecostal Theology in the Twenty-First Century', p. 18.
⁴⁷ Thomas, 'Pentecostal Theology in the Twenty-First Century', p. 19. See Kenneth J. Archer, 'Nourishment for our Journey: The Pentecostal *Via Salutis* and Sacramental Ordinances', *JPT* 13.1 (2004), pp. 76-96
⁴⁸ Thomas, 'Pentecostal Theology in the Twenty-First Century', p. 19.

Some of Thomas' methodological convictions are also found in his 2014 monograph on footwashing in John 13.[49] In it, Thomas offer 'new exegetical treatment based upon the incorporation of appropriate literary, philological, grammatical, and theological data'.[50] Looking through the lens of the NT, Thomas suggests that for the Johannine community, footwashing was a rite that 'signified the forgiveness of post-conversion sin'.[51] Based on his findings, he also suggests that the practice ought to be considered truly sacramental along with the rites of baptism and eucharist, though they are not 'magical rites', but need to be 'accompanied by faith'.[52] Later building on his earlier work on footwashing, Thomas calls for Pentecostal scholars to develop the sacraments within the context of the five-fold gospel.[53] Significantly, Thomas' work on the subject from a Pentecostal perspective has summoned responses from other Pentecostal scholars.[54]

Lastly, some of Thomas' methodological convictions can also be found in his recent work on anointed cloths.[55] He focuses on one aspect of Pentecostal worship practice that has drawn criticism by outsiders and embarrassment amongst some insiders. To 'contribute to a better understanding of the use of anointed cloths',[56] he first surveys 'the testimonies of this practice found in early Pentecostal periodical literature'.[57] After charting and reflecting on references to this practice in *The Apostolic Faith*,[58] *Bridegroom's Messenger*,[59] *The Latter*

---

[49] John Christopher Thomas, *Footwashing in John 13 and the Johannine Community* (Cleveland, TN: CPT Press, 2nd edn, 2014) which originally appeared in 1991. While Thomas' monograph on footwashing does foreshadow some of his future interests, it is important to note that there are no Pentecostal resources utilized in the original volume, though the topic itself is of relevance to the tradition. Thus, while his scholarly work is done with Pentecostal interests in view, he also engages relevant outside resources.

[50] Thomas, *Footwashing in John 13 and the Johannine Community*, p. 8.

[51] Thomas, *Footwashing in John 13 and the Johannine Community*, p. 180.

[52] Thomas, *Footwashing in John 13 and the Johannine Community*, p. 189.

[53] Thomas, 'Pentecostal Theology in the Twenty-First Century', pp. 3-19.

[54] See Macchia, 'Is Footwashing the Neglected Sacrament?', pp. 239-49; Lisa Stephenson, 'Getting Our Feet Wet', pp. 154-70.

[55] John Christopher Thomas, 'Toward A Pentecostal Theology of Anointed Cloths' in Lee Roy Martin (ed.), *Toward a Pentecostal Theology of Worship* (Cleveland, TN: CPT Press, 2016), pp. 89-112.

[56] Thomas, 'Toward A Pentecostal Theology of Anointed Cloths', p. 112.

[57] Thomas, 'Toward A Pentecostal Theology of Anointed Cloths', p. 89.

[58] Thomas, 'Toward A Pentecostal Theology of Anointed Cloths', p. 90.

[59] Thomas, 'Toward A Pentecostal Theology of Anointed Cloths', p. 90.

Rain Evangel,[60] *The Pentecostal Herald*,[61] *Church of God Evangel*,[62] and *The Bridal Call*,[63] Thomas moves to offer a 'narrative reading' of Acts 19.11-12.[64] Given his concise reading of Acts 19.11-12, Thomas reflects theologically on the reading by engaging a variety of scholarship – Pentecostal and non-Pentecostal. First, he states that these extraordinary miracles attributed to Paul are connected to the larger narrative underscoring the 'powerful presence of God's Spirit' in Luke-Acts.[65] Second, Paul was probably not aware of the circulation of the 'strips of cloth to the sick and possessed'.[66] He concludes that this understanding is 'consistent with the involuntary mediation of Jesus and Peter described before him'.[67] Third, Thomas notes the rich irony in this text contrasting these pieces of cloth resulted in deliverance of the demonic, and in the following text the seven sons of Sceva 'lose their clothing to a demon!'.[68] Lastly, the text exposes that these cloths operated as mediating materials through which the Spirit worked.[69]

Thomas concludes his study on anointed cloths with implications for Pentecostal practice. He states that though anointed cloths were widespread in their utilization within Pentecostal history, little attention has been given to the subject by Pentecostal scholars. He notes that French Arrington as well as Guy P. Duffield and Nathaniel M. Van Cleave's work both give short reflections on the practice.[70] However, outside of these two works, no scholarly Pentecostal work has offered a theological treatment of the subject. Thomas ends by stating that despite the 'misgivings of and embarrassment felt' by scholars, there should be 'no question about the biblical underpinning of

---

[60] Thomas, 'Toward A Pentecostal Theology of Anointed Cloths', pp. 91-92.
[61] Thomas, 'Toward A Pentecostal Theology of Anointed Cloths', p. 91.
[62] Thomas, 'Toward A Pentecostal Theology of Anointed Cloths', pp. 94, 100.
[63] Thomas, 'Toward A Pentecostal Theology of Anointed Cloths', pp. 96-97, 99, 100.
[64] Thomas, 'Toward A Pentecostal Theology of Anointed Cloths', p. 101.
[65] See Thomas, 'Toward A Pentecostal Theology of Anointed Cloths', pp. 104-106 (104).
[66] Thomas, 'Toward A Pentecostal Theology of Anointed Cloths', p. 106.
[67] Thomas, 'Toward A Pentecostal Theology of Anointed Cloths', p. 106.
[68] Thomas, 'Toward A Pentecostal Theology of Anointed Cloths', p. 107.
[69] Thomas, 'Toward A Pentecostal Theology of Anointed Cloths', p. 107.
[70] See French Arrington, *Christian Doctrine: A Pentecostal Perspective Volume Two* (Cleveland, TN: Pathway Press, 1993), p. 258, and Duffield and Van Cleave, *Foundations of Pentecostal Theology*, p. 398.

and support for the use of anointed cloths in worship'.[71] Thomas also suggests that it would be significant for the church to keep an 'intentional focus' on the ones needing prayer rather than on those who are praying for them.[72] This highlights the importance of the community in the practice. As seen in the text of Acts 19, the community is the one who played the primary role in distribution and practice.[73] Most significantly for this project, Thomas pushes the conversation forward by suggesting that anointed cloths be understood sacramentally.[74] Under his five-fold paradigm, he suggests that if anointing with oil functions as the Pentecostal sacramental sign of healing, then 'anointed cloths may well be a physical extension of this primary sign'.[75] This may be of particular use for those who have been separated from the community 'by distance and or infirmity'.[76]

Thomas' work on anointed cloths is an excellent example of the reception history methodology. This approach fits under the broader category of revisionist methodology. And since supervising Kimberly Alexander's project on Pentecostal healing, Thomas has aided in the method's dissemination.[77] Therefore, whether it is working from within a fivefold gospel paradigm or mining early Pentecostal periodicals, Thomas has been the major voice within Pentecostal theology calling scholars to hear untapped Pentecostal resources in order to revision Pentecostal theology into the twenty-first century. Certainly, this is only one aspect of his overall work, but it is arguably one of his most influential.

C.3 Mark Cartledge: The Empirical Approach

Mark Cartledge's work has been instrumental in forging another major approach to Pentecostal ecclesiology, which he terms 'empirical

---

[71] Thomas, 'Toward A Pentecostal Theology of Anointed Cloths', p. 108.
[72] Thomas, 'Toward A Pentecostal Theology of Anointed Cloths', p. 109.
[73] Thomas, 'Toward A Pentecostal Theology of Anointed Cloths', p. 109.
[74] Thomas, 'Toward A Pentecostal Theology of Anointed Cloths', p. 111.
[75] Thomas, 'Toward A Pentecostal Theology of Anointed Cloths', p. 111.
[76] Thomas, 'Toward A Pentecostal Theology of Anointed Cloths', p. 111.
[77] See McQueen, *Toward a Pentecostal Eschatology: Discerning the Way Forward*; Green, *Toward a Pentecostal Theology of the Lord's Supper: Foretasting the Kingdom*; Melissa Archer, *'I Was in the Spirit on the Lord's Day': A Pentecostal Engagement with Worship in the Apocalypse* (CPT Press, Cleveland, TN, 2015); Rick Wadholm, Jr, *A Theology of the Spirit in the Former Prophets: A Pentecostal Perspective* (CPT Press, Cleveland, TN, 2018); David R. Johnson, *Pneumatic Discernment in the Apocalypse: An Intertextual and Pentecostal Exploration* (CPT Press, Cleveland, TN, 2018).

theology'.⁷⁸ In his work on glossolalia, he used both qualitative and quantitative empirical methods from within a theological context to explore its nature and significance.⁷⁹ Cartledge describes this work as marking 'the beginning of a methodological journey' for him.⁸⁰ In a follow-up work entitled *Practical Theology*, Cartledge aims to 'situate the empirical-theological paradigm within a P/C (Pentecostal/Charismatic) theological framework'.⁸¹ He does this by first offering a methodological chapter that considers the connections between practical theology, social sciences, and Pentecostal/Charismatic spirituality.⁸² The second part of the book contains six individual studies on Pentecostal and Charismatic subjects. Notably, for this project, these studies primarily centered on ecclesiological concerns such as worship, liturgy, and spiritual gifts.⁸³

In his chapter on empirical approaches to theology, he describes qualitative and quantitative methods and 'their philosophical traditions' and then moves to give two examples of how he has conducted research using these traditions concerning Pentecostal and Charismatic themes.⁸⁴ First, in describing qualitative research, he states that the overall intention of such research is to 'provide a detailed description of the social contexts under investigation'.⁸⁵ Inexorably researchers move from description to analysis by explaining the contexts of certain 'beliefs, values, and behaviour'.⁸⁶ According to Cartledge, qualitative research focuses on the 'worldviews of the subjects under study' and tends to 'operate with an open and flexible research strategy rather than one which is overly prescriptive from the start'.⁸⁷ As a result, research problems tend to be focused on open and

---

⁷⁸ Cartledge uses 'the term "empirical theology" in the sense used by European scholars, which was established in 1988 with the publication of the *Journal of Empirical Theology*'. Mark Cartledge, *The Mediation of the Spirit: Interventions in Practical Theology* (Grand Rapids, MI: Eerdmans, 2015), p. 22.

⁷⁹ See Mark J. Cartledge, 'The Symbolism of Charismatic Glossolalia', *JET* 12.1 (1999), pp. 37-51; Mark J. Cartledge, *Charismatic Glossolalia: An Empirical Theological Study* (Aldershot: Ashgate, 2002).

⁸⁰ Cartledge, *The Mediation of the Spirit*, p. 23.

⁸¹ Cartledge, *The Mediation of the Spirit*, p. 23.

⁸² Mark Cartledge, *Practical Theology: Charismatic and Empirical Perspectives* (Eugene, OR: Wipf & Stock), p. xv.

⁸³ See Cartledge, *Practical Theology*, pp. 111-215.

⁸⁴ Cartledge, *Practical Theology*, p. 69.

⁸⁵ Cartledge, *Practical Theology*, p. 69.

⁸⁶ Cartledge, *Practical Theology*, p. 70.

⁸⁷ Cartledge, *Practical Theology*, p. 70.

general questions as opposed to firmly defined questions. Cartledge moves to describe major types of qualitative research approaches such as participant observation,[88] interviews,[89] focus groups or group interviews,[90] life histories,[91] oral history,[92] and documentary analysis.[93] Notably, he observes that all of these individual methods can be used 'in distinct qualitative approaches' such as 'grounded theory', 'ethnography', and 'case study'.[94]

Quantitative research, conversely, is similar to research used in the natural sciences that focuses on concepts of 'variables, control, measurement, and experiment'.[95] Individual qualitative methods include surveys,[96] experiments,[97] data mining,[98] and structured observation and interviews.[99] Quantitative research methods differ from qualitative research methods in that quantitative methods are often regarded as more 'scientific or factual' in their approach, while qualitative methods are more 'person-centered and have more in common with the arts'.[100] However, many modern social scientists use both kinds of methods, rejecting the 'polarized views of the past' and forging integrative empirical approaches.[101]

Nonetheless, Cartledge notes that one of the most significant differences between the two approaches lies in each of the respected tradition's presuppositions. In short, quantitative research has embraced positivism. Cartledge defines positivism as 'the belief that the methods and processes of the natural sciences are appropriate to the social sciences'.[102] Further, 'the appreciation that people are different from objects and things in the physical world because they have can have feelings, communicate, create meaning and are uniquely different from one another is not regarded as an obstacle to using the

---

[88] Cartledge, *Practical Theology*, pp. 70-71.
[89] Cartledge, *Practical Theology*, pp. 71-72.
[90] Cartledge, *Practical Theology*, pp. 71-72.
[91] Cartledge, *Practical Theology*, p. 72.
[92] Cartledge, *Practical Theology*, p. 72.
[93] Cartledge, *Practical Theology*, p. 73.
[94] Cartledge, *Practical Theology*, p. 73.
[95] Cartledge, *Practical Theology*, p. 73.
[96] Cartledge, *Practical Theology*, pp. 74-75.
[97] Cartledge, *Practical Theology*, p. 75.
[98] Cartledge, *Practical Theology*, p. 75.
[99] Cartledge, *Practical Theology*, pp. 75-76.
[100] Cartledge, *Practical Theology*, p. 74.
[101] Cartledge, *Practical Theology*, p. 74.
[102] Cartledge, *Practical Theology*, p. 76.

scientific methods'.[103] Qualitative research, conversely, belongs to a different rational construct. Qualitative methods philosophically reject the notion that the scientific method can be used on people since they are not objects. While qualitative approaches attempt to be 'flexible and more responsive to the subject's perspectives', this does not mean it is a 'second-rate approach'.[104] On the contrary, according to Cartledge, qualitative research often provides insights that are 'rich, deep, and meaningful'.[105] This has found true in Cartledge's work, specifically in his use of congregational studies.

In *Testimony in the Spirit,* Cartledge uses congregational studies to give due respect to the grassroots level of theological discourse.[106] The fundamental aim of this particular study was 'to listen to, record, and reflect upon the "ordinary theology" of congregational members in relation to a number of key themes', including discussions on liturgy and the sacraments.[107] Cartledge uses Jeff Astley's definition of ordinary theology as 'the theological beliefs and processes of believing that find expression in the God-talk of those believers who have received no scholarly theological education'.[108] This type of theology is grounded in 'attitudes, values and commitments, experiences and practices of individuals and communities', often described as the religious beliefs of the everyday person.[109] In reflecting back on his use of 'ordinary theology' testimonies and narratives, Cartledge states that he does not believe 'that ordinary theology should be allowed to dictate theological terms' neither does he believe 'academic discourse should set the agenda exclusively'.[110] He believes 'that experimentalist religious discourse should be respected as containing genuine theology'.[111] He admits that he has been at the forefront of arguing for

---

[103] Cartledge, *Practical Theology*, p. 76.
[104] Cartledge, *Practical Theology*, pp. 80-81.
[105] Cartledge, *Practical Theology*, p. 81.
[106] Mark J. Cartledge, 'Pentecostal Experience: An Example of Practical-Theological Rescripting', *JEPTA* 28.1 (2008), pp. 21-33; Mark J. Cartledge, *Testimony in the Spirit: Rescripting Ordinary Pentecostal Theology* (Farnham: Ashgate, 2010).
[107] Cartledge, *Testimony in the Spirit,* Chapter 3 (pp. 48-77).
[108] Jeff Astley and Leslie J. Francis (eds.), *Exploring Ordinary Theology: Everyday Christian Believing and the Church* (Explorations in Practical, Pastoral and Empirical Theology; Farnham: Ashgate, 2013), p. 1.
[109] Cartledge, *Testimony in the Spirit*, p. 34.
[110] Cartledge, *The Mediation of the Spirit*, p. 26.
[111] Cartledge, *The Mediation of the Spirit*, p. 26.

testimony to be considered valid theological discourse.[112] The result is a Pentecostal approach to theology constructed 'from below', and 'rooted in ordinary theological discourse of the ecclesial lifeworld'.[113]

In sum, for this project's purposes, Cartledge's description and use of qualitative research methods such as participant observation and interviews are especially helpful, for, as Cartledge notes, these methods can be properly considered 'field research', which attends to an important aspect of Pentecostal theology: testimony. Therefore, because of its centrality in Pentecostal practice, testimony is 'a legitimate mode of theological discourse that deserves to be explored empirically'.[114] This type of research also gives theologians research into 'concrete expressions of church'.[115] Cartledge notes that it is this aspect of his theology 'that invites further development', specifically his use of 'ordinary theology'.[116] He invites more projects to pay 'attention to the ordinary theology of adherents' which will continue to make a case for 'testimony as a legitimate theological mode'.[117] Therefore, Cartledge's empirical work has been at the forefront of its kind in Pentecostal theology.

C.4 Chris Green: The Integrative Approach[118]

As noted above, while Cartledge rightly finds three broad, existing groupings of ecclesiological method among Pentecostal scholars, he does not note that some scholars have utilized more than one of those specific methodologies together in a single project. While various Pentecostal scholars are using different methods in varying projects, Chris Green's monograph, *Toward a Pentecostal Theology of the Lord's Supper*, utilizes two of Cartledge's broad strands of method in a single project: the 'revisioning' methodology by engaging early Pentecostal periodicals,[119] and the 'ecumenical' methodology by dialoguing with outside voices within the greater church tradition in his

---

[112] Cartledge, *The Mediation of the Spirit*, p. 29.
[113] Cartledge, *Testimony in the Spirit*, p. 222.
[114] Cartledge, *The Mediation of the Spirit*, p. 24.
[115] Cartledge, *The Mediation of the Spirit*, p. 25.
[116] Cartledge, *The Mediation of the Spirit*, p. 25.
[117] Cartledge, *Testimony in the Spirit*, p. 231.
[118] As will become clear, I am not suggesting that Green is the only one to propose an integrative approach. Rather, I am suggesting that Green's work on the Lord's Supper has integrative elements that I will be seeking to follow.
[119] See Chapter 3 in Green, *Toward a Pentecostal Theology of the Lord's Supper*, pp. 72-181.

constructive chapter.[120] Green's work is not the only to do so, for Thomas' work on anointed cloths shows a similar approach.[121] Yet, Green's blending of Pentecostal periodicals, constructive ecumenical resources, and engagement with key biblical texts to aid in his constructive efforts is a particular integrative element that my project will seek to mimic.[122] Therefore, Green's work shows that there is an already-present blending of these methodologies, which will help lay the groundwork for my own constructive proposal. Particularly, I am proposing that the three ecclesiological 'strands' of method that Cartledge identifies, along with Green's engagement with key biblical texts, can complement one another if used together in a single project.

In Green's monograph, he devotes space to survey the scholarly Pentecostal literature surrounding the Lord's Supper. He then moves to include a careful reading of early Pentecostal periodical materials by looking at both Finished-Work and Wesleyan-Holiness streams. In doing this, he aims to 'search out and to sketch the contours of early Pentecostal sacramentality on its own terms'.[123] He then seeks to provide Pentecostal readings of scripture. As Thomas has noted, Pentecostal hermeneutical approaches 'envision an interpretive approach that is not beholden to pre-existing theological grids into which a Pentecostal approach must be force-fitted' and 'are far from the approach of fundamentalism or even the evangelical use of historical criticism'.[124] As Lee Roy Martin puts it, in this interpretive model 'the world within the text takes priority over the world behind the text'.[125] Following this type of approach to scripture, Green devotes a chapter in which he develops his interpretive model that engages the biblical texts that 'rings true to the form of life recognizable to Pentecostals as devotion to the God of the Gospel'.[126] Green then applies his

---

[120] See Chapter 5 in Green, *Toward a Pentecostal Theology of the Lord's Supper*, pp. 243-325.

[121] See Thomas, 'Toward A Pentecostal Theology of Anointed Cloths', pp. 89-112.

[122] See Chapter 4 in Green, *Toward a Pentecostal Theology of the Lord's Supper*, pp. 182-242.

[123] Green, *Toward a Pentecostal Theology of the Lord's Supper*, p. 3.

[124] John Christopher Thomas, '"Where the Spirit Leads" – The Development of Pentecostal Hermeneutics', *JB&V* 30.3 (December 2009), pp. 289–302 (301).

[125] Lee Roy Martin, *The Unheard Voice of God: A Pentecostal Hearing of the Book of Judges* (JPTSup 32; Blandford Forum: Deo Publishing, 2008), p. 14.

[126] Green, *Toward a Pentecostal Theology of the Lord's Supper*, p. 182.

Pentecostal hermeneutical model to three scriptural texts that speak to the 'meaning and purpose of the Eucharist-event'.[127]

After developing a hermeneutical model from which to proceed, Green calls for 'a literary/theological reading of scripture in the context of the worshipping and God-experiencing community, readings that remain sensitive to a text's canonical fit and that takes seriously the history of effects, always remaining focused on how the Spirit uses scripture to transform the community into Christ's ecclesia'.[128] Further, he seeks to draw 'heavily on the text's ... effective history, allowing what the texts have meant to other Christian readers, pre-modern, and contemporary' to shape his reading.[129] These readings are purposed to aid in the development of a Pentecostal theology of the Eucharist that makes sense in light of the 'whole counsel of Scripture'.[130]

From the onset, it should be noted that the influence of Thomas is perceived on Green's project on the Lord's Supper, particularly in his engagement in reception history efforts. However, in his own right, Green has also proven to be an ecumenically inclined Pentecostal theologian, which is reflected both in his monograph on the Lord's Supper as well as other sources.[131] In his constructive chapter, along with bringing Pentecostal scholarly voices, he regularly consults theologians outside the tradition, notably Rowan Williams and Robert Jenson.[132] Nonetheless, his engagement with early Pentecostal literature and Pentecostal readings of selected biblical texts provide the needed Pentecostal resources for his constructive chapter. Particularly, Green's methodology exposes the strength that results when Pentecostal resources are put into dialogue with ecumenical resources. Green effectively situates his project within the larger ecumenical conversation, while also maintaining to be thoroughly Pentecostal in his approach. Therefore, Green's work exposes that there

---

[127] Green, *Toward a Pentecostal Theology of the Lord's Supper*, p. 182.
[128] Green, *Toward a Pentecostal Theology of the Lord's Supper*, pp. 193-94.
[129] Green, *Toward a Pentecostal Theology of the Lord's Supper*, p. 3.
[130] Green, *Toward a Pentecostal Theology of the Lord's Supper*, p. 182.
[131] For one example, see his ecumenical approach in Chris E. Green, '"The Body of Christ, the Spirit of Communion": Re-Visioning Pentecostal Ecclesiology in Conversation with Robert Jenson', *JPT* 20.1 (2011), pp. 15-26.
[132] See Chapter 5 in Green, *Toward a Pentecostal Theology of the Lord's Supper*, pp. 243-325.

is already-present logic for integrating various methods into one project.[133]

D. A Pentecostal Programmatic Approach

As Kenneth Archer has argued, and as we have seen in this survey of scholarly literature, there are distinctive ways of doing Pentecostal theology among theologians.[134] Perhaps, though, it is time for Pentecostal theologians to again ask ourselves, if we were to articulate a Pentecostal approach to theology what might it look like?[135] Along with Archer, I agree that a fresh Pentecostal theological methodology must be thoroughly 'integrative'.[136] However, if an approach is truly going to be integrative, it should not merely respond to correct current approaches deemed to be useful, but rather to complement them.[137] Therefore, in what follows, I will move to articulate a harmonizing methodology that synthesizes contemporary ways of doing theology among Pentecostal scholars, in service to constructing a Pentecostal theology of water baptism that contributes to the greater ecumenical conversation.

Following this explanation of my methodological approach, then, I will include three chapters (Chapters 3-5) that will each focus on a particular denomination: The Foursquare Church (Chapter 3), the International Pentecostal Holiness Church (Chapter 4), and the Pentecostal Assemblies of the World (Chapter 5). These three

---

[133] My study, then, will seek to assimilate all three approaches articulated by Cartledge, Green's scriptural reading approach, along with engagement of denominational statements and scholarly resources to form an integrative *method* in constructing a Pentecostal theology of water baptism. This project certainly integrates, but I am using the methods differently than they have been used before to form one, unique holistic way of constructing theology. Most notably, while empirical qualitative approaches have been utilized by Pentecostal scholars, I am not aware of any work to date that uses qualitative fieldwork findings alongside other approaches to resource a larger *constructive* (rather than descriptive) theological project.

[134] Kenneth Archer, 'A Pentecostal Way of Doing Theology: Method and Manner', *IJST* 9.3 (2007), pp. 301-14 (301).

[135] Mark J. Cartledge, 'Pentecostal Theological Method and Intercultural Theology', *Transformation* 25.2/3 (2008), pp. 92-102 (92).

[136] Cartledge, 'Pentecostal Theological Method and Intercultural Theology', p. 95.

[137] However, this is not to say that these approaches ought to be used the same way they have been. As stated prior, I am using Cartledge's descriptive methodological categories constructively to resource my integrative method.

denominations were intentionally chosen, for together, they characterize a cross-section of Pentecostalism and are the most prominent denominations in terms of numbers for these cross-sections that have yet to be engaged in terms of the 'revisioning' strand of Pentecostal scholarship. Most significantly, these three denominations are varied enough from one another to characterize broadly North American Pentecostalism in all its diversity.[138]

As explained in the previous chapter, in each of these three chapters, I will (1) include a careful reading of the denomination's earliest Pentecostal periodicals looking specifically for references to water baptism, (2) summarize each denominational statement's section on water baptism, and, (3) engage the denomination's scholarly voices that speak to the subject of water baptism. These components will provide the necessary 'revisioning' resources for the whole of the project. Following these sections, I will also include (4) original interviews of present-day Pentecostals who have been water baptized, along with (5) my reflections as a 'participant observer' at a denominational church's water baptismal service.[139] As Cartledge notes, participant observation is often used with other qualitative research methods such as interviews.[140] Together, the interviews and observation reflections will provide a 'field study' perspective with which to also engage.[141] These three field study cases will provide the necessary 'empirical' resources for the whole of the project by utilizing ethnographic/netnographic research methods.[142]

---

[138] For example, The Foursquare Church is a primarily White Finished Work Pentecostal denomination, the International Pentecostal Holiness Church is a primarily White Wesleyan Pentecostal denomination, and the Pentecostal Assemblies of the World is a primarily Black (non-trinitarian) Oneness Pentecostal denomination.

[139] By using participant observation alongside interviews, I avoid testimonies being 'only interpreted in the light of other testimonies'. See Cartledge, *Testimony in the Spirit*, p. 19.

[140] Cartledge, *Practical Theology*, pp. 70-71.

[141] In paying attention to testimony in interviews, this study will respond to Cartledge's call for future work to examine 'more fully the notion of testimony as a legitimate theological mode'. See Cartledge, *Testimony in the Spirit*, p. 190.

[142] For a more detailed explanation of the field study/empirical technique, see Chapter 3 and Chapter 5. In short, in Chapters 3-4, I am conducting ethnographic research, utilizing participant observation and informal interviews. As Cartledge states, 'ethnography describes and interprets cultural and social settings primarily using participant observation, informal interviews, and extended time in the field'. (Cartledge, *Practical Theology*, p. 73). In the case of Chapter 5, I will be conducting virtual ethnography or 'netnography', due to the coronavirus pandemic at time of

Therefore, my approach will specifically explore (1) the 'ordinary theology' of *early* Pentecostals, (2) the 'ordinary theology' of *contemporary* Pentecostals in particular churches, and (3) how that triangulates with official denominational statements and scholarly denominational voices about water baptism.[143] This triangulation will explore whether or not theological denominational statements reflect the 'on the ground' perspectives of those who belong to the denomination – both early and contemporary. Finally, each of these three chapters will conclude by summarizing what each denomination can contribute to the construction of a Pentecostal theology of water baptism. These findings will provide the essential Pentecostal perspectives in moving towards a constructive account that is innovative in a way that holds promise for renewal of Pentecostal teaching and practice, and for ecumenical engagement.

Following these three chapters (Chapters 3-5), I will include a constructive theological engagement with scriptural texts (Chapter 6). By contributing theological readings of scripture, I hope to contribute a model for how Pentecostals can read water baptismal texts while also aiding in the development of a move towards thinking deeply about what a Pentecostal theology of water baptism might look like. My selection of biblical texts will directly relate to my revisioning and empirical work in Chapters 3-5 by choosing to work with scriptural texts that are frequently referenced by early Pentecostals and subsequently discussed with contemporary Pentecostals in my qualitative research.

Following the initial constructive work (Chapters 6), I will move to address what a distinctly Pentecostal theology of water baptism might look like (Chapter 7). This chapter will seek to develop a

---

research. Therefore, the particular approach I will be taking in Chapters 3-5 will be described in Chapter 3, though I will be moving from face-to-face research to virtual research in Chapter 5. For specifics of the relatedness of ethnography and netnography see Robert V. Kozinets, *Netnography: Doing Ethnographic Research Online* (Los Angeles, CA: Sage, 2013); Tom Boellstorff, Bonnie Nardi, Celia Pearce, and T.L. Taylor, *Ethnography and Virtual World: A Handbook of Methods* (Princeton: Princeton University Press, 2012); Alan Bryman, *Social Research Methods* (Oxford: Oxford University Press, 4th edn., 2004), chapter 23: 'E-Research: Using the Internet as an Object and Method of Data Collection', pp. 466-88.

[143] As noted earlier, ordinary theology is defined as 'the theological beliefs and processes of believing that find expression in the God-talk of those believers who have received no scholarly theological education'. See Astley and Francis (eds.), *Exploring Ordinary Theology*, p. 1.

Pentecostal theology of water baptism in a distinctly Pentecostal way. While this chapter will be resourced and oriented by the Pentecostal resources in prior chapters, it will also engage in critical conversation with dialogue partners selected from the wider Christian tradition – Protestant, Catholic, and Orthodox, historical and contemporary. This constructive chapter (Chapter 7) – along with my Pentecostal theological readings of scripture (Chapter 6) – will supply the 'ecumenical' resources for the whole of the project. The result is an original contribution to a Pentecostal theology of water baptism that is both Pentecostal but also ecumenically informed.

This study will conclude (Chapter 8) with a summary of the argument and will offer a handful of suggesting implications for further research.

In sum, this methodology seeks to be integrative but also well-rounded. It makes use of the strengths of each strand of Pentecostal scholarship, while also seeking to avoid the limits associated with each. In particular, the ecumenical engagement makes it germane for the wider theological conversation without becoming detached from its Pentecostal roots through the privileging of resources drawn from within the Pentecostal tradition. And while the project engages scholarly voices – both Pentecostal and ecumenical – it also makes room for 'ordinary' lay voices – both historical and contemporary. It also avoids the pitfall of becoming overly 'abstract' by including insights from empirical congregational studies, which is significant since 'Pentecostal theology is always practiced'.[144] Following this insight, I want to suggest that by attending to the practiced Pentecostal theology of ordinary believers, this project will become less speculative while also becoming more consistently Pentecostal. The intentional engagement with scripture also ensures that systematic theological work does not become detached from the biblical text. Finally, as my project seeks to explore the possibility of such an approach, I hope that it can contribute a meaningful methodology that is 'done in a holistic integrative manner'.[145]

---

[144] Wolfgang Vondey, *Pentecostal Theology: Living the Full Gospel* (London: Bloosmbury T&T Clark, 2017), p. 18. On this point Wolfgang Vondey has it right: 'Pentecostal theology as a form of mystical theology demands the constant availability to be practiced, and thus makes speculative theology as a purely intellectual or theoretical endeavor impossible'.

[145] Archer, 'A Pentecostal Way of Doing Theology', p. 314.

3

CLASSICAL PENTECOSTAL DENOMINATIONS AND WATER BAPTISM: THE FOURSQUARE CHURCH

A. Introduction

In this chapter, I will explore (1) the ordinary theology of early Pentecostals as it relates to the meaning and practice of water baptism in the Foursquare Church,[1] (2) the official denominational statements on the meaning and practice of water baptism,[2] (3) the scholarly articulations of water baptism by Foursquare scholars, and the (4) ordinary theology of contemporary Pentecostals in a particular Foursquare church.

My approach in this chapter – along with Chapter 4-5 – will seek to discover via revisioning and empirical methods the 'ordinary theology' of *early* denominational Pentecostals, the 'ordinary theology' of *contemporary* Pentecostals in particular denominational churches, and how these resources triangulate with the official denominational statements and scholarly denominational voices that discuss water

---

[1] For a comprehensive history of The Foursquare Church, see Nathaniel M. Van Cleave, *The Vine and the Branches: A History of the International Church of the Foursquare Gospel* (Los Angeles: ICFG Press, 1992); C.M. Robeck Jr, 'International Church of the Foursquare Gospel', in Sanley M. Burgess, Gary B. McGee, and Patrick H. Alexander (eds.), *DCPM* (Grand Rapids: Regency Reference Library, 1988), pp. 461-63.

[2] Foursquare's official 'Declaration of Faith' was compiled by Aimee Semple McPherson in 1927 and is still used in its original form today.

baptism.³ This triangulation will seek to explore the convergences and divergences between the various resources. Among other things, this method will help Pentecostal scholars begin to discover how, if at all, denominational statements and the scholarly and ministerial voices that engage such statements, truly reflect the praxis and applied spirituality of the denomination – at the beginning of the movement and in the present day.

While much of the chapter will focus on descriptive research, I will conclude by moving to summarize the findings and comment on potential contributions that The Foursquare Church can make to the construction of a Pentecostal theology of water baptism.

B. Hearing Early Pentecostal Ordinary Theology

Walter Hollenweger has argued that the first ten years of the Pentecostal movement serve as its 'heart' and not its 'infancy'.⁴ Many have followed Hollenweger in this assertion by choosing to mine and hear the spiritual practices and theological reflections of these earliest Pentecostals. These theological narratives have been used to judge, and at times, revise contemporary Pentecostal theology and practice.⁵ While methodologically this project seeks to make space for both historical and contemporary voices, the first part of this chapter will seek to listen to early Pentecostals. However, rather than looking at the first ten years of the Pentecostal movement as others have done, I will seek to start with Hollenweger's axiom but also move *within* and *beyond it*. I will explore whether this premise holds not only to the movement as a whole, but also to the individual denominations that emerge from the greater movement. Therefore, in this chapter, I will engage the first ten years of periodical literature associated with The

---

³ As noted earlier, ordinary theology is defined as 'the theological beliefs and processes of believing that find expression in the God-talk of those believers who have received no scholarly theological education'. See Astley and Francis (eds.), *Exploring Ordinary Theology*, p. 1.

⁴ Walter Hollenweger, *The Pentecostals* (Peabody: MA, Hendrickson Publishers, 1988), p. 551.

⁵ For example, see McQueen, *Toward a Pentecostal Eschatology*, pp. 1-325, and Thomas, 'Toward a Pentecostal Theology of Anointed Cloths', pp. 89-112.

Foursquare Church.⁶ This includes *The Bridal Call* and *The Bridal Call Foursquare*, which together ran from 1917 to 1926.

B.1 The Bridal Call (1917-1923)

The Bridal Call (*BC*), edited by Aimee Semple McPherson and published from 1917-1923, was a monthly publication that circulated sermons, testimonies, and updates on McPherson's ministry. The bulk of *BC* focused its attention on articulating bible-based teachings surrounding some of the major emphases of McPherson's ministry,⁷ namely Spirit baptism and physical healing. While the magazine also focused on teaching the 'Foursquare Gospel' of Christ as Savior, Healer, Baptizer in the Spirit, and Soon Coming King, McPherson also spent considerable time reporting on the progress of Angelus Temple and its upcoming activities.⁸ Noticeably, the publication also gave space to testimonies that spoke to the impact that McPherson and the ministry of Angelus Temple had on visitors following its opening. While certainly not the main topic, there are still many references made to the rite of water baptism – both through teachings and testimonies.

B.1.1 Water Baptism in *The Bridal Call*: Confessions and Articulations

In the second issue of *BC*, McPherson articulates the meaning of water baptism under the heading of 'What We Believe and Teach': 'Water Baptism is an outward sign of an inward work. Having reckoned ourselves and our old sinful lives nailed to the cross, we long to be identified with Him not only in His death but in His burial also'.⁹ Interestingly, in this statement, there is an absence of any language of identification with Christ's resurrection – only his death and burial. While in a later issue McPherson adds this point to her articulation of the meaning of water baptism,¹⁰ the focus throughout *BC* is

---

⁶ I will be following the same format in Chapter 4 (International Pentecostal Holiness Church) and Chapter 5 (Pentecostal Assemblies of the World).

⁷ Kenneth J. Archer, 'Early Pentecostal Biblical Interpretation', *JPT* 9.1 (2001), pp. 32-70.

⁸ Though Angelus Temple was founded in 1923, there were years of preparation and prayer leading up to its opening.

⁹ *BC* 1.2 (1917), p. 4.

¹⁰ In *BC* 1.9 (1918) p. 2. Further, in the same place, McPherson states that in baptism 'we outwardly show forth our reckoned unto death to sin, the burial by baptism into His death, the resurrection of the new man to walk in newness of life with Jesus, and our subsequent identification with Him'.

on identification and participation in Christ's *burial* in baptism.[11] Overall the teachings place a much higher emphasis on being buried with Christ than it does looking towards being raised with Christ in the rite. Significantly, 'visitors' to Angelus Temple use the same language of being 'buried' in baptism. In fact, at times visitors' language is almost identical to McPherson's in other places.[12]

The teachings also place a heavy emphasis on Jesus' baptism in the Jordan River. One might consider that this might be due to the Christological emphasis of the fourfold gospel and the emphasis of obedience regarding baptism: 'He went to the Jordan and was baptized, for He did not want to ask you to follow where He did not go … If you are going to follow Jesus you want to take every step he takes, don't you?'[13] Baptism, then, serves as the first step of obedience in the Christian life. When we are baptized, we are following 'the Shepherd' to 'Golgotha's brow' where we are 'crucified with Him', yet we 'do not plant our feet in the Shepherd's footsteps … on calvary'.[14] We continue to follow Christ 'to the tomb and are buried with Him in baptism in the watery grave' so that we may be 'raised up with Him to walk together with Him in newness of life'.[15]

Further, the only mention of *mode* in *BC* was immersion for adult believers: 'the way this beautiful ordinance is presented again and again during the week to changing audiences would be a delight to any immersionist'.[16] In one report, a woman gave her heart to Christ in her home kitchen and then ran to a baptismal service being held at the Mississippi River 'arriving just in time to be immersed'.[17] Some reports also discuss candidates 'standing waist-deep in the water' before being baptized,[18] and other reports from summer camps state that people were baptized by being immersed 'completely under' the water.[19] In some instances, 'whole families (were) baptized

---

[11] This is particularly intriguing considering the triumphalism championed throughout publication by focusing on 'fresh moves' of the Spirit. The focus on being buried in baptism rather than raised to new life, then, is significant.

[12] Perhaps this implies that from the beginning, McPherson had a heavy editorial hand throughout this publication.

[13] *BC* 7.6 (1923), p. 19.
[14] *BC* 7.1 (1923), p. 15.
[15] *BC* 7.1 (1923), p. 15.
[16] *BC* 7.6 (1923), p. 19,
[17] *BC* 4.4 (1920), p. 9.
[18] *BC* 7.1 (1923), p. 14.
[19] *BC* 3.10 (1920), p. 13.

together'.[20] A family of three, for example, 'joined hands behind them' right before descending together in the baptismal pool.[21] There are also reports of married couples being immersed 'simultaneously, side by side'.[22] In one case a 'family of eleven' was baptized together.[23] Another report records a time where 'two little children descend(ed) into the water smiling, testifying with uplifted hands'.[24] And though these children were 'little', they were old enough to 'follow the Shepherd' in baptism.[25]

Significantly, McPherson devoted a small section to clarify the official teaching on the 'Jesus only baptism' theology circulating at the time. Her response came after 'several inquiries' came through 'correspondence asking' about their position 'regarding the new teaching which advocates water baptism in Jesus' Name, and denies the tri-personality of the God-Head'.[26] In response, McPherson states:

> While we have always endeavored to keep away from controversy … we feel at this time that in justice to ourselves and to our readers we should make it very plain after two years of prayerful study we still believe more firmly than ever in the Father, and in His Son Jesus Christ, and in the Holy Spirit as three persons, and in water baptism according to our Lord's commission in Matt. 28:19.[27]

A few years later this same stance was reiterated: 'We still believe in Father – Son – and Holy Spirit, and in water baptism according to Matt. 28:19'.[28]

Lastly, perhaps one of the most intriguing teachings about water baptism comes from a guest writer, Elder A.B. Cox, who appears to have been asked to write an apologetic against cessationism. Within his teaching on 'The Baptism of the Holy Spirit', he appeals to many scriptures – especially in Acts – but then moves to discuss evidence in church history. After surveying a few of John Wesley's writings on the *charismata*, Elder Cox turns to 'quote some of our church

---

[20] *BC* 6.9 (1923), p. 18.
[21] *BC* 7.1 (1923), p. 14.
[22] *BC* 4.9 (1920), p. 18.
[23] *BC* 7.1 (1923), p. 14. While the ages of the children within the family of eleven are not recorded, the testimony is in the context of believer's baptism.
[24] *BC* 7.1 (1923), p. 15.
[25] *BC* 7.1 (1923), p. 15.
[26] *BC* 2.2 (1918), p. 13.
[27] *BC* 2.2 (1918), p. 13.
[28] *BC* 2.11 (1919), p. 16.

fathers'.²⁹ First, he quotes St. Augustine: 'We still do what the apostles did when they laid hands on the Samaritans and called down the Holy Spirit in laying on of hands. It is expected that the convert should speak in new tongues.'³⁰ St. Chrysostom is also quoted: 'Whosoever was baptized in the Apostle's day, he straightaway spoke with tongues'.³¹ Elder Cox names, quotes, and summarizes other various teachings from Origen, Gregory the Theologian, Gregory of Nyssa, and Jerome.³² While Elder Cox uses these early church theologians to write an apologetic against cessationism, he uncovers the connection between water baptism, the Spirit, and the *charismata* in the quotes of the church fathers.

B.1.2 Water Baptism in *The Bridal Call*: Scripture

In confessing and articulating the meaning of water baptism, *BC* appeals to and discusses many scriptural passages. Certainly, the most appealed to throughout the whole of *BC* were those scriptures surrounding Jesus' baptism by John (Mt. 3.13-17; Mk 1.9-11; Lk. 3.21-23; Jn 1.29-33). However, when referring to Jesus' baptism at the Jordan River, most often the scripture references were not quoted or cited but simply referenced as an event in the life of Christ. As noted earlier, even the baptistry at Angelus Temple was built and decorated so that one would 'gaze upon a scene from the River Jordan'.³³ Jesus' baptism was so fundamental to *BC*'s discussion of water baptism, it served as a hermeneutical lens at times. For instance, in one of Aimee's sermons, Jn 10.4 was quoted and situated within the context of Jesus' baptism at the Jordan:

---

²⁹ *BC* 3.10 (1920), p. 17.

³⁰ *BC* 3.10 (1920), p. 17. Elder Cox misquotes Augustine. The actual quote confirms that Augustine was speaking of water baptism:

In the first days ... they spoke in tongues that they hadn't learned, as the Spirit gave them to speak. These signs were appropriate for the time. For it was necessary that the Holy Spirit be signified thus in all tongues, because the gospel of God was going to traverse all tongues throughout the earth. That was the sign that was given, and it passed. Is it expected now of those upon whom a hand is imposed, so that they may receive the Holy Spirit, that they speak in tongues? Or, when we imposed our hands upon those infants, was any one of you paying attention to see if they would speak in tongues?

See Augustine, 'Homilies on the First Epistle of John', Boniface Ramsey (ed. and trans.), *The Works of Saint Augustine: A Translation for the 21ˢᵗ Century, Part 1, Vol. 14, Homily 6.10* (Hyde Park, NY: New City Press, 2008), p. 97.

³¹ *BC* 3.10 (1920), p. 17.
³² *BC* 3.10 (1920), p. 18.
³³ *BC* 6.9 (1923), p. 15.

'When the Shepherd putteth forth His sheep, He goeth before them; they know His voice and follow after Him.' Quickly the scenes wherein the Good Shepherd of the Bible went before His sheep, are sketched. Rapidly we are caught up and caused to stand, in fancy, beside the waters of the Jordan. We listen a few moments to the fiery words of John the Baptist then hold our breath and gaze with wondering love and adoration upon the Chief Shepherd himself, even Jesus Christ leading the way into the water of baptism.[34]

Water baptism, then, is about following the example of Jesus, who submitted himself to baptism at the Jordan river, mandating our submission to it. Notably, when one is baptized, they are 'taken up' to walk in Jesus' footsteps and participate in the scene of Jesus' baptism. Similarly, in another sermon, McPherson states, 'If you are going to follow Jesus you want to take every step He takes, don't you? Well. He went to the Jordan and was baptized, for He did not want to ask you to follow where He did not go.'[35] These two examples illustrate how often *BC* records Jesus' baptism at the Jordan River. This scriptural scene was often used to encourage believers to follow in Jesus' footsteps in water baptism, emphasizing obedience and imaginative participation.

However, *BC* also used Jesus' baptism to talk of Spirit baptism at times by separating Jesus' baptism at the Jordan from his reception of the Spirit at his baptism. For instance, in an article entitled 'The Three-fold Witness of the Baptism', McPherson states,

> One day the Lord showed me that God gives witness in THREES. 1 John 5:7, 8 – 'For there are THREE that bear record in heaven, the Father, the Word and the Holy Ghost; and these THREE are ONE. And there are THREE that bear witness in earth, the Spirit, and the water, and the blood: and these three agree in one.' It is true in Nature. Anything that can be grasped and seen has three dimensions – width, breadth and length; light has three primal colors and its ray has a three-fold action – light, heat and actinic (or chemical).[36]

---

[34] *BC* 7.1 (1923), p. 13.
[35] *BC* 7.6 (1923), p. 19.
[36] *BC* 4.4 (1920), p. 5.

McPherson continues to use this hermeneutic of 'three' to connect two scriptures recording Jesus' baptism (Mt. 3.14 and Jn 1.33) to Jesus' ministry of healing and deliverance (Luke 7) to argue that Spirit baptism contains three key indicators. According to the McPherson, as Jesus approached John for water baptism, one discerns that 'something from within John the Baptist told him who was coming, and he said, "Comest Thou to me, I have need to be baptized of Thee!"'.[37] McPherson then asserts that in Spirit baptism, one receives 'the testimony of the Holy Spirit to our hearts', and the 'sign from heaven' which is the Holy Spirit.[38] This 'sign from heaven over which we have no control, which surpasses conception and is miraculous' is 'the new tongues of Mark 16:17'.[39] Lastly, McPherson references the great miracles of healing and good works following in Luke 7. McPherson, then, appeals to two texts that record Jesus' baptism and uses them to argue for a 'three-fold witness' resulting from Spirit baptism, rather than water baptism. In McPherson's words, 'A person seeking the Baptism of the Holy Ghost and obtaining it, gets a three-fold witness'.[40]

Though Jesus' baptism at the Jordan was the major scriptural event appealed to when discussing water baptism, Acts 2.38 was also noted at times. In one of the earliest issues of *BC*, Acts 2.38 was one of the primary scriptural passages referenced under 'What We Believe and Teach' on water baptism.[41] Acts 2.38 was also referenced in teaching on Pentecost, in which the author ties together the 'events' of Spirit baptism, water baptism, and the forgiveness of sins:

> That same blessed presence was for all who would repent and believe that day, Peter is also inspired to make clear to the deeply convicted hearers 'Repent' he says, 'and be baptized (in water) every one of you in the name of Jesus Christ for the remission of sin, and ye shall receive the gift (baptism) of the Holy Ghost'. Three thousand repented and were baptized in water as necessary to receive 'that' which was 'seen' and 'heard'.[42]

---

[37] *BC* 4.4 (1920), p. 5.
[38] *BC* 4.4 (1920), p. 5.
[39] *BC* 4.4 (1920), p. 5.
[40] *BC* 4.4 (1920), p. 5.
[41] *BC* 1.2 (1917), p. 4. Romans 6.3-5; Acts 10.47-48; 19.4-5, Mk 16.16, and Mt. 23.19 were also referenced.
[42] *BC* 2.10 (1919), p. 8.

This teaching, then, connects water baptism, Spirit baptism, and the forgiveness of sins and seems to affirm that they are related. Yet, while they are held together in the context of this teaching, there is no further elaboration of how they ought to be held together theologically.

In another place, a writer re-tells the story of Pentecost and references Acts 2.38. Commenting on the event, the writer says that if the believers 'would but repent, and be baptized everyone in the name of Jesus Christ, for the remission of sins they too should receive this gift of the Holy Ghost'.[43] Therefore, though Acts 2.38 is referenced in connection to water baptism, there is no appreciable reflection on the theological significance of that connection.

B.1.3 Water Baptism in *The Bridal Call*: Testimonies and Reflections

Testimonies and reflections reveal that water baptism was a significant worship element at Angelus Temple. Angelus Temple held a baptismal service every Thursday evening. Many reports testify to how 'impressed' visitors were by the 'place and prominence of water baptism' at Angelus Temple.[44] Weekly numbers were regularly reported ranging from forty to one-hundred-fifty people being 'buried in baptism' each week.[45] Within the first three months of Angelus Temple's opening, 'more than one thousand were thus buried in baptism'.[46] Since McPherson's ministry extended outside the walls of Angelus Temple, reports of McPherson holding services other places are also present. Even when ministering at other churches, McPherson on occasion held water baptismal services for those who had been 'gleaned from the fields of the harvest' during a crusade or evangelistic meeting.[47] At one time, McPherson was also a part of a large baptismal service led by other ministers. In this instance, baptisms were held 'until the overworked baptistery sprung a leak' and had to be repaired.[48] Ironically, McPherson reported that the minister

---

[43] *BC* 2.6 (1918), p. 2.
[44] *BC* 7.6 (1923), p. 19.
[45] *BC* 7.6 (1923), p. 19.
[46] *BC* 7.1 (1923), p. 15.
[47] *BC* 4.10 (1921), p. 12. For instance, at a camp meeting at Long Branch, New Jersey, there was a water baptism service held for those who had responded in faith to Christ. See *BC* 1.2 (1917), p. 4.
[48] *BC* 5.5 (1921), p. 7.

who was performing the baptisms 'stated that this was the first time he ever heard of this happening in a Baptist church'.[49]

Many testimonies record the aesthetics of water baptism. Before Angelus Temple was finished being built, baptismal services sometimes took place at tent meetings. In one of these instances, the baptismal itself is described as being 'draped with myrtle and banked with fragrant carnations', floating on the water.[50] Further, one visitor at Angelus Temple describes its baptistry as the 'most beautiful baptistry in America'.[51] Another report indicates that the Temple's baptistry contained a painting of the 'River Jordan'.[52] Another testimony states that every Thursday, many were 'buried 'neath the flower stern watery grave in beautiful Angelus Temple baptistry'.[53] One visitor describes the scene this way: 'In this beautiful baptistry ... you gaze upon a scene from the River Jordan, whose waters flow beneath tropical foliage and palms – then come tumbling and cascading over rocks, pebbles, and moss into the white purity of the baptistry'.[54] The baptismal candidates were also dressed in white robes symbolizing 'purity' and 'righteousness'.[55]

Noticeably in *BC*, the altar was often an occasion for the experience of the presence of God which culminated in water baptism. In recounting a testimony, McPherson tells the readers that she instructed a 'brother' who responded to the altar call to 'just kneel right here at Jesus' feet'.[56] She then asked him, 'are you seeking salvation brother?'[57] He replies by asking for prayer saying that he has 'been a sinner for 89 years'.[58] McPherson says she loves the 'memory of his face at the water baptismal service on the next Thursday night where he is buried with Christ in baptism; the depth of feeling in his voice when as being lowered into the water, he exclaimed, ... "thank God

---

[49] *BC* 5.5 (1921), p. 7.
[50] *BC* 5.5 (1921), p. 9.
[51] *BC* 6.11 (1923), p. 14.
[52] *BC* 6.11 (1923), p. 14.
[53] *BC* 6.12 (1923), p. 25. While this account reinforces the importance of the aesthetics surrounding McPherson's baptismal, it also highlights the recurring theme throughout *BC* of being 'being buried' with Christ in baptism.
[54] *BC* 6.9 (1923), p. 15.
[55] *BC* 6.9 (1923), p. 15.
[56] *BC* 6.12 (1923), p. 15.
[57] *BC* 6.12 (1923), p. 15.
[58] *BC* 6.12 (1923), p. 15.

I am home at last!'".[59] Significantly, this testimony suggests that the altar is understood to take one to the very 'feet of Jesus'. The altar's ability to mediate the presence of Christ is significant here. However, this also sheds light on the fact that perhaps the altar crisis experience could overshadow the baptismal experience. Yet, there is still a relationship between these two events. One writer states that often people would 'give their hearts to Christ' and then go 'right into the water (to be baptized) clothes and all'.[60]

Other testimonies record people experiencing the presence of God in the waters of baptism. In one report from a revival meeting in San Francisco, 'power fell in the water' on 'those being baptized according to Jesus' command Mathew 28.19'.[61] They 'spoke, sang, and prophesied in the Spirit, whilst weeping, shouting and holy laughter prevailed throughout the entire hall. The power fell on the Pastor, as he spoke in tongues and the Spirit witnessed through interpretation whilst in the water.'[62] Significantly, this testimony links the *charismata* to water baptism instead of linking it to a separate, subsequent Spirit baptism experience.

There were also other reports of the Spirit 'falling' in water baptism: 'Upon some the power of the Holy Spirit so fell while in the water, that we could scarce get them out of the water'.[63] In a testimony received as a telegram, one person reported 'ministers baptizing "twenty-two in the Mississippi"' and as a result, God poured 'out His Spirit in a wonderful way'.[64] Another testimony records 'several ... gypsy converts' being baptized and the 'very presence of the Lord and the Holy Spirit, like a brooding dove' was 'felt throughout the place'.[65] Taken together, these testimonies reveal a relationship between the Spirit's presence and water baptism for some. In these instances, there was a mediation of the Spirit and his presence through the rite itself. In some cases, this presence manifested itself through the *charismata*, resulting in some becoming physically weak after such an encounter, and for others, a perceptible sense of the Holy Spirit's presence.

---

[59] *BC* 6.12 (1923), p. 15.
[60] *BC* 4.4 (1920), p. 9.
[61] *BC* 2.11 (1919), p. 15.
[62] *BC* 2.11 (1919), p. 15.
[63] *BC* 7.1 (1923), p. 15.
[64] *BC* 4.4 (1920), p. 7.
[65] *BC* 6.9 (1923), p. 18.

Another testimony includes a report of some seeing 'the face of Jesus smiling down ... surrounded by an innumerable company of angels' while in the baptismal waters.[66] Others described similar experiences of heaven opening in the waters of baptism, recalling Jesus' baptism at the Jordan. Picking up on this theme is a report of a special ecumenical water baptismal service held by 'five clergymen' who were 'immersing candidates':[67]

> Dressed in spotless white, many young women kneel upon the edge of the pool, lifting their hands to the open heavens, dedicating their lives for service at home or abroad, as hands are laid upon them, imploring God's blessing upon their lives (as) they are raised and with clasped hands and lifted faces, step down into the sparkling waters ... the glory in the faces of the people is a never forgotten scene ... in the sunlight, and mirrored in the placid waters beneath, as the throng takes up and makes the heavens echo with the song: 'Yes we will gather at the river; The beautiful, the beautiful river; Gather with the saints at the river; that flows by the throne of God.'[68]

Significantly, this testimony highlights the presence of God within the rite of baptism. By the 'lifting' of their hands and heads to the 'open heavens' and having 'hands laid upon them', the candidates signified their openness to experience Christ by the Spirit in/through water baptism. Those testifying understood those immersed to be participating in Christ's own baptism in the Jordan. Having been gathered 'with the saints at the river' they are being baptized in the river that takes them by the very throne of God.[69] Interestingly, this testimony also speaks to the *missional* aspect of baptism: here, baptism is understood to be an act of 'dedication' in which people lay their vocations before God, expecting to be sent out for 'service', either locally or globally.

---

[66] *BC* 4.4 (1920), p. 9.
[67] *BC* 6.4 (1922), p. 6.
[68] *BC* 6.4 (1922), p. 6.
[69] *BC* 6.4 (1922), p. 6.

B.2 *The Bridal Call Foursquare* (1923-1934)[70]

BCF, edited by Aimee Semple McPherson and published from 1923-1934, was a monthly publication that circulated sermons, updates on the ministry of McPherson and Angelus Temple, along with some testimonies. In the issues engaged (1923-1926), there are noticeably fewer testimonies of experiences of God's presence in the waters of baptism in *BCF* than in *BC*.[71] While *BCF* occasionally highlights articles from guest writers, much of the material comes from the teaching from McPherson. Testimonies mostly center on the ministry of McPherson, Angelus Temple, and reporting on the number of people saved, baptized in water, healed, and Spirit-baptized. Due to the weekly Thursday night baptismal service at Angelus Temple, water baptism does appear often in *BCF*. However, the bulk of content on water baptism comes in the form of confessions and articulations rather than in testimonies and reflections.

B.2.1 Water Baptism in *The Bridal Call Foursquare*: Confessions and Articulations

Concerning water baptism, one of the major accents of *BCF* was the reality of being 'buried' with Christ, borrowing language from Rom. 6.3-4. Therefore, in water baptism, one cannot skip the grave in trying to arrive at the empty tomb. McPherson puts it this way: 'Jesus did not jump from Calvary to Pentecost. They took Him to the grave. So reckoning my old life dead with Christ, crucified with Him, the thing to do was to be buried, buried in the waters of baptism, just as they buried Christ.'[72] Therefore, baptism identifies one with Christ's death just as much as it identifies the believer with his resurrection. This theme of being 'buried' with Christ, is also used to discuss another important theme in *BCF*: the forgiveness of sins.

Baptism is truly an act of 'washing'. In McPherson's words, 'just as the waters of the Jordan came out of Galilee and emptied into the Dead Sea, washing everything that they carried along with them, so

---

[70] While *BCF* ran from December 1923 to 1934, only issues between 1923-1926 are engaged since I am strictly covering the first ten years of the denomination's periodicals (1917-1926). Further, I have intentionally separated *BCF* from *BC* given the change in tone and content between the two publications. Angelus Temple's opening in 1923 marks a shift in focus and BCF reflects these differences. In other words – in my estimation – the publications should be treated as two separate periodicals, not just one publication re-named.

[71] Interestingly, it is not clear why this is so.

[72] *BCF* 10.7 (1926), p. 26.

from the Man of Galilee, even Jesus of Nazareth, has come pardon and cleansing, carrying our sins away into the Dead Sea of God's forgetfulness, to be remembered against us no more'.[73] However, it is not the mere washing of water that forgives sin, since Christ is the only one who can forgive sins. For *BCF*, the water rite grants the forgiveness of sins as 'Jesus is our Galilee and the Jordan is the cleansing stream of Calvary which carries our sins far away'.[74] Thus, water baptism can forgive sins due to the rite's ability to mediate the presence of Christ to those who are baptized. Christ, then, is the agent acting through the rite to wash the candidates clean of sin.

The relationship between salvation and water baptism is also affirmed in *BCF*, but not clearly articulated and expounded upon. McPherson admits that there is a clear relationship in scripture but denies that water baptism is necessary to salvation: 'Again, in Mark – he that believeth and is baptized, the same shall be saved. That does not mean if you are not baptized you won't be saved, but I do interpret that the two should go together.'[75] This ambiguity surrounding the relationship between salvation and water baptism is also reflected in the statements surrounding *BCF*'s articulated *ordo salutis*. While there is a clear preferred or normative understanding of the *ordo salutis*, there seems also to be some flexibility. This is reflected when McPherson states that the 'Divine plan of things is repentance unto salvation, water baptism, and the baptism of the Holy Spirit. Of course, you may be converted and receive the baptism of the Holy Ghost before an opportunity for water baptism comes.'[76] Even though sometimes there may be variance in timing between water baptism and Spirit baptism, the normative understanding is to undergo water baptism with Spirit baptism following. Therefore, 'the first step' is 'repentance, the second step (is) to be baptized in water, and the third (is) the baptism of the Holy Spirit'.[77] One might consider this articulated *ordo salutis* reflects the overall commitment to expressed individual faith: 'Having received faith and having been baptized, you may go on with the Lord to Pentecost … and by faith accept the baptism of the Holy Ghost that is for every one of God's

---

[73] *BCF* 9.9 (1926), p. 12.
[74] *BCF* 10.7 (1926), p. 26.
[75] *BCF* 10.7 (1926), p. 26.
[76] *BCF* 9.10 (1926), p. 11.
[77] *BCF* 10.7 (1926), p. 26.

children'.⁷⁸ Moreover, it is by and through faith that the individual can experience these various steps.

Further, baptism is for believers only. Infants are not baptized and only those children who had expressed faith in Christ should be baptized since they are themselves 'born again'.⁷⁹ As McPherson states, 'into the Baptismal waters come those whose life lies ahead of them – little children, the precious jewels of His Kingdom who have consecrated their lives to the service of the Master ... Young as many of them are, they have all been born again and many of them have been filled with the Holy Spirit.'⁸⁰ Anyone regardless of age or 'walk of life' can be baptized, as long as they are 'saved'.⁸¹ Whole families can be baptized together when all have proclaimed Christ as their Lord: 'Into these shimmering waters come families from all walks of life to fulfill this great command'.⁸² The reason that infant baptism should not be practiced is due to the lack of explicit teaching in the NT. McPherson states: 'though I looked through the Bible and tried to find where a baby was baptized – had really repented and was baptized – I could not find it. I challenge anybody to find recorded in the Bible where a baby was ever baptized'.⁸³ Thus, because there is no record of a 'baby' repenting and being baptized, the practice should be rejected. This speaks to the importance of individual faith expressed in *BCF*. For it is 'by faith we enter baptism'.⁸⁴ Water baptism is always reserved for those who can give 'confessions of faith'.⁸⁵ In fact, 'without faith ... baptism means nothing',⁸⁶ for it is 'by faith we consider ourselves buried with our Lord in baptism. By faith we are raised to walk with Him in newness of life.'⁸⁷

Despite *BCF*'s rejection of infant baptism, it affirms infant dedication. *BCF* records a testimony that shows how Angelus Temple practiced believer's baptism and infant dedication together: 'It was there in February 1924, I learned that Jesus Christ was the same

---

[78] *BCF* 10.7 (1926), p. 16.
[79] *BCF* 10.4 (1926), p. 32.
[80] *BCF* 10.4 (1926), p. 32.
[81] *BCF* 10.4 (1926), p. 32.
[82] *BCF* 10.4 (1926), p. 32.
[83] *BCF* 10.7 (1926), p 26.
[84] *BCF* 10.7 (1926), p. 16.
[85] *BCF* 8.6 (1924), p. 29.
[86] *BCF* 10.7 (1926), p. 16.
[87] *BCF* 10.7 (1926), p. 16.

yesterday, today, and forever. It was there I accepted him as my Savior and was baptized ... My wife and I not only want to serve the Lord all our days but also dedicated our precious little son.'[88] This testimony is also an example of the many reports of new converts being baptized. The weekly baptismal service at Angelus Temple provided a weekly opportunity for the newly converted to respond in obedience to the call for water baptism. Those attending the weekly baptismal service were encouraged to bring 'their new converts' so that they may be baptized.[89] Another testimony confirms that new 'converts come to the Temple and are buried with Him in the waters of baptism, at the Thursday evening service'.[90] In one case, someone listening to 'Radio KFSG' – the radio station owned by McPherson and used for ministry – 'gave' their 'heart to the Dear Lord' and came to Angelus Temple to 'be buried with Him in baptism'.[91]

Whenever anyone was baptized in Angelus Temple or under McPherson's ministry, they were 'gracefully immersed'.[92] By 1924, *BCF* reported that 'some ten thousand persons have been immersed since the Angelus Temple first opened its doors'.[93] In 1925, McPherson reported that 'a week ago tonight, eighty-eight were baptized in water, and the week before that, sixty-six. Yes, the revival is growing and going on, and there is no end in sight.'[94] All candidates were also baptized 'in the name of – The Father; The Son; and – The Holy Spirit'.[95] This is without exception in *BCF*.

Additionally, the teaching on water baptism in *BCF* and the presence of the weekly baptismal services held at Angelus Temple both witness to the centrality of water baptism for McPherson. In advertising the ministries of Angelus Temple, water baptism was one of the major components. Consider one example: 'Water Baptism (50 to 125 baptized each Thursday evening) and sermon of Aimee Semple McPherson with Altar Call. Music by the Temple Choir and Silver

---

[88] *BCF* 8.7 (1924), p. 25.
[89] *BCF* 9.8 (1926), p. 19.
[90] *BCF* 9.8 (1926), p. 20.
[91] *BCF* 8.11 (1925), p. 33.
[92] *BCF* 8.6 (1924), p. 27.
[93] *BCF* 10.4 (1926), p. 14.
[94] *BCF* 8.11 (1925), p. 28.
[95] *BCF* 8.8 (1925), p. 22.

Band under the direction of G.N. Nichols. Esther Fricke Green at the organ'.[96]

Another evidence of the centrality of baptism is found in the many records kept and reported regarding water baptism. For instance, whenever someone came to the altar for prayer they were given 'a registration card' which recorded the person's 'address, age, church standing, if any, and desire regarding baptism'.[97] Angelus Temple also recorded the number of people who followed through with baptism: 'More than twelve thousand persons have been buried with their Lord in Baptism. It is an almost unbelievable fact which cannot be disproved, for the actual records have been kept of everyone who is baptized in Angelus Temple'.[98] Many figures are detailed throughout *BCF* regarding water baptism. These figures were often used to highlight the 'revivalistic' nature of the ministry at Angelus Temple.

Finally, another important theme in *BCF* is the place of obedience in responding to water baptism. Therefore, the primary reason to be baptized is out of obedience. Believers must follow Jesus' example to be baptized. Those who submit themselves to baptism 'fulfill the command of Christ'.[99] As one newly baptized convert testified, 'I just obeyed the Lord'.[100] Water baptism, then, is done primarily out of obedience to Christ, though this obedience is not overly rote.

B.2.2 Water Baptism in the *Bridal Call Foursquare*: Scripture

In keeping with *BC*, the most prominent scriptures are those that recount Jesus' baptism at the Jordan (Mt. 3.13-17; Mk 1.9-11; Lk. 3.21-23; Jn 1.29-33). Since Jesus 'is the Shepherd, He leads the way. He goeth forth and His sheep follow'.[101] Jesus demonstrated the importance of baptism which means his followers must follow suit.

Also, in addition to Christ's baptism, another scriptural motif often referenced is that of being 'buried' in baptism, finding its roots in the language of Rom. 6.3. This scripture is largely referenced to argue for the necessity of being 'buried in baptism'. This scripture is also used to argue for baptism by immersion over-and-against

---

[96] *BCF* 8.7 (1924), p. 18.
[97] *BCF* 8.8 (1925), p. 26.
[98] *BCF* 10.4 (1926), p. 32.
[99] *BCF* 10.4 (1926), p. 32.
[100] *BCF* 8.4 (1924), p. 27.
[101] *BCF* 10.7 (1926), p. 23.

sprinkling: 'Therefore, we were buried, not sprinkled, but buried with Him by baptism into death'.[102] This emphasis of being 'buried' in baptism shows up throughout *BCF*.

Yet, the most impactful texts on McPherson's thoughts on water baptism come from the Gospels. In fact, at one place McPherson shares how she came to her convictions on water baptism:

> My father and mother did not believe in water baptism and I was never even sprinkled because of the beautiful dedication services of the Salvation Army ... (but) instead of refusing, I decided it would be better to trace it out myself ... First, John had been baptizing but he moved to a place on the river where there was much water ... Then I read Luke of the great commission wherein Jesus told the disciples to go into all the world and preach the Gospel and teach them to observe whatsoever He had commanded them, baptizing them in the name of the Father, Son, and the Holy Ghost. Again, in Mark – he that believeth and is baptized, the same shall be saved. That does not mean if you are not baptized you won't be saved, but I do interpret that the two should go together.[103]

Therefore, while she 'had been told' water baptism 'was no longer necessary', she began to 'study the Bible upon the subject ... and the light dawned!'. And rather than 'giving up (her) Methodist faith and teaching', she 'simply added to it'.[104] Therefore, while most of the scriptural references in *BCF* are indirect, McPherson certainly believed that scripture should be the primary source for instruction regarding water baptism, revealing a form of biblicism in her own thought.

B.2.3 Water Baptism in Bridal Call Foursquare: Testimonies and Reflections
In continuity with *BC*, *BCF* documents the importance placed on aesthetics and presentation regarding both water baptisms and the baptistry itself. The following testimony is a helpful description of the experience of water baptism at Angelus Temple:

> The Baptismal service each Thursday night is a very impressive scene. The lights are turned out by the electrician, the big Kimball

---

[102] *BCF* 10.7 (1926), p. 26.
[103] *BCF* 10.7 (1926), p. 26.
[104] *BCF* 8.5 (1924), p. 11.

organ is humming in soft tone, the curtain slowly rolls back and you see a beautiful picture of the winding River Jordan, with beautiful mountains and fertile valley. At the edge of the picture are seen artistically arranged cobblestones with water cascading down. A powerful, bright light is thrown upon the picture, which gives it a very realistic effect. The converts are gracefully immersed. Since the opening of the Temple over 5,363 have followed their Lord in the baptismal waters. Last month 128 were baptized at one service. This service always closes with a powerful altar call and makes a great impression on the unsaved.[105]

Other testimonies in *BCF* also expose the impression that the water baptismal service made on the viewers. One visitor to Angelus Temple stated that 'the (baptismal) ceremony in Angelus Temple is … outstanding in its presentation and beauty'.[106] Another testimony of an unknown author wrote about their experience of water baptism at Angelus Temple. This testimony was included in a larger article under the heading, 'The Beautiful Jordan':

Instantly, we are transported to that country, afar, where the feet of our Lord touched upon the hilltops and traversed the plains. Lying, stretched out before us is the beautiful Jordan River … flowing, as it were, right into our midst, the quiet water of the river seems to tumble and roll over the rocks and pour into the baptistry. The Evangelist, in white baptismal robes, steps down into the crystal waters. With hands uplifted, God's blessing is asked on the service to follow.[107]

The presentation and aesthetics surrounding baptism were important at Angelus Temple. This is most clearly reflected in the 'miniature reproduction of the River Jordan'.[108] Another testimony reveals that there was a complementary stained-glass window of the same biblical scene. According to a visitor – Urania Elizabeth Burgess – 'there is one window that I love perhaps a little more than other – the

---

[105] *BCF* 8.6 (1924), p. 27. Though there is little indication of how long these services lasted, one could speculate that they often lasted hours.
[106] *BCF* 10.4 (1926), p. 14.
[107] *BCF* 8.8 (1925), p. 22.
[108] *BCF* 9.2 (1925), p. 30.

Baptismal window. It depicts John baptizing Jesus in the beautiful river Jordan.'[109]

While there are many descriptive testimonies from visitors to Angelus Temple, in *BCF* there is a noticeable lack of references to experiencing God's presence in-and-through water baptism as was present throughout *BC*. As shown above, the bulk of the material on water baptism is either explicit teaching on the subject, reports recording the number of people being baptized, or visitors' testimonies of their experience viewing the baptismal services. Nonetheless, one notable testimony emphasizes experiencing God's presence in/through baptism.

An unnamed person testified that 'after being baptized in water, the Lord revealed to me that Divine Healing for our body is part of His plan of redemption for the children of men. My stomach was healed from that very hour.'[110] This testimony indicates that through water baptism, God imparted revelation of Jesus as Healer, and then acted as Healer by healing his or her stomach. The waters of baptism, then, mediated the presence of Christ in a way that opened the person up to receiving physical healing.

Aside from this brief testimony, though, *BCF* does not contain many testimonies of experiencing God's presence in/through baptism. This is especially surprising considering how often *BC* recorded such testimonies. However, *BCF* recorded fewer testimonies overall in comparison to *BC*, which may partially account for the discrepancy.

B.3 Hearing Early Pentecostal Ordinary Theology: Conclusions

In *BC*, water baptism was central to McPherson's ministry, and especially to the worship at Angelus Temple due to the Thursday night baptismal service. Those who were baptized were often fresh converts, saved through McPherson's ministry. Members of Angelus Temple were also often encouraged to bring their unsaved friends and family to the baptismal service in hopes that they would receive Christ and respond in water baptism. The number of people baptized was reported often in the pages of *BC* and was sometimes used to

---

[109] *BCF* 10.3 (1926), p. 26.
[110] *BCF* 9.9 (1926), p. 26.

validate the ministry that was taking place through McPherson and Angelus Temple.

In the explicit teaching on water baptism in *BC*, there was a strong emphasis on obedience to Christ – following in his footsteps to 'the Jordan'. This teaching on water baptism centered on obedience to Christ's command to be baptized and to participate in his death. Overall, the teaching tended to talk about water baptism in symbolic terms – the rite being an act that represented something outside of itself. This is heard in the reflections surrounding the scriptural narrative of Jesus' baptism, which was the central scriptural resource engaged. Ironically, while Jesus' baptism at the Jordan was referenced many times, there was no commentary on Jesus' reception of the Spirit while being water baptized. Further, Acts 2.38 was also referenced. However, exegetical and/or theological explanations on how forgiveness of sins, Spirit baptism, and water baptism relate were absent. And while the explicit teaching tended to talk of water baptism in symbolic terms, the implicit teaching – revealed through testimonies – exposed a more presence-driven understanding of the rite. Testimonies of power 'falling in the water' resulting in prophecy, glossolalia, and visions are present. And while the explicit teaching (confessions and articulations) highlighted the difference between water baptism and Spirit baptism, the implicit teaching (testimonies and reflection) expressed a close relationship between the two.

In *BCF*, most of the material on water baptism found was explicit teaching on water baptism, reports regarding the number of people being baptized, and visitor's testimonies of their experiences viewing the baptismal services at Angelus Temple. Teaching on water baptism centered on the theme of obedience, and its connection to salvation, among other relevant issues discussed in *BC*. As a result of the prominent ministry of McPherson and Angelus Temple, many *believers* were baptized, and in some cases, children dedicated. Like *BC*, much of the scriptural references in *BCF* were taken from the Gospels and focused on Jesus' baptism, though Rom. 6.3-4 was also a prominent, reoccurring scripture. Overall, water baptism and Spirit baptism were viewed as two different events. Yet unlike *BC*, testimonies recounting baptismal candidates experiencing God's presence in/through water baptism in *BCF* were largely absent.

C. Hearing Official Denominational Statements

Official Foursquare teaching on water baptism stems from two sources: The Foursquare Church's 'Declaration of Faith' and the latest edition of the 'Foursquare Licensing Process Guide', which is used for credentialing ministers. The 'Declaration of Faith' was compiled by founder Aimee Semple McPherson in 1927 and is still used in its original form today.[111] In the latest edition of the 'Foursquare Licensing Process Guide', there are discussion guides on each article in the Declaration of Faith that seek to expound upon each subject.[112] This treatment is more extensive and thorough than the original article contained within the Declaration of Faith.

C.1 The Foursquare Declaration of Faith

The Foursquare Church considers water baptism and the Lord's Supper to be its two 'ordinances'. The 'Declaration of Faith' asserts that the denomination believes water baptism should be administered in the name of the triune God, 'according to the command of our Lord'.[113] Additionally, water baptism is a 'blessed outward sign of an inward work' while also being 'a beautiful and solemn emblem *reminding* us that even as our Lord died upon the cross of Calvary so we reckon ourselves now dead indeed unto sin'.[114] According to the 'Declaration of Faith', believers are then buried into Christ's death by baptism while also participating in his resurrection, which mandates the believer to 'walk in newness of life'.[115] Interestingly, statements discussing mode are noticeably absent from the statement's treatment of water baptism, and perhaps simply assumes immersion.

C.2 Foursquare Licensing Process Guide

In the licensing guide, the section on water baptism discusses water baptism in the Old and New Testaments before turning to four 'Specific Questions' on (1) the relationship of baptism to salvation, (2) the official stance on infant baptism, (3) the mode(s) of baptism, and (4) the baptismal formula.

---

[111] The Foursquare Church's declaration of faith can be found at: http://foursquare-org.s3.amazonaws.com/assets/Declaration_of_Faith.pdf

[112] 'Water Baptism and The Lord's Supper' in 'Foursquare Licensing Process Guide' (Los Angeles, CA, updated November 2012).

[113] Aimee Semple McPherson, 'Declaration of Faith', p. 6. My emphasis.

[114] McPherson, 'Declaration of Faith', p. 6. My emphasis.

[115] McPherson, 'Declaration of Faith', p. 6. My emphasis.

First, the guide notes that 'especially since the Protestant Reformation of the 16th century', the church has been quite divided over the understanding and practice of water baptism.[116] That considered, 'we want to possess our understandings and pursue our practices with appropriate humility, focusing not so much on our precise (and partial! 1 Cor. 13:9, 12) understandings as on our obedient and powerful practice'.[117] Since many churches seem to neglect baptism, the Foursquare Church does not want to neglect to call people towards it. Those 'who are not baptized or who do not witness baptisms, can possess an impoverished and weak Christianity that is based on simply "receiving Jesus"', without 'repenting of our sins, obeying Jesus Christ, and dying to live again'.[118]

Moving towards discussion around water baptism in the OT, the guide notes three prefigurements: the creation act (Genesis 1), the salvation of Noah and his family through the waters (Gen. 6-9; 1 Pet. 3.20-21), and the deliverance of Israel out of the slavery of Egypt through the Red Sea (Exod. 14.19-15.22; 1 Cor. 10.1-2). All three of these scriptures anticipate the spiritual bath. Further, ritual washing, proselyte-baptism, and the baptism of John the Baptist are all a part of Christian baptism's Jewish background. In moving towards the NT, all of the OT 'prefigurements find their fulfillment in Jesus Christ' who was baptized by John to 'fulfill all righteousness'.[119] Significantly, 'in Acts and throughout the New Testament, baptism is related to repentance, faith, and the reception of the Spirit'.[120] In Romans, Paul states that the death and resurrection of Jesus 'is modeled by water baptism (Rom. 6.1-7)'.[121] As Col. 2.12 and 1 Pet. 3.20-21 display, 'Pharaoh's army is drowned! Through our faith, by which at baptism we renounce all allegiance to alien authorities, demonic influences that would seek to draw us back are cut off.'[122] Further, in baptism 'our sins are washed away'.[123] Most significantly, in water

---

[116] 'Water Baptism and the Lord's Supper', p. 2.
[117] 'Water Baptism and the Lord's Supper', p. 2.
[118] 'Water Baptism and the Lord's Supper', p. 2. One might consider this a critique of some forms of decisionism within Evangelicalism.
[119] 'Water Baptism and the Lord's Supper', p. 2.
[120] 'Water Baptism and the Lord's Supper', p. 3.
[121] 'Water Baptism and the Lord's Supper', p. 3.
[122] 'Water Baptism and the Lord's Supper', p. 3. One might discern that traditional baptismal liturgies might be in view here.
[123] 'Water Baptism and the Lord's Supper', p. 3.

baptism 'God's Spirit may come upon us in fullness even as it did first upon Jesus Himself, the 120 in the Upper Room and other believers through the ages'.[124]

In discussing the relationship of baptism to salvation, 'there is no question that water baptism apart from faith can save no one' for it is 'by grace through faith in Jesus Christ' that ultimately saves. But, while water baptism cannot save, 'it is closely linked with the forgiveness of sins (Acts 2.38), regeneration (John 3.5; Titus 3.5), and "salvation" (1 Pet. 3.20-21)'.[125] Since this is the case, in the NT, 'baptism is neither self-operative nor merely symbolic' for 'both the divine and human sides are given their proper due'.[126]

On the issue of infant baptism, the Foursquare Church follows 'the practice of infant dedication and then calling youth or adults who have come to personal faith to make a conscious, informed choice for baptism'.[127] One should keep in mind, though, that we will often encounter people 'in various stages of full conversion'.[128] Those who were baptized as 'an infant or small child comes to personal faith as an adult and wishes to obey the call to baptism, we will gladly baptize again'.[129] The disclaimer is made that this does not 'necessarily imply either a negative judgment on another church's baptism or any lack of respect or gratitude for the loving actions of parents'.[130] But what it does mean, then, is that it 'represents our support of a person's conscientious obedience in faith through the Spirit to the call of Jesus'.[131] Interestingly, the first footnote on infant baptism directs one to take a 'brief look at understandings in favor of both infant and adult baptism' in Jack Hayford's *Hayford Bible Handbook*.[132] In it, Hayford states that 'regarding the matter of baptizing infants, the most generous Christian view seems to be in the willingness of many to (1) honor the concerns that prompt infant baptism, and not denigrate the practice, and (2) emphasize the need for personal faith in Jesus Christ, at the earliest possible age of understanding, faith, and

---

[124] 'Water Baptism and the Lord's Supper', p. 3.
[125] 'Water Baptism and the Lord's Supper', p. 3.
[126] 'Water Baptism and the Lord's Supper', p. 3.
[127] 'Water Baptism and the Lord's Supper', p. 4.
[128] 'Water Baptism and the Lord's Supper', p. 4.
[129] 'Water Baptism and the Lord's Supper', p. 4.
[130] 'Water Baptism and the Lord's Supper', p. 4.
[131] 'Water Baptism and the Lord's Supper', p. 4.
[132] 'Water Baptism and the Lord's Supper', p. 4 n. 5.

repentance'.[133] While the guide does not directly engage Hayford's resource on this subject, it is significant that it footnotes such comments.

In approaching baptismal mode, 'our understanding of the Greek word *baptizo*' leads the Foursquare Church to practice immersion. However, 'we can imagine God honoring a baptism that, for some circumstantial or personal reason, is performed in the manner of sprinkling or pouring'.[134] And while 'at times Pentecostal churches have divided over whether to baptize in the name of Jesus or the trinitarian formula' the Foursquare Church has consistently recommended the use of the trinitarian formula since this is in keeping with Mt. 28.19 and it 'was the formula that predominated in the Early Church'.[135] Nonetheless, the Foursquare Church does not 'forbid the use of the formula, "in the name of Jesus", as long as it does not represent a polemic against a Trinitarian understanding'.[136]

C.3 Hearing Official Denominational Statements: Conclusions

In sum, the official teaching of the Foursquare Church states that water baptism is for believers, by immersion in the name of the triune God, in response to faith, and is symbolic in nature. Declaration of Faith's (DF) treatment of water baptism is quite concise, so much so, it fails even to reference mode. The Licensing Process Guide (LPG), though, explicitly states what was most likely assumed. Thus, the later LPG expounds upon the original teaching found in the DF, while also bringing more clarity and nuance to the issues discussed. Nonetheless, the teaching found in the LPG is quite consistent with the original treatment of water baptism found in the DF.

D. Hearing Foursquare Scholarly Voices

This section restricts itself to engagement with scholarly works that are written on water baptism by Foursquare scholars/ministers. Presently, three Foursquare scholars have engaged the subject of water baptism: Guy Duffield and N.M. Van Cleave, who co-authored a

---

[133] Jack Hayford (ed.), 'Baptism', in *Hayford's Bible Handbook* (Nashville: Thomas Nelson Publishers, 1995), p. 553.
[134] 'Water Baptism and the Lord's Supper', p. 4.
[135] 'Water Baptism and the Lord's Supper', p. 4.
[136] 'Water Baptism and the Lord's Supper', p. 4.

work on Pentecostal doctrine, and Kyle W. Bauer.[137] Except for Bauer, these engagements are marginal and are not the main subject of the engagement. Therefore, this subject has yet to be extensively engaged by scholars in the Foursquare Church.

D.1 Guy Duffield and N.M. Van Cleave

In 1983 Foursquare faculty members of L.I.F.E. Bible College, Guy Duffield, and N.M. Van Cleave, co-authored *Foundations of Pentecostal Theology*. Rather than being considered a systematic theology, the monograph is structured as a book of bible doctrines. According to the authors, the work is largely a compilation of 'scriptural teachings concerning the great doctrines of our faith'.[138] They note in their Introduction that they desired to publish a work that 'may be a means under God to ground and settle (Col. 1:23) our Pentecostal family throughout the world, and to encourage others to receive and enjoy all the blessings of a rich spiritual life in the fullness of the Holy Spirit'.[139] In the Introduction, Jack Hayford,[140] – founding pastor of Church on the Way in Van Nuys, CA – notes that this monograph began at his request 'during the years I served as President of L.I.F.E. Bible College at Los Angeles'.[141] Having since been re-published and re-printed by 'Foursquare Media', this work continues to serve as the authorized theological work of The Foursquare Church.

The treatment of water baptism is situated within the larger context of the 'ordinances' of the church, which are 'outward rites or

---

[137] Perhaps it is worth noting that Telford C. Work has briefly written on water baptism. He states that in water baptism, people cross over the borderline from one way of life into another as Eph. 4.22 suggests, and baptism also serves as a reminder of the hope in the Eschaton. Therefore, baptism is not an eschatological sign that breaks into the present from the future, but rather reminds the participant of the future. Thus, Work's articulation of the theological significance of water baptism is minimal and peripheral. Although Work attended a Foursquare church from 1997-2003, he is not included within this section since he has had no association with Foursquare for some time. See Telford C. Work, *Deuteronomy* (BTC; Grand Rapids: Brazos, 2009), pp. 55, 143; Telford C. Work, *Ain't Too Proud to Beg: Living Through the Lord's Prayer* (Grand Rapids: Eerdmans, 2007), p. 74.

[138] Duffield and Van Cleave, *Foundations of Pentecostal Theology*, p. xiv.

[139] Duffield and Van Cleave, *Foundations of Pentecostal Theology*, pp. xiv–xv.

[140] Hayford has written on water baptism in his book of Bible doctrines, *Grounds for Living*. However, due to the popular rather than academic nature of the work, I will not engage it in my scholarly sources section. See Jack W. Hayford, *Grounds for Living: Sound Teaching for Sure Footing in Growth* (Sovereign World: England, 2001), pp. 128-34.

[141] Jack W. Hayford, 'Introduction', in *Foundations of Pentecostal Theology*, pp. viii–ix.

symbolic observances commanded by Jesus, which set forth essential Christian truths'.[142] Duffield and Van Cleave note that 'the ordinances are sometimes called sacraments'.[143] The authors state that 'the ordinances observed by the Protestant churches are two in number, namely: Water Baptism and The Lord's Supper'.[144] Specifically, baptism is 'an outward sign of an inward work' or 'the visible sign of an invisible work of grace'.[145] We are to participate in water baptism because Jesus set an example for us by submitting to baptism himself. The mode of water baptism is by immersion because it is 'the biblical description of the manner of Jesus' baptism in the river Jordan'.[146] Further, the formula for water baptism is clearly stated by Christ: 'in the name of the Father and of the Son and of the Holy Spirit'.[147] Referring to the Foursquare 'Declaration of Faith', water baptism 'is a blessed outward sign of an inward work, a beautiful and solemn emblem' that reminds us that just as Christ died on the cross, so we are dead to sin, buried with Him, and raised from the dead so we may walk in newness of life in our baptism.[148]

Notably, the work dedicates less than 400 words to the subject in its entirety. They devote 20 pages to their treatment of Spirit baptism (pp. 304-25), but less than one full page to water baptism (p. 436).[149]

D.2 Kyle W. Bauer

The grandson of Foursquare pastor, Jack Hayford, and pastor at La Iglesia En El Camino Santa Clarita, in Santa Clarita, CA recently self-published a monograph on water baptism entitled *Watery Grave*.[150]

---

[142] Duffield and Van Cleave, *Foundations of Pentecostal Theology*, p. 442.
[143] Duffield and Van Cleave, *Foundations of Pentecostal Theology*, p. 442.
[144] Duffield and Van Cleave, *Foundations of Pentecostal Theology*, p. 442.
[145] Duffield and Van Cleave, *Foundations of Pentecostal Theology*, p. 442.
[146] Duffield and Van Cleave, *Foundations of Pentecostal Theology*, p. 443.
[147] Duffield and Van Cleave, *Foundations of Pentecostal Theology*, p. 443. Further, 'Statements about being baptized "in the name of Jesus" omit the longer formula, and emphasize the Christian baptism as distinct from John's baptism' (p. 443).
[148] Duffield and Van Cleave, *Foundations of Pentecostal Theology*, p. 443.
[149] See Green, *Toward a Pentecostal Theology of the Lord's Supper*, p. 18 n. 60.
[150] Kyle W. Bauer, *Watery Grave: To Die is to Live* (USA: Kyle W. Bauer, 2016). Notably, General Supervisor of the Foursquare Church, Tammy Dunahoo, sent an email to all licensed and ordained Foursquare pastors in the United States on June 7, 2017, encouraging them to read Bauer's *Watery Grave*. In her email, Dunahoo remarked that as she has been 'tracking the spiritual results reported each year' she has 'experienced a growing discomfort with the large gap between the number of decisions for Christ and the number of water baptisms. Last year, our U.S. churches reported 92,241 decisions yet only 12,981 water baptisms.' Remarking on the

From the beginning to the end, Bauer makes clear that water baptism is symbolic: water baptism is a 'symbolic passage into the fullness of life that is available to us in Jesus Christ'.[151] Bauer also states that 'baptism fully symbolizes the way that God the Father brings us into His family' and serves as 'the symbol of our salvation', while also stating that it is 'more than a rite or ritual that Jesus Christ established'.[152] So while baptism is a 'representation of our salvation' and 'the symbol of our union with Christ', baptism *also* 'releases the life, freedom, and power in our lives, and this power is to be effectuated and remain in force during our whole life'.[153] When one is 'immersed in the water of baptism' there is a release of a 'new, supernatural way of living'.[154] Following up on these statements, Bauer rhetorically asks the question, 'if it is only a symbol or a representation, then why do we need to do it at all?'[155] In answering this question he replies by stating that 'it is a step of obedience'.[156] One is left wondering how Bauer sees these proposals correlating.

Throughout the monograph, Bauer states that baptism is merely a symbol, while also stating that it is more than just a ritual. In the eight chapters, Bauer argues that water baptism is for 'freedom, purification, new life, access to God's promises, growing in God's family, and the power for living the way God does',[157] while also holding to

---

importance of baptism, Dunahoo states that 'it is far more than an ordinance of the church; it is a mark of one's identity, an initiation into the community of faith and a public witness of life in Christ'. As Kyle Bauer remarks in his portion of the email, *Watery Grave* was birthed out of sermons he preached in his local church in a desire to teach his congregation about the rite. While the book is more popular in style, due to the work's recent significance in The Foursquare Church and for its theological content, I have chosen to include it in this review. Tammy Dunahoo, 'A Message From General Supervisor Tammy Dunahoo', (Email: June 7, 2017), accessed September 26, 2017.

[151] Bauer, *Watery Grave*, p. 9.

[152] Bauer, *Watery Grave*, pp. 9-10. Reading Bauer's monograph, one wonders how Bauer understands baptism to be merely symbolic, while also bringing about dynamic, 'fullness of life'. This disjointedness is seen throughout the book. For instance, Bauer states that 'In baptism we are a new creation' and 'your sins will be forever drowned in the water grave of baptism', while concurrently stating that baptism is 'a symbol that … has no power in and of itself'. See Bauer, *Watery Grave*, pp. 22-23, 32.

[153] Bauer, *Watery Grave*, p. 11.
[154] Bauer, *Watery Grave*, p. 11.
[155] Bauer, *Watery Grave*, p. 12.
[156] Bauer, *Watery Grave*, p. 12.
[157] Bauer, *Watery Grave*, p. 14.

baptism as a symbol much like 'wedding rings' are 'representations of deep truths and spiritual realities'.[158] In the case of water baptism, the 'water is a physical representation of the spiritual reality of God's working in our lives'.[159] It is quite evident that Bauer attempts to hold together a meaningful, experiential view of baptism within a symbolic understanding of the rite. This comes even clearer when Bauer begins to discuss 'the three baptisms'.

Bauer states that 'though we have studied and applied the power that God offers us through the important symbol of baptism, the bible talks about three distinct baptisms'.[160] The first baptism is the 'Baptism *of* the Holy Spirit … not to be confused with the Baptism with/in the Holy Spirit' or water baptism.[161] The first is a spiritual 'work of the Holy Spirit that unites us to Christ and the family of God'.[162] The second baptism is that of water baptism that is a 'symbol of our salvation and repentance'.[163] Lastly, the third baptism is Spirit baptism which for Jesus 'occurred at the same time he was baptized in water … which ignited God's supernatural power for Jesus to live and minister'.[164]

Further, in sharing his testimony of water baptism, he records that at ten years of age, he 'came up from the water' with his hands lifted and was 'immediately baptized in the power of the Holy Spirit and began to speak in tongues'.[165] He shares that it was 'one of the most powerful experiences' of his life. He states that 'though many people do not experience the baptism of the Holy Spirit in the waters of baptism, it is still an expectation that we can receive the promise of the Father, the Holy Spirit, at the same time we are baptized'.[166] Bauer notes that this 'also happened to Jesus'.[167] Thus, rather than understanding Jesus' reception of the Spirit in water baptism as the prototype for believers, he understands Jesus' water baptism and Spirit baptism to have overlapped in a unique experience, and as a result,

---

[158] Bauer, *Watery Grave*, p. 23.
[159] Bauer, *Watery Grave*, p. 22.
[160] Bauer, *Watery Grave*, p. 78.
[161] Bauer, *Watery Grave*, p. 78. Emphasis original.
[162] Bauer, *Watery Grave*, p. 78.
[163] Bauer, *Watery Grave*, p. 78.
[164] Bauer, *Watery Grave*, p. 80.
[165] Bauer, *Watery Grave*, p. 112.
[166] Bauer, *Watery Grave*, p. 112.
[167] Bauer, *Watery Grave*, p. 113.

some today can experience this overlapping of receiving the Spirit in water baptism.[168]

Lastly, Bauer concisely comments on infant baptism at the very end of the monograph in an 'Addendum'. While he states that infant baptism for some serves 'as a testimony' to the parent's desire that their children would walk in 'the ways of God … we do not practice the baptizing of infants and small children in our tradition'.[169] Further, if one has 'already been baptized as a child, it is not at all inconsistent with the baptism that your parents provided for you' to be 'baptized as an adult'.[170] Rather, 'it would be more of a fulfillment of the step of dedication and faith' the parents took in baptizing their child.[171] Bauer, then, recommends 'the dedication of children' because it 'is actually very biblical', citing Luke 2.22 for support.[172]

In sum, Bauer's work talks of water baptism in symbolic terms, while at the same time, seeking to demonstrate that it is also *more* than just a symbol.

D.3 Hearing Foursquare Scholarly Voices: Conclusions

In conclusion, the above survey reveals that Foursquare scholarly articulations of water baptism are minimal. However, the Foursquare scholars and ministers that do speak to the rite echo the official denominational teaching by focusing on water baptism's symbolic nature. However, Bauer also discusses water baptism's relationship to Spirit reception in the context of Spirit baptism, referencing his testimony along with Jesus' baptism. Bauer, then, attempts to balance his emphasis on water baptism as a symbol, with an experiential possibility. For Bauer, water baptism is symbolic but can become a dynamic encounter with the Holy Spirit if Spirit baptism coincides with water baptism.

---

[168] Bauer does not suggest why everyone does not.
[169] Bauer, *Watery Grave*, p. 86.
[170] Bauer, *Watery Grave*, p. 86.
[171] Bauer, *Watery Grave*, p. 86.
[172] Bauer, *Watery Grave*, p. 86.

E. Empiricizing Pentecostalism: Contemporary Foursquare Ordinary Theology[173]

In moving from the revisioning to the empirical, I will be following Mark Cartledge in his use of qualitative research methods. In doing so, I aim to attend to testimony as an important mode of Pentecostal theology.[174] In Cartledge's words, 'Pentecostal discourse is encapsulated in the notion of testimony'.[175] For that reason, 'the role of testimony is an important aspect of P/C (Pentecostal/Charismatic) theology and a legitimate mode of theological discourse that deserves to be explored empirically'.[176] Cartledge holds that the 'narratives that people tell regarding their faith' should be understood as a 'grassroots level of theological discourse'.[177] Thus, his empirical work has invited 'experientialist religious discourse' because he believes it 'should be respected as containing genuine theology'.[178] Significantly, he notes that it is this aspect of his theology 'that invites further development'.[179]

Cartledge's use of 'ordinary theology' in his constructive efforts is particularly salient for my project.[180] Suggestively, he encourages more projects to replicate his methodology in terms of 'paying attention to the ordinary theology of adherents' by continuing to make a

---

[173] As previously noted, I am following Cartledge's use of Jeff Astley's definition of ordinary theology as 'the theological beliefs and processes of believing that find expression in the God-talk of those believers who have received no scholarly theological education'. See Jeff Astley and Leslie J. Francis, eds., *Exploring Ordinary Theology*, p. 1.

[174] See Cartledge, *Testimony in the Spirit*, pp. 1-219. For other works on the role of testimony within Pentecostalism see, for example, Cheryl Bridges-Johns, *Pentecostal Formation: A Pedagogy Among the Oppressed* (JPTSup 2; Sheffield: Sheffield Academic Press, 1993), pp. 87-91; Steven J. Land, *Pentecostal Spirituality: A Passion for the Kingdom* (JPTSup 1: Sheffield, Sheffield Academic Press, 1993), p. 112; Scott A. Ellington, 'The Costly Loss of Testimony', *JPT* 8.16 (2000), pp. 48-59; Marcela A. Chaván de Matviuk, 'Latin American Pentecostal Growth: Culture, Orality and the Power of Testimonies', *AJPS* 5.2 (2002), pp. 205-22.

[175] Cartledge, *The Mediation of the Spirit*, p. 18.
[176] Cartledge, *The Mediation of the Spirit*, p. 24.
[177] Cartledge, *The Mediation of the Spirit*, p. 25.
[178] Cartledge, *The Mediation of the Spirit*, p. 26. By stating that ordinary theology is 'genuine theology', Cartledge, as I read him, intends to argue that ordinary theology ought to be 'respected', yet that respect 'does not preclude theological evaluation or comment'. See Cartledge, *The Mediation of the Spirit*, p. 26
[179] Cartledge, *The Mediation of the Spirit*, p. 25.
[180] Cartledge, *Testimony in the Spirit*, p. 15.

case for 'testimony as a legitimate theological mode'.[181] Thus, in response, this section will provide a 'field study' perspective with which to engage by conducting ethnographic research. As Cartledge states, 'ethnography describes and interprets cultural and social settings primarily using participant observation, informal interviews, and extended time in the field'.[182] Therefore, my research strategy will include interviews with believers who have been water baptized in a present-day Foursquare church – listening for the *implicit* theology in their *explicit* statements on the rite and its meaning. It will also include my reflections as a 'participant observer' at a particular Foursquare church's water baptismal service.[183] As Cartledge notes, participant observation is often used with other qualitative research methods such as interviews.[184] Both the participant observation and interviews will also be put into dialogue with secondary denominational literature.[185] Therefore, by using (1) participation observation along with (2) interviews and (3) secondary denominational literature, 'ideas generated from one source of material can be checked by reference' to another source.[186] This triangulation can 'enhance the reliability of the results of research'.[187]

E.1 Fieldwork Technique

Before moving to my findings, a few introductory remarks on the methodological technique are in order. While operating under the general rubric of Cartledge's project, I will also be seeking to imitate elements of Sarah Coakley's 'fieldwork' technique, which complements Cartledge's approach to theology in several ways.[188] First, like Cartledge, she uses qualitative fieldwork methods instead of quantitative.[189] Like Cartledge, her use of qualitative research methods

---

[181] Cartledge, *Testimony in the Spirit*, p. 231.
[182] Cartledge, *Practical Theology*, p. 73.
[183] By using participant observation alongside interviews, I avoid testimonies being 'only interpreted in the light of other testimonies'. See Cartledge, *Testimony in the Spirit*, p. 19.
[184] Cartledge, *Practical Theology*, pp. 70-71.
[185] For secondary literature, I will be consulting various articles within Burgess, Stanley M., Gary B. McGee, Patrick H. Alexander (eds.), *DCPM* (Grand Rapids, MI, Zondervan, 1988), pp. 1-928.
[186] Cartledge, *Practical Theology*, pp. 70- 71.
[187] Cartledge, *Practical Theology*, p. 71.
[188] Sarah Coakley, *God, Sexuality, and the Self: An Essay 'On the Trinity'* (Cambridge, UK: Cambridge University Press, 2013), pp. 152-89.
[189] Coakley, *God, Sexuality, and the Self*, p. 165.

worked better with her project since she 'had no particular axe to grind theologically, and a little sense of what I was likely to find'.[190] These approaches to data gathering also helped her 'to see and understand' the ordinary theology of Pentecostal/charismatic Christians.[191] Further, Coakley's fieldwork is also significant for this project for three reasons: (1) She uses the fieldwork findings in the context of constructive/systematic theology,[192] (2) her fieldwork approach is only one of several methods used in her larger project, and lastly, (3) her approach is also brief enough to fit the findings within a more expansive project. Finally, my use of Coakley's technique is significant since Pentecostals have already begun to engage Coakley's work.[193] And since Christopher Stephenson believes that 'Coakley's fieldwork among charismatics is a welcome move', my appropriation of her work to classical Pentecostals can be understood as a suitable development in the dialogue between Coakley and Pentecostal theology.[194] All in all, Coakley's fieldwork provides a helpful prototype on how to situate empirical research within a larger project that seeks to utilize multiple approaches to theology, while also being suitable for Pentecostal use.

Following Coakley, I will use 'taped "in-depth" interviews with a range of informants, representative (in age, sex, and socioeconomic

---

[190] Coakley, God, *Sexuality, and the Self*, p. 165.

[191] Coakley, God, *Sexuality, and the Self*, p. 165.

[192] While Cartledge's empirical work has informed my approach, he is clear that his project on 'ordinary theology' is 'located within the discipline of practical theology, that took seriously the empirical approach to the subject coming from the Nijmegen school, associated with the *Journal of Empirical Theology* (Brill).' See Cartledge, *Testimony in the Spirit*, p. 13. Therefore, since my project is located within the discipline of systematic theology rather than practical theology, Coakley is a helpful dialogue partner. However, it is important to note upfront a major difference between my fieldwork and Coakley's: While Coakley is interested in correlating Ernst Troeltsch's typological categories to modern day charismatic groups, in turn interviewing two different church groups and comparing the divergent results, I am instead, like Cartledge, focusing on one congregation and interviewing more participants.

[193] For dialogue between Coakley and Pentecostal theologians, see Christopher A. Stephenson, 'Sarah Coakley's Théologie Totale: Starting with the Holy Spirit and/or Starting with Pneumatology?', *JPT* 26.1 (2017), pp. 1-9. Daniel Castelo, 'Charisma and Apophasis: A Dialogue with Sarah Coakley's *God, Sexuality, and the Self*', *JPT* 26.1 (2017), pp. 10-15. Chris E.W. Green, 'Prayer as Trinitarian and Transformative Event in Sarah Coakley's *God, Sexuality, and the Self*', *JPT* 26.1, pp. 16-22. Sarah Coakley, 'Response to My Critics in the *Journal of Pentecostal Theology*', *JPT* 26.1 (2017), pp. 23-29.

[194] See Stephenson, 'Sarah Coakley's Théologie Totale', p. 4.

terms) of the congregation as a whole'.[195] Thus, following both Coakley *and* Cartledge, I will be utilizing the qualitative/ethnographic research method of participant observation. By taking the 'stance of a participant-observer',[196] I will witness a worship service in which baptisms are present.[197] Like Cartledge, I will become a 'research participant' by taking part in the 'social setting while at the same time engaging in positive social interaction'.[198] Thus, I will be 'involved in the situation already, but take time to step back and analyze what is happening from a research perspective'.[199] By focusing on 'one congregation', I will be able to 'attend to the ordinary theology of the members in a particular context and take an inductive approach that treats the congregation as a case study'.[200] From each particular congregation, I will conduct 12-15 'in-depth interviews ... with individual members' yet, 'in some interviews more than one respondent was involved' due to the participant's schedule and/or preference.[201]

Like Coakley, I will describe the interviews as 'semi-structured'.[202] Following her lead, I will construct and ask five 'open-ended', 'basic questions' to all the informants and allow each informant to answer in their own ways, but I will allow 'other matters to emerge

---

[195] Coakley, *God, Sexuality, and the Self*, p. 165.

[196] For Coakley's participant observation comments, see Coakley, *God, Sexuality, and the Self*, pp. 166-68.

[197] Echoing Cartledge, 'this meant that I took notes throughout the service as well as participating in liturgical acts', yet I mostly 'watched what happened and made notes' of the water baptisms and 'how these were interpreted'. See Cartledge, *Testimony in the Spirit*, p. 23.

[198] Cartledge, *Practical Theology*, p. 71.

[199] Cartledge, *Practical Theology*, p. 71.

[200] Cartledge, *Testimony in the Spirit*, p. 21.

[201] Coakley, *God, Sexuality, and the Self*, p. 165, n. 19. Following Coakley, 'in choosing my informants I was partly guided by suggestions from the leaders of the congregations, and partly took the initiate myself in inviting people to fulfil representative roles'. Also, each interview took around an hour and was conducted in various places 'depending on convenience for the person or family concerned'. I also 'took time at the start of each interview to explain my undertaking, my background, and to answer any questions the informants had about the use I would make of what was said. Formal permission to tape the interviews was received in each case. I also took brief notes while conducting the interviews, and more extensive notes after each one'. See Coakley, *God, Sexuality, and the Self*, p. 165 n. 19.

[202] Coakley, *God, Sexuality, and the Self*, p. 168 n. 22. Twelve to fifteen in-depth interviews were done with individual members. Following Coakley, in some interviews more than one respondent was involved due to the participant's schedule and/or preference.

spontaneously'.²⁰³ Put differently, in addition to these 'open-ended queries, allowance' will be 'made for impromptu follow-ups to probe and clarify as needed'.²⁰⁴ These five basic questions will focus on (1) their own personal experience of water baptism,²⁰⁵ (2) the water baptisms of other believers, (3) various ways of baptizing (for example immersion or sprinkling), (4) the relationship between water baptism and Spirit baptism, and (5) the scriptural authority for practices of water baptism.

In reporting and organizing my findings, I will also follow the format forged by Coakley by first summarizing my findings through 'the interviews, tackling each theme in turn'.²⁰⁶ I will then briefly conclude by summarizing the discoveries.²⁰⁷ While I will use this technique in all three denominational chapters (Chapters 3-5), in this chapter I will be focusing on one Foursquare congregation, which is pseudonymously entitled: New Life Church.²⁰⁸

---

²⁰³ Coakley, *God, Sexuality, and the Self*, p. 168. The initial five questions to all informants were: 1. Will you describe your personal experience of water baptism? 2. What have you seen the Spirit do in other people's water baptisms? 3. Do you think there is any right way to do baptism? 4. What in your view is the relationship between water baptism and Spirit baptism? 5. What scriptures inform your view of water baptism? (and) What do Acts 2.38 and Romans 6.3-4 tell you about water baptism?

²⁰⁴ Bob L. Johnson Jr, 'On Pentecostals and Pentecostal Theology: An Interview with Walter Brueggemann', *Pneuma* 38.1-2 (2016), p. 126. According to Johnson, this is 'derived from accepted standards of qualitative data collection methods, specifically via interviews'. See, for example, Michael Q. Patton, *Qualitative Research and Evaluation Methods* (3rd edn; Thousand Oaks, CA: Sage Publications, 2002)'. Johnson, 'On Pentecostals and Pentecostal Theology', p. 126 n. 5.

²⁰⁵ While this first question relates specifically to water baptism, themes such as conversion, re-baptism, and 'stages' of conversion/sanctification naturally emerged. Follow up questions also sought to place water baptism in the context of the larger context of Christian initiation. For a multi-disciplinary theory of religious conversion in the context of Pentecostal ordinary theology, see Cartledge, *Testimony in the Spirit*, pp. 63-73.

²⁰⁶ Coakley, *God, Sexuality, and the Self*, p. 168.

²⁰⁷ From the outset, let me note the limitations in my approach. While I spend time with individual informants (12-15 from each church) over a few months, my participant observation is based on one baptismal service in each church. Further, following Coakley, my selection of informants was mostly in cooperation with the leadership of each church. See Coakley, *God, Sexuality, and the Self*, p. 165 n. 19. Lastly, all participating churches were in the Mid-Atlantic region of the USA, with churches located in Pennsylvania, Virginia, and Delaware. I am cognizant that such limitations influence findings and conclusions. Nonetheless, by drawing from Cartledge and Coakley's methods, I am confident that this approach will contribute meaningful discoveries.

²⁰⁸ Cartledge, 'The Symbolism of Charismatic Glossolalia', p. 37.

E.2 New Life Church[209]

New Life Church, located in Southern Pennsylvania, USA, began as a daughter church of another Foursquare church in 2014. After the initial launch, New Life Church held their first service in a large tent and then spent two years holding services at various places in the area including a local fire company, a pizza restaurant, and a skating rink. In the summer of 2016, the congregation moved into their permanent home at a former elementary school. The pastor of the church, Don (all names in this account are pseudonyms), formerly worked as a staff pastor at the parent Foursquare church and felt called by God to start a new church in a nearby town. Demographically speaking, the majority of the church is White/Caucasian and one family in attendance with Puerto Rican descent. Further, the average attendance of the congregation for the year of study (2018) was eighty-one.

E.3 Participant Observation: The Baptismal Service[210]

E.3.1 The Worship Service

As a daughter church of another Foursquare church, New Life Church was planted in 2014, and a year later, it moved into their current meeting space. A former elementary school, this newly renovated facility has been divided up into offices, meeting rooms, equipped with bathrooms, a kitchen space, and an open worship space, outfitted with a sound system, contemporary lighting, and a projector system.[211] Therefore, this church can be considered 'hi-tech in its use of media resources', though modest in its utilization.[212] Rather than pews or chairs, the worship space is furnished with round tables and chairs throughout the worship space, creating a relaxed and casual environment. Musical instruments such as guitars, a keyboard, and a drum set were present on the platform, along with a portable baptismal tank to the side of the platform.

---

[209] This information I gleaned from the leadership of the church and the church website.

[210] I am following Cartledge's format in reporting my participant observation. See Cartledge, *Testimony in the Spirit*, pp. 29-32. Further, all leaders/pastors/informants have been given pseudonyms.

[211] Cartledge, *Testimony in the Spirit*, p. 29.

[212] Cartledge, *Testimony in the Spirit*, p. 30.

E.3.2 Service Structure

This Sunday morning worship service featuring water baptisms was held on September 22nd, 2019. The worship service began at 10.30 am and concluded at noon, followed by baptisms and a lunch, commemorating the church's fifth anniversary. I was able to discern eight main units in this service. Additionally, for the service to flow between the main units, there were links. Following Cartledge's findings, there were also key individuals who 'link the units together, but they do so in relation to specific locations'.[213] For this service, there were three major locations: the platform, the baptismal tank, and the congregational seating. There were also 'key individuals who mediate these three zones': (1) The worship leader(s), who lead and facilitate the sung worship, (2) Pastor Don, who facilitates the transitions, links, baptizes the candidates, and manages the preaching and response times, and (3) Pastor Phil, the Lead (and visiting) Pastor of the parent Foursquare church, who presents the church with a Foursquare Charter Plaque, honoring their fifth anniversary as a church.[214]

The service begins with a 'greeting/welcome, a prayer',[215] and an invitation to worship from Pastor Don (unit 1). 'Then the music leader and the band lead the congregation in a time of singing', 'The Cross Has the Final Word' (unit 2).[216] After this song concludes, the worship leader instructs and leads the congregation into a greeting time (unit 3). This relational and informal greeting time might be considered a 'low church' equivalent to the 'high church' practice of 'passing the peace'. Following this greeting time, the worship team leads the congregation in four additional praise/worship songs: 'Blessed Be Your Name', 'Holy is the Lord', 'Call Unto Me', and Holy

---

[213] Cartledge, *Testimony in the Spirit*, p. 30.

[214] When a Foursquare church is opened, it opens as a district church. At this level, it is overseen by the Foursquare district council. Once it reaches 30 adult members, it moves to the status of charter church. Foursquare generates a plaque commemorating the date that the Foursquare board approves it as a charter church, and the plaque is presented by either a Divisional Superintendent, Area Pastor, or someone from the district office. According to Pastor Don, in this case, New Life Church was long overdue to become a charter church, and in conversation with the district, Pastor Don decided to have it presented on their five-year anniversary. Pastor Phil is both the Area Pastor and the Lead Pastor of the parent church. Thus, it was a natural fit for Pastor Phil to do the presentation.

[215] Cartledge, *Testimony in the Spirit*, p. 30.

[216] Cody Carnes, 'The Cross Has the Final Word' (Capitol CMG Paragon/ Writer's Roof Publishing, 2016).

is our King' (unit 4).[217] Echoing Cartledge's findings, there were two phases to the worship pattern. The first phase includes songs that are upbeat and celebratory, moving to a second phase which includes songs that are 'quieter and more reflective'.[218] Following the sung worship, Pastor Don transitioned into a time of announcements and collection of tithes and offerings (unit 5). During this time, Pastor Don invites a guest from Walk for Water to share about the 2019 Pennsylvania Walk for Water event.[219] Following this announcement, Pastor Phil – Lead Pastor of the parent church of New Life Church – makes his way to the platform to present the official Foursquare Charter Plaque from the corporate offices of The Foursquare Church. After some words of celebration and encouragement marking the momentous event within the life of the church, Pastor Don transitions into a time of the offering, where free will gifts are collected.

Pastor Don, then, moved into a sermon on a study of Job (unit 6). This sermon was birthed out a response of discerned, 'heaviness in the congregation'. Pastor Don noted that though they are 'celebrating five years' as a church, there are times in the Christian journey when one needs to grow close to God in times of suffering. Celebrations are wonderful, but one must also understand suffering, and 'how to give God glory amid suffering'. The biblical text Pastor Don reads and refers to throughout the sermon is Job 1.1-22. Towards the conclusion of the sermon, Pastor Don invites some of the worship team to the platform 'to play some instrumental music' during the conclusion to his sermon. Pastor Don concludes by inviting the congregation to respond to the sermon by praying a prayer along with him, humbling themselves before God, and committing their hearts to become servants who trust God during experienced difficulty. The tone of the sermon is instructional, ending with a time of reflection

---

[217] Matt Redman and Beth Redman, 'Blessed Be Your Name' (Thankyou Music, 2002); Chris Tomlin and Louie Giglio, 'Holy is the Lord' (sixsteps Music, 2003); Gary Wayne Sherrill, 'Call Unto Me' (Gary Wayne Sherrill Music, 1994), Rita Springer, 'Holy is our King' (Vineyard/Mercy Publishing, 1998).
[218] Cartledge, *Testimony in the Spirit*, p. 30.
[219] The Walk for Water event hopes to unite people in Pennsylvania around the need to bring safe water to hundreds of men, women, and children across the world.

and response.[220] Following the final prayer, Pastor Don announces that there will be a short break since he and the baptismal candidates need to change clothes in preparation for water baptism. He also announces that following the baptisms, the church will begin lunch together. Thus, the service moves back into a time of fellowship as the congregation awaits water baptisms (unit 7).

Approximately ten minutes later, Pastor Don and three baptismal candidates make their way forward to the baptismal (unit 8). After signaling for the congregation's attention, Pastor Don invites anyone who would like to have a better view of the baptisms to make their way up near the platform. While people are making their way forward, Pastor Don introduces the three baptismal candidates: a younger, male teenager (Victor), and an elderly couple (Sherry and Jerry).[221] Pastor Don also states: 'If someone else is interested in being baptized this morning, I would be happy to talk with you'. Pastor Don then proceeds to invite Victor into the baptismal, while sharing that he had recently had a 'nice long conversation' with Victor about his desire to be baptized. Pastor Don also shared that following their conversation, he felt that 'this young man's heart is right with the Lord'. Pastor Don continued to remark about Victor's growth in the Lord, evidenced by his mature faith. Pastor Don then asks Victor, 'Can you briefly share ... what baptism means to you?' In response, Victor shares a brief remark about Pastor Don's discussion with him on baptism at his home. Following Victor's remarks, the congregation applauds. Pastor Don then states:

> Based on your profession of faith, committing to live a Christ-centered life, and the old Victor is buried and dead with Christ and the new Victor to be resurrected with Christ, based on these things, I baptize you in the name of the Father, Son, and Holy Spirit.

In response, Victor is immersed and raised, and the congregation applauds and shouts.

Following a few pictures, Victor exits the baptismal, and Sherry and Jerry enter together. Pastor Don follows the same format,

---

[220] There is little participation from the congregation in unit 7, especially. The most participation from the congregation is focused within units 2 – 4.

[221] In keeping with the following section, I have chosen to provide pseudonyms for the baptismal candidates.

introducing Sherry and Jerry, sharing a few remarks about their faith, allowing them an opportunity to testify about what baptism means to them, and then baptizing them. It is worth noting that in his initial introduction, Pastor Don shares that Sherry and Jerry 'recently gave their hearts to the Lord'. Following Pastor Don's comments, Jerry was given a chance to speak. Jerry thanks everyone for praying for him, and shares how much his salvation means to him, stating, 'I can feel it'. Pastor Don, then, asks Sherry, 'Would you like to share anything?'; however, Sherry declined. At this point, Pastor Don shares that, 'Sherry is going to be baptized forward because she has a bad back', while also noting that 'even being in this tank right now, is a big step of faith for Sherry'. He remarked that initially, Sherry asked to be sprinkled due to fear of water. However, upon further discussion and reflection, she felt like she could overcome her fear 'in the power of Christ'. The congregation ensues with celebration and support. Pastor Don then baptizes Sherry forward using the trinitarian formula. Then, Pastor Don moves to immerse Jerry forward as well. Before concluding, Pastor Don asks the congregation: 'Is there anyone else here who might be interested, who has given their life to the Lord, but has never been baptized and that is a step you'd like to take now?' Following no response, Pastor Don announces that the church can begin lunch.

In sum, 'it can be seen that despite the lack of written liturgy there is a clear sequence of expected events'.[222] Pastor Don serves as the primary liturgical leader, 'and is the chief master of ceremonies that ensures there is a smooth transition' between units and zones.[223] The worship leader and team work in partnership with Pastor Don throughout the service to lead the congregation in sung worship, provide a 'musical atmosphere', and support transitions between units, especially units 1-4, and 6-7. Given Pastor Phil's position as the Lead Pastor of the parent church, he exercises a certain kind of authority in the service during his presentation time. However, this is irregular given the unique circumstances that brought Pastor Phil to this service. Therefore, while congregational participation is encouraged, at times – especially during sung worship – the liturgy is primarily handled by Pastor Don and the worship leader/team.

---

[222] Cartledge, *Testimony in the Spirit*, p. 32.
[223] Cartledge, *Testimony in the Spirit*, p. 32.

E.4 Interviews

E.4.1 Interview Participants

The interview participants at New Life Church were comprised of six men and nine women, 'representative (in age, sex, and socioeconomic terms) of the congregation as a whole'.[224] All participants were white/Caucasian but varied in age. The men were mostly middle-aged (Paul, Ralph, Barry), though Caleb and Shane were younger men, and Joshua was elderly. These men were employed in medicine (Joshua), home-keeping (Caleb), plumbing (Ralph), manufacturing (Barry), finances (Paul), and athletics (Shane). The women too were mostly middle-aged (Sally, Deborah, Barbara, Kourtney, Sarah, Nancy), yet Stephanie was younger, and Judy and Anne were elderly. These women were employed in finances (Stephanie), military (Deborah), home-keeping (Sarah), real estate (Kourtney), education (Nancy), and retired (Anne, Barbara, Sally, Judy).[225]

E.4.2 Interview Findings

Question 1: Personal Testimonies of Baptism
While the first question relates particularly to one's experience of water baptism, themes such as conversion, re-baptism, and 'stages' of conversion/sanctification naturally emerged in the conversations. My follow up questions also sought to place water baptism in the context of the larger context of Christian initiation. Most participants were baptized multiple times, either initially as an infant and then later as an adult, or in some case, baptized as an adult twice. However, even the participants who had not been baptized multiple times unanimously supported re-baptism. One of the main reasons they offered is the lack of personal choice in their infant baptism. According to one participant, their adult baptism 'felt like it was a more determined choice' (Barbara). For another, their earlier baptism as an infant was understood only as something for 'my parents but not for me' (Anne). One participant who was baptized twice as an adult stated that 'the second time was when I comprehended things' (Sally). The importance placed on cognitive understanding was an emphasis that came up frequently in the interviews. Speaking for those who had

---

[224] Coakley, *God, Sexuality, and the Self*, p. 165.
[225] Following Cartledge's focus group format, each informant is identified by their pseudonym, ethnicity, age, and occupation. See Cartledge, *Testimony in the Spirit*, p. 32.

been baptized multiple times, one person stated that, 'the second time I had a better understanding' (Sarah). Lastly, another reason given for getting rebaptized was that one woman felt 'God was calling' her to be baptized a second time (Barbara). All in all, the consensus pointed to water baptism being a repeatable act, and the most recent baptism being the one that really 'counted' because it was best understood.

Situating water baptism within Christian initiation, most participants understood baptism to be something following 'conversion'. While baptism is not necessary, it is important because it is a 'commitment ... and a profession of faith' (Stephanie) and a 'personal decision' (Shane). One participant stated that 'I wanted everyone to know ... to profess' (Deborah), while another said similarly, 'water baptism was a way of professing my faith in Jesus Christ – symbolizing belief in Jesus' (Paul). Put another way, water baptism is an 'outward showing to the body of Christ' that one is 'saved' (Ralph). And while some participants understood baptism to be an act of obedience (Barbara, Stephanie), the obedience theme was not as prevalent as the theme of profession of faith. Lastly, one participant connected their water baptism to entrance into the church (Barry).

But to the general question, 'Can you tell me about your personal experience of water baptism?', there were answers such as 'it wasn't unusual ... nothing dramatic or traumatic' (Nancy), while others reported, 'The Spirit was present' and 'I felt a great relief coming up like I had just gotten mud sprayed off me' (Caleb). Therefore, people's experiences of water baptism – particularly affective experiences – varied. Some reported 'no felt difference' during and after their baptism (Stephanie), while others stated that they emerged from the waters 'in the Spirit' (Sarah), 'crying like a baby – feeling the presence' (Sally) and feeling 'more special than ... before' (Judy). For another, their water baptism helped them 'finally able to feel the love of God' (Kourtney). Thus, significant variance was found in the personal testimonies surrounding the contributor's experiences of water baptism.

Question 2: Observations of Other's Baptisms

My second question centered on the participants' observations of others' water baptisms. Fortunately, there were many fresh instances on many of their minds because a 'good portion' of the church was 'baptized for the first time or the second time' a few months before my interviews (Barbara).[226] A few months prior, a guest pastor came to minister to this local congregation and held evening services for consecutive days. These nightly meetings also featured 'spontaneous ... water baptisms every night' (Barbara).

When reflecting upon their observations of other people's water baptisms, one woman stated that the baptisms she had witnessed have been 'nothing special'[227] (Stephanie), while one man stated that in most baptisms he has witnessed, people seem to be 'energized by it' (Barry). Others noted seeing people visibly 'at peace' (Joshua, Nancy) and others sensing a 'release' of some kind (Sarah, Nancy). One woman reported that after witnessing baptisms, it changed her understanding of its meaning: 'I used to believe it was symbolic ... but I have seen it be an opportunity for demonic oppression to be broken' (Kourtney). Another noted that he had seen multiple instances of 'people coming out of the water speaking in tongues' (Ralph). One man recounted a more detailed instance of this happening:

> I remember my wife coming out of the water speaking in tongues. I remember she told the people that she was desperate and convicted that she wanted to speak in tongues. She told the pastor, 'hold me under the water until I get it!' And when she came up out of the water, the pastor said, 'sister you got it' as she was praising the Lord with her new language. (Paul)

Another woman noted that at one point she sensed someone had 'received the Spirit of love' in the waters of baptism (Anne). Recounting a recent baptism she witnessed, Deborah stated that 'the most memorable was when' a fellow church member 'came up out of the water and was stunned ... it touched the audience. Something definitely happened to her'. Lastly, one man reported that one of his 'church friends struggles with many illnesses' and he witnessed her recently being 'refreshed and renewed' by God as she was coming up from the baptismal waters (Caleb).

---

[226] Many participants voluntarily discussed these revivalist meetings, all in positive terms.

[227] Shane also had not witnessed any baptisms that were particularly memorable.

Question 3: Ways of Baptizing

This third question – 'Do you think there is any right way to do baptism?' – was left open-ended initially. However, follow up questions centered on three issues: (1) mode, (2) formula (3), and those authorized to perform baptisms.

A few people stated that there is no right way to do baptism, the only consideration being that the candidate is old enough to choose the baptism for themselves. All participants held to believer's baptism and denounced all forms of infant baptism. As long as the baptism candidate is old enough to decide for themselves and their 'heart is in the right place … then it doesn't matter' (Caleb). Others offered a similar perspective with statements such as 'it's all a heart issue. It shouldn't matter … God is flexible' (Deborah), and 'I don't think it matters, as long as they are old enough' (Shane).

Perhaps the most consensus, though, centered around *mode*. According to one person, 'God honors any … but immersion is best' (Deborah). According to Shane, immersion is the correct mode, though 'if someone can't be immersed for medical reasons it doesn't invalidate the baptism'. Another stated that 'it should be submersion' because 'that's what they did in the bible' (Sarah). Put another way, 'it's not as meaningful without full immersion' (Nancy). Others echoed similar sentiments (Anne, Stephanie, Ralph, Joshua, Kourtney, Barry). However, one person argued for triple immersion: 'Immersing three times, once in the Father, once in the Son, and once in the Holy Ghost – that is best because fully submerged really cleanses you' (Sally).

Nonetheless, two participants diverged on this issue, by stating that mode does not ultimately make a difference. For example, one woman stated that even if she put her own 'head over the sink … that would still count' as a baptism (Barbara), and another stated that 'if the Holy Spirit would prompt' her, she would baptize a new believer 'with a water bottle if (she was) on the side of the road and (she did not) have a pond' (Judy). Therefore, while immersion is preferred overall, it should not discount other methods if practical concerns prevent full immersion.

The participants were less dogmatic about the formula. Commenting on whether one should be baptized in Jesus' name or the name of the Father, Son, and Holy Spirit, a few simply commented, it 'doesn't matter' (Sarah, Barry) and others were unsure (Ralph,

Stephanie). Others preferred the triune formula (Anne, Joshua, Nancy, Shane) due to historical precedent, their own experience, and Jesus' command in Mt. 28.19, while another woman preferred baptism in Jesus' name, 'because Jesus has to be there against the demonic. It is not just symbolic – used to think it was, but there is power in Jesus' name' (Kourtney).

Lastly, on the issue of 'who' is authorized to baptize, one participant thought that while 'friends and family have great intentions … I think we should entrust our pastor with that gift, blessing, and responsibility' (Deborah). Another stated that 'having an ordained pastor to baptize is best' and 'anyone *cannot* baptize' (Joshua), another citing 'discernment purposes' for the reasoning behind a pastor baptizing (Kourtney). Yet, for the rest of the participants, any Christian can baptize another Christian. In one man's words, 'ordination means nothing' (Ralph). Another woman, echoing a similar sentiment stated that anyone should be able to baptize since 'we are all priests in Jesus Christ' (Judy). One expressed that while it does not need to be a pastor, 'I do think it needs to be someone mature who understands what baptism is about. Someone who just got saved shouldn't be doing a baptism' (Sarah). Lastly, another stated that while 'a pastor should be involved' that does not exclude other believers from immersing another believer (Shane).

Question 4: Water Baptism and Spirit Baptism

My fourth question sought to tease out the relationship (if any) between water baptism and Spirit baptism. Interestingly, there was some disagreement on this issue. Though one contributor was simply 'not sure' (Anne) of their relationship, the other participants had a general understanding of their position. For some, water baptism and Spirit baptism are 'two separate things' (Joshua, Deborah) and 'not related' (Stephanie). Most emphasized the lack of relationship between these two events, stating that while water 'baptism is just getting splashed in water' (Barry), Spirit baptism is an ecstatic event where the believer receives empowerment. One participant summarized this view well: 'They are different. Water baptism is a confession of faith in Jesus Christ. Spirit baptism is the empowerment to be able to walk like Jesus' (Paul). Nonetheless, one participant who emphasized the lack of relationship between these two 'baptisms' assigned more efficacy to water baptism than the other by stating that, 'water baptism is the cleansing … it washes away the demonic influences' (Kourtney).

However, those who affirmed the lack of relationship between the two agreed that 'water baptism is first and then Spirit (baptism)' (Joshua). However, other participants stated that 'they can happen at the same time' (Paul).

Another affirmed that there are 'three baptisms: a blood baptism – being baptized into the body of Christ at salvation – then water baptism – repentance, outward showing – and then Spirit baptism. But I also believe if you are seeking, it can happen at the same time of water baptism, but if not, it can later' (Ralph). According to Judy:

> It all depends on what the Lord wants to do with you … in the Bible, sometimes it happens at the same time and other times it doesn't. Sometimes it happens at the same time, like Jesus. But they are two different things. So, they can overlap, but two different things.

Thus, the timing of these events depends entirely upon the freedom of the Spirit. In the words of one man, 'God can put the Spirit anywhere he wishes – water, stone, snow – Spirit can be anywhere. Based on my experience, it can happen separately, but … it just depends' (Caleb). But the consensus is well summarized by one contributor when she stated that, 'while it can happen at the same time, it is more of an exception. Most of the time baptism of the Spirit happens after water baptism' (Nancy).

One contributor argued that these two events 'happen simultaneously' (Barbara). And though 'sometimes the Holy Spirit doesn't manifest in you right away, it is more a growing thing … just because you don't have certain gifts doesn't mean you don't have it (Spirit baptism). But I think they happen at the same time when you receive water baptism, you at the same time receive your Holy Spirit baptism' (Barbara). Lastly, one participant (Shane) argued similarly by stating:

> I see them as connected in a sense. I tend to think of baptism and communion more as sacraments than just as symbols. I tend to think there is an actual quality that the Spirit is a part of that, so water baptism is a baptism of the Spirit in a sense. I have seen people who have received it at the same time, and others not. The Spirit is involved in water baptism, but the gifts may come later or not at all in someone's life.

Therefore, Barbara and Shane understood these events to happen concurrently, even if the 'evidence' is not initially seen or heard.

Thus, most of the participants understood water baptism and Spirit baptism as two separate, and unrelated events. A few understood the possibility of these two events overlapping in a single experience, though one argued that these two 'baptisms' are always conjoined and another that they are usually connected, indicating a diversity and breadth of theological influences shaping this community.

Question 5: Water Baptism and Scripture

The final, two-part question focused on scriptural reflection.[228] The first part sought to hear what scriptural verses, passages, or biblical events informed the interviewee's view of water baptism. While most could think of at least one verse, passage, or biblical event, two participants could not think of any (Deborah, Barry), and though the rest were able to think of something, there was not much additional reflection offered.

For Sarah, 'Jesus' baptism' was what informed her view the most. In her words, 'it was the next step for Jesus … and us. There are steps we need to take. It is about obedience – but it doesn't mean we aren't going to heaven if we aren't baptized'. Others stated that John the Baptist 'baptizing in the wilderness' came to mind (Barbara, Ralph). Anne replied by stating that 'Matthew 28 when Jesus tells leaders/preachers to baptize and teach' was the most formative passage. One other participant stated that 'the book of Acts is full. Acts is when the church started and it was like a big wave of the movement, people getting saved, baptized, moving in the gifts, in different order' (Paul). Also referencing Acts, Shane stated that the 'Ethiopian eunuch being baptized has informed my view' by showing him that baptism 'is a personal decision that everyone needs to be able to make, and the Holy Spirit is involved in it'. Lastly, Caleb connected baptism to 'when Gideon was grinding wheat and God asks him to take the sword and defend Israel. Gideon is afraid, and God tells him not to be afraid. God gives us courage in water baptism.'

In the second part of the question, I directed the participants to Rom. 6.3-4 and Acts 2.38 to read and reflect on its meaning and

---

[228] 'What scriptures inform your view of water baptism? (and) What do Acts 2.38 and Romans 6.3-4 tell you about water baptism?'

implications for water baptism.[229] In reflecting on Rom. 6.3-4, Deborah stated that 'it is about unity and oneness with Christ. You went down with Christ as separate beings and now you are one'. Baptism, then, is about becoming one with Christ. Another woman furthered this line of thought: 'it says "joined" in this verse and you are joined in marriage ... we are married to him and we become his bride. We are married to Christ (in baptism)' (Barbara). Sally, agreeing with the last two women stated that Rom. 6.3-4 teaches that 'we are a part of him now'.

Barry stated that Rom. 6.3-4 tells us that 'we should change once we are baptized. You should really change and live a different life. Be cleaner and better'. Echoing a similar sentiment, another man stated that this told him that in baptism, 'you are new creation, and the old person dies'(Joshua). For another, rather than unity, it is about 'association with his death for the forgiveness of sins' (Stephanie). Though baptism does not forgive sins, Christ does, and we must associate with him who can forgive our sins. Nancy echoed a similar perspective: 'My sins *were* forgiven and (now) they are buried. And they are in my past. And though I sin every day, there is power in being baptized. New life begins, and the old life is gone' (Nancy).[230] Kourtney, also emphasizing the newness of life baptism brings stated that baptism 'is the beginning of walking with Jesus ... starting new'.

Paul connected this verse with John 3 in saying 'That's why Jesus said to Nicodemus – you must be born again' because in water baptism 'we die to our old self and are raised to new life as a new self'. Another believed Rom. 6.3-4 was evidence of the necessity of immersion since it 'pictured' death and resurrection (Shane). One man, though, did not believe this verse was talking about water baptism at all: 'I believe in three baptisms. I believe he is talking about the first baptism. A baptism unto salvation, not water baptism' (Ralph). Lastly, Judy did not offer any thoughts on Rom. 6.3-4.

In reflecting on Acts 2.38, a few participants believed this verse provided an *ordo salutis*. For Nancy, Acts 2.38 'tells us that there are steps. Confess your sins, (and receive) the forgiveness of sins. He will then send the Holy Spirit after water baptism'. Barry also believed that this scripture taught that 'the Holy Spirit ... comes after water

---

[229] Acts 2.38 and Rom. 6.3-4 were selected due to these scripture's prominence in the early contemporary Pentecostal literature.
[230] My emphasis.

baptism'. In other words, 'after baptism, you receive the gift of the Holy Spirit' (Kourtney). For Shane, this verse showed that 'baptism follows repentance'. Following this line of thought, Joshua offered a rationale behind the importance of being baptized first: 'The old you needs to die first … in water baptism because you are not going to get the gifts of the Spirit in the old you'.

Yet, for two others, this same scripture proved that water baptism and Spirit baptism can happen simultaneously. One woman stated that Acts 2.38 shows that 'If you get baptized you get both – you get the water baptism and the gift of the Holy Spirit at the same time' (Barbara). Additionally, another argued that 'this scripture' teaches that you 'will receive the gift of the Holy Spirit (in water baptism). The gift of the Spirit can (be given) in water baptism, and sometimes it can happen in a different way' (Paul). One woman was admittedly puzzled because this verse seemed to indicate that 'the Holy Spirit comes at baptism' (Anne). She also stated that it was confusing to her because 'Peter also says that you must be baptized to have forgiveness of sins and the Holy Spirit' (Anne). Another woman had a similar reaction by stating that, 'We need to repent of our sins before getting baptized. Then you will receive the Holy Spirit – but (here in Acts 2.38) that doesn't apply. They were baptized with the Holy Spirit before they were water baptized' (Judy).

Others tended to focus on the topic of forgiveness of sins in reflecting on Acts 2.38: 'This is saying to me, through baptism, in Jesus Christ, the weight of our sins is taken off of us'. (Caleb) And while baptism 'is related to salvation (it) doesn't give you salvation' (Deborah).[231] But for Ralph and Stephanie, Acts 2.38 taught the validity of baptism in Jesus' name. For Stephanie, Acts 2.38 helped her see 'it needs to be in the name of Jesus … repentance must be first and then baptism'. But for Ralph, Jesus' name is valid, but not necessary: 'This shows someone *could* say Jesus' name'.[232] Sally also opted for an 'either/or' attitude towards baptismal formula: 'to be baptized in the name of Jesus Christ – they are all one – God, Holy Spirit … it doesn't matter'. Taken as a whole, there were varying interpretations

---

[231] This participant did not elaborate further on the ways baptism and salvation are related and unrelated.

[232] My emphasis. Ralph also stated that this was evidence 'that some people could come out of the water speaking in tongues'.

and perspectives on these baptismal texts. Further, these texts brought much dissonance to many interviewed.

E.5 Secondary Literature

According to the *DPCM*, The Foursquare Church's 'doctrinal position ... is found in the declaration of faith, penned by its founder', Aimee Semple McPherson.[233] The Foursquare Church is 'trinitarian with respect to the Godhead', thus trinitarian in respect to its baptismal formula. In fact, 'little separates the doctrinal positions of the ICFG from that of the Assemblies of God, except for minor nuances', and water baptism is no exception.[234] Along with 'all major Pentecostal denominations in the U.S.', The Foursquare Church practices 'water baptism by immersion'.[235] This 'preference ... may lie as much in the continuity of the demonstrative nature of regular worship services as in their finding scriptural support for the practice'.[236] Further, 'faith by the recipient' is a 'crucial concern' for those being baptized in The Foursquare Church. Thus, in The Foursquare Church water baptism is for those who can exert their faith, since 'no proxy faith is sufficient', and baptism is by immersion in the name of the triune God.[237]

E.6 Empiricizing Pentecostalism: Conclusions

My overall findings suggest that ordinary Pentecostal theology in The Foursquare Church is not uniform. However, despite noticeable divergences on a host of issues, my study reveals some noteworthy uniformity on other issues. First, both observation and interviews show an openness to spontaneous baptisms. Observation revealed that both prior to and following the water baptisms, Pastor Don inquired whether anyone in the congregation was interested in being baptized who had not planned to be baptized. Further, interviews also reveal that many participants were often (re)baptized spontaneously at revival services. This both emphasizes the leading of the Holy Spirit *to*

---

[233] C.M. Robeck, Jr., 'International Church of the Foursquare Gospel', in Stanley M. Burgess, Gary B. McGee, and Patrick H. Alexander (eds.), *DCPM* (Grand Rapids, MI: Zondervan, 1988), p. 462.

[234] C.M. Robeck, Jr., 'International Church of the Foursquare Gospel', p. 462.

[235] Harold Hunter, 'Ordinances, Pentecostal', in Stanley M. Burgess, Gary B. McGee, and Patrick H. Alexander (eds.), *DCPM* (Grand Rapids, MI: Zondervan, 1988), p. 654.

[236] Hunter, 'Ordinances, Pentecostal', p. 654.

[237] Hunter, 'Ordinances, Pentecostal', p. 654.

baptism while de-emphasizing catechesis in preparation of baptism. Further, both observation and interviews reveal the prominence of baptism as a 'profession of faith'. For this congregation, baptism is above all else a public profession of faith. This means that water baptism is deeply personal to the believer, while perhaps also suggesting that baptism is more an act of the believer than it is of God. Notably, the theme of 'burial' was also widely present throughout the study. For many, water baptism symbolizes the believer's burial of one's old, sinful nature. The often-used 'burial' language also signals the significance of Rom. 6.4 as a scriptural resource. Lastly, both observation and interviews show that believer's baptism by immersion is the 'right' way to baptize and infant baptism is inappropriate. Rebaptism was also consistently and unvaryingly affirmed. Perhaps above all, the meaning of baptism, explicitly stated, was understood to be an occasion to profess one's faith publicly.

Yet, despite such convergences, there were also many divergent findings on several issues. First, while many understood baptism to be merely symbolic, a few interviewed suggested that God works through the water rite. Some interviewed described their personal experiences and observations of baptism to be quite routine/ordinary, while others reported experiencing and observing affective and/or S/spirited experiences in water baptism. For one interviewed, water baptism delivers the new believer from evil spirits and spiritual strongholds. Others interviewed testified to feeling God's presence in water baptism and/or experiencing its effects following their baptism. Though observation shows a preference for the triune formula, the interviews revealed variance in opinion on baptismal formula. Informants were split between baptism in 'Jesus' name' and baptism utilizing a trinitarian formula, though one argued for triple (trinitarian) immersion. And though Pastor Don water baptized all three candidates observed, interviews reveal that some interviewed believe ordination is not required to perform baptisms. Most of the participants in the interviews also understood water baptism and Spirit baptism as two separate, unrelated events, which is consistent with the observation. However, a few understood the possibility of these two events overlapping in a single experience, though one argued that these two 'baptisms' happen simultaneously. Scriptural reflection also varied widely, with no one theme or scripture dominating the conversation.

Finally, these findings are overall consistent with the secondary literature on The Foursquare Church: trinitarian formula, immersion, and profession of faith by the recipient are all consistent themes in all three sources (observation, interviews, and secondary literature). However, the secondary literature did not make mention of the rich sacramentality at the *implicit* level of theological discourse embedded in testimony. Through testimonies and reflections, the interviews reveal some expect to meet God in/through the water rite.

F. Water Baptism in The Foursquare Church: Conclusions

As the research indicates, early Pentecostal ordinary theology generally corresponds with the official teaching of The Foursquare Church at the explicit level of theological discourse. This should come as no surprise since the official teaching on water baptism has not changed since the denomination's inception. And while the Licensing Guide and the scholarly denominational voices are more contemporary and robust in their exploration of the sacrament, they too affirm a symbolic understanding of the rite. Therefore, the teaching on water baptism found in the official teaching agrees with the explicit teaching on water baptism expressed in *BC* and *BCF*. Further, some findings from the empirical research methods (interviews and participant observation) were also consistent with these sources.[238]

However, the official teaching found in the Declaration of Faith does not take into consideration the implicit sacramentality found in the testimonies expressed in the early *and* contemporary Pentecostal ordinary theology (revisioning and empirical). My findings indicate that at the implicit level of theological discourse, *contemporary* ordinary theology has much resonance with *early* ordinary theology.[239] More specifically, this study of *contemporary* ordinary theology reveals that while explicit statements on the rite's meaning tend to fit within a symbolic view of the bath, the majority of testimonies and

---

[238] However, one noticeable divergence is that while early sources emphasize baptism as a step of obedience, contemporary empirical sources emphasize baptism as a profession of faith.

[239] See my earlier section engaging *The Bridal Call* and *The Bridal Call Foursquare*. As Cartledge states, Pentecostal theology is often 'encapsulated in the notion of testimony'. Cartledge, *The Mediation of the Spirit*, p. 18.

reflections on the participants own experience of water baptism (Question 1) *and* their observation of other people's water baptisms (Question 2) disclose at the implicit level of discourse, a presence-driven (or encounter-driven) understanding of the rite exists. While this is certainly not uniform, the occurrences are significant enough to indicate that while ordinary believers explicitly state that the rite is symbolic, there is an implicit expectation to meet God amid the ritual. Or put another way, at least some seem to have a sense that if the rite is truly important, then meeting God would be how that is done.

Thus, while The Foursquare Church's resources have much to contribute to the construction of a Pentecostal theology of water baptism, perhaps one of its greatest gifts is its highlighting of the typical Pentecostal disjunction between experiences of water baptism and the official theology of water baptism. Put another way, as typical in Pentecostalism, there is a disparity between theology and practice. In this way, the resourcing confirms Frank Macchia's suspicion that 'Pentecostal theology must still catch up to Pentecostal experience when it comes to the sacraments of the church'.[240] Hence, The Foursquare Church's historical and contemporary resourcing, while divided at points, is beneficial in its offerings.

Yet, we need to continue to apply the approach taken in this chapter to other Classical Pentecostal denominations to discover and identify the proper framework within which a Pentecostal theology of water baptism might be constructed. Therefore, in the next chapter, we continue with an examination of the International Pentecostal Holiness Church.

---

[240] Frank D. Macchia, 'Tradition and the *Novum* of the Spirit: A Review of Clark Pinnock's Flame of Love', *JPT* 6.13 (1998), pp. 31-48 (46).

4

CLASSICAL PENTECOSTAL DENOMINATIONS AND WATER BAPTISM: INTERNATIONAL PENTECOSTAL HOLINESS CHURCH

A. Introduction

In this chapter, I will follow the previous chapter's structure. As stated previously, this means that I will explore (1) the ordinary theology of early Pentecostals as it relates to the meaning and practice of water baptism in the IPHC,[1] (2) the official denominational statements on the meaning and practice of water baptism, (3) the scholarly articulations of water baptism by IPHC scholars, and (4) the ordinary theology of contemporary Pentecostals in a particular IPHC church.

Therefore, my approach in this chapter – along with Chapters 3 and 5 – will seek to discover the 'ordinary theology' of *early* denominational Pentecostals, the 'ordinary theology' of *contemporary* Pentecostals in a particular denominational church, and how these resources triangulate with the official denominational statements and

---

[1] The IPHC has been known as the Fire-Baptized Holiness Association (1895-1902), Fire-Baptized Holiness Church (1902-1911), the Pentecostal Holiness Church (1907-1975), and the International Pentecostal Holiness Church (1975-Present). For a comprehensive history of the International Pentecostal Holiness Church provided by preeminent Pentecostal historian Vinson Synan, see 'International Pentecostal Holiness Church History (Part 1-3)' (2017). *International Pentecostal Holiness Church History*. https://digitalshowcase.oru.edu/iphch/1; https://digitalshowcase.oru.edu/iphch/2; https://digitalshowcase.oru.edu/iphch/3. See also the IPHC Archives & Research Center's Historic Timeline: https://iphc.org/gso/archives/timeline/

scholarly denominational voices that discuss water baptism. This triangulation will seek to investigate the convergences and divergences between the various resources. Among other things, this method will help Pentecostal scholars begin to discover how if at all denominational statements and the scholarly and ministerial voices that engage such statements, truly reflect the praxis and applied spirituality of the denomination – at the beginning of the movement and in the present day.

Though much of the chapter will focus on the descriptive research, I will conclude by moving to summarize the findings and comment on potential contributions that the IPHC can make to the construction of a Pentecostal theology of water baptism.

B. Hearing Early International Pentecostal Holiness Church Ordinary Theology

Following the structure and logic of the previous chapter,[2] I will engage the first ten years of periodical literature associated with the IPHC: *The Pentecostal Holiness Advocate*. It is now to this periodical that we turn.

B.1 *The Pentecostal Holiness Advocate* (1917-1926)
The Pentecostal Holiness Advocate (PHA) was 'the official church organ' of the Pentecostal Holiness Church from 1917 until 1996. At its inception, G.F. Taylor was named editor, and served in this role until his resignation in 1925. He was replaced by J.H. King who served until 1929. In the years engaged (1917-1926), most of the content on water baptism was in the form of scriptural engagements with the subject, though confessions on the rite's meaning and testimonies of baptismal experiences are also present. For our purposes, the most extensive discussions surrounding water baptism are in the form of rejoinders to Oneness Pentecostal teachings on the subject. Yet there are also discussions about water baptism to distinguish it from Spirit baptism, and to clear up potential confusion about the relationship between the two. Finally, it is noteworthy how little *PHA* engages the subject of water baptism compared to the Lord's Supper.

---

[2] See Chapter 3.

B.1.1 Water Baptism in *The Pentecostal Holiness Advocate*: Confessions and Articulations

Water baptism is described in several ways in *PHA*, including as 'an outward testimony of an inward work',[3] 'the first ordinance of the church',[4] and 'the sign of allegiance to Christ'.[5] And since 'we do not find where this ordinance has been repealed … no Christian should be denied the right to baptism'.[6] Therefore, baptism is important *to* and *for* the Christian because this act is 'an act of obedience to our Savior'.[7] All Christians, then, should be allowed to 'follow the Lord in water baptism'.[8] Perhaps this is important primarily because it is a step of Christian obedience. This implies that the only reason that 'one would be kept out of heaven for not receiving it' would be if one 'failed to receive it through disobedience'.[9] Therefore, *PHA* confesses water baptism to be important (1) emblematically as an outward representation of an inward work and (2) as a step of obedience.

It is important to note, though, that these two emphases throughout *PHA* seem to insist that the rite is not necessary to salvation. Since water baptism simply represents an inward work of grace it may be dispensed with in extreme cases as that of the thief on the cross. Therefore, there must be those 'in heaven today who never received water baptism'.[10] If one were to teach that water baptism is 'a part of the atonement' it would insist 'that the death of Jesus is in itself insufficient'.[11] Here G.F. Taylor is speaking to Pentecostals who might be tempted by 'radical' teachings during this time. Contrary to these teachings, *PHA* instructs that baptism is not something necessary in the eyes of God.[12]

---

[3] *PHA* 9.35 (1926), p. 7.
[4] *PHA* 3.10 (1919), p. 2.
[5] *PHA* 3.10 (1919), p. 2.
[6] *PHA* 3.10 (1919), p. 2.
[7] *PHA* 9.35 (1926), p. 7.
[8] *PHA* 1.4 (1917), p. 13.
[9] *PHA* 3.42 (1920), p. 9.
[10] *PHA* 2.18 (1918), p. 8.
[11] *PHA* 3.42 (1920), p. 9.
[12] The only break in this overall narrative comes from a guest writer, Brother John W. Wilson, who was 'on the road to heaven' when he wrote to 'Brother Taylor and Advocate Family' on the issue of water baptism. He wrote that 'it is a Christian's privilege to be baptized in the water, should they deem it necessary to make the race successful to heaven'. Further, 'we must not forget the law of doing this,

While these statements might suggest that the writers did not consider water baptism to be important, other statements suggest that as a whole, there was a desire to find a middle position between water baptism being essential and conversely, being something completely unnecessary:[13] 'some make water baptism the only real thing in religion, another fights all the ordinances of the Christian church, and builds a whole theology on that text where Paul says the Jewish ordinances were nailed to the cross'.[14] Therefore, given the various statements on baptism, *PHA* as a whole offers no single coherent vision of baptism.

PHA, or least its editors and leading voices, also places importance on the use of the triune formula when baptizing:

> It is to be in the name of the Father, and of the Son, and of the Holy Ghost. Here Jesus recognizes the Trinity. The three Persons of the Godhead are mentioned here in consecutive order. A number of times Jesus spoke about His Father being a distinct and separate Person from Himself ... there are many scriptures that reveal the Holy Trinity, and water baptism should be administered in the name of the Holy Trinity.[15]

In addition to the above statement, G.F. Taylor states that 'baptism must be administered with the formula, "In the name of the Father, and of the Son, and of the Holy Ghost." All of this is *entirely* ceremonial, but it is a ceremony of the New Dispensation.'[16] It is important to note that this insistence on the triune formula was used as a boundary marker in some cases, against 'the Finished work' and the 'modern fad' of 'Unitarianism' among Pentecostals.[17] While some in 'the Finished work ... argue that baptism should not be given in any

---

not only in baptism, but in every respect as our Christian duties'. And though water baptism is essential to the 'race to heaven ... we won't be left aside on account of different baptisms then, for all will be in the highest place to all men on earth and more glory and more joy and true peace'. Therefore, Wilson seems to posit that baptism in water is essential to salvation, but those baptized with differing modes or formulas will not be kept 'out of heaven'. See *PHA* 3.46 (1920), p. 16.

[13] Considering the Wesleyan Holiness lineage of Pentecostal Holiness doctrines, practices, and commitments, one might discern an Anglican 'via media' or 'way between two extremes' influence here.

[14] *PHA* 2.17 (1918), p. 1.
[15] *PHA* 3.10 (1919), p. 2.
[16] *PHA* 1.18 (1917), p. 4. Emphasis mine.
[17] *PHA* 3.10 (1919), p. 2.

name',[18] and Oneness groups argue that it is necessary to 'baptize in the name of Jesus only',[19] the *PHA* consistently maintains that 'if you believe in Jesus, you will accept baptism in the name of the Father, and of the Son, and of the Holy Ghost (and) to do otherwise is to go contrary to His plain command'.[20]

Furthermore, several places in PHA give ample room for teaching that speaks against Oneness baptismal theology, which is consistently described as 'a serious error' or 'an error that grows out of another error, and an error that leads to other errors'.[21] Further:

> This error grew out of the error that we are sanctified when we are converted. It has led to the error that there is but One Person in God. Such is the position of the Unitarians. Unitarianism is almost sure to lead to Universalism, and many other serious errors. Jesus commanded us to baptize in the name of the Father, and of the Son, and of the Holy Ghost, and no man has a right to change it.[22]

F.M. Britton, an instrumental figure in the merger between PHC and the Fire-Baptized Holiness Church,[23] weighing in on the Oneness controversy argues that 'the so-called "one God, one name baptism", has caused much confusion'.[24] In his mind, 'they substitute water baptism in "the name of Jesus only" for the blood of Jesus' by teaching that baptism washes away sin.[25] Britton describes this

---

[18] *PHA* 3.10 (1919), p. 2. Taylor states that those in 'the Finished Work' who argue 'that to repeat a formula in administering baptism can mean nothing, as it is only a form' are mistaken. In reply, he states: 'I would like to know if baptism itself is not a form. Is there not as much form in the act of baptizing as there is in repeating a formula in words? If baptizing is to be done without repeating a formula, without doing it in the name of the Lord, what is the difference between baptism and getting wet in a rain or jumping into a pond? If we are to so carefully avoid formality, would it not be wise to just let the rain baptize us or to carelessly fall into the river? If it is such a mistake to repeat the name of the Father, and of the Son, and of the Holy Ghost over a candidate for baptism, it must be as great mistake to administer baptism in any form. Such would be the natural conclusion.' See *PHA* 3.10 (1919), p. 2.

[19] *PHA* 3.10 (1919), p. 2.
[20] *PHA* 3.10 (1919), p. 2.
[21] *PHA* 3.10 (1919), p. 2.
[22] *PHA* 3.10 (1919), p. 2.
[23] See C.W. Conn, 'Britton, Francis Marion' in Stanley M. Burgess, et al. (eds.), *DPCM* (Grand Rapids: Zondervan, 1988), p. 99.
[24] *PHA* 9.22 (1925), p. 14.
[25] *PHA* 9.22 (1925), p. 14.

teaching as 'an awful error'.[26] Another writer states that Oneness Pentecostals 'preach that Jesus is His own Father, and that there is no Son. They say that the Father, Son and Holy Ghost is utterly false, and that there is only one in the Godhead, and they say that if you are baptized in the name of the Father, Son and Holy Ghost you are baptized wrong.'[27] In response, he urges believers to fight 'it with all (their) might'.[28]

Interestingly, while *PHA* was firm on *formula*, it was much more flexible on *mode*, since 'The P.H. Church … gives right of choice as to mode of baptism'.[29] The most important thing in water baptism is what it signifies, not how it is administered. In affirming this position, a guest writer from Baxter Springs, Kansas wrote to 'Brother Taylor' stating that he or she has 'felt for some time that there should be published in the Advocate the main principles of the Pentecostal Holiness Church'.[30] In stating the beliefs and convictions of the church, he or she states that 'we give anyone the right to choose any mode of water baptism they believe in'.[31] Even in later years as 'the Convention' updated polity and doctrine on baptism, a free choice on the mode of water baptism was continually affirmed. This writer continues:

> Up to this time, the Holiness Church received members with or without water baptism. You know the Quakers do not believe in water baptism, and the Holiness Church was so organized as to let that class in, as many of them in North Carolina were enjoying the experience of holiness. This Convention made water baptism essential to membership; but the candidate was left free to choose his own mode of baptism, as had been the case from the beginning, and is so to this day.[32]

While there is no definitive reason other than ambiguity in scripture stated for why there was flexibility given to mode, it seems clear the desire for unity influenced the decision. One writer testifies to the fact that the PHC was born 'out of revival' unlike 'other churches

---

[26] *PHA* 9.22 (1925), p. 14.
[27] *PHA* 6.38 (1923), p.15.
[28] *PHA* 6.38 (1923), p.15.
[29] *PHA* 7.43 (1924), p. 9.
[30] *PHA* 3.6 (1919), p. 12.
[31] *PHA* 3.6 (1919), p. 12.
[32] *PHA* 4.47 (1921), p. 9.

(that) have been born out of strife and confusion'.[33] These 'subjects that have caused such divisions in the past are those such as the Trinity, eternal punishment, predestination, water baptism, the second coming of Jesus, divine healing, etc.'[34] Therefore, it is not so much that the writers of PHA considered mode to be unimportant, only that it was not essential in drawing boundaries over.

While there are no explicit articulations or confessions surrounding infant baptism, there is one statement that mentions the practice concerning Roman Catholicism. In discussing why missionaries should be sent to Christian nations, the author states that it is because Catholicism has failed to share the true gospel, and has instead 'enshrouded it with mystery and superstition'.[35] As a result, 'great numbers' have been 'baptized en masse, having been coerced or forced to accept Catholicism. The result was not the genuine conversion of the natives, but a kind of paganized Catholicism which has since prevailed.'[36] While more than anything, these statements expose the author's anti-Catholic sentiment, it also sheds light on the fact that this author understands the kind of infant baptism practiced in Catholicism to be illegitimate. Further, one writer states that no one 'should receive water baptism until he is saved', which seems to advocate for believer's baptism.[37]

Finally, another important issue within the discussion surrounding water baptism is a type of 'spiritual baptism' that is both related, yet also unrelated to water baptism:

> There is another condition here given, necessary for salvation. Jesus puts baptism as a condition of being saved. Hence, I am inclined to think that there is more than water baptism included in this baptism. Perhaps it refers to suffering as well as to water. There is a baptism of suffering, and I am sure one must have it in order to be saved eternally. He that believeth and suffers with Christ will be eternally saved, and he that believeth not, shall never be baptized, but shall be eternally damned. One must be saved from sin before he can be saved eternally. Simon Magus both believed and received water baptism, but he never was saved in any

---

[33] *PHA* 4.42 (1921), p. 8.
[34] *PHA* 4.42 (1921), p. 8.
[35] *PHA* 5.15 (1921), p. 7.
[36] *PHA* 5.15 (1921), p. 7.
[37] *PHA* 2.18 (1918), p. 8.

sense. Baptism has more than one meaning, and perhaps is the case here.[38]

For this writer, there is a 'baptism of suffering' that relates to water baptism in some way. As we will soon see, this is a major discussion point throughout *PHA*, especially in relation to the scriptural witness. Therefore, it is to these scriptures that we now turn.

B.1.2 Water Baptism in *The Pentecostal Holiness Advocate*: Scripture

In confessing and articulating the meaning of water baptism, *PHA* appeals to and discusses many scriptures. *PHA* does not attempt to articulate *much* on water baptism without an exposition or appeal to biblical texts, especially Rom. 6.3-7[39] and Acts 2.38. Other passages from the Gospels of Matthew (Mt. 3.15; 20.22-23) and Mark (Mk 16.9-20) were discussed, as well, along with others from the Pauline (1 Cor. 2.4; 10.2; 12.13; 15.29), Lukan (Lk. 12.50; Acts 2.4, 2.42; 8; 18; 19), Johannine (Jn 3.5), and Petrine (1 Pet. 3.21; 2 Pet. 1.4) corpora.

Seeking to explain Jn 3.5, one commentator states that 'the water refers to the water of life, and not water baptism. Water is a symbol of the Holy Spirit. Except a man be born from above he cannot enter the kingdom of heaven. If this water refers to water baptism, then no one could be saved without it.'[40] The writer continues: 'concerning the water and the Spirit ... the water in John 3:5 refers to the water of life mentioned in John 3.10. I think that the Baptism [*sic*] of Mark 16:16 refers to the crucifixion of the old man (Rom. 6.6) and may also take in the Baptism [*sic*] of the Spirit. I have no objection to the interpretation that includes water baptism with the others in Mark 16:16.'[41] Interestingly, the writer opts for an intertextual interpretation on this matter. While he has 'no objection' for water baptism to '*include* water baptism *with the other*' signs in Mk 16.16,[42] he seems uncomfortable interpreting Jn 3.5 and Mk 16.16 as referring to water

---

[38] *PHA* 2.18 (1918), p. 8.
[39] As we will see, most writers in *PHA* did not understand Rom. 6.3-7 to be referencing water baptism, but a spiritual baptism of suffering. Yet, because this interpretation went against the grain of most interpreters, water baptism was inevitably brought up in the discussions of Rom. 6.3-7.
[40] *PHA* 5.22 (1922), p. 9.
[41] *PHA* 5.22 (1922), p. 6. The capitalization of the two baptisms might suggest the writer wants to privilege those over water baptism.
[42] *PHA* 5.22 (1922), p. 6. My emphasis.

baptism, at least exclusively. Another writer commenting on Mk 16.16 states that 'this does not refer to water baptism'.[43]

Remarking on 1 Cor. 10.2, another writer states that the Red Sea is a 'perfect type of water baptism':

> Then God took them through the Red Sea, a perfect type of water baptism, for the Word says they were baptized unto Moses in the cloud and in the sea. How their hearts rejoiced and they praised God on the other side. And so will every one of you rejoice and praise God on the other side when you see you are freed from the enemy of your soul.[44]

Thus, he/she discerns a connection between water baptism and freedom for the Christian, especially freedom from the enemy. While there is no more commentary on this statement, it is significant because it communicates that water baptism may be regarded a part of the process of Christian rebirth, and it this connection harkens back to ancient baptismal liturgies. The connection between baptism and the Red Sea crossing is again picked up by another writer, yet he goes in a different direction with it. He states that 'any preacher who knows the truth can use the crossing of the Red Sea, the crossing of the Jordan, the tabernacle, and many other such things to illustrate repentance, pardon, justification, sanctification, baptism of the Spirit, divine healing, water baptism, second coming of Jesus, or almost anything else'.[45] It seems that this particular author understands there to be flexibility in the *uses* of biblical metaphors to illustrate the meaning of various scriptural themes, including water baptism. Since the crossing of the Red Sea and water baptism are both mentioned, it is clear 1 Cor. 10.2 must be one of the scriptures in view. However, one might consider that this statement has more to do with the author's scriptural exegesis than it does his or her theology of water baptism, considering there is no more elaboration on how these types connect to water baptism or any of the other biblical themes mentioned.

Various passages from Acts were also discussed. In an article entitled, 'What We Believe', F.M. Britton references water baptism in the context of an argument discussing Acts 8, 18, and 19 with the

---

[43] *PHA* 7.44 (1924), p. 16.
[44] *PHA* 5.15 (1921), p. 2.
[45] *PHA* 7.43 (1924), p. 10.

intent to 'prove that the same doctrines are plainly taught in both'.[46] The 'Samaritans were straightened or sanctified by this baptism'.[47] Referencing Rom. 6.3, 6 the same writer states that this 'baptism of suffering, or into Jesus Christ, had so straitened, or sanctified Peter and John that they taught the Samaritans how to be sanctified so that they could receive the Holy Ghost'.[48] Therefore, Britton seems to argue that the water baptism of the Samaritans was also an occasion for their sanctification or straitening.[49] This means that water baptism, at least in Romans 6 and Acts 18, is understood to have a sanctifying effect.

This understanding of the rite as a *sanctifying bath* is also repeated in a later issue. An anonymous writer states that Apollos, while preaching at Ephesus, was unaware that Jesus was the Messiah, and he and the other Ephesians were only followers of John the Baptist.[50] He then concludes that 'when they thus received water baptism, it is my thought that they were sanctified'.[51] Sanctification is not explicitly mentioned, but the writer states that it is implied due to its connection to water baptism.

This reasoning is also furthered by the same writer in connection to chapters 8 and 19 in Acts:

> Another thing is that there is evidence that these people were sanctified under the ministry of Philip. It is not so stated in so many words, but I believe it is implied ... there is a baptism unto the death of the old man, and we read in Romans that those who were baptized into Jesus Christ were baptized into His death, and that this death is the death of the old man ... I believe that these people received water baptism after they were truly saved and that when they consented to this baptism they met such conditions as brought about their sanctification. The same truth can be applied to the Ephesian brethren in the nineteenth chapter of Acts.[52]

For *PHA*, then, sanctification can be related to water baptism in that the rite is a primary occasion for sanctification to take place for the

---

[46] *PHA* 6.49 (1923), p. 3.
[47] *PHA* 6.49 (1923), p. 3.
[48] *PHA* 6.49 (1923), p. 3.
[49] *PHA* 6.49 (1923), p. 3.
[50] *PHA* 7.26 (1923), p. 10.
[51] *PHA* 7.26 (1923), p. 10.
[52] *PHA* 3.40 (1920), p. 2.

believer, as implied throughout Acts. So, while some considered the rite to be primarily concerned with obedience, others considered it a means to experience sanctification.

In contrast, however, G.F. Taylor's interpretation of Acts 19.5 states that 'water baptism may be implied, but I am sure it refers more directly to the baptism of Romans 6:3-7, which means a crucifixion of the old man. Study it also in connection with Luke 12:50 and Matthew 20:22, 23.'[53] While some of the Acts narratives may speak of water baptism, it may refer more directly to a baptism of suffering, which is a spiritual baptism of sorts.[54] The first type of baptism is water baptism, which 'is employed as a symbol'.[55] Then, second, there is 'the real baptism' which is found 'in 1 Corinthians 12:13, "For by one Spirit are we all baptized into one body … this is a baptism that brings oneness'.[56] Lastly, there is a baptism of suffering which as shown in Rom. 6.3-7, 'does away with our old man, the cause of division'.[57] *PHA* consistently speaks of texts in light of these three, separate categories of 'baptisms'. In discussing the baptism mentioned in Romans 6, one author states that it 'looses from sin: absence of the old man and his deeds … one accord; great joy; continual praises to God. The gift of the Holy Ghost.'[58] Therefore, the reception of the Spirit is often associated with a baptism of repentance or suffering, but not truly separate for baptism in every case.

Others spoke differently of these baptisms. In another article, entitled 'Baptized into one Body', an author quotes 1 Cor. 12.13 and states that he or she had recently listened to a sermon 'in which the preacher took the position that the above quotation means Holy Ghost baptism. And that all believers receive this baptism when regenerate.'[59] According to this author, this is an error that is spreading due to a lack of proper spiritual knowledge.[60] The writer sought to 'advance a few thoughts which may shed some light' on the 'true meaning' of the passage.[61] After arguing for a subsequent 'Holy

---

[53] *PHA* 2.2 (1918), p. 16.
[54] *PHA* 2.2 (1918), p. 16.
[55] *PHA* 1.7 (1917), p. 3.
[56] *PHA* 1.7 (1917), p. 3.
[57] *PHA* 1.7 (1917), p. 3.
[58] *PHA* 1.7 (1917), p. 3.
[59] *PHA* 4.30 (1920), p. 2. Grammar and spelling original.
[60] *PHA* 4.30 (1920), p. 2. Grammar and spelling original.
[61] *PHA* 4.30 (1920), p. 2.

Ghost baptism', the writer moves to discuss the differences between 'water baptism', 'Holy Ghost baptism', and 'baptism into death'.[62] In sum, the author advances the view that these three baptisms serve different purposes. Water baptism is strictly for church membership purposes, Spirit baptism is for a relationship with the Holy Spirit and to be endued with power, and the last baptism mentioned in Romans 6 is for a spiritual baptism of death to sin.[63]

After articulating these three different types of baptism, the author turns back to the original question: 'What does the Apostle mean by saying, "We are baptized by one spirit into one body?"'.[64] In response, the author states that all Christians become members in the church through 'the Spirit of Christ, for we are told that if we have not the Spirit of Christ we are none of His, or in other words, not members of His body'.[65] Yet:

> the Spirit of Christ ... is *not* the Holy Ghost. It is not the personality of Christ, but the Holy Spirit or principle that belongs to Him by divine nature and is imparted to us ... So we see that it is this Spirit or principle of Christ by which we become possessors of the nine spiritual gifts and become members of the body of Christ and receive the precious gift of the Holy Ghost baptism.[66]

While this teaching is perhaps unclear on several points, it appears at the least, that the author is arguing that (1) there are three 'baptisms' spoken of in scripture: water baptism, Spirit baptism, and baptism into Christ's death, (2) 1 Cor. 12.13 is *not* referring to 'Holy Ghost baptism' but to 'baptism into death' that unites us to Christ and his church, and finally, (3) that 'the Spirit of Christ' or 'the principle of Christ', (which/who is not 'The Holy Ghost') is imparted to believers in preparation of receiving the subsequent 'Holy Ghost baptism' where one receives the Holy Spirit. In order to keep the sharp distinction between water baptism and Spirit baptism, the author distinguishes between the Holy Spirit/Holy Ghost as the third person in the Godhead, from the 'principle of Christ' or 'holy spirit', which is a new nature, but not an indwelling person. Also, in this rendering

---

[62] *PHA* 4.30 (1920), p. 2.
[63] *PHA* 4.30 (1920), p. 2.
[64] *PHA* 4.30 (1920), p. 2.
[65] *PHA* 4.30 (1920), p. 2. Italics mine.
[66] *PHA* 4.30 (1920), p. 2. Italics mine.

water baptism serves to unite one to the church, which suggests that baptism is as much for the community as it is for the baptized one.[67] Therefore, not only is Rom. 6.3-7 understood to reference the 'third baptism' (baptism into Christ's death), but 1 Cor. 12.13 is as well.

In a Q&A section entitled 'Question Box', someone wrote in asking the question: 'Does Jesus refer to water baptism in Luke 12:50?' In reply, the writer responded by saying, 'He refers to a baptism of suffering or His sufferings on the cross'.[68] G.F. Taylor also connects 'the verse that speaks of one being baptized for the dead' (1 Cor. 15.29) to this 'baptism of suffering':[69]

> I think that being baptized for the dead means to be baptized in the name of a dead Christ ... This (passage) may refer to water baptism, or it may go farther than that and refer to spiritual baptism unto the death of the old man. Then connecting it with Rom. 6:4 we can see that we are void of the resurrection life of Jesus.[70]

Hence, for some in the *PHA*, water baptism has little to do with being buried and participating in Christ's death, since this takes place in a separate baptism. However, there are minority voices that upend this narrative at times.

Lastly, *PHA* contains many references to Acts 2.38. Commenting on this verse, G.F. Taylor states, 'this text is used by some to teach that water baptism is essential to salvation; by others, to teach that it is essential to the Baptism of the Holy Spirit; by others, to teach that water baptism should be administered in the name of Jesus only. We do not believe that the text teaches any of these things.'[71] Instead, 'Peter was preaching to people who had crucified Jesus in the open, and their sin was of such a nature as to demand that they now are baptized in the name of the very one whom they had crucified'.[72] He also states that 'there is no doubt that Peter referred first to water baptism, but this does not exclude another application of the word ... since the word baptism has various shades of meaning'.[73] He argues that by looking to Rom. 6.3-4, one can interpret this baptism to

---

[67] *PHA* 4.30 (1920), p. 2.
[68] *PHA* 7.27 (1923), p. 10.
[69] *PHA* 8.32 (1924), p. 9.
[70] *PHA* 8.32 (1924), p. 9.
[71] *PHA* 8.31 (1921), p. 4.
[72] *PHA* 8.31 (1921), p. 4.
[73] *PHA* 8.31 (1921), p. 4.

also mean 'a baptism of death', which would imply that 'Peter's command to those Jews to be baptized in the name of Jesus carried with it the thought of being crucified with Christ ... (and) on these grounds all their sins, both outward and inward, would be taken away'.[74] Therefore, 'it cannot be shown that water baptism is required before the Baptism of the Holy Spirit'.[75]

In another instance, an anonymous author asked Taylor to 'explain why Jesus was baptized' since 'water baptism is for the remission of sins'.[76] In response, the editor replied, 'water baptism is not for remission of sins. No scripture teaches it thus when properly understood'.[77] While the original writer might have been appealing to Acts 2.38, Taylor does not acknowledge it and provides no commentary on it.

In another issue, however, Taylor does argue another explanation of Acts 2.38. Significantly, he states that 'the "remission of sins", must *mean the act of taking sins away*'.[78] He goes on to say:

> We believe that Jesus Christ shed His blood for the remission of all sin, whatever it may be in nature ... still, you will notice the following phrases: 'Baptism of repentance for the remission of sins' ... these verses insisted that there are conditions as well as grounds on which God grants pardon. Now, so far as the merits of pardon are concerned, they are all in the shed blood of Jesus Christ ... Nothing can be added to it or taken from it ... yet, it is clear that a man must meet certain conditions before this price will be turned to his individual credit.[79]

Therefore, Taylor appears to state that water baptism is a condition for receiving the remission of sins. While pardon is granted through the blood of Christ, one is only able to receive it through the condition of baptism. These statements stand in considerable tension with other statements of his.

A similar text that gets only one treatment is 1 Pet. 3.21. In expounding upon it the writer states:

---

[74] *PHA* 8.31 (1921), p. 4.
[75] *PHA* 8.31 (1921), p. 4.
[76] *PHA* 1.35 (1917), p. 16.
[77] *PHA* 1.35 (1917), p. 16.
[78] *PHA* 1.29 (1917), p. 4. Emphasis original.
[79] *PHA* 1.79 (1917), pp. 4-5.

The parenthetical expression refers to water baptism, and this has its place, and is right and proper, but mere water baptism alone has no saving virtue. The baptism that counts is the inward work of grace, the regenerating forces and virtues of the atonement and resurrection of Jesus Christ. The ark was a type of Christ, and those saved in it are prophetical of those who are saved by the grace of God.[80]

The author seems to suggest that though this text speaks of water baptism, there is more to this text than meets the eye. As this demonstrates, there is much 'grey area' regarding comments on baptism in *PHA*.

B.1.3 Water Baptism in *The Pentecostal Holiness Advocate*: Testimonies and Reflections

The bulk of testimonies and reflections in *PHA* centered around reporting baptisms taking place in local congregations and camp meetings. Most reports follow a standard format: 'Nine were baptized in water one week ago yesterday, and we expect to have another baptizing a week from next Sunday'.[81] Consistently, reports also showed that believers of all ages were baptized: 'We had a water baptizing ... the oldest one was seventy-six years of age, Sister Martha Campbell. The youngest was little Sister Dollie Ginger, nine years of age.'[82] These same testimonies say that children (most likely infants) were 'consecrated': 'The last Sunday we baptized ten in water and consecrated six children which made a total of forty-six baptized this quarter and thirty-eight children consecrated'.[83] In another report, one writer states that they recently water baptized 'thirty-six at Mabeiskraal and consecrated thirteen children. We had five blessed days in the Lord at Mabeiskraal. We left there and went to Rasegae Stad. There we baptized fourteen adults and consecrated one child.'[84] Therefore, it seems that standard practice was water baptism for believers and 'consecration' for infants.

Water baptism was also used to validate true revival: 'At my last writing I was in LaGrange, GA., in a tent meeting. Had just started.

---

[80] See *PHA* 5.5 (1921), p. 10.
[81] *PHA* 4.45 (1921), p. 13. Misspelling original.
[82] *PHA* 5.15 (1921), p. 11.
[83] *PHA* 4.45 (1921), p. 6.
[84] *PHA* 3.46 (1920), p. 10.

The Lord gave the victory, and several were saved and sanctified, one received the Holy Ghost. Three were baptized in water and were added to the church.'[85] In other cases, water baptism was connected to accepting members into the church.[86] This seems to suggest that, in some cases, baptism was understood to be a performative act, joining people as members to the community.

One of the more interesting testimonies comes from J.C. Yearout, recounting a story of a bedside baptism. He states that someone 'about three weeks before he died ... wanted to be baptized'.[87] As a result, Yearout 'called for his pastor, Brother G.W. Stanley, and as many of the saints as could come to his home'.[88] Consequently, there was a large crowd that sang and prayed with this man. Brother Stanley then baptized the man 'by pouring the water in the name of Jesus'.[89] Notably, pouring was used instead of immersion, and this man was said to be baptized in the name of Jesus instead of the triune God. This implies that while the confessions and articulations surrounding water baptism consistently states that the only valid baptismal formula is the triune formula, this testimony and reflection reveals that some of those 'on the ground' baptized in the name of Jesus.

Most noticeably, testimonies of sensational or extraordinary experiences in water baptism are unusual in *PHA*. The testimonies and reflections *might* suggest that water baptism was understood to be a lesser theme. Consider following report as one example: 'In February Bro. Wiley came and preached eleven days. He went home and came back, he and Brother Vaughn, and had a wonderful meeting. *Many* were saved, sanctified, and baptized with the Holy Ghost, and *some* baptized in water.'[90] One might consider the fact that many were saved and only some were water baptized is revealing.

B.2 Hearing Early International Pentecostal Holiness Church Ordinary Theology: Conclusions

In conclusion, throughout the pages of *PHA* various subjects on water baptism were discussed. There were many scriptural engagements on the subject, most notably centered around Rom. 6.3-6 and Acts

---

[85] *PHA* 2.18 (1918), p. 5.
[86] *PHA* 6.46 (1923), p. 3.
[87] *PHA* 3.46 (1920), p. 6.
[88] *PHA* 3.46 (1920), p. 6.
[89] *PHA* 3.46 (1920), p. 6.
[90] *PHA* 7.26 (1923), p. 11. Emphasis mine.

2.38. Overall, great attention was given to affirming the importance of baptism as a step in one's discipleship. Water baptism was also often understood as one baptism among others, including Spirit baptism and a distinct baptism of suffering. While it was mainly understood as merely a symbol, a few statements talked of water baptism being an entry into sanctification. However, the importance of the rite was quite often downplayed, especially in comments made by the periodical's first editor, G.F. Taylor. Overall, the contributors did not present a coherent vision of baptism in *PHA*.[91]

As noted earlier, a few guest writers' confessions and testimonies scattered throughout *PHA* reveal that some minority voices thought more highly of the rite's importance. Often, readers would submit questions for the editor asking for an explanation on scriptures that spoke of baptism concerning salvation or 'remission of sins'. My reading of the material, then, indicates that the loudest, majority voice (the editors) had a consistently 'low' view of water baptism, while other guest writers and the readership, at times, expressed an implicitly 'high' view of the rite. Nevertheless, the publication spoke in varying ways about water baptism.

C. Hearing Official Denominational Statements

Official IPHC teaching on water baptism stems from one source: 'The IPHC Constitution Disciplines and Manuals'. Notably, this document has been updated twenty-six times since the original 1911 'Constitution and General Rules of the Pentecostal Holiness Church'.[92]

C.1 International Pentecostal Holiness Church Constitution Disciplines and Manuals

Historically, the IPHC has considered water baptism and the Lord's Supper to be its two 'ordinances', though footwashing has been observed, even if it is not elevated to the status of an 'ordinance': 'Each individual member of the Pentecostal Holiness Church shall have

---

[91] G.H. Taylor's contradictory statements on Acts 2.38 are but one example of this.
[92] According to denominational minutes, this guide was updated in the following years: 1913, 1917, 1921, 1925, 1929, 1933, 1937, 1941, 1945, 1949, 1953, 1957, 1961, 1965, 1969, 1973, 1977, 1981, 1985, 1989, 1993, 1997, 2001, 2005, 2009, 2013.

liberty of conscience in the matter of footwashing'.[93] From the beginning, the official statements on water baptism centered solely upon flexibility on mode and believer/infant baptism. For instance, the statement on water baptism in the earliest manual says: 'All candidates for baptism shall have the right of choice between the various modes as practiced by the various evangelical denominations. Christian parents and guardians shall have liberty of conscience in the baptism of their children.'[94]

Meaning and formula, then, are absent from the earliest official statements on water baptism for the central concern at the time was freedom of choice in baptizing adults or children through various modes. However, the manual prescribes a baptismal charge to be implored/prayed over the candidate, which gives a deeper look into the meaning of water baptism.

> Dearly Beloved: The last command of our risen Lord was to go into all the world and preach the gospel to every creature, and His Representative, the blessed Holy Spirit, throughout the Book of Acts enforced this command through the apostles in relation to all who believed in Christ; therefore it is our bounden duty as possessors of His grace to conform to this great commission, both in the preaching of the Word and the administration of the ordinance of baptism, as opportunity affords ... This act of yours, coming seeking baptism in the name of the Lord, is a public testimony of your professed subjection to Christ and the grace vouchsafed to you in the pardon and cleansing of your soul from sin. But that you may further declare your determination to walk in the commandments of the Lord and in faith of Christ.[95]

According to this baptismal charge, baptism is understood to be a command that must be obeyed. And by obeying this command from Christ, the candidate's baptism serves as a 'public testimony of ...

---

[93] 'Constitution and General Rules of the Pentecostal Holiness Church' (1911), p. 5

[94] 'Constitution and General Rules of the Pentecostal Holiness Church' (1911), p. 4.

[95] 'Constitution and General Rules of the Pentecostal Holiness Church' (1911), p. 22.

professed subjection to Christ'.[96] Thus, baptism is an act of obedience and a public profession of faith.

Nonetheless, as noted earlier, there have been many updates and revisions by committees to the official manual throughout the years, including notable changes in the statements surrounding water baptism. From 1911-1925 the statement on water baptism remained unchanged. Yet, in 1925 the manual added two features to the statement. The formula was clarified by adding, 'baptism shall be administered according to the divine command of our blessed Lord, "In the name of the Father, and of the Son, and of the Holy Ghost"', and it was supported by referencing Mt. 28.19-20 at the end of the statement.[97] Except for this addition on formula, the statement was left unchanged until 1933. At this point, one declaration was added: 'All who unite with any local church on the profession of their faith in Christ shall further confess Christ by receiving water baptism as early as convenient'.[98] What was implicitly taught in the 1911 manual through the charge to candidates, then, was explicitly added in the official statement on water baptism in 1933.[99]

In 1945, there was a striking addition to the statement. From 1911-1945, one part of the official statement had read, 'Christian parents and guardians shall have liberty of conscience in the baptism of their children'; yet, in the 1945 manual, the statement was changed to read:

> Christian parents and guardians shall have liberty of conscience in the *dedication or* baptism of their children. When a child is dedicated or baptized, he or she shall be taken under the watch-care of the church until the age of discretion and responsibility is reached, and then the child received into full fellowship of the church according to his own desire and profession of faith.[100]

---

[96] 'Constitution and General Rules of the Pentecostal Holiness Church' (1911), p. 22.

[97] 'Discipline of the Pentecostal Holiness Church' (1929), p. 24. One might consider that this point was clarified considering the Oneness baptismal teaching coming to prominence among Pentecostals in this time.

[98] 'Discipline of the Pentecostal Holiness Church' (1933), p. 37.

[99] Perhaps this is a sign of a need for greater theological coherence surrounding baptism.

[100] 'Discipline of the Pentecostal Holiness Church' (1945), p. 44. My emphasis.

Therefore, for the first-time infant dedication was said to be an option alongside infant baptism.[101] The relationship between infant dedication, infant baptism, and the church was also clarified. Significantly, the added statement also signals an understanding of children not being 'full members' until they have reached 'the age of discretion and responsibility'.[102] Thus, only those who have 'professed' their faith, are considered to be in 'full fellowship' with the church.[103] Notably, Lk. 18.15-17 was added alongside Mt. 28.19, 20 as official, scriptural support for infant dedication.

As significant as this alternation is, the 1957 manual made a perhaps even more significant change. In this update, all mentions of parental choice on mode, baptism, and dedication were omitted. In 1965, the statement was shortened further by omitting 'the right of choice between the various modes as practiced by the various evangelical denominations' from the earlier statement.[104] Therefore, by 1957 every part of the original 1911 statement had been omitted and replaced.

Most recently in 2009, the statement was altered for the last time:[105]

> Water Baptism is intended only for those who have professed faith in the Lord Jesus Christ. It is a God-given *illustration* of each Christian's identification with Christ in His death, burial, and resurrection. Obedience to this ordinance demonstrates the believer's public confession of this fact to others.[106]

The most recent statement clearly emphasizes the motifs of obedience to this ordinance and identification with Christ, not in participation or imitation, but in a mental exercise of recognition with Christ. The statement also adds that baptism is intended for those who have professed faith in Christ.

---

[101] Despite the shift, this seems to have been standard practice already, as seen in *PHA*'s discussion of children being 'consecrated'. My emphasis.
[102] 'Discipline of the Pentecostal Holiness Church' (1945), p. 44.
[103] 'Discipline of the Pentecostal Holiness Church' (1945), p. 44.
[104] 'Discipline of the Pentecostal Holiness Church' (1945), p. 44.
[105] The latest statement on water baptism in 2013 manual reads the same as the 2009 statement.
[106] 'International Pentecostal Holiness Church Manual' (2009), p. 53. My emphasis.

Therefore, in sum, not only has the official statements on water baptism changed considerably over the years, it has changed so much so that the current manual's description of water baptism has been completely rewritten since the original 1911 statement.

C.2 Hearing Official Denominational Statements: Conclusions

In sum, much of the official IPHC teaching on water baptism has changed significantly over the years. Originally, the IPHC's statement on water baptism was most concerned with parental choice in mode and timing with regards to the baptism of their children. Yet most recently, the IPHC's statement emphasizes believer's baptism and the dedication of children, fundamentally shifting away from the theological framework at work in the early period. Yet, the IPHC has also been uniformly trinitarian in its water baptismal formula. Though water baptism has been consistently understood as an act of obedience, this motif has shifted weight from imitating Christ to obeying the ordinance. Therefore, significant shifts have taken place on issues such as parental choice, infant/believer baptism, mode, and the stated meaning of water baptism.

D. Hearing International Pentecostal Holiness Church Scholarly Voices

This section restricts itself to engagement with scholarly works that are written on water baptism by IPHC scholars/ministers. Presently, seven IPHC scholars have engaged the subject of water baptism: J.H. King, Noel Brooks, Paul Beacham, Harold D. Hunter, Terry Tramel, Frank G. Tunstall, and A.D. Beacham, Jr. We now turn to summarize these scholar's contributions to the subject.

D.1 J.H. King[107]

J.H. King was a founder and noteworthy General Superintendent of the IPHC (1917-1945). While he wrote on many topics as a major

---

[107] Since J.H. King served as the editor of the *Pentecostal Holiness Advocate* (*PHA*) from 1925-1929, his work has already been probed indirectly through my engagement of the *PHA*. Nonetheless, due to King's monumental importance to the IPHC, I will also be engaging other works where he discusses water baptism.

voice within the IPHC and the broader Pentecostal movement, his overall treatment of water baptism was peripheral.[108]

According to Tony Moon, a leading King scholar, 'reflecting his Methodist Episcopal heritage' King often called the rite 'the sacrament of baptism'.[109] King stated that he was 'thoroughly indoctrinated by Methodistic tenets of faith … (and) came into full sympathy with its spirit and polity',[110] and nothing had ever removed him from it.[111] King's overall theology of baptism, then, shows alignment with his Methodist roots.[112] One evidence is the way he framed his opposition to Oneness Pentecostalism's teaching on water baptism.

Moon has pointed out that King regularly used his 'Bible conference work' and 'pulpit Scripture exposition ministry' to 'make a dent in the rampant problem of Pentecostals "running wild" after the "new and sensational"'.[113] According to King, 'unitarian anti-Trinitarianism' and 'Jesus name water baptism' were both examples of this.[114] Thus, combating the Oneness teaching, King argued for a trinitarian baptismal formula, with *no* allowance made for Jesus' name baptism. King, serving as General Superintendent of the IPHC during the rise of Oneness Pentecostalism, 'surely endorsed' the need to 'refine and

---

[108] I was told this through personal correspondence with Tony Moon via telephone on September 2, 2018. Further, the fact that King never discusses his own baptism in his autobiography, I believe, is telling. It is especially striking considering the amount of detail King provides about other minor happenings in his lifetime. See Joseph H. King, *Yet Speaketh* (Franklin Springs, GA: The Publishing House of the Pentecostal Holiness Church, 1949).

[109] J.H. King, 'Pacific Coast Missionary Society', p. 5 in Tony G. Moon, *From Plowboy to Pentecostal Bishop: The Life of J.H. King* (Lexington, KY: Emeth Press, 2017), p. 201 n. 28. See also *The Doctrines And Discipline of the Methodist Episcopal Church, South* (Nashville, TN: Barbee & Smith, 1890); *Manual of the Methodist Episcopal Church* (New York: Phillips & Hunt, 1888).

[110] King, *Yet Speaketh*, p. 43.

[111] King was associated with the Methodist Episcopal Church, (South) from 1885-1890 and subsequently the Methodist Episcopal Church, (North) from 1891-1898. In August 1898, King joined the Fire-Baptized Holiness Church in Anderson, South Carolina. See David A. Alexander, 'Bishop J.H. King and the Emergence of Holiness Pentecostalism', *Pneuma* 8.1 (1986), pp. 159-83 (176-77).

[112] One example is King's flexibility on mode and infant baptism/believer's baptism. In the section on the sacraments, the 1988 *Manual of the Methodist Episcopal Church* states: 'Let every adult person, and the parents of every child to be baptized, have the choice of either sprinkling, pouring, or immersion'. See, *Manual of the Methodist Episcopal Church*, p. 233.

[113] Moon, *From Plowboy to Pentecostal Bishop*, p. 304.

[114] Moon, *From Plowboy to Pentecostal Bishop*, p. 304.

add more details to its official theology'.¹¹⁵ As a result of King's insistence, the 'Trinitarian formula of Matthew 28:19 was inserted into the "Ordinances" section of the polity manual as a requirement for water baptism'.¹¹⁶ King drew upon 'four affirmations of American Methodism's 1784 Twenty-Five Articles of Religion' to address 'the subject of the divine Trinitarian nature of traditional, historic, orthodox Christian fashion'.¹¹⁷

Reflecting on his early years in his autobiography, King detailed that 'no one knew God in deep spirituality, and we were but one step removed from heathen superstition and abominations'.¹¹⁸ However, at the age of nine, King experienced a Baptist revival and witnessed 'forty professions of faith'.¹¹⁹ These forty people were also baptized in water. As he describes this event, he discloses some of his understanding of water baptism:

> As a little boy I stood by the pool and saw the venerable old man, Rev. Hamilton Hayes, stand in cold water to baptize forty candidates. It took a long time to do it. In my ignorance I verily thought that as each candidate went up out of the water they left their sins in it, and the water carried their sins away. Bible truths were little known in all that country, and hence I had no one to teach me the truth of forgiveness, and the new birth. The sermons delivered by the preachers of the Methodist and Baptist churches were but in the bear [sic] twilight of gospel truth. If the facts were fully known concerning those candidates baptized that day, they would probably show that but few of them were saved, or born of the Spirit.¹²⁰

In this passage King connects true baptism to a lived life of faith. Baptism alone does not save or signal that one is truly born of the Spirit. Water baptism must be followed by a lived life of service to God to be understood as genuine.

At other times, King described baptism as a symbolic act. For instance, when discussing Rom. 6.3-4, King stated that the Romans 'had been baptized symbolically into Christ's death in the baptism of

---

[115] Moon, *From Plowboy to Pentecostal Bishop*, p. 423.
[116] Moon, *From Plowboy to Pentecostal Bishop*, p. 423.
[117] Moon, *From Plowboy to Pentecostal Bishop*, p. 423.
[118] King, *Yet Speaketh*, p. 19
[119] King, *Yet Speaketh*, p. 24
[120] King, *Yet Speaketh*, p. 25.

water'.[121] Through baptism 'they were to reckon themselves to be dead indeed and to sin because they had passed through it symbolically'.[122] King states that water baptism is symbolic but also that the Spirit is present in the act of baptism: 'The Holy Spirit is the baptizing agent, we are the subjects, and death is the element into which we are plunged; the effect is the death and burial of the "old man"; the resurrection to a life wholly renewed in God's image of holiness, the result'.[123] Yet, in discussing Jesus' baptism, King does not connect baptism to the work of the Spirit but instead connects it to Spirit baptism. For King, Jesus' baptism by John 'refers to both His baptism in water and the baptism of the Holy Ghost'.[124] So while 'the Trinity was manifested in His baptism ... with us, it is the actual incoming of the Father, Son, and Spirit to abide in the Pentecostal baptism'.[125]

Finally, at one place King connects water baptism to grace when he states that 'baptism in water has its sign, the fact of grace imparted, and we must never lose sight of this if we expect to keep baptism up to its Scriptural standard'.[126] One might suggest that this statement most resembles his Methodist roots, with its emphasis on baptism as a means of grace.[127] Yet, as demonstrated above, King had a myriad of ways of describing the meaning of baptism. Perhaps based on King's background, he is suggesting an understanding of baptism that is symbolic, but not merely so – one that is also a means of grace.

D.2 Noel Brooks[128]

Noel Brooks became a part of the English Pentecostal Holiness Church in 1954, where he served as a pastor of the Pentecostal Holiness Church in Bristol. Later, he served in many roles for the English Pentecostal Holiness Church, such as Director of Evangelism, General Superintendent of the British Conference, and founder

---

[121] J.H. King, *From Passover to Pentecost* (Franklin Springs, GA: LifeSprings Resources, 2004), p. 64.
[122] King, *From Passover the Pentecost*, p. 64.
[123] King, *From Passover the Pentecost*, p. 65.
[124] King, *From Passover the Pentecost*, p. 109.
[125] King, *From Passover the Pentecost*, p. 110.
[126] King, *From Passover the Pentecost*, p. 144.
[127] For instance, the *Manual of the Methodist Episcopal Church* (1888) states that baptism is a 'means of grace' (p. 235).
[128] Though my study is limited to US forms of the IPHC, Brooks' ministry and writing was highly influential in the US church as a British minister.

of the British Bible College in Bristol.[129] Brooks also published widely on several subjects through books and a weekly column in the PHA, making him an important voice within the IPHC in the States.

In one publication, Noel Brooks discusses baptism in connection to Rom. 6.3-5.[130] Commenting on this passage he states, 'this death, burial and resurrection is linked with Christian baptism'.[131] However, 'baptism itself ... as a mere religious rite' cannot 'automatically and inevitably accomplish this'.[132] For 'without living, personal faith in Christ, baptism is ... useless'.[133] In Christian baptism, 'inward realities of repentance and faith are dramatized in a public ceremony', making faith vital for baptism.[134] Immersion also provides a 'vivid picture' of being 'symbolically buried'.[135] This public picturing that serves as a declaration that one is 'dead to (their) former life'.[136] Therefore, when one is baptized, he or she 'cannot go on living' their 'former independent life'.[137] Moreover:

> When, as symbolized in baptism, he dies to his former life of sin is raised to the new life of holiness, he cannot 'continue in sin'. When he is severed from the old Adam and grafted into the second Adam, he cannot 'continue to sin' he is committed henceforth to the life of holiness. He cannot 'continue in sin' and 'abide in Christ' *at the same time*.[138]

Baptism testifies to a new life of holiness in the believer.

Brooks also believes, like King and Taylor before him, that baptism should be done in the name of the triune God, for 'when you baptize people you are actually baptizing them into the Name of the Father, the Son, and the Holy Spirit, which means into union with Them, into union with the Trinity'.[139] Unfortunately, in Brooks' view,

---

[129] https://sites.google.com/a/swcu.edu/archives/noel-brooks---biography, Accessed October 5, 2018.
[130] Noel Brooks, *Fingertip Holiness: Studies in Practical Holiness* (Muse Memorial Lectures, Southwestern Christian University, Oklahoma City, OK, 1975), pp. 8-10.
[131] Brooks, *Fingertip Holiness*, p. 8.
[132] Brooks, *Fingertip Holiness*, p. 8.
[133] Brooks, *Fingertip Holiness*, p. 8.
[134] Brooks, *Fingertip Holiness*, p. 8.
[135] Brooks, *Fingertip Holiness*, p. 9.
[136] Brooks, *Fingertip Holiness*, p. 9.
[137] Brooks, *Fingertip Holiness*, p. 10.
[138] Brooks, *Fingertip Holiness*, p. 10. Original emphasis.
[139] Noel Brooks, *The Biblical Basis for Missions* (Franklin Springs, GA: Advocate Press, 1976), p. 53. Brooks also mentions Mt. 28.19 in connection to Eph. 4.5,

baptism is often neglected because there has 'been such an abuse of baptism in the formal churches through the centuries as a formal liturgical act'.[140] He then sees the need to now recover the NT's view of baptism.[141] While Brooks is 'not worried so much about the mode of baptism' he is 'concerned about the purpose ... that is baptism into union with Jesus'.[142]

Significantly, Brooks is critical of IPHC doctrines when they depart from the traditional Wesleyan and Anglican positions, as he understands them.[143] Significant for our purposes, he chides the IPHC's doctrinal statements for calling the Lord's Supper a sacrament and water baptism an ordinance.[144] He also expresses dissatisfaction with the 'anti-sacramental' view of water baptism put forth.[145] Hence, though Brooks emphasizes water baptism as a symbolic and declarative act, he also understands it to be effective when accompanied by faith and performed in the name of the triune God.

D.3 Paul Beacham

Paul Franklin Beacham served as the IPHC's general superintendent from 1946-1949. Notably, he wrote two catechisms for the church: *Primary Catechism* and *Advanced Catechism*.[146] While the date of publication for both is unknown, these two concise catechisms serve as major guiding publications for the distribution of foundational

---

stating that Paul is likely referring to water baptism in this phrase, yet also stating that 'the "one baptism" cannot be merely the outward rite performed in a formal manner, but must, in Paul's mind, mean also its profound spiritual significance'. Thus, water baptism, for Brooks, is separate from, yet connected to, a 'spiritual baptism'. See Noel Brooks, *Ephesians: Outlined and Unfolded* (Franklin Springs, GA: Advocate Press, 1976), p. 147.

[140] Brooks, *The Biblical Basis for Missions*, p. 53.
[141] Brooks, *The Biblical Basis for Missions*, p. 53.
[142] Brooks, *The Biblical Basis for Missions*, p. 53.
[143] Chris E. Green, 'In Word and Spirit: Critical and Constructive Reflections on Theological Method in the Work of Noel Brooks', in Marilyn A. Hudson (ed.), *Mosaic: Papers in Honor of Noel Brooks* (1914-2006) (Norman, OK: Whorl Books, 2012), pp. 3-27 (6).
[144] Green, 'In Word and Spirit', p. 6. For support, Green cites *PHA* 54.24 (1971), p. 14.
[145] Green, 'In Word and Spirit', p. 6. For support, Green cites *PHA* 54.23 (1971), p. 26.
[146] Paul F. Beacham, *Primary Catechism: For the Home, Sunday School and Bible Classes* (Franklin Springs, GA: Board of Publication of Pentecostal Holiness Church, nd), pp. 1-31; Paul F. Beacham, *Advanced Catechism: For the Home, Sunday School and Bible Classes* (Franklin Springs, GA: Board of Publication of Pentecostal Holiness Church, nd), pp. 1-32.

teaching for the IPHC. In *Primary Catechism*, Beacham includes twenty-six lessons on specific topics lettered A-Z.[147] While Beacham covers a variety of topics, water baptism is absent throughout every lesson. And though there are many topics that water baptism would have appropriately fit within, the author evidently did not deem it worthy of treatment.[148]

However, in Beacham's *Advanced Catechism*, water baptism is discussed in the last section, 'Chapter XII – Miscellaneous'. In response to a question asking how many 'ordinances' Christ instituted, the answer reads, 'Two, water baptism; and the sacrament of the Lord's Supper'.[149] Further, the following question: 'Is water baptism essential to salvation?' is answered: 'It is not essential in the sense of moral necessity, for it does not in any degree cleanse one from sin. However, it is necessary to perfect obedience, as all believers are commanded to be baptized. It is an outward sign of the New Covenant, just as circumcision was of the Old Covenant.'[150]

Therefore, while water baptism is not essential to salvation, it is 'necessary to perfect obedience' because of Christ's command to participate in water baptism.[151] Baptism, then, 'does not impart saving grace', and it is 'possible for one to receive' baptism 'without actually appropriating salvation by faith'.[152] This 'ordinance', then, 'cannot impart salvation to a graceless soul; but their observance

---

[147] The following topics were addressed: 'The Creator' (Lesson A), 'Angels' (Lesson B), 'Man' (Lesson C), 'Good and Evil' (Lesson D), 'God's Love' (Lesson E), 'Jesus Christ' (Lesson F), 'The Holy Ghost' (Lesson G), 'The Bible' (Lesson H), 'Salvation' (Lesson I), 'Sanctification' (Lesson J), 'Baptism with the Spirit' (Lesson K), 'Divine Healing' (Lesson L), 'Temptation' (Lesson O), 'Privileges' (Lesson P), 'Duties' (Lesson Q), 'Conduct' (Lesson R), 'Heaven' (Lesson S), 'Hell' (Lesson T), 'Christ's Second Coming' (Lesson U), 'Death' (Lesson V), 'Old Testament' (Lesson W), 'New Testament' (Lesson X), 'Places' (Lesson Y), 'Bible Characters' (Lesson Z).

[148] This is even more startling when one looks further into specific questions that were given treatment such as 'When will the great White Throne judgment take place?' (p. 23), 'How many years between Moses and Malachi?' (p. 25), 'What is the distance from Dan to Beersheba?' (p. 28), and 'What is the distance from Jerusalem to the Dead Sea, and Mediterranean Sea?' (p. 29).

[149] Beacham, *Advanced Catechism*, p. 25. One might consider it to be revealing that water baptism was understood to be only an 'ordinance', while the Lord's Supper was called 'the sacrament' (p. 25).

[150] Beacham, *Advanced Catechism*, p. 26.

[151] Beacham, *Advanced Catechism*, p. 26.

[152] Beacham, *Advanced Catechism*, p. 26.

communicates more grace to a true believer'.[153] Beacham seeks to hold a position that understands water baptism to be 'necessary to perfect obedience' without being 'essential'. However, he does not apply this same logic to the issue of Spirit baptism. When asked 'Does everyone need this Baptism?', meaning Spirit baptism, Beacham answers: 'Yes, and God has commanded that we seek and obtain it'.[154] One might also consider it ironic that Beacham discusses Acts 19.6 in the context of Spirit baptism, but fails to address its relation to the greater context of water baptism.

In sum, then, in Beacham's writings, water baptism was a marginal, or 'miscellaneous' issue, with no explicit connection to any 'major topics' such as Spirit baptism.[155]

D.4 Harold D. Hunter[156]

IPHC ecumenist and theologian, Harold D. Hunter, published a formal, Pentecostal response to *Baptism, Eucharist, and Ministry*.[157] However, Hunter's response is largely descriptive rather than constructive.[158] Hunter notes that Pentecostals have traditionally preferred the term 'ordinance' rather than 'sacrament'.[159] He also states that Pentecostals resist 'magical ingredients sometimes pressed into this sacrament'.[160] Pentecostals often rebaptize and immersion is considered to be the 'New Testament precedent'.[161] And though not all Pentecostals practice the trinitarian formula, most do. Finally, Hunter states that Pentecostals view baptism as an external rite 'directed by scripture and observed by the people of God' and has no 'self-contained efficacy'.[162]

---

[153] Beacham, *Advanced Catechism*, pp. 26-27.

[154] Beacham, *Primary Catechism*, p. 13.

[155] Again, it is telling that Beacham's only treatment of water baptism is in 'Chapter XII – Miscellaneous' (pp. 25-26) in *Advanced Catechism*.

[156] Harold Hunter was affiliated with the Church of God of Prophecy from 1966-1991, the Church of God (Cleveland, TN) from 1991-1995, and the IPHC from 1995-Present. Though some of his writings included within this section were written before he joined the IPHC, I have chosen to include them considering his current status with the IPHC.

[157] Harold D. Hunter, 'Reflections by a Pentecostalist on Aspects of BEM', *JES* 29.3-4 (1992), pp. 317-45.

[158] Green, *Toward a Pentecostal Theology of the Lord's Supper*, p. 30.

[159] Hunter, 'of BEM', p. 329.

[160] Hunter, 'Reflections by a Pentecostalist on Aspects of BEM', p. 331.

[161] Hunter, 'Reflections by a Pentecostalist on Aspects of BEM', p. 333.

[162] Harold D. Hunter, 'Ordinances, Pentecostal', in Burgess, et. al. (eds.), *DPCM*, pp. 947, 949.

Speaking prescriptively, Hunter has also sought to argue for a 'distinct work of the Spirit which effects charismatic activity in the life of the believer' over-and-against the proposals set forth by J.D.G. Dunn and F. Dale Bruner.[163] In doing so, he distances the reception of the Spirit from water baptism, utilizing scripture and patristic literature.[164] Therefore, for Hunter, 'no strict connection can be made between baptism and salvation, primarily because baptism may not be a sacramental conferral of the Spirit but may be given in response to the bestowal of the Spirit'.[165]

D.5 Terry Tramel

Former Professor of Bible and Theology at Southwestern Christian University and current Director of Global Outreach and Leadership development for IPHC World Missions, Terry Tramel, briefly mentions water baptism in relation to Spirit baptism in one work. For Tramel, 'producing a pattern for water baptism in regard to Spirit baptism is virtually impossible'.[166] This is because, in Acts, water baptism took place before Spirit baptism at Samaria (Acts 8) and Ephesus (Acts 19).[167] Yet, for Saul (Acts 9) and Cornelius' household (Acts 10), Spirit baptism came before water baptism.[168] Therefore, as Tramel sees it, Spirit baptism and water baptism are related, but scripture does not prescribe a particular standard for their ordering.

D.6 Frank G. Tunstall

According to IPHC minister and former president of Southwestern Christian University Frank Tunstall, Jesus established the 'sacraments' to 'help His followers remember His death and resurrection'.[169] Baptism, then, is a 'public pledge of a believer's fidelity to the Lord, binding him to his commitment of loyalty and distinguishing him from the world'.[170] Baptism helps 'remember' Jesus' sacrifice.[171]

---

[163] Harold D. Hunter, *Spirit Baptism: A Pentecostal Approach* (Eugene, OR: Wipf & Stock, 2009), p. ix.
[164] Hunter, *Spirit Baptism*, pp. 98, 132-34, 144.
[165] Hunter, *Spirit Baptism*, p. 98.
[166] Terry Tramel, *The Beauty of the Balance: Toward an Evangelical-Pentecostal Theology* (Franklin Springs, GA: LifeSprings Resources, 2009), Kindle location 5077.
[167] Tramel, *The Beauty of the Balance*, Kindle location 5077.
[168] Tramel, *The Beauty of the Balance*, Kindle location 5078.
[169] Frank G. Tunstall, *Our Awesome Lord: A Captivating Pentecostal Christology* (Lake Mary, FL: Creation House, 2008), p. 268.
[170] Tunstall, *Our Awesome Lord*, p. 272.
[171] Tunstall, *Our Awesome Lord*, p. 272.

For Tunstall, scripture testifies to the importance of a trinitarian formula and expresses a 'symbolic' and 'illustrative' view of the sacrament.[172] And 'by not making water baptism a priority for salvation, Paul was teaching that the ordinance imparted no saving merit'.[173] Instead, Paul teaches that baptism gives 'public testimony to an inward work of saving grace Jesus had already wrought through the Holy Spirit'.[174] Finally, though immersion is the most 'desirable' among modes, sprinkling and pouring are also valid.

D.7 A.D. Beacham, Jr.

The current Presiding Bishop of the IPHC, A.D. 'Doug' Beacham, Jr., has written briefly on water baptism. Due to his influence and prominence within the IPHC, his voice on the subject is key. While he has written several works, the most relevant to this project is his book on bible doctrines, *Light for the Journey*.[175] In it, he attempts to provide a 'contemporary way of reflecting on the great truths of the Christian faith' using 'the Fourteen Articles of Faith' of the IPHC.[176] In his thirteen lessons on doctrinal subjects, he broaches the subject of water baptism in lesson thirteen, 'The Meaning and Mission of the Church'. When discussing the mission of the church – identified with the so-called 'Great Commission' – Beacham states: 'Discipleship includes baptism and teaching. Water baptism is the public evidence that a sinner has been born again and belongs to Christ. It is a statement to the world and to the local church that this person is a follower of the Lord.'[177] Thus, water baptism serves as an individual public profession of faith. But aside from these brief comments, water baptism is not mentioned in the rest of the book.

D.5 Hearing International Pentecostal Holiness Church Scholarly Voices: Conclusions

In conclusion, the above survey reveals that IPHC scholarly articulations of water baptism are scant, at least in comparison with treatments of sanctification and Spirit baptism, and perhaps even the Lord's Supper and eschatological issues. Nonetheless, the IPHC

---

[172] Tunstall, *Our Awesome Lord*, p. 272.
[173] Tunstall, *Our Awesome Lord*, p. 272.
[174] Tunstall, *Our Awesome Lord*, p. 273.
[175] A.D. Beacham, Jr., *Light for the Journey: A Fresh Focus on Doctrine* (Franklin Springs, GA: LifeSprings Resources, 1998), pp. 1-125.
[176] Beacham, *Light for the Journey*, p. 5.
[177] Beacham, *Light for the Journey*, p. 115.

scholars/ministers that discuss water baptism tend to focus on the rite's symbolic significance and as an act of obedience and public profession of faith. However, J.H. King and Noel Brooks, at times, also speak of baptism's effectiveness as a means of grace. Thus, some voices discuss baptism almost entirely in baptistic terms (Beacham, Tramel, Tunstall, Beacham, Jr.), while others discuss it more Wesleyan/Anglican terms (King, Brooks).[178] Perhaps worth underscoring further, water baptism is often left out in doctrinal discussions almost entirely, except for a few scattered remarks.

E. Empiricizing Pentecostalism: Contemporary International Pentecostal Holiness Church Ordinary Theology[179]

As described in detail earlier,[180] in moving from the revisioning to the empirical, I will be following Mark Cartledge in his use of qualitative research methods. In doing so, I aim to attend to testimony as an important mode of Pentecostal theology. In Cartledge's words, 'Pentecostal discourse is encapsulated in the notion of testimony'.[181] In response, this section will provide a field study perspective with which to engage. This research strategy will include interviews with believers who have been water baptized in a present-day IPHC church – listening for the *implicit* theology in their *explicit* statements on the rite and its meaning. It will also include my reflections as a 'participant observer' at a particular IPHC church's water baptismal service.[182] As Cartledge notes, participant observation is often used with other qualitative research methods such as interviews.[183] Both the participant observation and interviews will also be put into

---

[178] Since most of Hunter's engagement with the subject is descriptive, his own voice is not as discernable as others.

[179] As previously noted, I am following Cartledge's use of Jeff Astley's definition of ordinary theology as 'the theological beliefs and processes of believing that find expression in the God-talk of those believers who have received no scholarly theological education'. See Astley and Francis (eds.), *Exploring Ordinary Theology*, p. 1.

[180] For a more detailed look at my fieldwork technique, see Chapter 3.

[181] Cartledge, *The Mediation of the Spirit*, p. 18.

[182] By using participant observation alongside interviews, I avoid testimonies being 'only interpreted in the light of other testimonies'. See Cartledge, *Testimony in the Spirit*, p. 19.

[183] Cartledge, *Practical Theology*, pp. 70-71.

dialogue with secondary denominational literature.[184] Therefore, by using (1) participation observation along with (2) interviews and (3) secondary denominational literature, 'ideas generated from one source of material can be checked by reference' to another source.[185] This triangulation can 'enhance the reliability of the results of research'.[186] Thus, in this chapter, I will be focusing on one IPHC congregation, which is pseudonymously entitled: Faith Assembly. It is to these sources that we now turn.

E.1 Faith Assembly[187]

Faith Assembly, located in Southeast Virginia, USA, was founded in 1932. The church was founded by two women who felt a desire to establish a 'full gospel place of worship'. Significantly, all nine charter members were women, and thus, the church was affectionately nicknamed 'The Ladies' Church' by the IPHC Conference, which it joined in 1932. Since its founding, the church has moved locations multiple times, building new buildings (1938/1960/1989). Under the current leadership of Pastors Larry and Sally Jones (all names in this account are pseudonyms), the church began to reach new demographics and establish new ministries. Demographically speaking, roughly 60% of the congregation are Black and 40% are White. Faith Assembly has two different meeting locations/campuses. Combined, the average attendance of the congregation for the year of study was two hundred sixty.

E.2 Participant Observation: The Baptismal Service[188]

E.2.1 The Worship Service

One can assume that worship space at one time was 'traditional' which is evidenced by the pews, traditional church balcony, and chandeliers lighting the room. However, more recently the space has been updated, most notably, with colored lighting, a contemporary

---

[184] For secondary literature, I will be consulting Stanley M. Burgess, Gary B. McGee, Patrick H. Alexander (eds.), *DCPM* (Grand Rapids, MI, Zondervan, 1988), pp. 1-928.
[185] Cartledge, *Practical Theology*, pp. 70-71.
[186] Cartledge, *Practical Theology*, p. 71.
[187] This information I gleaned from the leadership of the church and the church website.
[188] I am following Cartledge's structure and format in reporting his participation observation. See Cartledge, *Testimony in the Spirit*, pp. 29-32. Further, all leaders/pastors/informants have been given pseudonyms.

backdrop design, sound system, and projector system.[189] This means that the words of songs can be projected onto two screens on either side of the platform. Therefore, this church can be considered hi-tech in its use of media resources.[190] Musical instruments such as guitars, a keyboard, and drum set were present on the platform, along with a portable baptismal tank.

E.2.2 Service Structure

This Sunday night baptismal service was held on August 4th, 2019. This special Sunday night baptismal service began at 6.00 PM and concluded at 7.00 PM. In this hour-long service, I was able to discern seven main units. Additionally, for the service to flow between the main units, there were links. Following Cartledge's findings, there were also key individuals who linked the units together in relation to specific locations.[191] For this service, there were three such locations: the platform, the altar, and congregational seating. There were also key individuals who mediate these three 'zones': (1) The worship leader(s), who led the sung worship; (2) Lead Pastor Larry, who facilitates the transitions and links while also managing the preaching and response times; (3) Pastors Jerry and Cliff, who baptize the candidates; and (4) the elders/pastors, who are invited by Pastor Larry to give instruction or testimony.

The service begins with a greeting, an invitation for the congregation to stand, brief comments on the importance of baptism, and an opening, spontaneous prayer (unit 1). As Pastor Larry welcomed the church, he lightheartedly commented on the rainy weather and related it to the meaning of baptism: 'if we were a sprinkling church, we would just let you go outside, but no, we are a full dunking church'. Yet, Pastor Larry almost immediately transitioned into a more serious tone, exhorting the candidates to allow God to calm their nerves, and urged the congregation 'to create an atmosphere of honor and reverence' by focusing on Christ. He continued: 'Baptism is about thanking God for all he has done'. Because, in spite of the fact that baptism is just 'an outside sign', it points to the 'sacrifice of Jesus who has paid the price'. Pastor Larry concluded this first unit with a prayer of thankfulness.

---

[189] Cartledge, *Testimony in the Spirit*, p. 29
[190] Cartledge, *Testimony in the Spirit*, p. 30.
[191] Cartledge, *Testimony in the Spirit*, p. 30.

Then, the worship team led the congregation in a time of worship, singing 'Glorious Day',[192] an upbeat, celebratory praise song (unit 2). During worship, the congregation moves with the rhythm of the music.[193] Following the song and a 'clap offering', Pastor Larry instructs the congregation to be seated. He then asks the baptismal candidates to make their way out of the sanctuary to prepare for their baptisms (unit 3). As the baptismal candidates rise, the congregation claps in celebration. Pastors Jerry and John receive the candidates and take them to the appropriate place to give them some 'instruction and time to prepare'. During this transition, the worship team is seated, though the keyboard player continues to accompany following Pastor Larry's request.

Pastor Larry follows this time by preaching a brief, fifteen-minute sermon on 'the significance of baptism and why we do what we do' (unit 4). Beginning his sermon, Pastor Larry refers the congregation to the projector screen, and he reads Mt. 28.18-20 (NIV). He then states: 'This is why we baptize in the name of the Father, and of the Son, and of the Holy Spirit'. But as Matthew 28 states, baptism is just the beginning. After people are baptized, they need to be taught and then released. Yet, to set the stage for his teaching, Pastor Larry begs the questions: 'But what is water baptism? What does it represent?'

First, he differentiates between Spirit baptism and water baptism. While Spirit baptism is about empowerment for the whole of Christian life, water baptism is about death and resurrection, a sharing in Christ's experiences. Thus, baptism is 'death to ourselves'. While he does not explicitly reference Rom. 6.3-5, he does state that 'Paul says baptism is about our dying and rising with Jesus'. Significantly, the media graphic on the projected screens was entitled, 'Baptism: from death to life'. Baptism, then, announces this truth as opposed to effecting the reality of it because it is a 'symbol of dying to ourselves' and of our new resurrected life with Christ. Thus, 'the candidates are telling us that, as a symbol, they have already died to themselves'. Just as going under the water represents death to self, coming up from the water represents raising with Christ. The baptized are thus identified imaginatively with Christ's life.

---

[192] Kristian Stanfill; Jason Ingram; Jonathan Smith; Sean Curran, 'Glorious Day' (Kristian Stanfill Publishing Designee; sixsteps Music, 2017).

[193] Cartledge, *Testimony in the Spirit*, p. 30.

Following the sermon, Pastor Larry calls Pastor Jerry, Pastor Cliff, and the baptismal candidates to make their way forward (unit 5). Following Pastor Jerry and Pastor Cliff, the candidates walk down the middle aisle onto the platform. Pastor Larry exclaims that any family members or friends of the candidates can come near the altar and platform to take pictures or videos. Pastor Jerry follows this instruction by stepping into the (portable) baptismal tank and then exhorts the congregation: 'This is about celebration. Right? ... Amen?' The congregation responds in clapping. The keyboard continues to play throughout this time of baptism. Pastor Jerry then proceeds to baptize four candidates, asking them to state their name and then state which campus they normally attend. Following the candidates answering, Pastor Jerry baptized them using the trinitarian formula. After each baptism, the congregation would respond in shouting, clapping, some exclaiming 'Hallelujah' and/or 'Amen'. After Pastor Jerry baptized four candidates, Pastor Jerry exited the baptismal tank and Pastor Cliff entered. Pastor Cliff followed the same format as Pastor Jerry in baptizing the final four candidates.

After the final candidate is baptized, the worship team returns to the platform and leads the congregation in singing 'In the River' (unit 6).[194] The congregation responds in expressive and vibrant praise. As the song concludes, Pastor Larry calls forward Pastor Daniel, the pastor of a house-church plant in a nearby town. Pastor Larry asks Pastor Daniel to close the time with a word of prayer. Before praying, Pastor Daniel testifies to God's working in the church and ministry and then concludes the time thanking God for the service.

Therefore, despite the lack of written liturgy there is a clear sequence of expected events.[195] Pastor Larry serves as the 'the chief master of ceremonies that ensures there is a smooth transition' between units and zones.[196] The worship leader and team work in partnership with Pastor Larry to lead the congregation in sung worship, and support transitions between units throughout. Yet Pastor Larry does release authority in the service by allowing Pastors Jerry, Cliff, and Daniel to lead various elements. Significantly, while Pastor Daniel was asked only to conclude the service with prayer, he felt the

---

[194] Chris Quilala; Joshua Silverberg; Mark Alan Schoolmeesters; Ryan Williams, 'In the River' (Capitol CMG Amplifier; Jesus Culture Music, 2015).
[195] Cartledge, *Testimony in the Spirit*, p. 32.
[196] Cartledge, *Testimony in the Spirit*, p. 32.

freedom to also give a lengthy testimony before the prayer. Nonetheless, the overall service structure and flow were primarily handled by Pastor Larry and the worship team, particularly the keyboard player.

E.3 Interviews[197]

E.3.1 Interview Participants

The interview participants were comprised of six men and eight women, 'representative (in age, sex, and socioeconomic terms) of the congregation as a whole'.[198] Some participants were black/African American (8), while others were white/Caucasian (6), varying in age. The men were mostly middle-aged (Jason, Phil, Shane, Joseph, Cody), though Sam was younger. These men were employed in manufacturing (Jason, Cody), marketing (Sam), finance (Phil), public speaking (Shane), and construction (Joseph). The women too were mostly middle-aged (Isabella, Carla, Linda, Jerri, Erin, Marie, Jane), though Kristen was younger. These women were employed in administration (Isabella, Jerri, Jane), cosmetology (Carla), military (Linda), writing and editing (Erin), finance (Marie), and education (Kristen).[199]

E.3.2 Interview Findings

Question 1: Personal Testimonies of Baptism
While the first question relates mainly to one's experience of water baptism, themes such as conversion, re-baptism, and 'stages' of conversion/sanctification naturally surfaced in the conversations. My follow up questions also sought to place water baptism in the context of the larger context of Christian initiation. Nine of the fourteen participants had been baptized twice, either initially as an infant/child/teen and then later as an adult, or in some case, was baptized as an adult twice. Isabella reported that she was first baptized as a teen, yet desired to be baptized again since 'a lot of things happened between when I rededicated my life to the Lord and when I

---

[197] Following the last chapter, the interviews will be composed of five basic questions that focus on (1) the participant's own personal experience of water baptism, (2) the water baptisms of other believers, (3) various ways of baptizing (for example immersion or sprinkling), (4) the relationship between water baptism and Spirit baptism, and (5) the Scriptural authority for practices of water baptism.

[198] Coakley, *God, Sexuality, and the Self*, p. 165.

[199] Following Cartledge's focus group format, each informant is identified by their pseudonym, ethnicity, age, and occupation. See Cartledge, *Testimony in the Spirit*, p. 32.

was filled with the Holy Spirit and fire'. She reported that after those events, she felt compelled to be baptized again. So, she asked the Lord: 'Why do I need to get baptized again? In response, God said, "because of the newness and the need to lay everything behind"'. Others stated that a lack of understanding the first time they were baptized necessitated their second baptism (Jason, Linda, Jane), while others stated that they did not choose their infant baptism (Shane, Marie). Jane stated that, 'as an adult, it was a whole new meaning. I was really a whole new person'. Additionally, Joseph stated that he felt that he needed to be fully immersed since he was 'only sprinkled the first time'.

Most participants also understood baptism to be something following 'conversion'. Baptism is necessary because it is 'identification with Jesus Christ' (Joseph), an action that signifies 'starting over' (Marie), an 'outward representation of what happened inwardly' (Linda), an act of 'confession to Jesus as my Lord and Savior' (Phil), a 'reaffirmation of my faith in Jesus' (Sam), a 'public confession' (Jane) or put another way, 'an outward showing of our faith' (Carla). For Jason, baptism is 'a form of repentance of sin', while Jerri stated that it was an obligatory act since church 'membership required water baptism'.

In answering the general question, 'Can you tell me about your personal experience of water baptism?', there were answers such as, 'it wasn't anything special' (Kristen), though others reported, 'it was awesome. I'll never forget it' (Carla), 'I felt the power of God all over me' (Jason), and 'I felt different' (Cody). Consequently, people's experiences of water baptism differed. However, most reported some sense of felt or observed change. Carla stated that she 'felt like a new person, and (her) sin was gone and cleansed'. Similarly, Shane stated that after his baptism he 'felt clean', while Joseph reported feeling 'jittery'. Marie was told by multiple people that she 'looked more beautiful' following her baptism, whereas Jerri 'felt more attacked spiritually'. Phil and Carla both testified to feeling a new sense of freedom following their baptism. Therefore, personal testimonies surrounding the participant's experiences of water baptism differed considerably from each other. However, most participants reported feeling or experiencing a sensed difference following their baptism.

Finally, three participants also associated *glossolalia* and water baptism in their testimonies. Two participants reported feeling pressured to speak in tongues as they came up from the waters, though did not

(Kristen, Linda), whereas Jason did not report feeling pressured, but did report his experience of speaking in tongues as he came up out of the water.

Question 2: Observations of Other's Baptisms

My second question focused on the participant's observations of others' water baptisms. First, several participants stated that they had observed a change in lifestyle in people following their baptisms (Jason, Sam, Isabella, Jerri). Jason noted that oftentimes he has noticed that 'people's lives were transformed after that moment' (of baptism). Those who were struggling with fornication or drugs were delivered through a process of breaking off'. Sam, too, reported something similar. He stated that often 'people change their lives. Have a fresh start.' Sam stated that he observed a recently baptized family member 'walking (their) faith out' commenting that 'people around him could see the difference. It was a significant moment at baptism, but also seeing the change in his life and intensity of his relationship with the Lord following' was most substantial. Isabella, too, described a time when a friend of hers was baptized and told her, 'Isabella, I am different. I feel this tingle inside of me.' She replied by telling her friend, 'I hear you. Now I am going to watch you.' After watching her the following year, Isabella testified that her friend 'grew and is still growing'. But rather than reporting a positive change like others, Jerri stated that she has known 'a bunch of people who backed away' following their baptism.

Some participants also observed joy (Phil, Erin, Jane) and peace (Shane) on people's faces as the baptized came up from the water, though others stated that there was 'nothing extra' (Kristen) or 'nothing much' (Marie) regarding baptisms they have observed. Yet, Joseph reported seeing many who began 'jumping and shouting' following their baptisms. He stated: 'I don't deny the Spirit's doing that. I just know I didn't experience it that way.' Carla, too, reported seeing some 'come out of the water screaming, crying, and praising. Tears were everywhere.' Linda recounted one woman whose response to water baptism made a profound impression on her: 'She came up out of the water praying in tongues, and bowing down all four directions – north, south, east, west. It made me a believer (in water baptism). It was authentic and amazing.' Lastly, Cody stated that he has observed 'the Spirit of the Lord working on their hearts'.

Question 3: Ways of Baptizing

The general question – 'Do you think there is any right way to do baptism?' – was followed up with questions centered on three issues: (1) mode, (2) formula, (3) and those authorized to perform baptisms.

First, there was great variance on the issue of mode. Half of the participants considered immersion to be the correct mode (Joseph, Kristen, Jason, Erin, Shane, Linda, Cody), while the other half believed immersion *and* sprinkling are valid (Marie, Sam, Phil, Carla, Jerri, Jane, Isabella). However, there were different reasons and qualifications given for each of their thinking. For some, immersion is preferred because 'it identifies you with dying to sin' (Joseph), 'it is more illustrative of dying to old and rising to the new' (Kristen), though some stated it is because 'the bible is clear' (Erin), and we should follow Jesus' example (Shane, Linda). Conversely, Marie stated that she thinks infant baptism and adult baptism are 'equally valid', thus 'immersion is best for adults, and sprinkling for infants'. Agreeing with Marie, Phil stated that 'full immersion is best for adults, and sprinkling is good for babies'. Others offered similar comments along these lines (Carla, Jane). Sam stated that though immersion might 'have a bigger impact', sprinkling can also be valid *for adults*. Isabella and Jerri, too, are flexible on mode, though believe only adults should be baptized. Jerri stated that because 'infants aren't able to make that choice and profess and declare faith' they should not be baptized, though she recommended sprinkling for those who might have a fear of water. Isabella stated that she thinks Christians too often 'get hung up on mode'. She considers both sprinkling and immersion as valid.

Second, commenting on whether one should be baptized in Jesus' name or the name of the Father, Son, and Holy Spirit, a few simply commented, 'either one' (Jane, Kristen) while one was unsure (Erin). Some favored the triune formula (Isabella, Carla, Jerri, Phil, Sam, Cody, Linda, Shane) because it is instructive about God's nature and because Jesus commands a trinitarian formula in Mt. 28.19. Isabella, though, stated that a trinitarian formula is needed because it signifies Jesus' baptism with the Father's affirmation and the Holy Spirit's descent. Marie, conversely, simply stated that she preferred baptism in Jesus' name. Finally, Joseph sought a compromise between the two modes by stating that we should baptize 'In the name of the Father, Son, and Holy Spirit, in the name of Jesus'.

Lastly, on the issue of 'who' is authorized to baptize, the participants were once again divided. Some believed that only pastors should be authorized to baptize (Cody, Isabella, Marie, Carla, Jason, Jane), while others stated that any believer should be able to baptize (Jerri, Joseph, Sam, Phil, Linda, Shane, Erin, Kristen). Cody stated that 'it should be done by "clean hands" – someone who is ordained'. Others agreed. Marie sated, I 'personally feel like it should be a pastor doing it' and Jane said that 'someone performing a baptism needs some credentialing, such as a pastor'. Yet, for other participants, any Christian can baptize another Christian. As one man put it, 'ordination is a worldly classification' (Shane). Linda stated that the one baptizing 'doesn't need to be a pastor as long as they have a relationship with Christ'. Phil, Erin, and Kristen all consider insistence upon ordained clergy to administer baptism to be 'legalism'.

Question 4: Water Baptism and Spirit Baptism
My next question aimed to tease out the relationship (if any) between water baptism and Spirit baptism. With one exception (Sam), Spirit baptism and water baptism were understood to be two separate events. When distinguishing between them, I received answers such as, 'water baptism is our public declaration, and Spirit baptism is God giving us the Spirit' (Shane), or 'baptism symbolizes our death. Baptism in the Holy Ghost is us being empowered' (Cody). For Jane, water baptism is a public act while Spirit baptism is a private, personal experience: 'Water baptism requires someone else. Baptism with the Holy Spirit can be more private with evidence of speaking in tongues.' The participants overall posited water baptism as a human act and Spirit baptism was a divine act. Jerri summarized these explanations well when she stated that, 'water baptism is our part, and the other (Spirit baptism) is God's part'.

This question, for a few, led to further discussions on the order of events in a believer's life. Jason stated that people 'do not have control over which one comes first'. The order of events is completely up to the Spirit. In other words, it is different for everyone (Phil, Erin, Linda). Joseph, however, understood Spirit baptism to be synonymous with conversion: 'When we get saved, the Holy Spirit comes and fills us. You have to get saved before you get baptism. The Holy Spirit is in conversion, not baptism.' Thus, for Joseph, there is clear order: salvation – which is Spirit baptism – then water baptism.

However, Sam understood Spirit baptism and water baptism to be the same. He stated:

> Water baptism is a connection with the Holy Spirit. He is a perfect gentleman and the Comforter. He is a presence that rests on you through your baptism and after that because the Holy Spirit is about transformation. There is a presence there in water baptism. When John the Baptist baptized Jesus, the dove – the Holy Spirit – came on Jesus. Sometimes the feeling of baptism is different because of the Holy Spirit's presence.

Therefore, Sam understood water baptism and Spirit baptism to be synonymous due to Jesus' reception of the Spirit in his baptism. Jason, too, drew a potential relationship between water baptism and Spirit baptism. He maintained that one might be Spirit-baptized during water baptism, though they remain two separate events that may happen simultaneously. Lastly, Shane who maintained a strong distinction between the two, later stated: 'I personally believe every time someone is (water) baptized heaven is opened up, like in Jesus' baptism. And the Holy Spirit lands on us when we are (water) baptized.' Therefore, because of Jesus' example, we receive the Spirit in water baptism, though Spirit baptism is a later event that is for empowerment by the Spirit.[200] Hence, most of the participants understood water baptism and Spirit baptism as two separate, unrelated events. The one exception is Sam who understood them to be one and the same.

Question 5: Water Baptism and Scripture

The final, two-part question focused on scriptural reflection.[201] The first part of the question sought to understand what scriptural verses, passages, or biblical events informed the interviewee's view of water baptism. While most could think of at least one verse, passage, or biblical event, two participants could not think of any (Cody, Phil).

Overwhelmingly, Jesus' baptism by John dominated the conversations. Jesus' baptism was said to be the most formative scriptural

---

[200] Though Mike did not attempt the explain these assertions in further detail, it is worth noting the inconsistency inherent within these statements. If nothing else, it reveals a common dilemma many Pentecostals face when attempting both to establish Christ's baptism as paradigmatic and argue for a traditional account of subsequence

[201] 'What scriptures inform your view of water baptism?' and 'What do Acts 2.38 and Rom. 6.3-4 tell you about water baptism?'

event for all participants who responded.[202] Still, the question – 'What scriptures inform your view of water baptism?' – was answered in varying ways. For a few, Jesus' baptism demonstrated the importance of obedience, since even Jesus was baptized 'to fulfill all righteousness' (Isabella, Jane, Shane, Carla, Kristen, Erin, Jason). Jason put it this way: 'If God himself was baptized, we should too. Why would his followers not be baptized too?' Further, two participants (Shane, Linda) mentioned that Jesus' baptism initiated his public ministry, thus revealing the importance of our ministry following baptism. For others, Jesus' baptism most supremely demonstrated the importance of immersion: 'We see that John the Baptist fully submerged Jesus' (Joseph).

Yet, perhaps one of the more surprising findings was how Jesus' baptism informed participants on the relationship between water baptism and the Spirit (Linda, Kristen, Marie, Jason, Sam), especially considering the lack of relationship expressed earlier in Question 4. Nonetheless, for some participants, Jesus' reception of the Spirit at his baptism is instructive for us and our baptism. Kristen was the most explicit: 'The Holy Spirit descended on Jesus (at his baptism) and that is when the Holy Spirit descends on us'. Sam, too, said it similarly: 'Jesus baptism shows the sacredness … the presence of the Holy Spirit in baptism'. Additionally, Jerri focused on Jesus' baptism as proof of the trinitarian nature of our baptism and the command to baptize using the triune formula. Therefore, though Jesus' baptism was widely referenced, participants diverged on their interpretations of its significance for the meaning of baptism. Finally, Linda referenced one other scripture (1 Cor. 1.14) in stating, 'Paul said he was glad he did not baptize anyone. This shows me that baptism can be very divisive.'

In the second part of the question, I directed the participants to Rom. 6.3-4 and Acts 2.38 to read and reflect on its meaning and implications for water baptism.[203]

Reflecting on Rom. 6.3-4, many participants discussed how baptism replaces the old with the new. Some focused on the 'old' being wiped away while others focused more on the 'new' being imparted. Carla stated it this way: 'baptism tells me that because of the sins that

---

[202] Therefore, this excludes Wesley and Jon.
[203] Acts 2.38 and Rom. 6.3-4 were selected due to these scripture's prominence in the early contemporary Pentecostal literature.

I had committed in my life, my old (wo)man died and I came up new in Christ in water baptism'. Focusing more on the 'new' life, Shane stated that 'part of going through baptism means we are actually new. We are completely new. We are a new creation. Everything of old is passed away. Not a renewed version – a totally new version.' Linda, talking in eschatological terms stated that baptism is a 'precursor to what we will get when we die – a new body'.

There were other reflections, though, that did not center upon the old/new motifs. Cody stated that this passage discusses the importance of obedience. He further argued that 'water baptism is not a requirement to get to heaven because of the thief on the cross, but we should still follow the scriptures and be baptized'. One participant (Phil) linked this verse to 'the rapture', stating that this scripture speaks to the resurrection of the dead that will happen when Christ comes again. Lastly, Sam did not think it spoke to water baptism at all, but instead 'talks about crucifying the flesh and deliverance'.

In reflecting on Acts 2.38, a few participants believed this verse provided an *ordo salutis*. For Jane, Acts 2.38 'lays the blueprint. First, we have to come with a repentant heart, water baptism comes after and you know you are forgiven, then we receive the gift of the Holy Spirit. It is available for everyone.' Linda also believed that this scripture showed that 'there is an order to things'. For others, this shows that baptism is connected to the forgiveness of sins. Jason stated that just like the Jews had murdered Jesus and had to repent and be forgiven, so Christians need to be baptized and forgiven for other sins. Sam focused on the forgiveness motif as well. However, he pointed out that forgiveness did not come about through 'the water, but about the meaning behind what was happening. It wasn't natural but supernatural. There was a symbolic going down and drowning those addictions, habits, etc.'. Therefore, the forgiveness of sins is connected to water baptism, though in contrast with the way they read Romans 6.

Yet, for four others, Acts 2.38 confirmed that water baptism and the Holy Spirit are related. For instance, Phil stated that this showed him that 'like Jesus was baptized and received the Spirit, so the same will happen to us'. However, others sought to connect water baptism to the Spirit in a more indirect way. First, Erin stated that 'The Holy Spirit did come upon Jesus when he was water baptized and because of that, you are also given a gift in baptism (the Holy Spirit), but you have to open the gift. The baptism with the Holy Spirit happens when we open the gift, and it takes you deeper.' Carla also understood water baptism to make way for Spirit baptism: 'our water baptism will be sealed with the baptism with the Holy Spirit'. Isabella, too, argued that 'when we get baptized in water, we receive the gift of the Holy Spirit' but the 'gift of the Holy Spirit is not the baptism with the Holy Spirit. That comes later.'

Therefore, in sum, there were significantly differing interpretations and perspectives on these baptismal texts.

E.4 Secondary Literature

According to the *DCPM*, the IPHC is 'one of the oldest and largest Pentecostal denominations in the U.S.'[204] While the IPHC practices 'water baptism by immersion ... under the influence of J.H. King, the Pentecostal Holiness Church officially sanctions sprinkling'.[205] Thus, the IPHC embraces multiple modes as valid. Yet, with whatever mode is chosen, the trinitarian formula must be used. Also, 'parents may follow the Wesleyan pattern and have their infants baptized or merely dedicated if they prefer'.[206] Significantly, the IPHC's endorsement of infant baptism played an important role in forming 'affiliations with the Iglesia Metodista Pentecostal de Chile (MPC)' in 1967 'and the Igreja Metodista Wesleyana do Brasil in 1984'.[207] Thus, the IPHC's unique flexibility on mode and infant baptism/dedication is almost unrivaled among Classical Pentecostal denominations. However, outside the discussions of mode and formula, the IPHC's discussion around water baptism is marginal.

E.5 Empiricizing Pentecostalism: Conclusions

My general findings indicate that ordinary Pentecostal theology in the IPHC is far from consistent. However, even with evident disagreements on many issues, my findings indicate some striking consistency

---

[204] Vinson Synan, 'International Pentecostal Holiness Church', in Stanley M. Burgess, Gary B. McGee, and Patrick H. Alexander (eds.), *DCPM* (Grand Rapids, MI: Zondervan, 1988), p. 466.

[205] Harold Hunter, 'Ordinances, Pentecostal', in Stanley M. Burgess, Gary B. McGee, and Patrick H. Alexander (eds.), *DCPM* (Grand Rapids, MI: Zondervan, 1988), p. 654.

[206] D.J Wilson, 'Church Membership', in Stanley M. Burgess, Gary B. McGee, and Patrick H. Alexander (eds.), *DCPM* (Grand Rapids, MI: Zondervan, 1988), p. 197.

[207] Synan, 'International Pentecostal Holiness Church', p. 468.

on other matters. Both observations and interviews speak of baptism as a death to the old way of life. Particularly in my observation of the baptismal service, Rom. 6.3 was in the background of much of the teaching surrounding baptism, though it was never directly referenced. Interviewees also discussed baptism as the death of one's old, sinful nature and as a resurrection into a new life with Christ. Baptism as a personal profession of faith was another recurring theme in both observation and interviews. This implies that baptism is understood to be a deeply personal matter, which is another consistent theme. Absent from observation, but consistent within the interviews, is the prominence of Jesus' baptism for informing the participant's view of the rite. Water baptism and Spirit baptism were also consistently but not uniformly understood to be two separate, unrelated events. Lastly, the trinitarian formula was standard with little exception.

However, regardless of such convergences, there were also many divergent findings. On the issues of mode and authority to baptize the informants were divided. Some also considered infant baptism legitimate alongside believer's baptism, while others considered infant baptism illegitimate. Overall, these findings undermine the consistency noted within the service observation: The sole mode used was immersion, only adult believers were baptized, and only pastors baptized the candidates. Further, some interviewed explained their personal experiences and observations of baptism to be quite ordinary, while others reported experiencing and observing extraordinary experiences in water baptism. Also, most participants in the interviews understood water baptism and Spirit baptism as two separate events, which is consistent with comments made during the observation. However, when later reflecting on Jesus' baptism, some understood the Spirit to be received in water baptism.

Finally, the finding surrounding the divergence on the issue of mode is consistent with the secondary literature on the IPHC. As the secondary literature notes, the baptismal mode has been flexible from the beginning of the IPHC. The primacy of the trinitarian formula in both observation and interviews, too, is consistent with secondary literature.

F. Water Baptism in The International Pentecostal Holiness Church: Conclusions

As the research indicates, early Pentecostal ordinary theology generally corresponded with the official teaching of the IPHC at the explicit level of theological discourse, though not uniformly. The *IPHC Constitution and the Manuals*, several scholarly/ministerial voices, and many early voices in *PHA* considered the rite merely representative. However, some minority voices in *PHA* and several scholarly/ministerial voices thought more highly of the rite's importance. Findings from the empirical research methods also reveal conflicting opinions on the water rite. Adding to the discord is the fact that much of the official IPHC teaching on water baptism has changed substantially, profoundly shifting away from the theological framework at work in the early period.[208]

However, significant for this study is the implicit sacramentality found within some testimonies expressed in early and contemporary Pentecostal ordinary theology (revisioning and empirical).[209] Also, the findings of the contemporary fieldwork reveal that while explicit statements on the rite's meaning tend to fit within an emblematic view of baptism, some significant testimonies and reflections on the participants' own experience of water baptism (Question 1) *and* their observation of other people's water baptisms (Question 2) disclose at the implicit level of discourse, a presence-driven understanding of the rite. Further, comments on Jesus' baptism and the relationship between the Spirit and water baptism (Question 5), seem to undermine earlier comments on the lack of the relationship between the two. While these findings are not uniform, its minority presence supports my earlier finding (Chapter 3) which indicates that while most ordinary believers explicitly state that the rite is merely symbolic,

---

[208] The most significant shift over the years has been over infant baptism. Early on, infant baptism was considered a legitimate option, though today it is not officially stated as recognized. However, to my knowledge the practice has never been officially condemned.

[209] Notably, there are fewer *early* than *contemporary* testimonies of sacramental experiences of baptism in the sources engaged. As noted earlier, this is perhaps due to a heavy editorial hand in *PHA*, whose editor consistently articulated a 'low view' of water baptism. A few guest writers' confessions and testimonies scattered throughout *PHA* reveal that there were some minority voices who thought more highly of the rite's importance.

among some there is an implicit expectation to meet God amid the ritual.[210]

Moreover, while IPHC resources have much to contribute to the construction of a Pentecostal theology of water baptism, perhaps one of its greatest gifts is the historical flexibility on mode and the issue(s) of infant baptism/believers' baptism. As has been noted, this is a unique feature within Pentecostalism.[211] And since the IPHC's affirmation of infant baptism has already played an important role in forming affiliations with global Methodist denominations,[212] perhaps in a more general way, it can provide Pentecostal theologians the opportunity to construct theologies of water baptism that dialogue ecumenically with traditions who hold to infant baptism.

Yet, we need to continue to apply the approach taken in this chapter to one other Classical Pentecostal denomination. This will allow us to continue to discover and identify the proper framework within which a Pentecostal theology of water baptism might be constructed. Therefore, in the next chapter, we continue with an examination of the Pentecostal Assemblies of the World.

---

[210] Notably, there is more evidence of this found in Chapter 3.
[211] Synan, 'International Pentecostal Holiness Church', p. 468.
[212] Synan, 'International Pentecostal Holiness Church', p. 468.

5

CLASSICAL PENTECOSTAL DENOMINATIONS AND WATER BAPTISM: PENTECOSTAL ASSEMBLIES OF THE WORLD

A. Introduction

In this chapter, I will follow the same structure used in the previous chapters. Therefore, I will explore (1) the ordinary theology of early Pentecostals as it relates to the meaning and practice of water baptism in the PAW,[1] (2) the official denominational statements on the meaning and practice of water baptism, (3) the scholarly articulations of water baptism by PAW scholars, and the (4) ordinary theology of contemporary Pentecostals in a particular PAW church.[2]

---

[1] For history of the Pentecostal Assemblies of the World, see D.A. Reed, 'Pentecostal Assemblies of the World', in Stanley M. Burgess, Gary B. McGee, and Patrick H. Alexander (eds.), *DCPM* (Grand Rapids: Regency Reference Library, 1988), pp. 700-701; James C. Richardson, Jr., *With Water and Spirit: A History of Black Apostolic Denominations in the U.S.* (Washington, DC: Spirit Press, 1980), pp. 51-62; Talmage L. French and Allan H. Anderson, *Early Interracial Oneness Pentecostalism: G.T. Haywood and the Pentecostal Assemblies of the World (1901-1931)* (Eugene, OR: Pickwick, 2014).

[2] As noted in Chapter 2, in this chapter I will be conducting virtual ethnography or 'netnography' due to the coronavirus pandemic at the time of research. Therefore, I will be taking the same approach as in Chapters 3-4, though I will be moving from face-to-face research to virtual research. Further, because I am unable to attend a baptismal service (participant observation), I will seek to adjust and offset this limitation by (1) viewing a Sunday morning worship service via Facebook Live (participant observation) and (2) conduct an interview with the pastor of the PAW church on the church's baptismal ritual (informant interview).

My approach in this chapter – along with Chapter 3-4 – will seek to discover via revisioning and empirical methods the 'ordinary theology' of *early* denominational Pentecostals, the 'ordinary theology' of *contemporary* Pentecostals in particular denominational churches, and how these resources triangulate with the official denominational statements and scholarly denominational voices that discuss water baptism. This triangulation will seek to explore the convergences and divergences between the various resources. Among other things, this method will help Pentecostal scholars begin to discover how if at all denominational statements and the scholarly and ministerial voices that engage such statements, truly reflect the praxis and applied spirituality of the denomination – at the beginning of the movement and in the present day.

While much of the chapter will focus on descriptive research, I will conclude by moving to summarize the findings and comment on potential contributions that the PAW can make to the construction of a Pentecostal theology of water baptism.

B. Hearing Early Pentecostal Assemblies of the World Ordinary Theology

B.1 *The Christian Outlook* (1923-1932)

TCO is the official publication of the Pentecostal Assemblies of the World (PAW) and is still in publication today.[3] The periodical began in 1923 with Elder G.T. Haywood serving as its inaugural editor until his sudden death in 1931. Following Haywood, Elder S.K. Grimes took the role of editor. In the years engaged in this study (1923-1932), the subject of water baptism features quite prominently in the periodical. Confessions and teachings, exegesis on the subject, and testimonies from the field are all prevalent throughout *TCO*. In fact, water baptism was one of the most consistent subjects engaged in the first ten years of *TCO*.

---

[3] The earliest available issue is *TCO* 1.4 (April, 1923). Speculatively, that would make January *TCO* 1.1 (January, 1923) the first issue. In some cases, issue numbers are not available for every issue. As a result, when the issue is unknown, the month will be included with the year of publication.

B.1.1 Water Baptism in *The Christian Outlook*: Confessions and Articulations

In *TCO*, one of the most important theological aspects of water baptism is its connection with 'New Birth' doctrine, which one writer summarizes in these terms: 'to be baptized in Jesus' Name, to receive the Holy Ghost and to speak in other tongues is to be born of the water and spirit into that very Kingdom that began on the day of Pentecost'.[4] A.D. Urshan expresses this doctrine when he states that salvation is found in being 'baptized in water and Spirit in His name'.[5] Every Christian, then, must obey this 'command of God'.[6] If one is not baptized in the name of Jesus and Spirit-baptized, they are not born again.

Thus, it is of vital importance for believers to 'follow in His footsteps ... and be baptized in His name', expecting salvation.[7] Speaking as the Presiding Bishop of the PAW, Elder G.T. Haywood states, 'he that believeth, and is BAPTIZED, shall be saved',[8] for 'the sins of our flesh are put off by baptism in the name of Jesus Christ'.[9] The salvific nature of baptism, according to A.D. Urshan, is 'the backbone of our faith, which we cannot compromise upon for the sake of membership'.[10] Water baptism, then, is an indispensable part of the faith since it is essential to the 'New Birth'.

Another important theme that emerges from the literature is the emphasis of scripture over-and-against 'tradition'. Oneness proponents believed that trinitarians undermined the plain reading of scripture by appealing to the long-held tradition of the trinitarian formula. For Haywood, it is much more vital to 'stand for the Apostles' Doctrine' which is 'Baptism in Jesus name for the remission of sins' than to succumb to man's tradition.[11] Readers are often warned 'not [to] allow [themselves] to be deceived by man-made theological theories and religious speculations' but instead simply '[to] obey Acts 2:38 and

---

[4] *TCO* 6.12 (1928), p. 173.
[5] *TCO* (March, 1924), p. 307.
[6] *TCO* 9.2 (1931), p. 30.
[7] *TCO* 2.9 (1924), p. 475.
[8] *TCO* 7.8 (1929), p. 111. Original emphasis.
[9] *TCO* 6.1 (1928), p. 3.
[10] *TCO* (March, 1924), p. 311.
[11] *TCO* (November, 1924), p. 481.

be born of water and the Spirit, in the Name of Jesus Christ'.[12] This emphasis upon scripture over-and-against 'tradition' and 'theological theories' is a reoccurring theme throughout. For instance, one writer states that while many people claim that water baptism is simply an 'ordinance ... an outward sign of inward purity ... such an expression cannot be found in the Word of God'.[13] And though it is 'commonly stated that baptism does not save us ... the Word of God says' it does.[14] In doing so, they were arguing for a 'higher' view of baptism than their trinitarian counterparts.

This emphasis is also expressed in the confessions surrounding *mode* and *formula*. Candidates were required to be baptized by immersion in the name of Jesus, for 'to be born of water means to be dipped in water and come forth out of water ... done in the Name of the Lord Jesus Christ'.[15] This too was a rejection of tradition, especially for those who 'would advise sprinkling'.[16] By contrast, one writer notes, 'there are many ministers who ... ridicule water baptism as though it was a man's doctrine', but Oneness Pentecostals consistently understood scripture 'to prove it to be of divine origin'.[17] One writer, in my estimation, speaks on behalf of the whole in his or her comments on mode:

> Sprinkling is not baptism at all. That is only man's tradition. It is not to be found in the Word of God that children or men are to be sprinkled with water. But the Bible does read that man must be born of water ... You will see that sprinkling has never been used in the Bible at all. Therefore, if you have not been buried *under* the water, you have never been baptized at all. We will give $50 to any man who can show us in the New Testament where man or child was sprinkled.[18]

---

[12] *TCO* 8.9 (1930), p. 133. One can see in this statement that Jn 3.5 and Acts 2.38 are operating together to form this New Birth doctrine. This is also seen the following statement: '"Jesus' Name," is inseparably connected with being born of water and ALL HAVE TO take on His Name'. See *TCO* 6.12 (1928), p. 172. Original emphasis.

[13] *TCO* 9.2 (1931), p. 30.

[14] 1 Peter 3.20-21 is probably in view here.

[15] *TCO* 8.8 (1930), p. 119.

[16] *TCO* (September, 1923), p. 199.

[17] *TCO* 8.5 (1930), p. 69.

[18] *TCO* 9.2 (1931), p. 30. My emphasis.

Instead, they insisted that anything short of immersion in Jesus' name was unscriptural.[19] In Haywood's words, 'there are many who are opposed to baptism by immersion because of their traditional teachings upon the subject', but scripture is clear: 'the only way to be baptized in the NAME of the Father, and of the Son, and of the Holy Ghost is in Jesus' Name' by immersion.[20]

For the writers of *TCO*, scripture is clear on both *mode* and *formula*, and its witness must be trusted. And to get this right is of vast importance because much *is* at stake. Without true baptism, there is no salvation and remission of sins. Baptism, then, must not be deferred. As one writer states, 'delay not ... to be baptized',[21] because nothing should be allowed to 'stand between you and your God'.[22] If it is necessary, the believer should be ready to say, 'Hinder me not!' to whoever shall stand in the way.[23]

It is also important to note that when one is baptized in Jesus' name, they are affirming a scriptural position on the doctrine of God, as well as the practice of water baptism, over the 'traditional' positions. By submitting to baptism in Jesus' name, they are affirming that the 'the Father, Son and Holy Ghost "are one" ... and that in Christ Jesus dwelleth all the fulness of the Godhead in bodily form'.[24] In other words, 'there is positively no just reason for baptizing in Jesus' name as a matter of fact. The only solution – the only reason – the only just reason to offer for baptism in Jesus name is, in the fact, that, the Fulness of God indwells Christ'.[25] Affirming baptism in Jesus' name, then, is affirming the Oneness doctrine of God as well. Expounding on this doctrine of God in connection with water baptism, E.N. Bell states,[26]

---

[19] *TCO* 6.7 (1928), p. 99.
[20] *TCO* (February, 1924), p. 283. Original emphasis.
[21] *TCO* (September, 1923), p. 199.
[22] *TCO* (September, 1923), p. 199.
[23] *TCO* (September, 1923), p. 199.
[24] *TCO* (June, 1924), p. 385.
[25] *TCO* 8.6 (1930), p. 86. Misspelling original.
[26] E.N. Bell was the first general chairman of the General Council of the Assemblies of God. During the early years of the Oneness controversy, Bell was rebaptized in Jesus' name. However, he returned to the trinitarian camp not long after. See W.E. Warner, 'Bell, Eudorus N.' in Stanley M. Burgess, et al. (eds.), *DPCM* (Grand Rapids, MI: Zondervan, 1988), p. 53.

> When Jesus commanded to 'baptize in the name of the Father and of the Son' they understood what the Father's name was for Isaiah had told them it was the Lord (42:8) and Jesus had opened their understanding that they might understand the Scriptures (Luke 24:25). Knowing also that God was a Spirit (John 4:24) and that the Lord was the Spirit (2 Cor. 3:17) they could completely obey the command of Jesus by commanding baptism merely 'IN THE NAME OF THE LORD'[27] as Peter did in Acts 10:48 or in the name of the Lord Jesus as under Paul in Acts 19:5 … I can in all sincerity say that I do not now believe Christ ever meant to baptize with the phrase 'Father and Son' at all … I prefer to use the real name common to both Father and Son as the Lord commanded me to baptize in 'The Name', not in a relationship phrase which is no proper name at all. Lord, help the dear brethren to see that father and son are by no means a proper name. Recognizing the whole Godhead always present in Jesus, the apostles baptized either in a part or all of His name.[28]

Accordingly, by being baptized in Jesus' name, one is affirming the Oneness of God and receiving the power that is contained in his 'Name'.

Finally, and perhaps most interestingly, the overall narrative of privileging scripture over 'man's tradition' is diverted from and then nuanced on three occasions.[29] First, in appealing to Church history, Haywood argues for water baptism to be accompanied by *glossolalia*:

---

[27] Original emphasis.
[28] *TCO* 4.3 (1926), p. 46. In an earlier issue, E.N. Bell shares a brief testimony on how this 'new vision of Jesus' has personally impacted him:

> If people knew what God is putting in my soul by a brand new vision of Jesus and the wonders hid in His mighty and glorious name, they would cease pitying me for being baptized in the Name of the Lord Jesus Christ and begin to shout and help me praise the Lamb that was slain who is now beginning to receive some honor and praise, but who will eventually make the whole universe – sea, earth and sky, reverberate with universal praise and honor to His great Name.

See *TCO* 4.2 (1926), p. 21. Perhaps it is important to note that Bell died in 1921. This means that the writers of TCO were still using his testimony, probably written in 1915, as justification for their position. This is 10 years after the conflict and Bell's rebaptism, which he later recanted.

[29] In this literature, 'tradition' is not univocal. Sometimes it is used as a shorthand for popular opinions, while other times it is used more technically and exactly to refer to the Christian tradition.

We here quote the words of St. Chrysostom, who lived 400 years after the death of Christ: Whoever was baptized in apostolic times (days) he straightway spake with tongues ... one in the Persian language, another in the Roman, another in the Indian, and another in some other tongue. And this made manifest to them that were without that it was the Spirit in the very person speaking. Wherefore the Apostle calls it 'the manifestation of the Spirit, which is given to every man to profit withal.' That the members of the body of Christ were baptized therein and spake with tongues is further shown by the words of Augustine, who lived several hundred years after the apostles: 'We still do what the apostles did when they laid hands on the Samaritans and called down the Holy Spirit on them in laying on of hands. It is expected that the converts should speak in new tongues.'[30]

Haywood also sought to provide an apologetic using church history for using the name of Jesus in water baptism:

> The trinitarian formula and triune immersion were not uniformly used from the beginning, nor did they always go together. The 'Teaching of the Apostles' indeed prescribed baptism in the name of the Father, Son and Holy Ghost, but on the next page speaks of those who have been baptized in the name of the Lord – the formula of the New Testament. In the third century baptism in the name of Jesus Christ was still so widespread that Pope Stephen, in opposition to Cyprian of Carthage, declared it to be valid. –Ency. Brit. Vol. 3, page 365. We only have to get a full proof of the fact that baptism in the name of Jesus Christ was the earliest formula of baptism.[31]

And lastly, an unidentified author argued that 'since ... the close of the apostolic age the Christian Church has used' the triune formula in baptism while 'the Church of the apostolic age used the name of the Lord Jesus Christ in the same rite, according to the Acts and the apostolic Epistles'.[32]

---

[30] *TCO* (September, 1926), p. 138. Significantly, Haywood possibly "borrowed" this information from earlier Pentecostal periodicals. See *The Bridal Call* 3.10 (1920), pp. 17-18.
[31] *TCO* (June, 1928), p. 79.
[32] *TCO* 7.10 (1929), p. 150.

Therefore, while these two writers utilize the history of the church and early church theologians to provide an apologetic against the triune formula and 'second blessing' theology, the Oneness writers also demonstrate that they believe in some instances the tradition of the church is an important resource in affirming theological confession and articulation.

B.1.2 Water Baptism in *The Christian Outlook*: Scripture

While Oneness Pentecostals appealed to many scriptures, Acts 2.38 was arguably *the* single most significant and informative verse for forming and authenticating the Oneness theological convictions on water baptism. Acts 2.38's formula of baptizing 'in Jesus name' proved to Oneness adherents (1) the biblical precedent of baptizing in Jesus' name, (2) the biblical foundation of affirming that baptism is for the 'remission of sins', and (3) the connection between water baptism and Spirit baptism. For some, these theological articulations were undeniably found in the reading of this scripture, causing one writer simply to declare, 'Acts 2:38 is right'.[33] As Haywood saw it, 'Any person reading ... the words recorded in Acts 2:38 ... cannot help but see that baptism in the name of Jesus Christ was preached and confirmed in the early days of the gospel'.[34] And for Haywood, this message was a central part of the gospel: 'In reading the Book of Acts you will find what was preached as the "gospel of the kingdom." Repentance and baptism for the remission of sins were to be preached in all the world in His (Jesus') name, beginning at Jerusalem.'[35]

At times, writers interpreted other scriptures in light of Acts 2.38. For instance, one writer argues that 'Acts 2:38 is ... the fulfillment of Matthew 28:19'.[36] This suggests that explanatory preference was provided to the apostle's baptizing in Jesus' name over Jesus' command to baptize in the name of the Father, Son, and Holy Spirit. This prioritizing of Acts 2.38 is seen consistently in the treatment of Jesus' command in Mt. 28.19. This is because 'if Acts 2:38 isn't the fulfilling of Matt. 28:19, then the Word of God contradicts itself. Hence there would be two ways of baptizing'.[37] To further the point, another

---

[33] *TCO* 3.1 (1925), p. 13.
[34] *TCO* (August, 1926), p. 115.
[35] *TCO* 4.2 (1926), p. 19.
[36] *TCO* 3.1 (1925), p. 18.
[37] *TCO* 6.1 (1928), p. 13.

writer states that 'when it says to baptize in the Name of the Father, and of the Son, and of the Holy Ghost. It doesn't say names, But Name in the singular. And Jesus is the Name of the Father, Son and Holy Ghost.'[38] The Oneness doctrine of God also serves as a hermeneutical stimulus, since 'Father', 'Son', and 'Holy Ghost' are interpreted to be titles for the name of Jesus. Since this is the case, in Haywood's words, 'why should there be any objections to one saying, "I baptized you in the Name of Jesus Christ"? Why should that be termed such a terrible error when it is mentioned in Matt. 28:19?'[39]

Acts. 2.38 and Acts 2.4 were referenced together at times to argue for the 'New Birth' doctrine. As one contributor said, 'Baptism in water in the name of Jesus, according to Acts 2:38, and the reception of the Holy Ghost according to Acts 2:4 starts the new life'.[40] Similarly, Acts 2.38 was coupled with Romans 6.3 to argue for baptism in Christ's name.

> As in Acts 2:38, 'Repent, and be baptized every one of you in (into) the name of JESUS CHRIST for the remission of sins and ye shall receive the gift of the Holy Ghost.' And in Romans 6:3, we read, 'Know ye not, that many of us as were baptized into JESUS CHRIST were baptized into his death?'[41]

Thus, Acts 2.38 was the primary biblical source and was placed into dialogue with many other scriptures to generate a consistent thread of scriptural witness. However, other scriptures in Acts were referenced as well. For example, in referring to Acts 19, Haywood comments:

> They 'baptized in water in Jesus name' and afterwards Paul laid in his hands on them, and they were filled with the Holy Ghost. HAVE YOU EVER HAD AN EXPERIENCE LIKE THIS? If not, then you are not sealed ... Go somewhere and ask the preacher to 'baptize you in Jesus Name' and you SHALL receive the Holy Ghost. See Acts 2:38.[42]

---

[38] *TCO* 6.1 (1928), p. 14.
[39] *TCO* (May, 1928), p. 63.
[40] *TCO* 6.7 (1928), p. 101.
[41] *TCO* 6.10 (1928), p. 150. Emphasis original.
[42] *TCO* (March, 1924), p. 319. Original emphasis.

Haywood argues that water baptism in Jesus' name should be accompanied by Spirit baptism soon afterward.

Another author uses this Acts 19 account to argue that since 'the disciples of John were rebaptized in the Name of the Lord Jesus' then baptism should be followed by Spirit baptism with accompanying 'tongues … in the Name of Jesus for the Holy Ghost'.[43] The key issue for many writers was that scriptures in Acts – as a whole – use 'the name JESUS CHRIST when baptizing the dear brothers and sisters'.[44] For example, 'in Acts 8.6, "Only they were baptized in the name of the Lord Jesus"' and 'in Acts 10:48' and 'Acts 19:5', all were baptized in Jesus' name.[45] Acts, then, served as a major scriptural resource for Oneness theologizing, especially, Acts 2.38.

In addition to Acts 2.38, Oneness Pentecostals received other prominent scriptures received in ways that reinforced their theology of Oneness baptism, such as Jn 3.5. This verse was a significant scriptural resource to argue for water baptism's salvific effect. Haywood states, 'If one has not been baptized in water and the Holy Spirit he cannot claim to be "born again". Conversion is one thing, but to be "born of the Spirit" is another.'[46] Conversion was understood to be something separate from being 'born of the Spirit' (referencing John 3.5) and becoming 'born again'. Affirming this position further by offering a commentary on the verse, one writer states that in Jn 3.5, 'Jesus declares that even a righteous Pharisee must be born of the baptismal water and of the Holy Ghost in order to be saved'.[47]

Overall, early Oneness Pentecostals were convinced that 'too many' Christians as a whole 'jump over the 5th verse of the third chapter of John's Gospel',[48] and hence fail to see the salvific element embedded within water baptism. They criticized Christians for attempting to 'hide behind the thief on the cross to evade the subject of baptism'.[49] The writer explains,

> There is no refuge there. The thief on the cross believed in the death, burial and resurrection of our Lord Jesus Christ even

---

[43] *TCO* 6.7 (1928), p. 99.
[44] *TCO* 6.10 (1928), p. 149. Original emphasis.
[45] *TCO* 6.10 (1928), p. 149.
[46] *TCO* 7.8 (1929), p. 112.
[47] *TCO* (September, 1923), p. 179.
[48] *TCO* 1.4 (1923), p. 13.
[49] *TCO* (February, 1923), p. 4.

before he had 'given up the Ghost'.... There is no doubt but what that thief would have been 'buried with him by baptism' had he lived to see the day of Pentecost fulfilled. There is no refuge in the thief on the cross. Our refuge is in Jesus Christ alone. We must be baptized into Him.[50]

The thief on the cross, then, does not compromise the truths found in Jn 3.5. In this scripture, it is indisputable that 'only one "family" will be saved – those who are born of water and Spirit ... See John 3:3-5'.[51] There is no exception in salvation – one must be 'born of water (Come forth up and out of the water) and of the Spirit (Come forth up and out of the Spirit, being soaked with same and clothed upon with)' or 'he cannot enter into the Kingdom of God'.[52] John 3.5, then, helped confirm baptism's vital importance to Christian salvation.

While Acts 2.38 and Jn 3.5 were significant throughout early Oneness literature, other scriptures were important in supporting and strengthening Oneness baptismal theology. John 3.5 was tied with Paul's statement in Eph. 4.5 to argue for 'one baptism', containing two 'vital elements':

> Paul tells us that there is one Lord, one faith, one baptism. Jesus tells Nicodemus, this Baptism is a birth. Which makes only one Baptism, composed of two vital elements, water and Spirit (blood). For the life is in the blood and the Spirit is life.[53]

This emphasis on 'one baptism' can be seen throughout the literature. One writer, Leona Burnison, argues that since 'Paul ... declares that there (is) One Lord, One Faith. One Baptism (Eph. 4:5) ... then there is just one.'[54] Further, they reasoned, most Pauline scriptures argued for only 'one' baptism. For example, in one case Eph. 4.5 and 1 Cor. 12.13 are brought together to argue this point: 'In 1 Cor. 12:13 we read that "by one Spirit we are all baptized into one body, whether we be Jews or Gentiles" and in Ephesians 4:5 we see that there is

---

[50] *TCO* (February, 1923), p. 4.
[51] *TCO* 2.9 (1924), p. 475. In another issue, 1 Pet. 3.20-21 is also referenced and used to argue that 'Baptism saves'. See *TCO* (June 1925), p. 104.
[52] *TCO* 7.7 (1929), p. 98.
[53] *TCO* 3.1 (1925), p. 18.
[54] *TCO* 6.1 (1928), p. 13.

"one baptism" and "one body" also (verse 4)'.[55] Because of this, the church is composed of a 'people ... who have truly repented of their sins, and have been baptized into the Name of JESUS CHRIST for the remission of their sins ... and have been baptized into the one body by the Holy Ghost (1 Cor. 12:13)'.[56] Affirming this position, Haywood states that 'all who are baptized by that "one Spirit" ... are members of that one body'.[57]

Further, passages in Romans were received by Oneness Pentecostals as supportive of their view. One writer, Wm. Boaz Macgregor, references Rom. 6.3-4 indirectly when he states that, 'our sins are not remitted until we are *buried* with Christ in baptism'.[58] Another author, engaging Rom. 6.4 directly, argues for the Oneness doctrine of God and baptism in Jesus' name by stating, 'we are buried with HIM by baptism into death, not THEM, HIM!'[59] This scripture is also significant for another author because it 'typifies death to the allurements of the world. (Rom. 6:3-13)'.[60]

Surprising is the fact that the mentions of the baptism of Jesus were sparse. In an indirect reference to Jesus' baptism, Haywood declares that 'when you are immersed in the Name of Jesus Christ for the remission of sins, heaven will open up unto you immediately'.[61] However, this reference notwithstanding, the lack of references to Jesus' baptism is noteworthy since Haywood notes Jesus' filling 'with the Holy Spirit at the River of Jordan'.[62] Considering Oneness Pentecostalism's consistent emphasis upon the relationship between water baptism and Spirit baptism, one might consider this an opportune resource. Yet, little attention was given to those texts, likely because of how trinitarians used the passage to refute the Oneness position.

B.1.3 Water Baptism in *The Christian Outlook*: Testimonies and Reflections

There were many testimonies and reflections surrounding water baptism and Spirit baptism among early Oneness Pentecostals. In fact,

---

[55] *TCO* (September, 1926), p. 133.
[56] TCP 4.2 (1926), p. 27. Original emphasis.
[57] *TCO* (November, 1924), p. 489.
[58] *TCO* 4.7 (1926), p. 101. My emphasis.
[59] *TCO* 3.1 (1925), p. 18. Original emphasis.
[60] *TCO* (June 1925), p. 106.
[61] *TCO* (November, 1923), p. 213.
[62] *TCO* (November, 1923), p. 231.

water baptism along with Spirit baptism were the two most consistently reported events in the early literature. Usually, these correspondents would state the number of water baptized and then the number Spirit baptized.[63] As a whole, testimonies seemed to reveal that there were more people water baptized than Spirit baptized, because water baptism preceded Spirit baptism.[64] For example, one report states, 'Eleven were baptized in Jesus's name, nine received the Holy Ghost and others were seeking'.[65] Sometimes after being water baptized, candidates experienced Spirit baptism immediately.[66] Others, however, experienced a gap in time between these two events. For instance, Elder C.B. Gordon shares that one person 'was baptized in the name of Jesus' and then one hour later 'was filled with the Holy Ghost'.[67] This suggests that though they believed that speaking in tongues was part of the conversion experience, Spirit baptism was still in some sense a subsequent experience. One could be saved, baptized in water, and still seeking Spirit baptism.

---

[63] Additionally, the reported number baptized and the number Spirit baptized were usually different. For example, see *TCO* 4.3 (1926), p. 45; *TCO* (April, 1924), pp. 325, 329, 331, 336, 345; *TCO* 7.9 (1929), pp. 130, 131; *TCO* 6.7 (1928), pp. 104-105; *TCO* 6.10 (1928), pp. 140-41, 148; *TCO* 7.4 (1929), pp. 54, 60-61; *TCO* 3.7 (1925), pp. 126-27, 129, 132; *TCO* 5.8 (1927), p. 121, 124; *TCO* 5.10 (1927), p. 153; *TCO* 7.7 (1929), p. 103; *TCO* 4.7 (1926), pp. 106-107, 109; *TCO* 4.2 (1926), p. 25; *TCO* 4.2 (1926), p. 29; *TCO* 6.12 (1928), pp. 177, 179-80; *TCO* 5.2 (1927), pp. 22, 25, 28, 29; *TCO* 7.10 (1927), pp. 140, 144, 147-49; *TCO* 6.1 (1928), pp. 9-12; *TCO* (September, 1926), p. 138; *TCO* 2.9 (1924), p. 408, 470-71, 473; *TCO* 6.12 (1928), pp. 177, 179, 180; *TCO* 5.2 (1927), pp. 22, 25, 28-29; *TCO* 7.10 (1927), pp. 140, 144, 147-49; *TCO* 6.1 (1928), p. 9-12; *TCO* (September, 1926), p. 138; *TCO* 2.11 (1924), p. 200, 202, 205; *TCO* (November, 1924), p. 490; *TCO* (April, 1924), p. 347; *TCO* (June, 1923), p. 137; *TCO* 1.4 (April, 1923), p. 12; *TCO* 3.1 (1925), pp. 8, 13; *TCO* (March, 1924), pp. 295, 299, 304, 306, 313; *TCO* 9.9 (1931), pp. 111, 116-18; *TCO* 9.12 (1931), pp. 152-53; *TCO* 9.4 (1931), pp. 57-61; *TCO* 9.11 (1931), pp. 138-40; *TCO* 9.2 (1931), pp. 24-29; *TCO* 9.1 (1931), pp. 7-8, 10-12; *TCO* 8.11 (1930), pp. 169-73; *TCO* 8.9 (1930), pp. 137, 139-40; *TCO* 8.8 (1930), pp. 124-25; *TCO* 8.7 (1930), pp. 107-109; *TCO* 9.1 (1931), pp. 75-76; *TCO* 8.5 (1930), p. 67; *TCO* 8.5 (1930), pp. 69, 73, 76-78; *TCO* 8.6 (1930), p. 92; *TCO* 7.8 (1929), p. 118; *TCO* 7.8 (1929), p. 120; *TCO* 3.1 (1925), p. 17; *TCO* 4.3 (1926), p. 44.

[64] In Haywood's words, 'many are receiving the Holy Ghost *after* being baptized in Jesus' name'. My Emphasis. *TCO* (April, 1924), p. 325.

[65] *TCO* 8.5 (1930), p. 73.

[66] For example, one writer reports that 'twenty-five have been baptized in the Name of Jesus and *all* have received the Holy Ghost with the evidence of speaking in tongues as the Spirit gives utterance'. *TCO* 4.3 (1926), p. 44. My emphasis.

[67] *TCO* 4.2 (1926), p. 29.

Typically, after being baptized in Jesus' name, the newly baptized were 'still seeking for the promise' of Spirit baptism.[68] However, the newly baptized were always encouraged never to 'give up' on receiving Spirit baptism after they were baptized 'in Jesus' name'.[69] The testimonies, though, reveal flexibility in the timing of these two events. One writer – J.K. Solomon – reporting on his own experience of being baptized in the Jordan River states: 'I received my baptism of the Holy Spirit, that was before I went to the Jordan. The next day we went down to the Jordan.'[70] Therefore, some did receive 'the Holy Ghost before water baptism'.[71]

Testimonies also reveal there to be some who believed they had encountered the Spirit in water baptism. One pastor, summarizing an experience of someone in his or her congregation, reports, 'having believed on the Lord and been baptized in water' this believer 'realized she had something that she did not possess before conversion ... it was the Spirit of Jesus'.[72] Other testimonies reveal that some received 'the baptism with the Holy Ghost as (they) "came up out of the water"'.[73] Sister Margret Reed testified that as a man 'was baptized in Jesus' name and upon coming up out of the water, the power of God fell and he was filled with the Holy Ghost, speaking in tongues'.[74] Another report reveals a Baptist preacher being rebaptized in Jesus' name who after coming 'up out of the water', jumped out, and began running 'around the church, hollering, "Power! Power!!"'.[75] Some who were 'baptized in water ... came out of the water speaking in tongues'.[76] There was a widespread expectation to meet the Spirit in the waters of baptism, manifesting itself through

---

[68] *TCO* 8.6 (1930), p. 86. One pastor in the same issue reports: 'there are nine here yet to have been buried with him in baptism, who have not yet received the Holy Ghost'. See *TCO* 8.6 (1930), p. 92.
[69] *TCO* 4.7 (1929), p. 109.
[70] *TCO* 8.6 (1930), p. 89.
[71] *TCO* 7.4 (1929), p. 61.
[72] *TCO* (June, 1925), p. 114.
[73] *TCO* 1.4 (1923), p. 13.
[74] *TCO* 5.2 (1927), p. 28.
[75] *TCO* 2.9 (1924), p. 470.
[76] *TCO* 2.9 (1924), p. 470.

the *charismata* and other dramatic experiences.[77] One pastor recounts another one of these sensational experiences:

> We have seen more than 200 coming up out of the water speaking in tongues. We have seen hundreds slain under the power of God in the waters and floating as long as half an hour at the time, many speaking in tongues.[78]

Oneness Pentecostals sometimes reported demonic oppression being broken as a result of the baptism ritual. As one person put it, 'since the day that I was baptized in the name of Jesus Christ, the Lord cast all the evil spirits out'.[79] Testimonies of physical healings were also present, such as one man who was baptized 'who had been on crutches for about 35 years' and afterward was able to 'walk out and leave his crutches in the church'.[80] Another elderly 'woman ... who had dropsy was baptized and is now getting better'.[81] Lastly, in another case, 'a Baptist preacher was baptized in Jesus' name and was healed in the water'.[82] Thus, whether it was receiving 'power ... in the water',[83] receiving the 'Holy Ghost ... before getting out of the tank,[84] or receiving 'heal(ing) in the water',[85] it is clear that there was consistent anticipation for 'God's Spirit' to be 'poured out in power' in water baptism.[86]

The only break in narrative of water baptism as an opportunity to meet God comes from Elder J.R. Ledbetter, a missionary to Liberia, Africa. He reports that 'nearly every Wednesday, our fast day, *we* baptize from three to four in Jesus' name and *the Lord* baptizes nearly all of them with the Holy Ghost'.[87] Ledbetter seems to posit water baptism as man's work, and Spirit baptism as God's work. However, this

---

[77] In one instance, this 'power' evidenced itself in a 'native' from West Africa, 'Brother Peter Chea', testifying that when he was 'baptized in Jesus' Name' he gave 'up four wives and kept one'. See *TCO* 1.4 (1923), p. 9

[78] *TCO* 6.7 (1928), p. 195.

[79] *TCO* 6.7 (1928), p. 106.

[80] *TCO* 7.4 (1929), p. 60.

[81] *TCO* 6.11 (1928), p. 163.

[82] *TCO* 8.11 (1930), p. 172.

[83] *TCO* 6.11 (1928), p. 161.

[84] *TCO* 9.1 (1931), p. 75.

[85] *TCO* 8.11 (1930), p. 172.

[86] *TCO* 4.7 (1929), p. 103. For more testimonies of encountering the Spirit in the waters of baptism, see *TCO* 7.6 (1929); p. 79, *TCO* 7.7 (1927), pp. 103-10;. *TCO* 6.7 (1928), p. 103; *TCO* 4.7 (1929), pp. 103, 109.

[87] *TCO* 7.7 (1929), p. 101. Emphasis mine.

might be an exception to the rule, for many others understood water baptism to be a place to encounter the Spirit.

Testimonies also reveal that rebaptism was prominent, due to the nature of their belief in the efficacy of the formula. In one case, Timothy D. Urshan, a missionary to Jerusalem, shared his testimony of being rebaptized in Jesus' name:

> Before this time I was immersed according to the usual form 'in the name of the Father, and of the Son, and of the Holy Ghost,' ... but when I learned that Jesus Christ was 'the name' of the Father, Son and Holy Ghost I was ready to be baptized in Jesus' name ... so Brothers and Sisters, if you have not been baptized in Jesus' name, obey God at once.[88]

For Urshan, re-baptism was an issue of obedience tied to the promise in Act 2.38. Testimonies consistently affirmed this position. Many were rebaptized when they learned that Jesus' name is the only valid formula to be used in baptism. Following this revelation, many submitted to the 'Lord and obeyed' by being 'baptized in Jesus' name'.[89] In one instance, a person reported being 'obedient to the word' by being baptized in 'fourteen below zero' weather.[90] This is the price some Oneness Pentecostals paid for 'following Jesus in baptism'.[91]

The command to be baptized in Jesus' name extended even to children. One notes all 'little folks' (children) were 'baptized in Jesus name' by immersion.[92] Timothy Urshan shares that his 'two ... own children, Lydia and Josiah' were 'baptized at Jordan' through immersion.[93] And while many testimonies do not reveal the age of the children baptized, a few do. In one case a 'five-year-old girl that made quite an impression on the people' was immersed.[94] One missionary to China also reports that he or she 'baptized six women, two girls of fifteen years of age and thirteen boys, ranging from ten to sixteen years of age'.[95] Thus, children were baptized, but they were understood to be immersed as believers. For despite their age, children as

---

[88] *TCO* 5.8 (1927), p. 117.
[89] *TCO* 9.12 (1931), p. 152.
[90] *TCO* (March, 1924), p. 313.
[91] *TCO* 4.7 (1926), p. 103.
[92] *TCO* 8.5 (1930), p. 67.
[93] *TCO* 8.8 (1930), p. 121.
[94] *TCO* 8.5 (1930), p. 77.
[95] *TCO* 7.10 (1929), p. 144.

young as 'six years old were baptized' and even sought 'the Holy Ghost as honestly as an older person'.[96] Yet, they rejected the idea of infant baptism as efficacious. In one report condemning pedobaptism, a missionary to Switzerland reports,

> the class of people here is hard to reach, as they have their own church and ... their babies are baptized, and because of this some little children have told our children they are going to hell since they had not been baptized when infants. Then these same children swear and take the name of the Lord in vain. The young people in this place are all seeking pleasure.[97]

The writer, then, understands the 'swearing' and 'seeking pleasure' to demonstrate the expected ills of infant baptism. Other missionaries had to deal with the issue of pedobaptism when they began evangelizing people in other nations. Some missionaries ministered in places where there were 'no churches who immerse ... except' theirs.[98] However, despite the difficulty for some pastors and missionaries, Oneness Pentecostals resolutely and passionately advocated for immersion in Jesus' name for the remission of sins.

B.2 Hearing Early PAW Ordinary Theology: Conclusions

In conclusion, teaching on water baptism centered on the themes of the New Birth doctrine, the efficacious nature of being baptized in the Name of Jesus, the illegitimacy of any baptismal mode besides immersion, and baptism's inextricable connection with Spirit baptism. This theology was derived from how they received the baptismal passages taken from the book of Acts, particularly Acts 2.38, though Jn 3.5 was another prominent scripture referenced throughout. Overall, water baptism and Spirit baptism were viewed as two different events, yet closely related, since they are the two events that make up the New Birth. Reports and testimonies overall – with only one exception – reveal an understood expectation to meet the Spirit of God within the rite of baptism. Yet, this report has also uncovered variation in the timing between water baptism and Spirit baptism in early PAW ordinary theology. Though some received Spirit baptism concurrently with water baptism, others received one before the

---

[96] *TCO* 8.5 (1930), p. 76.
[97] *TCO* 1.4 (1923), p. 12.
[98] *TCO* (June, 1925), p. 112.

other. Therefore, while the New Birth doctrine was dogmatic, testimonies reveal that in practice there was flexibility in the *ordo salutis*.

TCO also reveals a 'sacramental' perspective, which is one of two main schools of thought within Oneness Pentecostalism.[99] As seen in the early literature, 'by incorporating the third stage of Spirit baptism into the new birth' this sacramental group 'transfers the initial entry of the Spirit from the traditional conversion experience to the Pentecostal one' which creates a 'highly exclusive theology of salvation ... in which one is neither truly born again nor indwelled by the Spirit until the three stages of Acts 2:38 are completed'.[100] Haywood and Urshan prove to be two of the major proponents of this school of thought.

While this study not only confirms Reed's assessment, it also adds something to the current body of research. The early Oneness baptismal theology surveyed almost universally expresses a sacramental view not only at the *explicit* level through teachings, confessions, and theological articulations, but also an *implicit* level of theological discourse found in testimonies and personal reflections.[101] As seen throughout, there is a deeply sacramental character to the testimonies in which those being baptized experience the presence of the Spirit through baptism. Baptism, then, is an opportunity to encounter the presence of God.

---

[99] According to David Reed,

Oneness soteriology from the earliest years has been divided into two main schools of thought. One follows the baptistic tradition of the AG in which the new birth is experienced in conversion. Baptism in the name of Jesus conforms the believer to the NT pattern of Christian initiation. Spirit baptism is a second work of grace that gives the Christian power for ministry ... the other position, expressed in sacramental terms, identifies all three elements in Acts 2:38 as constituent of the new birth. To be born of water and Spirit (John 3:5) means to be baptized in the name of Jesus and to receive the Pentecostal experience of Spirit baptism ... The insistence that baptism is for 'the remission of sins' (Acts 2:38) draws the charge of baptismal regeneration.

See Reed, 'Oneness Pentecostalism', p. 651.

[100] Reed, 'Oneness Pentecostalism', p. 650.

[101] By using the term 'sacramental', I am suggesting that this group understood water baptism to facilitate divine encounter.

C. Hearing Official Denominational Statements and Scholarly Voices[102]

Official PAW teaching on water baptism and scholarly treatment of the subject stems from three sources: the 'What We Believe Pamphlet', *Fundamentals of the Apostolic Faith*, and *The Birth of the Spirit*.

C.1 Pentecostal Assemblies of the World Statement of Faith: 'What We Believe Pamphlet'

The PAW 'What We Believe Pamphlet' seeks to provide the reader with a basic knowledge of what the denomination believes while also giving a brief overview of the history of the 'oldest Oneness Pentecostal organization'.[103] According to the pamphlet, the doctrines discussed 'are the results of special discussions held at various times by the Board of Bishops of the Pentecostal Assemblies of the World'.[104]

For our purposes, the first subject addressed is the sacraments: water baptism, the Lord's supper, and footwashing. About baptism, the first statement asserts: 'We Believe In: The one baptism, as recorded in Acts 2:4; 10:44-48; 19:1-6, is evidenced by the speaking of other tongues as the Spirit gives utterance as the initial evidence thereof'.[105] Further, 'The New Birth ("being born again"), includes water baptism in Jesus' Name',[106] more specifically using the formula, 'IN THE NAME OF THE LORD JESUS CHRIST FOR THE REMISSION OF SINS'.[107] This is emphasized multiple times throughout the pamphlet, perhaps since one can only 'experience the new birth' by being 'baptized with the Holy Spirit (Ghost) with the initial evidence of speaking in tongues'.[108] John 3.3, 5, and Acts 2.38 are

---

[102] While the previous two chapters held two separate sections for denominational statements and scholarly voices, considering the sources available, I have chosen to treat all sources within one section. The two 'scholarly' voices (G.T. Haywood and Francis Leonard Smith) were both presiding bishops of the PAW when they wrote their works, making their treatment of the issues binding for the denomination.

[103] 'What We Believe Pamphlet' (Indianapolis, IN: The Department of Publications of the Pentecostal Assemblies of the World, Inc.), p. 2. No publishing date is given.

[104] 'What We Believe Pamphlet', p. 5.
[105] 'What We Believe Pamphlet', p. 5.
[106] 'What We Believe Pamphlet', p. 6.
[107] 'What We Believe Pamphlet', p. 6. Original emphasis.
[108] 'What We Believe Pamphlet', p. 7.

given for support of this position.[109] Though, baptism for the remission of sins is reserved for 'persons who have reached the age of understanding and NO BAPTISM of infants under any condition'.[110]

Because 'the Apostles always administered baptism in His Name from the day of Pentecost forward' and 'there is no biblical record of one person ever being baptized … using the formula: In the name of the Father, and of the Son, and of the Holy Ghost (St. Mark 28:19)',[111] baptism in Jesus' name is the only valid formula. To illustrate the severity of this point, the author states that 'without the NAME of Jesus, baptism does not carry the substantiation of Calvary'.[112] Comments also expose that the baptismal formula is deeply connected to the Oneness doctrine of God.

Like baptism in Jesus' name, 'baptism in the days of the Apostles was ALWAYS by immersion' as well.[113] For the PAW, this is well illustrated in Paul's statement that baptism is a burial (Rom. 6.4).[114] Thus, all other 'modes of baptism (sprinkling, pouring, or infant baptism) are all inventions of men without biblical substantiation'.[115] Therefore, these modes 'are without Apostolic sanction of approval',[116] making immersion the only valid baptismal mode.

C.2 G.T. Haywood

G.T. Haywood, the founder of the PAW, served as the Bishop of the church until he died in 1931. During his tenure as Bishop, he wrote a booklet entitled, *The Birth of the Spirit: In the Days of the Apostles*.[117] As the Foreword states, this booklet was written 'because of the great controversy over what is the Birth of the Spirit'.[118] Haywood, then, seeks to present 'facts upon the subject as they are found within the Word of God'.[119] More specifically, he aims to follow the book of

---

[109] While Acts 2.38 is quoted, Acts 2.28 is given as the reference.
[110] 'What We Believe Pamphlet', p. 6.
[111] Though Matthew 28.19 is quoted, it is attributed to Mark's gospel. 'What We Believe Pamphlet', p. 7.
[112] 'What We Believe Pamphlet', p. 8. Original emphasis.
[113] 'What We Believe Pamphlet', p. 8. Original emphasis. Many Scriptural references were given: Mk 1.10; Acts 8.38, 39; Rom. 6.4; Mt. 12.40.
[114] 'What We Believe Pamphlet', p. 8.
[115] 'What We Believe Pamphlet', p. 8.
[116] 'What We Believe Pamphlet', p. 9.
[117] G.T. Haywood, *The Birth of the Spirit: In the Days of the Apostles* (Christ Temple Book Store [Indianapolis, IN]), pp. 1-40. The exact year of publication is unknown.
[118] Haywood, *The Birth of the Spirit*, 'Foreword' (unnumbered page).
[119] Haywood, *The Birth of the Spirit*, 'Foreword'.

Acts to come to the 'one conclusion as to what constituted The Birth of the Spirit in the Days of the Apostles'.[120] The treatment of water baptism in Haywood's book, then, is situated within the larger context of a discussion on the meaning of being born of the Spirit.

According to Haywood, when Jesus told Nicodemus in John 3 that one needed to be 'born of water and the Spirit', that was just 'another way of saying, "He that believed and is baptized, shall be saved"'.[121] Other biblical authors use the word 'baptize' instead of 'birth' to convey the same truth. Put another way, 'scripture will interpret scripture if we seek to rightly divide the word of truth. To be born of "water and the Spirit," and "believe and is baptized" (John 3:5 and Mar. 16:16), are proven to be synonymous terms expressing the one and self-same thing.'[122] Therefore, scripture as a whole witnessed to the fact that 'baptism of water and the Holy Ghost' make up the 'New Birth'.[123]

When discussing water baptism 'from an Apostolic point of view', Haywood emphasizes that it 'is a command of God'.[124] Yet this command of God is not optional because baptism is 'a saving medium'.[125] Therefore, while 'it is said, by many, to be an ordinance, that is, "an outward sign of inward purity" such an expression cannot be found in the Word of God'.[126] It is much more than a mere ordinance. Baptism *saves*. But baptism saves only '"by the resurrection of Jesus Christ from the dead." (I Pet. 3:20, 21).'[127] Moreover, baptism in Jesus' name is vital: 'To be saved by water baptism, it must be administered in the name of Jesus, for there is "no other name under heaven given among men, whereby we must be saved"'.[128] 'Water alone', then, 'does not save us'; the water must wash over the recipient with the power of the blood of Christ, since 'the blood and the name of an individual are inseparable'.[129] Hence, immersion in Jesus' name is the only correct formula and mode. As Haywood states, 'If you have

---

[120] Haywood, *The Birth of the Spirit*, 'Foreword'.
[121] Haywood, *The Birth of the Spirit*, p. 3.
[122] Haywood, *The Birth of the Spirit*, p. 5.
[123] Haywood, *The Birth of the Spirit*, pp. 5-6.
[124] Haywood, *The Birth of the Spirit*, p. 23.
[125] Haywood, *The Birth of the Spirit*, p. 24.
[126] Haywood, *The Birth of the Spirit*, p. 23.
[127] Haywood, *The Birth of the Spirit*, p. 24.
[128] Haywood, *The Birth of the Spirit*, p. 24.
[129] Haywood, *The Birth of the Spirit*, p. 24.

never been baptized in the name of JESUS CHRIST, you have never been immersed properly'.[130] Conversely, if one is immersed in the name of Jesus, one is 'guaranteed' to 'receive the baptism of the Holy Ghost as (they) "come up out of the water"'.[131]

C.3 Francis Leonard Smith

Francis Leonard Smith became Presiding Bishop of the PAW in 1974 and served two three-year terms.[132] During his time serving the PAW, he wrote what later became *Fundamentals of the Apostolic Faith*.[133] In it, Smith seeks to produce a 'simplified text in language the average reader can understand'.[134] Smith's treatment of water baptism, while present, is not substantial. Nevertheless, *Fundamentals of the Apostolic Faith* is a significant publication within PAW literature.

Notably, water baptism is discussed within the chapter on soteriology, rather than ecclesiology. Baptism is a 'requirement' for every Christian 'to fulfill', for 'believing unto repentance is demonstrated by yielding to God's will'.[135] And though 'there are many who claim that baptism is not essential', Jesus' words in Mk 16.16 prove otherwise.[136] According to 1 Pet. 3.21, 'baptism is a figure that saves us, and that it is the answer of a good conscience toward God'.[137] When discussing the 'new birth', Smith states that in 'John 3:5 and Titus 3:5 we learn that the "new birth" or regeneration is accomplished by the baptism of the Holy Ghost',[138] thus leaving out water baptism. Lastly, though Smith states that the 'mode of baptism will be discussed in another chapter', the subject of baptism is not brought up again later in the book.[139] Speculatively, one might assume that water baptism was intended to be brought up again within the discussion on ecclesiology.

---

[130] Haywood, *The Birth of the Spirit*, p. 24. Original emphasis.
[131] Haywood, *The Birth of the Spirit*, p. 40.
[132] Francis Leonard Smith, *Fundamentals of the Apostolic Faith* (Indianapolis, IN: The Department of Publications of the Pentecostal Assemblies of the World, Inc., 1998), p. 1.
[133] Smith, *Fundamentals of the Apostolic Faith*, pp. 1-61.
[134] Smith, *Fundamentals of the Apostolic Faith*, p. 4.
[135] Smith, *Fundamentals of the Apostolic Faith*, p. 37.
[136] Smith, *Fundamentals of the Apostolic Faith*, p. 37.
[137] Smith, *Fundamentals of the Apostolic Faith*, p. 37.
[138] Smith, *Fundamentals of the Apostolic Faith*, p. 31.
[139] Smith, *Fundamentals of the Apostolic Faith*, p. 37.

C.4 Hearing Official Denominational Statements and Scholarly Voices: Conclusions

The official teaching of the PAW states that water baptism is for believers by immersion in the name of Jesus, and is a significant component of the New Birth, making water baptism essential for salvation. G.T. Haywood's treatment of water baptism reaffirms the official denominational teaching on the subject, expounding and bringing greater clarity to its statements. Nonetheless, Haywood seems to suggest a closer relationship between Spirit baptism and water baptism than the official teaching. This is seen in his statement assuring readers that when one is properly immersed in Jesus' name, the candidate will receive Spirit baptism as they come up out of the baptismal waters. Smith's treatment is brief, so much so, he fails to reference mode. Leonard also equates the New Birth solely with Spirit baptism, while the official teaching and Haywood's work associate both Spirit baptism and water baptism with the New Birth. Nonetheless, despite such variances, all sources agree on most issues of water baptism.

D. Empiricizing Pentecostalism: Contemporary Pentecostal Assemblies of the World Ordinary Theology[140]

As described in detail earlier,[141] in moving from the revisioning to the empirical, I will be following Mark Cartledge in his use of qualitative research methods. Therefore, participant observation, interviews, and secondary denominational literature will be put into dialogue

---

[140] As previously noted, I am following Cartledge's use of Jeff Astley's definition of ordinary theology as 'the theological beliefs and processes of believing that find expression in the God-talk of those believers who have received no scholarly theological education'. See Astley and Francis (eds.), *Exploring Ordinary Theology*, p. 1. Further, empirical theology refers to the use of empirical research methods in practical theology developed in Europe and should not be confused with the American version of this designation associated with process theology. As stated earlier, Cartledge notes that, 'it was first categorized as an approach by the practical theology department at Nijmegen University, under the influence of Johannes A. van der Ven. Since the founding of the *Journal of Empirical Theology* in 1988, it has become a well-established approach within practical theology.' See Cartledge, 'Practical Theology: Attending to Pneumatologically-Driven Praxis', p. 166.

[141] For a more detailed look at my fieldwork technique, see Chapter 3.

with one another.¹⁴² By using (1) participation observation along with (2) interviews and (3) secondary denominational literature, 'ideas generated from one source of material can be checked by reference' to another source.¹⁴³ This triangulation can 'enhance the reliability of the results of research'.¹⁴⁴

And while this chapter will follow the same format as Chapters 3-4, there is one methodological adjustment: this chapter will shift from ethnographic research (Chapters 3-4) to netnographic research (Chapter 5).¹⁴⁵ While 'ethnography describes and interprets cultural and social settings primarily using participant observation, informal interviews, and extended time in the field',¹⁴⁶ netnography draws from the traditions of ethnography and applies them to online research. According to Robert Kozinets, 'netnography is participant-observational research based in online fieldwork. It uses computer-mediated communications as a source of data to arrive at the ethnographic understanding and representation of a cultural or communal phenomenon.'¹⁴⁷ Therefore, the following fieldwork will follow the earlier framework, yet shift from face-to-face data gathering to online data gathering.¹⁴⁸ As with ethnography, netnography has both strengths and limitations.¹⁴⁹ Nevertheless, the approach taken will

---

¹⁴² For secondary literature, I will be consulting Burgess, Stanley M., Gary B. McGee, Patrick H. Alexander (eds.), *DCPM* (Grand Rapids, MI, Zondervan, 1988), pp. 1-928.
¹⁴³ Cartledge, *Practical Theology*, pp. 70-71.
¹⁴⁴ Cartledge, *Practical Theology*, p. 71.
¹⁴⁵ As noted in Chapter 2, in this chapter I will be conducting virtual ethnography or 'netnography' due to the coronavirus pandemic at the time of research. Therefore, I will be taking the same approach as in Chapters 3-4, though I will be moving from face-to-face research to virtual research.
¹⁴⁶ Cartledge, *Practical Theology*, p. 73
¹⁴⁷ Kozinets, *Netnography*, p. 60.
¹⁴⁸ This suggests that interviews and participant observation will be mediated via technology of some kind (Skype, Zoom, Email, Facebook Live, etc.). Netnography, then, draws from the traditions of ethnography and applies them to online research by using computer-mediated communications as a source of data.
¹⁴⁹ Though some sociologists have argued that 'online interactions can be and are as rich and varied as traditional interactions', there can be limitations of virtual ethnography/netnography: a holistic description of any informant is unfeasible, body language and tone of voice can be stifled compared to face-to-face communications, among others. However, there are also strengths of netnography. As Kozinets notes, the revelatory depth in which some communicate online is a great strength. See Katelyn McKenna and Gwendolyn Seidman, 'You, Me, and We: Interpersonal Processes in Electronic Groups' in Yair Amichai-Hamburger (ed.), *The*

stay consistent with previous chapters and continue to give a 'thick' description with which to engage. It is to these sources that we now turn.

D.1 New Horizons Fellowship[150]

New Horizons Fellowship, located in North Delaware, USA, was established as a daughter church of a nearby PAW church in 1999. The founding and current pastor, William (all names in this account are pseudonyms), held the church's first official service in October of that year. In June 2011, New Horizons Fellowship was able to purchase their church facility. After some renovation, New Horizons Fellowship was able to hold their first service in their newly purchased facility on Easter, 2012. Demographically speaking, the whole of the church is black/African American and contains members of all ages. Further, the average attendance of the congregation for the year of study (2020) was seventy.

D.2 Participant Observation: The Worship Service[151]

D.2.1 The Worship Service

The worship space is traditional, though it does contain some modern elements. The worship space is equipped with pews, an organ, and a large pulpit. However, the space is also outfitted with an updated sound system, drum set, and some modern décor. The organ and drum set are adjacent to the platform, while the microphones for the worship leader and supporting vocalist are on the platform, in front of the pulpit.

D.2.2 Service Structure

This Sunday morning worship service was held on March 22nd, 2020. The worship service began at 10.00 AM and concluded at 11.00 am.[152] In this service, I was able to discern five main units.

Social Net: Human Behavior in Cyberspace (Oxford: Oxford University Press, 2005), pp. 192-93; Kozinets, *Netnography*, p. 116.

[150] The following information I gleaned from the leadership of the church and the church website.

[151] I am following Cartledge's structure and format in reporting his participation observation. See Cartledge, *Testimony in the Spirit*, pp. 29-32.

[152] From discussion with church leadership, services have been shortened because of the coronavirus. Services usually begin at 10.00 am and conclude between 11.45 am and noon. Further, though many joined to view online via Facebook Live, there were still those who were physically present.

Furthermore, for the service to move between the main units, there were links. Following Cartledge's findings, there were also key individuals who link the units together, but they do so in relation to specific locations. There were three major locations: the platform, the altar, and the congregational seating. There were also key individuals who mediate the zones: (1) The worship leader(s) who lead the sung worship, (2) Lady Sandra who facilitated some of the transitions and links,[153] (3) James and Nancy Smith who were invited by Lady Sandra to give testimony, and (4) Pastor William who managed some of the transitions, the preaching, and response times.

The service begins with the worship leader and assisting vocalists singing acapella, 'Praise the Name of Jesus' (Unit 1).[154] The congregation responds by standing, joining in with singing, and with many giving spontaneous praise. As the worship leader sporadically shouts, 'hallelujah' and 'thank you Jesus' the congregation responds in several ways: lifting of arms, clapping of hands, jumping, swaying, dancing, and repeating 'hallelujah' and 'thank you Jesus'. Following the first song, the worship leader introduces, 'I Love to Praise His Name',[155] with the organ and drums accompanying. The congregation responds similarly to worship. Towards the conclusion of the song, one woman seated toward the front of the church began passionately shouting with arms lifted. As the shouting continues for a few minutes, the organ and drums continue to play. Others from the congregation respond enthusiastically, laying hands on her, praying for her, and praising God.

As the congregation and music begin to settle, Lady Sandra enters the platform and gives an exhortation: 'The fact that we are all here is a miracle, so we might as well give God a hallelujah and praise!' (Unit 2). The congregation responds by raising hands, clapping, and shouting as the drummer crashes the cymbals and the organist continues to play. Following such praise, Lady Sandra begins speaking of God's protection and healing, moving into a time of prayer. Lady Sandra, then, prayed for (1) protection for the congregation amid the coronavirus, (2) healing for all people present in the gathering, including those with known ailments, (3) and faith 'since we still serve an awesome God!' Lady Sandra begins asking the congregation to

---

[153] Lady Sandra is married to Pastor William.
[154] Roy Hicks Jr, 'Praise the Name of Jesus' (Latter Rain Music, 1976).
[155] Mississippi Mass Choir, 'I Love to Praise His Name' (Malaco Records, 2011).

remember past miracles that God has enacted in their lives to stir up trust and faith, amid current uncertainty. Lastly, Lady Sandra invites James and Nancy Smith to share a testimony.

With the worship leader, supporting vocalists, and Lady Sandra still on the platform, James and Nancy make their way to the altar (Unit 3). Many applaud as James and Nancy make their way forward, some shouting 'hallelujah' and 'thank you Jesus'. Lady Sandra hands James the microphone. James follows by briefly giving testimony to how God had 'come through' and 'answered their prayers' after four years of waiting. People respond in applause and shouts of praise. James finishes by stating how his wife's faith encouraged him through the long season of waiting. He then hands the microphone to his wife, Nancy. As a result, Nancy shares a more detailed account. According to Nancy, her daughter was diagnosed with kidney failure four years prior. After years of dialysis, prayer, and loss of hope, their daughter had recently received word that she was matched with a new kidney and approved for a kidney transplant. In response, someone in the congregation began waving a tambourine, others shouting 'amen' and/or 'hallelujah'. Nancy, then, finishes her testimony with a prayer of thankfulness and then prays a healing prayer for those who might need a 'touch' from God. Following the prayer, the worship leader and band begin playing an upbeat, spontaneous chorus on 'wonder', 'power', and 'miracles'. The worship leader then instructs the congregation: 'Put your hands together, let us give God some praise!' The people respond in applause.

As the congregation is applauding, Pastor William – who has been sitting on the left side of the platform – stands up and makes his way to the pulpit (Unit 4). The organ and drums continue to play, while the worship leader and vocalist exit the platform. After a few minutes of continued praise, the music eases. Pastor William reads Psalm 46. Following the reading, Pastor William states that 'he wanted to share a word of encouragement'. He declares that this word of encouragement is that 'while we are social distancing, we need to practice getting right with God'. Because 'death is before us and God is judging the world right now', we need to begin to 'examine ourselves'. The tone of the sermon is serious, though Pastor William moves between challenge and encouragement, to move people towards 'getting right with God'. Throughout the sermon, many respond with shouting 'amen' and 'hallelujah'. Towards the end of the sermon, Pastor

William begins to become more passionate in his communication, and as a result, many congregants begin standing up, lifting their arms, clapping their hands, and shouting 'amen'. As he nears the end of his sermon, Pastor William mentions that he needs to 'cut the message short' due to time limitations, but states: 'Do not be weary. Instead, press into Jesus!' He encourages the congregation to have faith and look to God as their refuge and strength.

Following the sermon, Pastor William – accompanied by drums and organ – leads the congregation in singing, 'Just a Little While' (Unit 5).[156] Following this song, Pastor William moves into a time of collecting tithes and offering and then concludes the service.

Therefore, 'it can be seen that despite the lack of written liturgy there is a clear sequence of expected events'.[157] Pastor William serves as the 'the chief master of ceremonies that ensures there is a smooth transition' between units and zones, with Lady Sandra playing a supporting role.[158] The worship leader and instrumentalist – particularly the organist – work in partnership with Pastor William to lead the congregation in sung worship, and support transitions between units throughout. Yet Pastor William does release authority in the service by allowing spontaneous manifestations, congregational response, and testimonials to take place. Nonetheless, the overall service structure, flow, and transitions were mainly handled by Pastor William, Lady Sandra, and the organist.

D.3 Interviews

D.3.1 Clergy Interview: Baptismal Ritual[159]

In seeking to gain insight into New Horizons Fellowship baptismal ritual, I conducted a semi-structured interview with Pastor William. Through questioning, Pastor William sought to provide an outline for how their church performed baptisms. Therefore, what follows is

---

[156] E. M. Bartlett, 'Just a Little While' (Albert E. Brumley & Sons Publishing, 1921).

[157] Cartledge, *Testimony in the Spirit*, p. 32.

[158] Cartledge, *Testimony in the Spirit*, p. 32.

[159] As stated earlier, because I am unable to attend a baptismal service due to the coronavirus pandemic, I am seeking to adjust and offset this limitation by (1) viewing a Sunday morning worship service via Facebook Live (participant observation) and (2) conduct an interview with the pastor on the church's baptismal ritual (informant interview). In this section I hope to gain insight into what a typical water baptism service might look like via an interview with the Pastor of the church: Pastor William.

an overview of my interview with Pastor William regarding his church's baptismal practices.

According to Pastor William, the church only baptizes those who can profess their faith. Therefore, the church will baptize believers of all ages, including children who have come to Christ in their trust. In their community, 'deacons are permitted to baptize' along with the minister. This means that the deacons usually 'do the baptisms unless I am requested by the candidate to perform it myself, which is very rare, but it does happen'. Nevertheless, whoever performs the baptism first asks the candidate publicly 'why they want to be baptized to make sure they are doing this on their own and that they understand what they are doing'. Following a proper response, the candidate is 'then taken to change clothes and then brought to the pool'.

Once the candidate is brought to the pool,[160] they are baptized in Jesus' Name. In Pastor Williams' view, Jn 3.3-7, Acts 2.38, and Rom. 6.1-15 all witness to the importance of baptism in the name of Jesus and its salvific currency. He declares that his church practices baptism out of the belief that there is 'One Lord, one faith, and one baptism, which is in the name of Jesus'. In his view, because 'the Scripture tells us whatever you do, do it all in the Name of Jesus for there is no other name given whereby we must be saved and that at the Name of Jesus every knee shall bow and every tongue confess that He is Lord', all baptisms in New Horizons Fellowship *must* be done in the name of Jesus. Therefore, each candidate is baptized with the following formula:

> My dear brother or sister, according to your faith and confidence that you have in the death, burial, and resurrection of our Lord and Savior Jesus Christ, I now baptize you in the Name of Jesus for the remission of sin and you shall receive the gift of the Holy Ghost. Therefore, being buried in Him, rising to walk in the newness of life.

Finally, reflecting on his own experience, Pastor William stated that though he does not remember his personal experience since he 'was just seven years old', he has witnessed God do mighty things in baptism. In many cases, he testified to have seen 'many lives change immediately watching the outward change with some coming up out

---

[160] According to Pastor William, the church uses a portable tank for baptisms.

of the water'. In a few instances, he has witnessed 'people being under the influence of alcohol get baptized and get out sober'. Additionally, some people have come out of the water speaking in tongues. However, in Pastor Williams' view, 'one can be still be Spirit-filled before being water baptized'. Yet, regardless of what one might witness, the most important thing to recognize is that 'water baptism and Spirit baptism makes one complete and enables one to receive the full plan of salvation'.

D.3.2 Interview Participants

The interview participants were comprised of three men and nine women, 'representative (in age, sex, and socioeconomic terms) of the congregation as a whole'.[161] All participants were black/African American, varying in age. The men were all middle-aged. The men were employed in music production (Jarrett), education (Buck), and law enforcement (Brenton). The women too were mostly middle-aged (Melissa, Dinah, Layla, Bettie, Julietta, Sallie), though Suzanna was younger, and Terri and Ivy were older. These women were employed in healthcare (Melissa), technology (Sallie), counseling (Suzanna), business (Julietta), non-profit leadership (Bettie), human resources (Dinah), disabled (Layla), and retired (Terri, Ivy).[162]

D.3.3 Interview Findings

Question 1: Personal Testimonies of Baptism

While the first question relates mainly to one's experience of water baptism, themes such as conversion and rebaptism surfaced in the conversations. Four of the twelve participants had been baptized twice, either initially as an infant or young child and then later as an adult, or in some case, some were baptized multiple times as an adult. Terri, for instance, was raised Catholic and baptized as an infant. Later in a Protestant church, she was baptized again as an adult. However, most recently she was baptized again because 'she finally understood what it meant to be baptized and the true meaning of being baptized in Jesus' name'. Sallie too was baptized 'at twelve in the Name of the Father, Son, and Holy Ghost, and then again at the age of twenty-five in the Name of Jesus after getting a better

---

[161] Coakley, *God, Sexuality, and the Self*, p. 165.
[162] Following Cartledge's focus group format, each informant is identified by their pseudonym, ethnicity, age, and occupation. See Cartledge, *Testimony in the Spirit*, p. 32.

understanding'. Others referenced increased understanding as a reason for choosing to be baptized again (Melissa, Julietta).

All participants baptized once were baptized in Jesus' name (Bettie, Jarrett, Suzanna, Ivy, Buck, Layla, Dinah, Brenton). However, Jarrett – 'raised Apostolic Holiness, knowing the doctrine of water baptism' – was baptized at eight years old and today wonders if he 'should do it again because of greater understanding'. Conversely, Layla – who was also raised as an 'Apostolic Pentecostal' – was baptized at age nine and feels no need to seek baptism again.

In answering the general question, 'Can you tell me about your personal experience of water baptism?', there were answers such as 'it felt like a weight had been lifted … I was forgiven of my sins' (Dinah), 'I felt a filling and a presence that I had never felt before was moving in me' (Brenton), 'I felt clean and new' (Buck), and 'all I remember was the water being cold' (Ivy). Therefore, people's experiences with water baptism varied. However, most recounted some sense of felt change. Some, such as Terri, shared moments of ecstasy: 'When I was baptized, I remembered crying, jumping, feeling drunk, and speaking by the Holy Ghost'. Others simply reported feeling 'safe and free' (Melissa) or 'overcome in joy' (Suzanna).

Question 2: Observations of Other's Baptisms

My second question focused on the participants' observations of others' water baptisms. Significantly, all participants reported witnessing a significant change in others due to their baptisms. A few reported observing shifts in people's lives following the rite. Terri shared that she has seen 'changes and newness' in people, both as they come out of the water and in their lives following. Bettie, too, shared that she has 'seen lives transformed through water baptism – watching their lives take a 360 turn around'. Jarrett shared that he has noticed general changes 'in visage and countenance all due to water baptism'.

In answering the question, many focused on their observations of people's experiences in the moment of baptism. Buck notes several examples: 'I have witnessed heavily intoxicated people snapped out of drunkenness, those who are demon-possessed immediately placed in their right minds, sadness turn to gladness, and many come up out of the water speaking in tongues'. Along with Buck, other participants observed persons coming up in the waters speaking in 'tongues', 'a heavenly language', or 'an unknown language' (Anthony,

Sallie, Julietta, Bettie, Layla, Jarrett, Melissa), though Julietta stated that she has also witnessed others who come up 'very calm'. Suzanna, too, stated that she has 'seen many baptisms, some with immediate praise and some without'.

Still, many miraculous events were associated with baptism. According to Dinah, she has viewed 'God do many miraculous works' through baptism. In her words, 'some were healed of their illness or condition, some felt that they were free of their burdens and sins, some were so grateful to God, and others received the gift of the Holy Spirit as they came up out of the water'. Layla, too, is confident that she has seen many 'receive the gift of the Holy Ghost' in baptism due to the visible nature of God's working. Similarly, Jarrett stated that he has observed 'the descent of the Holy Ghost with the evidence of speaking in tongues while still in the pool'. Anthony too shared that he has 'witnessed persons speaking in tongues and see on their faces an indescribable shift in their physical appearance, if just for a moment or two'. Further, he has noticed 'a look that people have when they are filled with the Holy Spirit that cannot be replicated at any other time except at baptism'.

Lastly, there were also reports of some 'crying', 'sobbing', and 'looking overwhelmed' because of their experience in baptism (Terri, Julietta).

Question 3: Ways of Baptizing

The general question – 'Do you think there is any right way to do baptism?' – was followed up questions centered on three issues: (1) mode, (2) formula, (3) and those authorized to perform baptisms.

First, there was little disagreement on mode. All participants believed immersion was the proper mode. However, Julietta also thought that 'for babies – not babies in Christ, actual infants – we should sprinkle or pour'. And Buck stated that 'if conditions don't allow or provide for immersion, we should seek the guidance of the Holy Ghost so as to not let the desiring soul leave without being born of the water'. Further, the reasons given for immersion varied. For some, immersion is preferred because 'it is an act of dying to oneself that is to be buried and rising in the newness of Jesus Christ' (Terri) or as Brenton put it: 'The action of immersion in water depicts dying and being buried with Christ. The action of coming out illustrates Christ's resurrection'. A few people gave this reason, appealing to Rom. 6.1-11 either directly or indirectly (Jarrett, Bettie, Sallie, Dinah).

Melissa stated that immersion is best because 'immersion allows remission of sins'. For others, the word 'baptism' means to 'immerse, dip' (Bettie, Jarrett) or 'plunge' (Dinah). For Dinah, Jesus' example is enough to persuade us of the validity of immersion over other modes.

Remarking on whether one should be baptized in Jesus' name or the name of the Father, Son, and Holy Spirit, all argued for baptism in Jesus' name since 'without Jesus, we cannot be saved' (Brenton). For some, by being baptized in Jesus' name one achieves 'remission of sins' (Bettie), and even salvation itself (Layla). Many understood scripture to teach baptism in Jesus' name only. Since the Father, Son, and Holy Spirit are titles of the one name of Jesus, baptism in Jesus' name is the only valid formula (Sallie, Buck, Ivy, Bettie, Layla, Dinah, Melissa). As Buck shared, 'The only direction (in scripture) given was to be in the name of Jesus Christ, not the titles that He holds'. Though, one participant stated that one could use either formula if it was understood that 'the Father, Son, and Holy Ghost are three titles of the one name of Jesus' (Terri). Further, as one is baptized in the name of Jesus, they are 'placing faith in Jesus Christ to receive the gift of the Holy Spirit from the Father' (Brenton). For Jarrett, baptism in the name of Jesus is crucial for 'this action in this manner produces this result – the remission of sins'.

Finally, on the issue of who is authorized to baptize, the participants were divided. Some believed that pastors or deacons should be the only ones authorized to baptize (Dinah, Bettie, Layla). For Ivy, 'bishops and evangelists' should also be authorized to baptize alongside pastors and deacons. For other participants, anyone who is 'saved, living a life of holiness and is trained to baptize safely should be authorized to baptize' (Melissa). Others echoed similar statements (Buck, Brenton). Nonetheless, others were 'unsure' (Julietta, Terri). For Brenton, because 'Jesus commanded his disciples to baptize and none held a title within a priesthood' this implies that anyone who feels a 'calling on their life' should be allowed to baptize (Brenton). Sallie believed that anyone who has been 'baptized in Jesus Name can perform a baptism, but to maintain order in the church those that have been ordained as pastors, deacons or elders should perform baptisms'. Suzanna offered similar comments. Finally, Jarrett stated that while 'organizational polity limits the rite to ordained ministers', he believes that 'all those committed to gospel ministry have authority to perform the sacrament of baptism'.

Question 4: Water Baptism and Spirit Baptism

My next question aimed to tease out the relationship (if any) between water baptism and Spirit baptism. For all informants, Spirit baptism and water baptism were understood to be two separate events. When distinguishing between them, I received answers such as, 'Water baptism identifies us with the death, burial, and resurrection of Jesus Christ, and cleanses us; while the Spirit baptism is the infilling of the Holy Ghost which gives us the power to live clean and do the work of the Lord' (Layla), 'the relationship between water baptism and Spirit baptism is simply the submerging of one with water and some submerging one in the spirit' (Ivy), and 'I would say one is physical – water baptism – while the other is spiritual – Spirit baptism' (Jarrett). For one participant, 'Water baptism cleanses the flesh, and the Holy Spirit baptism cleanses the heart' (Brenton). Julietta stated that baptism is an act associated with cleansing, yet she associated Spirit baptism with tongues, only: 'Water baptism represents the washing of our sins, we go down dirty, but come up clean. I believe Spirit baptism is more of a verbal baptism.'

Though the participants often conceived of the relationship between the two differently, many were emphatic that both were vital. For instance, I received statements such as 'both are necessary' (Suzanna), 'they go hand in hand' (Melissa), 'you need both' (Dinah), and 'one compliments the other' (Jarrett). Bettie speaks on behalf of these voices when she states that 'both are vital to the salvation plan'. Both baptism and 'the Holy Ghost baptism is essential for the new birth experience to be complete' (Bettie). Yet for most, the 'order doesn't matter' (Suzanna). Melissa, though, stated that the usual order is 'you get baptized and then receive the Holy Spirit'. However, Melissa does state that it is still *possible* for someone to 'believe the word and receive the Holy Spirit before they are baptized and when this happens baptism usually follows'. Thus, for many of the informants, the order is secondary. The important issue is that 'the process of being born again is not complete until you have been born of the water and of the Spirit' (Sallie).

Finally, though water baptism was considered essential for salvation for all informants, symbolic language was used by some to explain the rite (Terri, Brenton, Bettie, Ivy, Jarrett). For instance, Terri shares that 'water baptism is the outward appearance as a symbolic act whereby a new Christian identifies with Christ's death, burial, and resurrection. It is also a public profession of repentance and faith in Jesus'. Brenton, too, states that 'water baptism is a picture of what our Lord has done for us, immersion symbolizes being baptized into Christ's death'. Baptism as a symbolic act, though, is still 'necessary for salvation' (Buck).

Question 5: Water Baptism and Scripture
The final, two-part question focused on scriptural reflection.[163] The first part of the question sought to understand what scriptural verses, passages, or biblical events informed the interviewee's view of water baptism. All participants were able to think of at least one scriptural passage or verse.[164] In answering the first questions, the participants stated (or quoted) Acts 2.38 (Melissa, Jarrett, Layla, Bettie, Suzanna, Ivy, Buck), Jn 3.5 (Julietta, Terri, Buck, Brenton), Rom. 6.3-4 (Jarrett, Bettie, Sallie), Mk 16.16 (Dinah, Melissa), Gal. 3.27 (Dinah, Buck) and Mt. 3.16 (Bettie). In expounding on the scriptures, the participants' associated baptism with the forgiveness of sins, identification with Christ, death to sin, and salvation. Significantly, Bettie was the only one who referenced Jesus' baptism. In expounding upon its significance, she stated that Jesus' baptism is significant because it 'proves full immersion'. Therefore, all candidates should 'be lowered in the water like Jesus'.

In the second part of the question, I directed the participants to Rom. 6.3-4 and Acts 2.38 to read and reflect on its meaning and implications for water baptism in more detail.[165] In reflecting on Rom. 6.3-4, Layla stated, 'water baptism identifies with the death, burial, and resurrection of Jesus Christ, and cleanses us'. Others shared that Rom. 6.3-4 attests to the importance of immersion (Melissa, Sallie, Bettie). For instance, Sallie shared that 'immersion is the proper way to baptize. Romans 6 speaks of being buried with Christ through baptism. Immersing in water is the only one that symbolizes being buried.' Still, some participants stated that it talks of 'death to sin'

---

[163] 'What Scriptures inform your view of water baptism? (and) What do Acts 2.38 and Rom. 6.3-4 tell you about water baptism?'
[164] Verses were either directly referenced, quoted, or summarized.
[165] Acts 2.38 and Rom. 6.3-4 were selected due to these Scripture's prominence in the early contemporary Pentecostal literature.

(Buck, Melissa, Terri). Finally, other comments centered around the theme of obedience (Dinah, Suzanna).

In reflecting on Acts 2.38, Bettie stated that 'Acts 2:38 refers to the salvation process of repenting of our sins and believing the good news, confessing it and being baptized in water' (Bettie). Others stated that it taught that 'everyone is mandated to be baptized' (Suzanna).[166] Buck and Sallie stated that it teaches baptism in the name of Jesus is essential for the forgiveness of sins. Reflections were also offered on the relationship between water baptism and the Holy Spirit, such as 'this teaches that the Holy Ghost is given through water Baptism' (Melissa), 'if we repent and are baptized in the name of Jesus, we will receive the Holy Ghost' (Julietta), and 'this speaks to our relationship with Christ, through which is the only way to be saved and have life eternal, by receiving the Holy Spirit' (Brenton). Lastly, two participants stated that this passage teaches that 'water baptism is essential to salvation and the new birth process' (Dinah) and 'water baptism is necessary for the remission of sin' (Melissa).

Hence, there were differing interpretations and perspectives on these baptismal texts overall.

D.4 Secondary Literature

According to the *DCPM*, the Pentecostal Assemblies of the World is 'one of the oldest interracial Oneness Pentecostal organizations' which is 'predominantly black'.[167] Further, the 'PAW adheres strictly to the Oneness "new birth" teaching' which is connected to its theology of water baptism.[168] This 'new birth' teaching is often expressed 'in sacramental terms' by 'identifying all three elements in Acts 2:38 as constituent of the new birth'.[169] Thus, 'to be born of water and Spirit (John 3:5) means to be baptized in the name of Jesus and to receive the Pentecostal experience of Spirit baptism'.[170] Baptism, then, 'cleanses from sin' and is for the 'remission of sins' and because of that, 'draws the charge of baptismal regeneration'.[171] However, proponents emphasize that for baptism 'to be efficacious

---

[166] Ivy echoed similar statements.
[167] Reed, 'Pentecostal Assemblies of the World', pp. 700-701.
[168] Reed, 'Pentecostal Assemblies of the World', p. 701.
[169] D.A. Reed, 'Oneness Pentecostalism' in Stanley M. Burgess, Gary B. McGee, and Patrick H. Alexander (eds.), *DCPM* (Grand Rapids: Regency Reference Library, 1988), p. 651.
[170] Reed, 'Oneness Pentecostalism', p. 651.
[171] Reed, 'Oneness Pentecostalism', p. 651.

the water must be accompanied by an active faith and invocation of the name of Jesus. In the words of Haywood, "To be saved by water baptism, it must be administered in the name of Jesus".[172] Though this teaching is embraced by other Oneness groups, it is especially embraced by the PAW, since 'the roots of this teaching are traced to Haywood'.[173] Thus, the PAW embraces a sacramental understanding of the rite in connection to its theology of 'the Name'.

D.5 Empiricizing Pentecostalism: Conclusions

My general findings indicate that ordinary Pentecostal theology in the PAW is not entirely consistent. Nevertheless, even with apparent differences on some issues, my findings reveal many uniformities on a host of other matters. Ordinary Christian participants reported witnessing a significant change in people due to their baptisms. Pastor William, too, commented on seeing people's lives change following the rite. Additionally, the clergy interview is consistent with the ordinary Christian interviews in that all have at one time observed individuals coming up from the baptismal waters speaking in tongues. Also, there was little disagreement on mode. Both the clergy interview and ordinary Christian interviews uphold immersion to be the proper mode, with only one participant advocating for sprinkling or pouring in the case of infant baptism.[174] All interviews upheld baptism in the name of Jesus as the correct mode, though one ordinary Christian participant stated that a triune formula could be used if understood within a Oneness framework. Each interview also stated that Spirit baptism and water baptism were two separate events, though the participants often conceived of the relationship between the two differently. Lastly, Pastor William's observed releasing of others in the worship service seems to support his interview claim that he releases others within his congregation – such as deacons – to baptize candidates.

Still, there were also several divergent findings. The informant's experiences of water baptism varied. Though most recounted some sense of felt change, some stated feeling little to nothing. Also, on the issue of authority to baptize, the informants were divided. Along

---

[172] Reed, 'Oneness Pentecostalism', p. 651.
[173] Reed, 'Oneness Pentecostalism', p. 651.
[174] All other ordinary Christian participants and Pastor William denied the validity of infant baptism.

with Pastor William, some stated that deacons and ministers are authorized to baptize, though others suggested that any Christian is authorized to baptize. And while most discussed baptism in salvific or sacramental terms, others discussed baptism in symbolic terms. Scriptural reflection also varied widely, though Acts 2.38, Jn 3.5, and Rom. 6.3-4 were most consistently referenced.

Finally, the overall findings cohere with the secondary literature. The emphases upon Acts 2.38 and Jn 3.5, the New Birth, baptism in Jesus' name, immersion, remission of sins, and the overall efficacious nature of baptism are mostly constant. Overall, all sources support the finding that the PAW embraces a sacramental understanding of water baptism concerning the name of Jesus.[175]

E. Water Baptism in the Pentecostal Assemblies of the World: Conclusions

As the research indicates, early PAW ordinary theology generally corresponded with the official teaching of the PAW and the scholarly engagements with the rite. Though the empirical research found variance within interviews, overall findings were consistent with the other sources engaged. Significantly, the theology of baptism in the PAW has been mostly consistent, perhaps due in part to its attachment to the New Birth doctrine and the non-trinitarian doctrine of God. However, Spirit baptism may have taken some prominence over water baptism even within discussions on the New Birth, as seen in Smith.

However, significant for this study is the explicit and implicit sacramentality expressed in early and contemporary Pentecostal ordinary theology (revisioning and empirical). My findings indicate that at both the explicit *and* implicit levels of theological discourse, Oneness Pentecostal theology reveals a presence-driven understanding of the rite.[176] This finding adds much to my earlier findings (Chapters 3-4) that suggest while trinitarian Pentecostal believers explicitly state

---

[175] Though the participant observation does not support this claim directly, it provides the necessary context for the other sources that do.

[176] The only exception comes in the form of interview comments that seem to articulate a merely symbolic view of the bath.

that the rite is symbolic, among some, there is an implicit expectation to meet God amid the ritual.[177]

Therefore, perhaps one of the PAW's greatest gifts towards constructing a Pentecostal theology of water baptism is its emphasis upon God's action in baptism, and its drawing a closer connection between water baptism and Spirit baptism. Further, Oneness Pentecostals may have more readily recognized the spiritual significance of the rite than some trinitarian Pentecostals.[178] Therefore, perhaps the PAW can challenge trinitarian Pentecostal theologians to construct theologies of water baptism that take seriously these concerns.

Yet, now that we have discovered and identified the proper framework within which a Pentecostal theology of water baptism might be constructed (Chapters 1-5), we will in the next chapter *begin* constructing a Pentecostal theology of water baptism by providing theological readings of scriptural texts.

---

[177] Notably, there is more evidence of this found in Chapter 3.

[178] Josiah Baker, '"One Lord, One Faith, One Baptism?": Between Trinitarian Ecumenism and Onenesss Pentecostals', *JPT* 29.1 (2020), p. 104.

6

WATER BAPTISM IN THE CHURCH'S SCRIPTURE

A. Introduction

As I described in Chapter 2, my constructive approach will include discerning engagement with scriptural texts. In this way, I hope to contribute a model for how Pentecostals can read biblical texts which refer, either explicitly or implicitly, to water baptism while also developing a constructive Pentecostal theology of water baptism that is deeply shaped by the witness of scripture.[1] But before proceeding, a few introductory remarks are in order.

First, my reading of these texts is indebted to and fits within the context of Pentecostal hermeneutics.[2] In John Christopher Thomas' comprehensive survey, he outlines its development over the last few decades.[3] Significantly, he notes that Pentecostal hermeneutical approaches 'envision an interpretive approach that is not beholden to pre-existing theological grids into which a Pentecostal approach must

---

[1] In the theological reading of scripture, exposition is particularly related to doctrinal issues and scriptural texts are read with deliberate and specific theological questions in mind. See Stephen E. Fowl (ed.), *The Theological Interpretation of Scripture: Classic and Contemporary Readings* (Oxford: Blackwell, 1997), and Francis Warson, *Text, Church, and World: Biblical Interpretation in Theological Perspective* (Edinburgh: T&T Clark, 1994).

[2] Joel Green has stated that Pentecostal scholars – perhaps more seriously than any others – have sought to identify both 'how they are influenced and how they ought to be influenced by their theological and ecclesial commitments in their reading of Scripture'. See Joel B. Green, *Practicing Theological Interpretation* (Grand Rapids, MI: Baker Academic, 2011), p. 12.

[3] Thomas, '"Where the Spirit leads"', pp. 289–302.

be force-fitted'[4] and 'are far from the approach of fundamentalism or even the evangelical use of historical criticism'.[5] As Lee Roy Martin puts it, in this interpretive model 'the world within the text takes priority over the world behind the text'.[6] Further, Thomas asserts that Pentecostals view scripture as 'dynamic and inviting, a veritable universe of terrain that awaits readers and hearers who identify with and long for the experiences to which scripture and a variety of communities of the Spirit testify'.[7] Therefore, Thomas has proposed a hermeneutical model narrated in Acts 15 that comprises three central components: the believing community, the activity of the Holy Spirit, and scripture.[8] Building upon Thomas' proposal, Ken Archer has constructed a narrative strategy that seeks to be 'faithful to the Pentecostal community's ethos and yet sensitive to current academic methodological perspectives concerning the interpretation of scripture'.[9]

As noted earlier, Chris Green's work on Pentecostal hermeneutics and the theological interpretation of scripture is something I will be seeking to follow. In one of the major sections of Chris Green's published PhD thesis, *Toward a Pentecostal Theology of the Lord's Supper*, he sets out to engage the biblical text in a way that 'rings true to the form of life recognizable to Pentecostals'.[10] The hermeneutical model proposed calls for 'a literary/theological reading of scripture in the context of the worshipping and God-experiencing community, readings that remain sensitive to a text's canonical fit and that takes seriously the history of effects, always remaining focused on how the Spirit uses scripture to transform the community into Christ's ecclesia'.[11]

---

[4] While Thomas does not give many specifics, one might consider complementarian, cessationist, and dispensational Evangelical readings are just a few approaches that Thomas might believe are incompatible with Pentecostal theology.

[5] Thomas, '"Where the Spirit Leads"', p. 301.

[6] Martin, *The Unheard Voice of God*, p. 14.

[7] Thomas, '"Where the Spirit Leads"', p. 301.

[8] John Christopher Thomas, 'Women, Pentecostals and the Bible', *JPT* 5 (1994), pp. 41-56; John Christopher Thomas, 'Reading the Bible from Within Our Traditions: A Pentecostal Hermeneutic as Test Case' in Joel Green and Max Turner (eds.), *Between Two Horizons: Spanning New Testament Studies and Systematic Theology* (Grand Rapids, MI: Eerdmans, 2000), pp. 108-22.

[9] Kenneth Archer, *A Pentecostal Hermeneutic for the Twenty-First Century: Spirit, Scripture and Community* (JPTSup 28; London and New York: T&T Clark International, 2004), p. 156.

[10] Green, *Towards a Pentecostal Theology of the Lord's Supper*, p. 182.

[11] Green, *Towards a Pentecostal Theology of the Lord's Supper*, pp. 193-94.

Green's scriptural readings are purposed to aid in the development of a Pentecostal theology of the Eucharist that makes sense in light of the 'whole counsel of scripture'.[12]

Yet Green's engagement with the biblical text as a theologian has continued to develop since the publication of his monograph on the Lord's Supper. The publication of his *Sanctifying Interpretation* (2015)[13] signaled an expansion of how he seeks to engage scripture. In other publications, he has continued to attempt to work out the hermeneutics he proposed in *Sanctifying Interpretation*.[14] Most recently, Green has provided a Christological reading of Psalm 88 which signals his continuing interest in providing fresh theological interpretations of scripture within the broader context of Pentecostal hermeneutics.[15] Yet, what features of his most recent work signal this development?

I want to suggest that Green's latest works on scriptural engagement have at least three consistent features that demonstrate development in his approach since his work on the Lord's Supper.[16] First, Green has paired his earlier literary approach with a more expansive canonical approach.[17] His later readings, then, encourage greater interaction with premodern exegetes and theologians.[18] By approaching scriptural texts in light of their canonical status, he reads scripture

---

[12] Green, *Towards a Pentecostal Theology of the Lord's Supper*, p. 182.

[13] Chris E.W. Green, *Sanctifying Interpretation: Vocation, Holiness, and Scripture* (Cleveland, TN: CPT Press, 2015). For further comments on Green's monograph, see Andrew Ray Williams, 'Review of *Sanctifying interpretation: Vocation, Holiness, and Scripture* by Chris E.W. Green', *JEPTA* 38.2 (2018), pp. 184-85. For an updated edition, see Chris E.W. Green, *Sanctifying Interpretation: Vocation, Holiness, and Scripture* (Cleveland, TN: CPT Press, 2nd edn., 2020).

[14] For example, see Chris E.W. Green, 'Provoked to Saving Jealousy: Reading Romans 9–11 as Theological Performance', *Pneuma* 38.1-2 (2016), pp. 180–92; Chris E.W. Green, 'Does (Not) Nature Itself Teach You?: Pentecostal Reflections on a Troubled and Troubling Text', *Pneuma* 38.4 (2016), pp. 456-75.

[15] Chris Green, '"I am Finished": Christological Reading(s) and Pentecostal Performance(s) of Psalm 88', *Pneuma* 40.1-2 (2018), pp. 150-66.

[16] Surely, there are more than just three. Yet, by naming *at least* three common features, I hope to demonstrate some of the differences between his earlier and later approach(es).

[17] Green's canonical approach should not be confused with Brevard Child's canonical approach to scripture. In fact, Green's approach has much more in common with William Abraham's 'canonical theism' approach. In short, Green is assuming Christian tradition and the rule of faith should carry authority in our Scriptural readings. See William James Abraham, *Canon and Criterion in Christian Theology: From the Fathers to Feminism* (Oxford and New York: Oxford University Press, 1998), pp. 25-26.

[18] Green, 'Does (Not) Nature Itself Teach You?', pp. 457-75.

through the lens of the theological tradition and subsequently constructs readings that can be fitted to Pentecostal theology and spirituality.[19] While some biblical scholarship has tended to fragment theology into disconnected disciplines and the bible into disconnected testaments,[20] Green's approach exposes his commitment to constructing readings to and for the church by reading scripture 'under the rule of faith'.[21]

Another important facet of Green's reading method is his emphasis on interpretive performance.[22] His most recent works consistently emphasize how scripture acts more like a mirror, at times than a window.[23] His emphasis upon the reader's response to the text is consistent, though he holds that this type of interpretation is always in service of reading with and for the Christian virtues:

> The Spirit uses Scripture to trouble us in any number of ways – wowing us, disturbing us, provoking us, puzzling us, boring us. The sacred texts 'instruct us for salvation' (2 Tim. 3.15) not so much by delivering sacred knowledge to us, but by 'training us in righteousness' (2 Tim 3.16), driving us and leading us into the imaginatively and affectively transformative experience of interpretation as the different kinds of difficult Scriptures work on our affections and imaginations in different ways … these moments occasion the formation of certain personal and corporate virtues (e.g. humility, patience, and courage) that are vital to the work of faithful priestly mediation.[24]

---

[19] Green, 'Does (Not) Nature Itself Teach You?', p. 456.

[20] Daniel J. Treier, 'Contemporary Theological Hermeneutics' in Kevin J. Vanhoozer (ed.), *DTIB* (Grand Rapids, MI: Baker Academic, 2005), p. 790.

[21] Green, *Sanctifying Interpretation*, p. 145. According to Kathryne Greene-McCreight, 'the Rule of Faith is a basic "take" on the subject matter and plot of the Christian story, which couples the confession of Jesus the Redeemer with God the Creator. Since it is generally understood to be drawn from Scripture, in biblical interpretation it is reapplied to Scripture.' See Kathryne Greene-McCreight, 'Literal Sense' in Kevin J. Vanhoozer (ed.), *DTIB* (Grand Rapids, MI: Baker Academic, 2005), p. 456.

[22] See Green, 'Provoked to Saving Jealousy', pp. 181-92; Green, '"I am Finished"', pp. 1-17; Chris E.W. Green, 'The Music of God: Scriptural Interpretation as Aesthetic Performance' in William Oliverio and Kenneth J. Archer (eds.), *Constructive Pneumatological Hermeneutics in Pentecostal Christianity* (London: Palgrave Macmillan, 2017), pp. 103-19.

[23] Green, 'Does (Not) Nature Itself Teach You?', p. 471.

[24] Green, *Sanctifying Interpretation*, p. 127.

Green's hermeneutical approach, then, wants to empower the reader to be led by the Spirit into the pains of interpretation for one's shaping into the image and likeness of Christ.

Another significant feature of Green's reading approach is its ecumenical scheme. While some Pentecostal scholars have sought to construct readings that revision their distinctive tradition, Green consistently seeks to contribute in discussion with wider ecumenical currents. Thus, his work often expresses theological readings constructed by means of an interface with mostly non-Pentecostal sources. And though his contribution is to Pentecostal theology broadly, the distinctiveness of his contribution is often brought about through the ecumenical interchange. This is not to say that Green's readings are not Pentecostal – for they are – but his contributions are often marked by utilization of ecumenical resources in conversation with Pentecostal spirituality. It is worth noting, then, that Green's scriptural readings are distinctively ecumenical in their construction.[25]

Therefore, Green's scriptural approach is distinctive among Pentecostal scholars. And in many respects, he is one of the primary voices within Pentecostal theology to provide readings of scripture as a constructive theologian. It is my hope, then, to follow Green by offering readings of the same kind, though I will follow him on some facets more than others.[26]

A.1 A Distinctly Pentecostal Reading

From the onset, I must state that as a Pentecostal, I admittedly bring my Pentecostal experience with me as I come to the text.[27] Because they give voice to what I have experienced, I will privilege Pentecostal voices in my readings. This does not mean that I will not allow ecumenical voices to shape my readings – in fact, ecumenical engagement will be widely present – but it does mean that these readings

---

[25] Surely other Pentecostal scholars who engage Scriptural texts are in dialogue with ecumenical sources. Nonetheless, I think it is worth noting that Green utilizes and relies upon a wider range of sources than most.

[26] In particular, I follow Green's canonical and ecumenical approaches quite closely.

[27] As Brad East notes, 'theological interpretation presupposes the biblical texts' social and religious location in the life and worship of the church ... Christians read Christian Scripture best when they read it as the Christians they are'. See Brad East, 'The Hermeneutics of Theological Interpretation: Holy Scripture, Biblical Scholarship and Historical Criticism', *IJST* 19.1 (2017), pp. 35, 38.

will be aimed to be noticeably Pentecostal in their approach and content.

Finally, my selection of biblical texts directly relates to my earlier work hearing early and contemporary voices (See Chapters 3-5). I have chosen to engage scriptural texts that were frequently referenced by early Pentecostals and subsequently discussed with contemporary Pentecostals in my qualitative research. Thus, the following section sets out in providing theological readings of two texts – Rom. 6.1-11 and Acts 2.37-40 – that can press us to think more carefully and deeply about the purpose and significance of water baptism, especially as it relates to the work of the Spirit in our lives. Though in the end, my goal in these readings is to hear from God.[28] As Joel Green has argued, the primary agenda of theological commentary of Scripture is to 'present an alternative framework within which to construe our lives' and call for a 'creative transformation of the stories by which we make sense of our lives and of the world'.[29] Consequently, I hope that these readings renew and transform our imaginations and desires to become more faithful in our witness to Christ as the baptized and baptizer.

B. Reading Strategy

My reading strategy is a form of 'interested exegesis', determined by its ecclesial location and its concern with encountering the God who is mediated through the scriptures.[30] Further, this theological reading strategy emphasizes the 'potentially mutual influence of Scripture

---

[28] According to Peter Althouse and Robby Waddell, this is the ultimate reason for reading scripture. See Robby Waddell and Peter Althouse, 'The Pentecostals and Their Scriptures', *Pneuma* 38.1-2 (2016), p. 121.

[29] Joel B. Green, 'Commentary' in Kevin J. Vanhoozer (ed.), *DTIB* (Grand Rapids, MI: Baker Academic, 2005), p. 126.

[30] Green, *Practicing Theological Interpretation*, p. 44. As Brad East has stated,

> What has come to be called 'theological interpretation of Scripture' is a wooly and somewhat indefinable thing, hardly a movement, more a loose collection of trends and shared interests and practices grouped under the same name. It is characterized by increased focus on, among other things, hermeneutical questions: the nature and authority of Scripture; the interpretive roles of biblical scholars, theologians, and ordinary believers; the relationship between Scripture and history; the function of doctrine and dogma in reading the Bible; and much more.

East, 'The Hermeneutics of Theological Interpretation', pp. 30-31.

and doctrine in theological discourse and, then, the role of Scripture in the self-understanding of the church and critical reflection on the church's practices'.[31] Towards this aim, I begin first with attention to the interpretative context of the passage and then contextualize my reading within the broader Pentecostal theological tradition through a history of interpretation, and then lastly, progress to read it theologically, dialoguing with those inside and outside the Pentecostal tradition towards a constructive reading, one that takes into account Pentecostal spirituality and theology.[32]

C. 'Buried in Baptism': Romans 6.1-11

> What then are we to say? Should we continue in sin in order that grace may abound? By no means! How can we who died to sin go on living in it? Do you not know that all of us who have been baptized into Christ were baptized into his death? Therefore we have been buried with him by baptism into death, so that, just as Christ was raised from the dead by the glory of the Father, so we too might walk in newness of life. For if we have been united with him in a death like his, we will certainly be united with him in a resurrection like his. We know that our old self was crucified with him so that the body of sin might be destroyed, and we might no longer be enslaved to sin. For whoever has died is freed from sin. But if we have died with Christ, we believe that we will also live with him. We know that Christ, being raised from the dead, will never die again; death no longer has dominion over him. The death he died, he died to sin, once for all; but the life he lives, he lives to God. So you also must consider yourselves dead to sin and alive to God in Christ Jesus.[33]

C.1 Introduction: Romans 6.1-11

While other texts consider merit, I have chosen Rom. 6.1-11, 'because of how frequently early Pentecostals used the passage' in the context of their discussions of water baptism, as demonstrated throughout Chapters 3-5 of this work.[34] This Pauline text has also been thought

---

[31] Green, *Practicing Theological Interpretation*, p. 44.
[32] Green, 'Does (Not) Nature Itself Teach You?', p. 456.
[33] For both Rom. 6.1-11 and Acts 2.37-40 I am utilizing the NRSV.
[34] Green, *Toward a Pentecostal Theology of the Lord's Supper*, p. 208.

to be an important reference to water baptism not just by Pentecostals, but by many in the Christian tradition.

C.2 The Interpretive Framework: Literary Context and Outline

Romans 6.1-11 is situated within the larger section of Paul's discussion of life in Christ and the Spirit (5.12-8.39).[35] According to Stanley Porter's literary reading, one sub-section (Rom. 6.1-7.6) within this larger discussion is 'further divided into two complementary sub-sections, the first concerning one's status in Christ (Rom. 6.1-14) and the second concerning one's new-found obligations to Christ (Rom. 6.15-7.6)'.[36] No doubt that there are various ways to outline this passage, and it is nearly impossible to determine surely where exactly any given passage begins or ends. Nonetheless, following Craig Keener and J. Ayodeji Adewuya, my engagement will be limited to Paul's discussion of becoming 'Dead to Sin and Alive in Christ' in Rom. 6.1-11, assuming vv. 12-23 belong together.[37]

In Rom. 5.1-11, Paul uses Abraham as an example for believers, and similarly in this section, 'Paul applies insights gleaned from the contrast with Adam in 5:12–21'.[38] Concepts such as 'sin, death, the Law vs. grace, life' that were first introduced when 'Paul began to tell the story of Adam in 5.12-21' arise again in 6.1-11 as Paul seeks to 'address a series of questions that arise out of his telling of the Adam story in comparison to the Christ story' in Romans 5.[39] According to James Dunn, Paul's address in Romans 6 is still determined by the Adam/Christ contrast of 5.12-21 which means 'the death here spoken of is the death of Adam and those in Adam and of the Adamic epoch'.[40]

---

[35] Craig S. Keener, *Romans* (Eugene, OR: Cascade Books, 2009), p. 79.

[36] Stanley E. Porter, *The Letter to the Romans: A Linguistic and Literary Commentary* (Sheffield: Sheffield Phoenix Press, 2015), p. 131.

[37] See Keener, *Romans*, pp. 79-82; J. Ayodeji Adewuya, *Transformed by Grace: Paul's View of Holiness in Romans 6-8* (Eugene: OR, Cascade Books, 2004), pp. 1-116 (19). Some theological commentaries have also outlined the passage in this way. For example, Karl Barth, *The Epistle to the Romans* (London: Oxford University Press, 1950), pp. 188-207.

[38] Keener, *Romans*, p. 79.

[39] Ben Witherington III, *Paul's Letter to the Romans: A Socio-Rhetorical Commentary* (Grand Rapids, MI: Eerdmans, 2004), p. 154.

[40] James D.G Dunn, *Romans 1-8* (Word Biblical Commentary; Dallas: Word, 1988), pp. 307-308.

Therefore, this section continues Paul's earlier discussion, while at the same introducing 'a set of varied graphic images to exemplify and illustrate the life of the follower of Christ'.[41] These images include such things as death and life, burial, crucifixion, and resurrection, among others. And significantly for this project, many of these images are discussed in the context of water baptism. As Luke Timothy Johnson has stated, 'it is noteworthy also for the role played by baptism in his argument, making it clear that, for Paul, baptism was not a mere ritual of initiation but powerful participation in the death and resurrection of Jesus',[42] which he makes clear by using these various images to demonstrate.

Thus, in my constructive reading, I will adopt these images to structure my engagement with how this passage speaks of water baptism. Yet, before I begin my constructive reading, I will look at how Pentecostals have historically read and interpreted Rom. 6.1-11.

C.3 History of Interpretation

C.3.1 Introduction

In seeking to identify the most relevant literature to engage, it is important to first look at the history behind Pentecostal scholarship. Paul Lewis has helpfully noted that the first 100 years of Pentecostalism can be divided into four periods: (1) The Period of Formulation (1901-1929), (2) The Period of Entrenchment and Adaptation (1929-1967), (3) The Period of Challenge (1967-1984), and (4) The Period of Reformulation (1984-Present).[43] Certainly, trajectories of Pentecostal theology in the twentieth century can be outlined in other ways,[44] yet I find Lewis' most helpful in outlining a history of interpretation.

Lewis notes that the first period was a time of theological exploration, which is reflected in early Pentecostal periodical literature.[45]

---

[41] Porter, *The Letter to the Romans*, p. 132.

[42] Luke Timothy Johnson, *Reading Romans: A Literary and Theological Commentary* (Macon, GA: Smyth & Helwys Publishing, 2001), p. 101.

[43] Paul Lewis, 'Reflections on a Hundred Years of Pentecostal Theology', *CJPCR* 12 (February 2003): http://www.pctii.org/cyberj/cyberj12/lewis.html

[44] See also, John Christopher Thomas, '1998 Presidential Address: Pentecostal Theology in the Twenty-First Century', *Pneuma* 20 (1998), pp. 3-4. Wonsuk Ma, 'Biblical Studies in the Pentecostal Tradition: Yesterday, Today, and Tomorrow', in Murray W. Dempster *et al* (ed.), *The Globalization of Pentecostalism* (Irvine, CA: Regnum Books, 1999), pp. 52-69.

[45] Lewis, 'Reflections on a Hundred Years of Pentecostal Theology'.

Significantly, the second *phase* of the first *period* centered most upon the issue of water baptism.⁴⁶ In the second period, there is a 'narrowing of theological perspectives within the Pentecostal framework, yet a gradual appropriation of Fundamentalist/Evangelical theological models and issues'.⁴⁷ The theological literature of this period is marked by the publishing of 'books, usually written to popular audiences for the purpose of establishing of traditional perspectives'.⁴⁸ According to Lewis, these 'doctrinal guides' were not critically reflective but rather they were presentations of 'biblically-based doctrines in a logical way'.⁴⁹ The third period came about as a result of the Charismatic Renewal and the Third Wave Movement. Concerning theological literature, Lewis notes that during this time 'there were not any major publishing houses or journals by Classical Pentecostals except for the Society for Pentecostal Studies (SPS) journal *Pneuma* (started in 1979). So there were limited theological forums for such discussions.'⁵⁰ Finally, Lewis notes that the current period – which he entitles 'The Period of Formulation' – represents the 'theological re-visioning of the Pentecostal movement'.⁵¹ Major journals such as the *JEPTA, AJPS,* and *JPT* have been established alongside 'denominational presses, Sheffield University {sic} as part of the *JPT* supplement series' and others.⁵²

Therefore, in developing a Pentecostal history of interpretation of Rom. 6.1-11, I will adopt Lewis' structure for organizational purposes, with one exception. Since my previous engagement with early periodical literature was limited to only three denominations and the years between 1917-1929, my history of interpretation will reflect those limits. Thus, I will exclusively focus on the second half of Lewis' first period (1917-1929), and only engage early IPHC, Foursquare, and PAW periodical literature. Therefore, the following subsections will seek to summarize the various ways Pentecostals in those traditions have typically engaged and interpreted Rom. 6.1-11.

---

⁴⁶ Lewis, 'Reflections on a Hundred Years of Pentecostal Theology'. Though water baptism was an important issue during this time, my earlier research suggests that this claim may be overstated.
⁴⁷ Lewis, 'Reflections on a Hundred Years of Pentecostal Theology'.
⁴⁸ Lewis, 'Reflections on a Hundred Years of Pentecostal Theology'.
⁴⁹ Lewis, 'Reflections on a Hundred Years of Pentecostal Theology'.
⁵⁰ Lewis, 'Reflections on a Hundred Years of Pentecostal Theology'.
⁵¹ Lewis, 'Reflections on a Hundred Years of Pentecostal Theology'.
⁵² Lewis, 'Reflections on a Hundred Years of Pentecostal Theology'.

C.3.2 The Period of Formulation (1917-1929)

For many early Pentecostals, Rom. 6.1-11 was thought to speak of water baptism. This scripture was also often referenced to argue for the necessity of being fully immersed in baptism over-and-against sprinkling.[53] Significantly, even when Rom. 6 was not *directly* referenced, it was at times *indirectly* referenced by early Pentecostals substituting 'buried' for 'baptized', utilizing the language of Rom. 6.3. Early Oneness Pentecostals also understood this text to be speaking of water baptism, emphasizing that in baptism the Christian is being baptized 'into Christ Jesus'.[54] This passage, then, occasionally served as a proof text for the necessity of being baptized in the name of Jesus. Therefore, many Finished Work Pentecostals and Oneness Pentecostals interpreted Rom. 6.1-11 to be speaking of water baptism.

Some early Pentecostals – particularly Wesleyan Holiness Pentecostals – understood Rom. 6.1-11 to be referencing not the rite of washing but a spiritual experience. Summarizing this teaching, G.F. Taylor writes that Rom. 6.3-4 speaks of 'a baptism of death' which implies that 'Peter's command to those Jews to be baptized in the name of Jesus carried with it the thought of being crucified with Christ … and on these grounds, all their sins, both outward and inward, would be taken away'.[55] For some, then, Rom. 6.1-11 references sanctification, not water baptism, although this spiritual reality is symbolized or predicted by the rite.

Early in his writing, J.H. King often linked Romans 6 with sanctification.[56] King understood the baptism in Rom. 6.1-11 to be a

---

[53] For example, see *BCF* 10.7 (1926), p. 26.
[54] *TCO* 7.10 (1928), p. 150.
[55] *PHA* 8.31 (1921), p. 4.
[56] For instance, in an 1907 issue within *The Bridegroom's Messenger*, King discusses the meaning of Rom. 6.1-8:

> The baptism deals with the sin question to its full and final destruction, and it is one baptism in nature, and could be administered at the same time if we could endure the process; but as it is we have to receive it in two installments, as it were – that is, in the experiences of justification and sanctification. As it is a baptism of suffering or death, it sustains the same relation to justification as sanctification, and in this case it is as much of a baptism in the one experience as the other … Sanctification is a subtraction, a taking away of that which is opposed to justification in the heart, and it is more of a subtraction than an addition … It is a baptism into death. Death is the element into which we are

spiritual baptism where one is sanctified by experiencing a death to the old sin nature. Yet, it appears that at some point King began to transition his thought on this passage, later writing that Rom. 6.1-11 references water baptism. In 1927, King states:

> He is speaking of those who had been baptized into the symbol of Christ's death ... going down beneath the water was regarded as death even by the heathen and Greeks; and being rescued, or raised out of it, was a symbol of life, or resurrection. In the ceremony of baptism, which elevated the same conception, the fact of death was set forth on the going down, and the fact of life in the raising up out of it. Since this truth was known to those to whom this epistle was addressed, and they had been baptized symbolically into Christ's death in the baptism of water, they were to have fellowship in His death in heart.[57]

At some point, then, King understood Rom. 6.1-11 to discuss not only sanctification but also water baptism.[58] So for at least some Wesleyan Holiness Pentecostals, Rom. 6.1-11 was connected to sanctification *and* water baptism.

C.3.3 The Period of Entrenchment and Adaptation (1929-1967)

Pentecostal scholarship in the second period engaged Rom. 6.1-11 infrequently. However, the scholarship available reveals that for some, Rom. 6.1-11 was thought to speak of water baptism, and for others, it referred to a separate, 'spiritual' baptism, yet in other cases, sanctification.

Myer Pearlman understood Rom. 6.1-4 to prove that 'the Scriptural, original mode is by immersion, which is true to the symbolical meaning of baptism, namely death, burial, and resurrection (Rom. 6:1-4)'.[59] Romans 6.1-4, then, clearly articulated baptism via immersion due to how immersion pictures death, burial, and resurrection.

---

immersed. We pass through a process of death in thus being submerged ... Death is the element which expresses the nature of the baptism'. See *TBM* 1.4 (1907), pp. 2-3.

[57] *PHA* 11.25 (1927), pp. 9-11. Later King published this same information in King, *From Passover to Pentecost*, p. 64.

[58] Prominent Pentecostal Holiness theologian Noel Brooks also understood Rom. 6.1-11 to reference water baptism. For one example, see Brooks, *Fingertip Holiness*, pp. 8-10.

[59] Myer Pearlman, *Knowing the Doctrines of the Bible* (Springfield, MO: Gospel Publishing House, 1937), Kindle location 5924.

On another occasion, citing Rom. 6.4, Pearlman states that 'this act of resurrection from spiritual death is symbolized in water baptism'.[60] Therefore, this verse also spoke to the symbolic nature of water baptism. However, he also cites Rom. 6.11 concerning sanctification: 'There are three deaths in which the believer must take part ... (1) Death in sin – our condemnation ... (2) Death for sin – our justification ... and (3) death to sin – our sanctification'.[61] This third death, for Pearlman, is attested to in Rom. 6.11.

Assemblies of God theologian and church officer Ernest Williams does not discuss Rom. 6.1-11 in much detail, but he does reference the passage multiple times in connection to water baptism. Christian baptism signifies our identification with Christ in death to sin.[62] Further, Williams argues against triple immersion, utilizing Rom. 6.3-4. He states that this practice is 'erroneous' since water 'baptism signifies identification with Christ in His death, burial, and resurrection'.[63] Further, 'since the Father and the Holy Spirit did not die to save, baptism should be single in act'.[64] Thus, for Williams, Rom. 6.1-11 refers to water baptism and instructs us on the issues of death to sin, identification with Christ, formula, and mode.

Former general overseer of the Church of God of Prophecy M.A. Tomlinson fleetingly references Rom. 6.3-4 when he argues for water baptism as the 'outward manifestation to the world that the person is a new creature and has left his old sinful life and taken on a new life in Christ'.[65] Romans 6.1-11, then, communicates that water baptism is a 'figure of the death, burial, and resurrection of Jesus'.[66] For Tomlinson, this text communicates that 'complete immersion' is necessary since that is the only way that death, burial, and resurrection are 'figured'.[67] However, Rom. 6.6-7 also references sanctification:

---

[60] Pearlman, *Knowing the Doctrines of the Bible*, Kindle location 4046.
[61] Pearlman, *Knowing the Doctrines of the Bible*, Kindle location 4380.
[62] Ernest S. Williams, *Systematic Theology, Volume III* (Springfield, MO: Gospel Publishing House, 1953), p. 150.
[63] Williams, *Systematic Theology, Volume III*, p. 152.
[64] Williams, *Systematic Theology, Volume III*, p. 152.
[65] M.A. Tomlinson, *Basic Bible Beliefs* (Cleveland, TN: White Wing Publishing House and Press, 1961), p. 20.
[66] Tomlinson, *Basic Bible Beliefs*, p. 20.
[67] Tomlinson, *Basic Bible Beliefs*, p. 21.

The Adamic nature or inbred sin that is a part of every person who is not sanctified is also referred to as the 'old man'. And the 'old man' can be put off or crucified. Paul said ... 'Knowing this, that our old man is crucified with him, that the body of sin might be destroyed, that henceforth we should not serve sin. For he that is dead is freed from sin.' (Romans 6:6, 7) ... to put off the old man and have him crucified, one must go to Jesus.[68]

Tomlinson, then, believes Rom. 6.1-11 to speak of both water baptism as well as sanctification.

Finally, Church of God missionary James Slay argues that Rom. 6.1-5 is key to understanding 'the mode and efficacy' of water baptism.[69] On mode, Slay states that 'though the New Testament Scriptures plainly teach immersion ... as the church grew older and more worldly-minded, it sought to accommodate itself to the demands of a new paganism and took on the ancient rite of pouring water'.[70] Slay then invites the reader to 'study the Scriptures which develop the proper concept of baptismal mode' and quotes Rom. 6.1-5.[71] For Slay, Rom. 6.1-11 testifies to the necessity of immersion. He also believes that these verses express the symbolic nature of baptism by referencing the death, burial, and resurrection.[72] This implies that baptism is a public declaration or 'showing on the part of the believer that he has died to self and sin and allowed the old un-regenerated person to be buried that the new man might arise'.[73] Since pouring or sprinkling cannot 'symbolize' this truth, both should be rejected.

C.3.4 The Period of Challenge (1967-1984)

As Lewis notes, there were limited theological publishing forums during the third period. Still, there were a few voices within these years that engaged Rom. 6.1-11. For example, Elim Pentecostal Church minister J. Lancaster understands Rom. 6.1-4 to be speaking of an inner spiritual baptism.[74] He notes that 'the baptism which effectually

---

[68] Tomlinson, *Basic Bible Beliefs*, p. 10.
[69] James L. Slay, *This We Believe* (Cleveland, TN: Pathway Press, 1963), p. 99.
[70] Slay, *This We Believe*, p. 99.
[71] Slay, *This We Believe*, p. 99.
[72] Slay, *This We Believe*, p. 99.
[73] Slay, *This We Believe*, pp. 99-100.
[74] Though Lancaster was British, and thus falls outside the scope of my limits, I have chosen to include him anyway considering his influence during this period of theological development.

introduces the penitent sinner into the body of Christ is not the sacrament of water baptism, but the inner work of the Spirit in his heart (Romans 6:1-4; 1 Corinthians 12:13), of which water baptism is the outward sign'.[75] He states that 'though there has been much controversy over the exact meaning of Romans 6:1-11 ... it seems clear to the writer that the "baptism" in view here is not the outward rite but the inward work of the Spirit for which the outward rite is a symbol'.[76] He continues:

> We are thus baptised or immersed into Christ, united with Him in His death and resurrection by faith and the operation of the Holy Spirit, not merely in a technical sense, but in a real, moral, spiritual sense ... in the same way, we are 'baptised into one body' not merely by undergoing a rite, but by the regenerating work of the Spirit, which incorporates us spiritually but actually into Christ and His Church ... Unless water baptism points to an inner event which has either preceded it or is taking place simultaneously it has no validity.[77]

Therefore, Lancaster understands water baptism to be merely a symbol of a greater inward work of God, and Rom. 6.1-11 is referring to this inner work of the Spirit – a spiritual baptism.

In 1983, Foursquare faculty members of L.I.F.E. Bible College, Guy Duffield, and N.M. Van Cleave, co-authored *Foundations of Pentecostal Theology*. This book of doctrines discusses Rom. 6.1-11 a handful of times. First, the authors quote Rom. 6.2-7 and connect this passage to water baptism directly:

> In describing the new birth as a resurrection, we must realize that it is preceded by a death. Believers have been crucified with Christ and have also been raised together with Him. Both of these truths become a spiritual reality through identification with Christ in His death, burial, and resurrection ... This is symbolized in the ordinance of water baptism by immersion.[78]

---

[75] J. Lancaster, 'The Ordinances', in P.S. Brewster (ed.), *Pentecostal Doctrines* (Cheltenham: Elim, 1976), p. 80
[76] Lancaster, 'The Ordinances', p. 84.
[77] Lancaster, 'The Ordinances', p. 84.
[78] Duffield and Van Cleave, *Foundations of Pentecostal Theology*, p. 235.

Notably, Duffield and Van Cleave argue that water baptism symbolizes what has happened in salvation. The authors also state that 'the spiritual significance of water baptism is taught in the epistles', using Rom. 6.3 as an example.[79] Lastly, they discuss the whole of Rom. 6.1-11 in relationship to dying to sin/salvation. By appealing to the passage, the authors state that 'there is no Bible teaching to the effect that some Christians have died to sin and others have not'.[80] Since Paul in Rom. 6.6 states that 'our old self was crucified with Him' this is 'considered to be an accomplished fact'.[81] Indeed, 'what a triumph this suggests!'.[82] Yet, Duffield and Van Cleave note that Paul's admonition in Rom. 6.12-13 proves 'progressive sanctification'.[83]

C.3.5 The Period of Reformulation (1984-Present)

Though Pentecostals in the past three periods varied on whether Rom. 6.1-11 spoke of water baptism or sanctification, a cursory glance of contemporary Pentecostal scholarship suggests that Pentecostal scholars within the present period unequivocally understand Rom. 6.1-11 to speak of water baptism. And while there are various nuances between the various theologians' positions, when Rom. 6.1-11 is consulted, it is often in the context of water baptism. In this section, I will briefly summarize five exemplary interpreters[84] – Amos Yong, Frank Macchia, Simon Chan, Matthias Wenk, and J. Ayodeji Adewuya – on their engagements with Rom. 6.1-11 to provide a framework with which to engage.[85]

First, in Yong's *Renewing Christian Theology*,[86] each of eleven chapters follows and expands upon one of the eleven statements in the World Assemblies of God Fellowship Statement of Faith. In his chapter on Article 7, 'The Ordinances of the Church', Rom. 6.4 is

---

[79] Duffield and Van Cleave, *Foundations of Pentecostal Theology*, p. 443.
[80] Duffield and Van Cleave, *Foundations of Pentecostal Theology*, p. 247.
[81] Duffield and Van Cleave, *Foundations of Pentecostal Theology*, p. 247.
[82] Duffield and Van Cleave, *Foundations of Pentecostal Theology*, p. 247.
[83] Duffield and Van Cleave, *Foundations of Pentecostal Theology*, p. 247. Interestingly, for Duffield and Van Cleave, Romans 6 does discuss sanctification, yet quite unlike the early Wesleyan-Holiness Pentecostal reading of this passage.
[84] Green, 'Does (Not) Nature Itself Teach You?', p. 461.
[85] While there are certainly others that could be engaged, I am aiming to keep my engagement focused on a few prominent voices within Pentecostal scholarship that speak of and reference Rom. 6.1-11 directly.
[86] Amos Yong, *Renewing Christian Theology: Systematics for a Global Christianity* (Waco, TX: Baylor University Press, 2014).

one of the texts referenced in support of the Article.[87] He states that 'baptism into the name of Jesus and of the triune God identifies association with the life, death, and resurrection of Jesus (Rom 6.1-4; Col 2.12)'.[88] In *The Spirit Poured Out on All Flesh*, he seeks to show the 'connection between ecclesiology and soteriology that sees salvation effected through baptism: the death and burial of the unbelieving individual in and with Christ and his or her resurrection into a new life, existence, and community, the living body of Christ'.[89] Further, for Yong, Rom. 6.3-5 'underscores the relationship between baptism and Christian initiation'.[90]

Speaking descriptively, Yong states that more deeply than evangelical or Pentecostal churches, 'the Orthodox emphasize baptismal participation in the death and resurrection of Christ – themes highlighted in Romans 6:1-4 and Colossians 2:11-13'.[91] Yet, seeking to contribute a 'renewalist' vision of the rite, Yong prefers to use associative over participative language.[92] He also envisions baptism to save by positioning the believer into the body of Christ whereby the Spirit transforms the individual and community into the likeness of Christ. So, it is not that baptism achieves salvific effects automatically, but it is through the fellowship of the Spirit and the 'new matrix of relationship that is the body of Christ' that 'facilitates ongoing conversion, repentance, and the power of the Spirit in anticipation of the full salvation to come'.[93]

For Frank Macchia, the sacraments 'point to the grace implied in all of life and also to God's desire to renew creation into the very dwelling place of God'.[94] Yet, when speaking of Spirit baptism and referencing Rom. 6.5, he states that 'the symbol of water baptism itself points to this fulfillment'.[95] Thus, water baptism points towards

---

[87] Yong, *Renewing Christian Theology*, p. 131.
[88] Yong, *Renewing Christian Theology*, p. 157.
[89] Amos Yong, *The Spirit Poured Out on All Flesh: Pentecostalism and the Possibility of Global Theology* (Grand Rapids, MI: Baker Academic, 2005), p. 92.
[90] Yong, *The Spirit Poured Out on All Flesh*, p. 128.
[91] Yong, *Renewing Christian Theology*, p. 138.
[92] Yong, *Renewing Christian Theology*, p. 157.
[93] Yong, *Renewing Christian Theology*, p. 157.
[94] Macchia, *Baptized in the Spirit*, p. 248.
[95] Frank D. Macchia, *Jesus the Spirit Baptizer: Christology in Light of Pentecost* (Grand Rapids, MI: Eerdmans, 2018), p. 303. He says something similar earlier in *Baptized in the Spirit*: 'The difference between John the Baptist's rite and that which endured

the experience of Spirit baptism. Commenting on Rom. 6.1-5, Macchia argues that 'in baptism, we are buried with Christ in order to rise to newness of life'.[96] As v. 5 states specifically, in 'water baptism we ritually die and rise with Christ in a way that not only points to the basis of our baptism in the Spirit but ahead to its horizon, our resurrection from the dead'.[97] Macchia also connects our descent into the water in water baptism as a death that participates into Christ's:

> Our descent into the water is like descending into a tomb. But unlike Christ's descent into forsakenness, we descend 'with him' (Rom. 6.4), meaning in solidarity with him. As such, all that dies in the tank is what is self-bound by flesh or what contradicts his love. In descending, we are already being drawn into the embrace of the Spirit. Dying with Christ leads to our sharing in his rising again. The watery *tomb* then becomes a *womb* from which we rise in newness of life centered on Christ and led of the Spirit.[98]

Macchia links death and resurrection in the act of water baptism. By 'being buried with him in baptism (Rom. 6.3-4) … our death is now defined in solidarity with his death'.[99] Yet, 'Romans 6:3 and Colossians 2:12 identify water baptism as being also "raised" with God *by God*'.[100] Thus, Macchia understands Rom. 6.1-4 to speak of water baptism bringing us into solidarity with Christ by the Spirit. Yet, he also sees the effects of water baptism to point towards Spirit baptism.

Conversely, Simon Chan argues that 'the Spirit should be seen as objectively given at baptism'.[101] Thus, Chan's reading of Rom. 6.1-11, though brief, suggests that he understands this participation with Christ to be more than symbolic association. For Chan, since Rom. 6.4 suggests that 'just as Christ was raised from the dead through the glory of the Father, we too may live a new life'.[102] Further, 'baptism is a drowning of the entire sinful self, a death and burial – but out of

---

in Christian contexts is that John's baptism looked forward to Spirit baptism while Christian baptism lives from it and points to its fulfillment' (p. 248).

[96] Macchia, *Jesus the Spirit Baptizer*, p. 333.
[97] Macchia, *Jesus the Spirit Baptizer*, p. 333.
[98] Macchia, *Justified in the Spirit*, p. 288.
[99] Macchia, *Baptized in the Spirit*, p. 249,
[100] Macchia, *Baptized in the Spirit*, p. 70. Original emphasis.
[101] Chan, *Pentecostal Theology and the Christian Spiritual Tradition*, p. 90.
[102] Chan, *Liturgical Theology*, p. 118.

death new life emerges'.[103] Chan notes that is because of Paul's language of burial, death, and resurrection in the context of water baptism that 'Cyril of Jerusalem in his mystagogical sermons speak of the waters of baptism as "at once your grave and your mother"'.[104] Chan, then, sees Rom. 6.1-11 to be referring to the waters of baptism as a place of death and new birth within the process of Christian initiation.

Swiss Pentecostal NT scholar Matthias Wenk has stated that Rom. 6.1-11 speaks both of water baptism and sanctification: 'Because of the argument in Romans 6, baptism is often, and almost exclusively, associated with purification and the elimination of sin'.[105] Yet, Rom. 6.1-11 also speaks of 'the rite of baptism', which is 'associated both with the believer's new life with Christ as well as with the new community of the people of God'.[106] Wenk's brief comments on Rom. 6.1-11 shows a desire to link water baptism and sanctification/purification.

Church of God (Cleveland, TN) biblical scholar J. Ayodeji Adewuya believes that in Rom. 6.1-11, Paul 'draws out the implications of the believers' faith-union with Christ, the outward expression of what was baptism'.[107] Addressing Rom. 6.3, Adewuya considers that when 'Paul refers to baptism, the primary reference is to water baptism'.[108] By the time Romans was written, 'the word baptize in its usage had virtually become a technical expression of the rite of water baptism'.[109] Thus, rather than this serving as a 'mere metaphor for Spirit baptism', baptism here is 'better understood as a reference to water baptism'.[110] For Adewuya, baptism is a 'pictorial representation of spiritual regeneration'.[111] Baptism, then, represents the 'believer's confession of having died to sin and of having been raised

---

[103] Chan, *Liturgical Theology*, p. 118
[104] Chan, *Liturgical Theology*, p. 118.
[105] Matthias Wenk, 'The Church as Sanctified Community' in John Christopher Thomas (ed.), *Toward a Pentecostal Ecclesiology: The Church and the Fivefold Gospel* (Cleveland, TN: CPT Press, 2010), p. 120.
[106] Wenk, 'The Church as Sanctified Community', p. 120.
[107] Adewuya, *Transformed by Grace*, p. 19.
[108] Adewuya, *Transformed by Grace*, p. 23. Notably, Adewuya cites 1 Cor. 1.13-17; 12.13; 15.29; Eph. 4.5 for support.
[109] Adewuya, *Transformed by Grace*, pp. 22-23.
[110] Adewuya, *Transformed by Grace*, p. 23.
[111] Adewuya, *Transformed by Grace*, p. 23.

up spiritually to a new life'.[112] Baptism attests to what has happened provisionally on the cross and experientially at conversion – baptism into Christ's death.[113] In sum, Adewuya believes Rom. 6.1-11 refers to water baptism, which symbolizes 'spiritual union with Christ'.[114]

C.3.6 Conclusions

During the period of formulation (1917-1929), early Pentecostal literature understood Rom. 6.1-11 primarily in two ways. First, many early Pentecostals understand the passage to be an important water baptismal text. Others – especially in the Wesleyan-Holiness wing of Pentecostalism – understood it to be speaking of sanctification. Interestingly, one finds something similar in the Pentecostal literature in the second period of engagement (1929-1967), with some development. While Rom. 6.1-11 was engaged infrequently during this period, the available scholarship reveals that Rom. 6.1-11 was thought to be speaking of either, (1) water baptism, (2) a spiritual baptism, or (3) sanctification. The third period (1967-1984) – as noted previously – is defined by limited theological publishing forums. As a result, there is not a lot of published theological scholarship, resulting in a limited engagement. However, those who did engage Rom. 6.1-11 understood it to speak of an inner spiritual baptism or water baptism, thus showing a decline in the sanctification interpretation.

Finally, the current period of Pentecostal scholarship (1984-present) consistently recognizes Rom. 6.1-11 to refer to water baptism. However, within this broad consensus, there are nuances between contemporary scholars on the meaning of baptism according to Rom. 6.1-11. Further, since my constructive reading fits within this current body of literature, I will conclude this history of interpretation by putting the five contemporary scholars surveyed into dialogue with one another to show the congruences and incongruences between the five voices.

C.3.7 The Contemporary Dialogue

Amos Yong emphasizes how Rom. 6.1-11 associates the believer with the death, burial, and resurrection of Christ. While he links salvation to water baptism, he places it within the broader context of the life

---

[112] Adewuya, *Transformed by Grace*, p. 23.
[113] Adewuya, *Transformed by Grace*, p. 23.
[114] Adewuya, *Transformed by Grace*, p. 24.

of the church, which continues to affect repentance and ongoing transformation. Macchia has a similar emphasis as Yong when discussing Rom. 6.1-11, though with some difference. Macchia, like Yong, sees it to discuss how water baptism identifies us with Christ by bringing us into solidarity with his death, burial, and resurrection. Yet, for Macchia baptism anticipates and is fulfilled in Spirit baptism. Therefore, we participate in Christ's resurrection not so much in water baptism, but Spirit baptism. Chan emphasizes identification with Christ, yet he seems to place more currency on the rite of water baptism than Yong and Macchia. Because of baptism, new life emerges. By linking sanctification and baptism, Wenk is unique. Certainly, Yong, Macchia, and Chan's emphasis on the death and burial that is brought about through water baptism hints at this connection. However, what the others made implicit, Wenk has made explicit. Water baptism, for Wenk, is a purification rite. Lastly, Adewuya discusses baptism in purely symbolic terms. For Adewuya, water baptism simply attests to something that has already happened earlier in conversion. Baptism pictures and represents spiritual regeneration.

In sum, while there are differences in conclusions among contemporary Pentecostal scholars, what all share is the conviction that Rom. 6.1-11 is an important baptismal passage. Therefore, as I move to my constructive reading, I aim to situate my thoughts on the text within this broader context among Pentecostal scholars, in dialogue both with Pentecostal and ecumenical voices. It is now to this passage that we turn our attention to.

C.4 'United with Him'

C.4.1 Baptism as Crucifixion and Death

In Romans 6, an earlier question, 'why not ... do evil so that good may come?' (3.8), is now asked differently: 'should we continue in sin in order that grace may abound?' (6.1).[115] Paul seeks to answer those who are suggesting that an emphasis on grace must mean authorization to sin and responds emphatically: 'By no means!' (6.2). For Paul, one who has 'died to sin' cannot 'go on living in it' (6.2). And interestingly, baptism plays an important part in his argument, 'making it clear that, for Paul, baptism was not a mere ritual of initiation but a

---

[115] Johnson, *Reading Romans*, p. 101.

powerful participation' in the death of Jesus.[116] Though 'the evidence that baptism was associated specifically with the death and resurrection of Jesus is – apart from the present passage – scant',[117] Paul connects death (and then later, resurrection) with the water rite. Jesus also connects death with baptism in a question to his disciples (Mk 10.38-39): 'Are you able to … be baptized with the baptism that I am baptized with?'. This question in Mark, along with the section of Col. 2.12–3.11 that bears much resemblance to our current passage,[118] signals a relationship between baptism and death. Yet, what does this connection infer about the meaning of baptism?

By sharing in the death of Christ in baptism, the baptized die to the Adamic nature of sin.[119] As Barth puts it, in baptism 'one man dies and another is born', for the 'the man over whom sin has power and dominion has died'.[120] Baptism, then, 'is about personal identity' because 'it answers the question, "Who am I?"' as 'Paul expects the Romans to know'.[121] The Christian is one who has now participated in Christ's death, and is now dead to sin, because 'being baptized into Christ Jesus' death is the same as dying to sin'.[122] This is how pre-modern interpreters read Rom. 6.1-3. Tellingly, Augustine argues that 'to be baptized into the death of Christ is nothing else but to die to sin, just as he died in the flesh'.[123] Augustine is right: death has come by way of crucifixion 'so that the body of sin might be destroyed, and we might no longer be enslaved to sin' (6.6). By living into his or her crucifixion, the baptized are freed from their prior enslavement to sin. Chrysostom adds that though 'baptism has made us dead to sin once and for all', we must also 'strive to maintain this state of affairs, so that however many commands sin may give us, we no longer obey it but remain unmoved by it, as a corpse does'.[124]

---

[116] Johnson, *Reading Romans*, p. 102.
[117] Johnson, *Reading Romans*, p. 102. This is particularly the case if we neglect the unclear reference to being 'baptized for the dead' in 1 Cor. 15.29.
[118] Johnson, *Reading Romans*, p. 102.
[119] Porter, *The Letter to the Romans*, p. 133.
[120] Barth, *The Epistle to the Romans*, p. 193.
[121] Peter J. Leithart, *The Baptized Body* (Moscow, Idaho: Canon Press, 2007), p. 4.
[122] Porter, *The Letter to the Romans*, pp. 132-33.
[123] Augustine, *Against Julian* 1.7.33.
[124] Chrysostom, *Homilies on Romans 10* in Gerald Bray (ed.), *Romans* (Vol. VI of *Ancient Christian Commentary on Scripture: New Testament*; Downers Grove, IL: InterVarsity Press, 1998), p. 153.

Therefore, by participating in baptism we have died to sin, yet this new life or state of sanctification is something we must live into, or 'strive to maintain'. Put another way, 'this death is grace'.[125]

Baptism as a sanctifying bath 'demonstrates the liberation of believers from the power of sin',[126] for as Paul puts it, 'whoever has died is freed from sin' (6.7). This also means that 'the death of sin' is left behind 'and life in the divine righteousness [is] ahead'.[127] Because as Paul states in 6.8, if we have died with Christ, we believe that we will also live with him. All in all, participating in the death of baptism, brings life to the believer. Yet, baptism as death is not the full picture, since Rom. 6.1-11 talks of burial as well.[128]

C.4.2 Baptism as Burial

As shown earlier, despite triumphalist tendencies[129] early Pentecostals connected baptism to burial often citing Rom. 6.4.[130] Yet, early Pentecostals did not often comment extensively upon its meaning. Frank Macchia, though, has specified that understanding baptism as a burial 'means that our death is now defined in solidarity with his (Christ's) death. Just as his death was an act of the pouring out of a life through the eternal Spirit (Heb 9.14) that was shown to be indestructible and victorious (7.16), so our death "with him" takes on the supreme act of an indestructible life poured out for God's kingdom as well.'[131] Baptism as Macchia explicates is sharing *in* Christ and his mission. This sharing in Christ's death through burial, though, is not just one of solely death to sin, but it is also a death to the *self*, as our *self* becomes one with the goals of God's Kingdom. The baptized are now called to live into the baptized life, which is life now 'hidden with Christ, in God' (Col. 3.3) and sent out for the sake of others.

Macchia's suggestion that this burial or pouring out is enacted through the Spirit also means that baptism is carried out by the Spirit. It is through the Spirit that the baptized can participate in Christ's

---

[125] Barth, *The Epistle to the Romans*, p. 194.
[126] Jürgen Moltmann, *The Church in the Power of the Spirit* (Minneapolis: Fortress Press, 1993), p. 238.
[127] Moltmann, *The Church in the Power of the Spirit*, p. 238.
[128] Moltmann, *The Church in the Power of the Spirit*, p. 238.
[129] See David J. Courey, *What Has Wittenberg to Do with Azusa?: Luther's Theology of the Cross and Pentecostal Triumphalism* (New York, NY: Bloomsbury T&T Clark, 2015).
[130] See especially Chapter 3.
[131] Macchia, *Baptized in the Spirit*, p. 249.

death. The Spirit's involvement in Jesus' baptism points to his involvement in Christian baptism. Mark Cartledge has also noted that Pentecostals have often understood baptism to be an 'experience of the Holy Spirit'.[132] On this point, then, 'contemporary experience and Scripture cohere'.[133] Certainly, this connects with Rom. 6.3 in which Paul associates water baptism with being '"buried" and "raised" with Christ *by God*'.[134] As Ben Witherington has stated, 'neither Rom. 6.3 nor 1 Cor. 12.13 ... speak(s) of human administrants of baptism ... baptism seems to be "by" the Holy Spirit' (1 Cor. 12.13).[135] When one is 'buried' or 'plunged into His death'[136] the Spirit is acting upon the baptized, bringing her into solidarity with Christ's death and burial. This suggests that water baptism has less to do with our actions than it has to do with God's actions. It is God that uses our baptism to identify us 'with the death of Christ' (6.3).[137]

According to Origen, by being 'buried together with Christ 'we have died to sin' as well.[138] By being 'entombed in the water',[139] we are dying to our former self, which prepares us to be resurrected to new life by the Spirit. This implies that being buried in baptism is the first step into this newly available process of sanctification. As Alexander Schmemann has argued:

> The sacrament of forgiveness is baptism, not because it operates a juridical removal of guilt, but because it is *baptism into Christ Jesus*, who is the Forgiveness ... Baptism is forgiveness of sins, not their removal. It introduces the sword of Christ into our life and makes it the real conflict, the inescapable pain and suffering of growth. It is indeed after baptism and because of it, that the reality of sin

---

[132] Cartledge, *Testimony in the Spirit*, p. 79.
[133] Cartledge, *Testimony in the Spirit*, p. 79.
[134] Macchia, *Baptized in the Spirit*, p. 70. Emphasis original.
[135] Witherington, *Paul's Letter to the Romans*, p. 157.
[136] Witherington, *Paul's Letter to the Romans*, p. 158.
[137] Miroslav Volf, *Exclusion and Embrace: A Theological Exploration of Identity, Otherness, and Reconciliation* (Nashville, TN: Abington Press, 1996), p. 25.
[138] Origen, *Commentary on the Epistle to the Romans* in Gerald Bray (ed.), *Romans* (Vol. VI of *Ancient Christian Commentary on Scripture: New Testament*, Downers Grove, IL: InterVarsity Press, 1998), p. 155.
[139] See Mt. 27.60.

can be recognized in all its sadness, and true repentance becomes possible.[140]

Therefore, being baptized 'into Christ' brings one into the person of forgiveness. Being buried in baptism does not simply give pardon from the past but imparts grace for the present and hope for the future.[141] Our eyes, too, now buried, help us 'recognize … the reality of sin', making true repentance and continual transformation possible.[142] As Daniel Tomberlin has stated, baptism bestows 'salvific grace' to the baptized because of a real 'Christo-Pneumatic presence' that cleanses and sanctifies.[143]

Baptism as burial also speaks to the issue of mode. In the accounts of Jesus' baptism, Jesus 'came up from out of the water' (Mt. 3.16; Mk 1.10), signaling the early association of baptism and immersion. The use of burial language in Rom. 6.4 draws an even clearer correlation between baptism by immersion and literal human burial.[144] In fact, the act of being submerged into the waters and subsequently rising in baptism embodies and dramatizes the act of being buried and rising in resurrection. Therefore, 'the *immersion* into the waters seems to have been the enactment of being *buried* with the crucified messiah'.[145] As Schmemann puts it, 'it is in this water that we now baptize – i.e. immerse – man, and this baptism is for him, baptism

---

[140] Alexander Schmemann, *For the Life of the World: Sacraments and Orthodoxy* (Crestwood: NY, SVS, 1973), pp. 78- 79.

[141] Robert Jenson notably takes issue with the assertion that sanctification as progress begins at baptism: 'Sanctification … is often misunderstood as a progress, kicked off, as it were, by baptism. This has obviously to be false. Baptism initiates into the life which God's three persons, Father, Son and Spirit, live among themselves; what would we progress to from that? Rather, sanctification is the continual *return* to baptism … Baptism is always there as a fact in my past; I can always, as Luther said, "creep" back to it and begin anew'. Robert Jenson, *A Large Catechism* (Delhi, NY: American Lutheran Publicity Bureau, 1999), p. 50. Agreeing with Jenson, I trust baptism initiates us into the life of God, yet as Schemmann argues, 'we (still) constantly fall away from the new life we have received' and still journey towards 'that total transformation and transfiguration of life which alone makes "saints"'. (p. 78) Thus, whether one wants to state that we journey back *to* baptism to begin anew, or forward *in* baptism towards the *telos*, I believe the most significant point is that baptism initiates us and sustains us in the life of God.

[142] Schmemann, *For the Life of the World*, p. 79.

[143] Daniel Tomberlin, 'Believers' Baptism in the Pentecostal Tradition', *ER* 67.3 (October 2015), p. 430.

[144] Porter, *The Letter to the Romans*, p. 133.

[145] Johnson, *Reading Romans*, p. 104.

"into Christ" (Rom. 6.3)'.[146] Thus, while pouring or sprinkling are not invalid modes, we might propose that they are deficient in embodying the true character of baptism as burial and subsequently, resurrection. As Orthodoxy shows us, this does not necessarily exclude infant baptism, but by affirming the biblical and theological priority of immersion, it allows baptism to 'give witness' and even 'testify'.

And though burial is an important aspect of water baptism, for the baptized Christian, 'death cannot be the last word' for 'the last word for us is not death, but life'.[147] As Emil Brunner has stated, 'God's No to sin that he has uttered in the Cross has now become our No. The significance of this No, however, and its force, is the Yes of God. It is not the death (and burial) of Jesus but his resurrection which is God's last word.'[148] Therefore, burial is the prelude to resurrection.

C.4.3 Baptism as Resurrection

For Paul, since believers 'have been united with him in a death like his, we will certainly be united with him in a resurrection like his' (6.5). And while Paul does not explicitly link the coming up out of the water with the resurrection of Jesus, that would be the apparent connection, and one made by Col. 2.12 explicitly.[149] Additionally, Christ's resurrection and our being baptized into Christ are closely identified.[150] Certainly, then, we can affirm that baptism '*imprints* in believers a certain identity, namely, the paschal reality of the crucified and raised messiah', and this 'identity that they have "put on," (is) his obedient death and his sharing in God's new life'.[151]

This work of participation and identification with/in Christ's resurrection is a work of the Spirit (Rom. 8.11). Luke Timothy Johnson puts it this way:

> Paul could not be clearer in his conviction that the life of believers is one that, through the gift of the Holy Spirit, shares in the resurrection power of Christ: 'I have been crucified with Christ; it is

---

[146] Schmemann, *For the Life of the World*, p. 73.
[147] Fleming Rutledge, *Not Ashamed of the Gospel: Sermons from Paul's Letter to the Romans* (Grand Rapids: MI, Eerdmans, 2007), p. 185.
[148] Emil Brunner, *The Letter to the Romans: A Commentary* (Philadelphia, PA: The Westminster Press, 1959), p. 50.
[149] Johnson, *Reading Romans*, p. 104.
[150] Porter, *The Letter to the Romans*, p. 134.
[151] Johnson, *Reading Romans*, p. 104. Emphasis original.

no longer I who live but Christ who lives in me' (Gal 2:20) … Romans (8.11) shows that what Paul stated in Galatians was not simply the expression of a personal mysticism but rather his sober estimate of the new creation in which Christians now participate (2 Cor 5:17).[152]

Therefore, baptism into Christ does not merely have a judicial character, but a relational one. The relational Spirit of God baptizes us into the *person* of Christ, enacting the transformation from death to life. Not only is the baptized person joined into the fellowship of Christ and shares in Christ's body, he or she also 'shares in the Spirit that inhabits and animates the body and participates in the resurrection power of Jesus'.[153] Thus, baptism 'is new life in the Spirit, and the dawn of the new creation and the glory of God'.[154] By participating in Christ's death, we have gained freedom from sin (6.7; 6.10), and his resurrected life has given us new life (6.8; 6.11).

Baptism, then, is not simply an outward profession of faith, but an inward imparting of identity. Even the free-church, non-sacramentalist Miroslav Volf argues for a fundamental change in identity as a result of baptism. He states that, 'by participating in the death and resurrection of Christ through faith and baptism … the self is both "de-centered" and "re-centered" by one and the same process'.[155] When one is crucified with Christ, he or she receives a new center – which 'is the story of Jesus Christ, which has become the story of the self. More precisely, the center is Jesus Christ crucified and resurrected who has become part and parcel of the very structure of the self'.[156] Yet, our identity is not 'simply erased', for 'by the process of de-centering, the self … received a new center that both transformed and reinforced the old one'.[157] Whether Volf holds this change to be one that is imparted sacramentally or not, I want to suggest that baptism enacts and completes a radical alteration in our identity. In baptism, there is a fundamental change in self – one not of obliteration, but transformation. Baptism changes us, making us into who we ought to be through the Spirit's transformative work.

---

[152] Johnson, *Reading Romans*, p. 104.
[153] Peter J. Leithart, *1 & 2 Kings* (Grand Rapids, MI: Brazos Press, 2006), p. 201.
[154] Moltmann, *The Church in the Power of the Spirit*, p. 238
[155] Volf, *Exclusion and Embrace*, p. 71.
[156] Volf, *Exclusion and Embrace*, p. 71.
[157] Volf, *Exclusion and Embrace*, p. 71.

This new identity also comes with a new mission. Just as 'Christ rose from the dead to fill the reign of God on earth, so we rise in baptism with Christ for the same purpose'.[158] Being baptized does not divide us safely from others.[159] In actuality, the baptized life is marked by journeying 'into the depths of the world's despair'.[160] According to Steven Land, Pentecostals have often understood baptism to be an 'acceptance of the call to become a holy witness in the power of the Holy Spirit'.[161] Baptism as resurrection, then, means that we are sent out from baptism in resurrection power for the sake of the world. As Veli-Matti Kärkkäinen has noted, there is a 'deep and wide connection between liturgy, sacramental life, and missionary orientation' found in the book of Acts (2.42-47).[162] This implies that the missional life flows from the baptized life, since this baptized life participates in the mission of the Resurrected One.

C.4.4 Conclusions

What can this reading tell us about what a Pentecostal theology of water baptism might look like? What are the implications for Pentecostal spirituality?[163] I want to suggest that in the end, this reading exposes the need to rework our theological framework, doctrinal language, and missional practices.

First, this reading calls for a re-examination of the relationship between water baptism and our share in Christ's crucifixion and death of sin. Agreeing with much of the scriptural witness, baptism and the forgiveness of sins are indeed related and connected.[164] Given the way Pentecostals have read this text, Pentecostals are likely to say that forgiveness of sin is not *solely* contained within the act, but instead, it is *a* way God has chosen to use to cleanse the believer. This must also mean that baptism is associated with sanctification. Perhaps the Wesleyan-Pentecostal emphasis upon sanctification as a 'second work' following justification can be maintained within the context of the water rite. This should not summon Pentecostals back to a doctrine

---

[158] Macchia, *Baptized in the Spirit*, p. 249.
[159] Green, *Sanctifying Interpretation*, pp. 23-24.
[160] Green, *Sanctifying Interpretation*, p. 24.
[161] Land, *Pentecostal Spirituality*, p. 110
[162] Veli-Matti Kärkkäinen, *Hope and Community* (Grand Rapids: MI, Eerdmans, 2017), p. 360.
[163] Green, '"I Am Finished"', p. 15.
[164] For example, see Acts 2.38; Acts 22.16; 1 Cor. 12.13; 1 Pet. 3.21.

of sinlessness following baptism, but it should summon us towards understanding water baptism as the initiation into the sanctified life, one that continually progresses forward towards realizing what has been proclaimed *to* and *about* us.

Second, it suggests a reformulation in our doctrinal language. When referring to baptism, Pentecostals ought to consider abandoning representative language for participatory language. If baptism is sharing and partaking in the very life of Christ, then symbolic language does not get to the heart of what God is up to in baptism. God is *active* in baptism. Our action, if any, is merely putting our faith in God's action. The Spirit of God, who is at the center of the sacrament, leads us into sharing in Christ's crucifixion, death, burial, and resurrection, so that we may be found in Christ. This implies that the Spirit does not simply act later in Spirit baptism, for the Spirit is the one filling and nurturing us throughout our Christian initiation into Christ, from beginning to end. Thus, participatory language – rather than associative language – must be at the forefront of our testimonies of baptism.

Finally, this reading calls for changes in our missional practices. Since we now share in Christ's life, we also share in his mission. Paradoxically, baptism brings us into the fellowship of the church, while also simultaneously pushing us outside itself, for the sake of others. Put another way, baptism makes one an insider in a community that is ultimately concerned about outsiders. Baptism, then, is not just an ecclesial act, but a missional one as well. We are re-made not merely for ourselves, but for the sake of our neighbor, and the good of the *cosmos*. Baptism is not simply a call to evangelizing the unsaved, but one marked by subversive, Spirit-led living in the societal, political, ecological, and familial environments that we inhabit.

D. Repentance, Water Baptism, and the Spirit: Acts 2.37-40

> Now when they heard this, they were cut to the heart and said to Peter and to the other apostles, 'Brothers, what should we do?' Peter said to them, 'Repent, and be baptized every one of you in the name of Jesus Christ so that your sins may be forgiven; and you will receive the gift of the Holy Spirit. For the promise is for you, for your children, and for all who are far away, everyone whom

the Lord our God calls to him.' And he testified with many other arguments and exhorted them, saying, 'Save yourselves from this corrupt generation.'

D.1 Introduction: Acts 2.37-40

Early Pentecostals engaged Acts 2.37-40 – especially Acts 2.38 – frequently in discussions on water baptism.[165] This text is also one of the more theologically significant passages on water baptism in Luke-Acts, and has caused much debate both within and outside Pentecostalism on water baptism's relationship to repentance, the forgiveness of sins, and the Holy Spirit. These reasons – in addition to the ecumenical interest in this text – justify a detailed examination of this passage.

D.2 The Interpretive Framework: Literary Context and Outline

According to John Christopher Thomas, the structure of Acts is one 'aspect ... that has not yet received the attention it deserves'.[166] In response, Thomas has sought to provide a structure of the text by following the literary markers in the book, which is 'more in keeping with how the narrative describes this unfolding drama'.[167] This approach to Acts also permits 'the text to define the geographical progression in its own terms'.[168] As a result, Thomas has proposed that the primary theme that holds Acts together is the charismatic activity of the Holy Spirit. For our purposes, Thomas situates Acts 2.37-40 within the larger section of 1.6-2.47: 'The Anointing of the Charismatic Community in Jerusalem'.[169] Another literary approach to Acts locates 2.37-40 inside the larger thought group concentrating on events that occurred on the day of Pentecost (Acts 2.1-47).[170] Craig Keener has also pointed out that one way to structure Peter's speech (2.14-40) is to 'see the addressees in 2:14, 22, 29, and 37 as structural

---

[165] Green, *Toward a Pentecostal Theology of the Lord's Supper*, p. 208.
[166] John Christopher Thomas, 'The Charismatic Structure of Acts', *JPT* 13.1 (2004), p. 20. As Thomas astutely notes 'often the meaning of a book is closely connected to its structure' pp. 19-30 (29).
[167] Thomas, 'The Charismatic Structure of Acts', p. 29.
[168] Thomas, 'The Charismatic Structure of Acts', p. 29.
[169] Thomas, 'The Charismatic Structure of Acts', p. 30.
[170] Charles H. Talbert, *Reading Acts: A Literary and Theological Commentary* (Macon, GA: Smyth and Helwys, 2005), p. 23.

markers'.¹⁷¹ Therefore, while there are various ways to outline this passage (and it is near impossible to determine where exactly any given passage begins or ends), we will take 2.37-40 together since scholarly commentators frequently delineate it as one unit.

In this section following Peter's inspired sermon, the hearers are given a response and a promise. Conscious-tormented over their people's corporate failure in rejecting and killing Christ, the crowd inquires what to do (2.37) – 'that is, in order to be saved (the issue raised in 2:21)'.¹⁷² Francis Martin has noted that in Acts 2.37-41, 'Peter's response includes four elements: repentance, baptism in the name of Jesus, the forgiveness of sins, and reception of the Holy Spirit'.¹⁷³ Structured around these major themes, this constructive reading will seek to expose how these elements relate to water baptism. However, before I begin my constructive reading, we will look at how Pentecostals have typically read and interpreted Acts 2.37-40.

D.3 History of Interpretation

D.3.1 Introduction

In keeping with my reading of Rom. 6.1-11, I am following Paul Lewis' outline of the four periods of Pentecostalism to organize my Pentecostal history of interpretation: (1) The Period of Formulation (1901-1929), (2) The Period of Entrenchment and Adaptation (1929-1967), (3) The Period of Challenge (1967-1984), and (4) The Period of Reformulation (1984-Present).¹⁷⁴

---

¹⁷¹ Craig Keener, *Acts, Volume 1: An Exegetical Commentary* (Grand Rapids, MI: Baker Academic, 2012), p. 863.

¹⁷² Keener, *Acts, Volume 1*, p. 971.

¹⁷³ Francis Martin (ed.), *Acts* (Downers Grove, IL: InterVarsity Press, 2014), p. 35.

¹⁷⁴ Paul Lewis, 'Reflections on a Hundred Years of Pentecostal Theology', *CJPCR* 12 (February 2003): http://www.pctii.org/cyberj/cyberj12/lewis.html As noted previously, in developing a Pentecostal history of interpretation, I will adopt Lewis' structure for organizational purposes, with one exception. Since my previous engagement with early periodical literature was limited to only three denominations and the years between 1917-1929, my history of interpretation will reflect those limits. Thus, I will exclusively focus on the second half of Lewis' first period (1917-1929), and only engage early IPHC, Foursquare, and PAW periodical literature. The following sub-sections, then, will seek to summarize the various ways Pentecostals have engaged and interpreted Acts 2.37-40. While not exhaustive, the review aims to highlight some of the major voices within the four periods described by Lewis, while also highlighting how Pentecostals have read Acts 2.37-40.

D.3.2 The Period of Formulation (1917-1929)

As we discussed previously, early Pentecostals regularly engaged Acts 2.37-40, especially v. 38. Notably, both trinitarian and Oneness Pentecostals consistently thought of Acts 2.38 to be an important verse on the topic of water baptism. Though trinitarian and Oneness Pentecostals differed on their interpretations of Acts 2.38, it was nonetheless a regularly discussed verse among both groups.

For Oneness Pentecostals, Acts 2.38 was arguably the most significant verse that spoke of water baptism. For many of the writers of *The Christian Outlook* this verse proved (1) the biblical precedent of baptizing in Jesus' name, (2) the biblical foundation of affirming that baptism is for the 'remission of sins', and (3) the close relationship between water baptism and Spirit baptism.[175] Thus, Acts 2.38 summarized 'full salvation'. G.T. Haywood states this belief well: 'The apostles standard of salvation was summarized in these few words, "Repent, and be baptized, every one of you in the name of Jesus Christ for the remission of sins and ye shall receive the gift of the Holy Ghost"'.[176] For Haywood, if one has not been water baptized in Jesus' name with the accompaniment of Spirit baptism, then that person has not been fully saved.[177] No doubt, other nuanced interpretations of Acts 2.38 within Oneness Pentecostalism emerged. However, for our purposes, it is enough to note that Oneness Pentecostals consistently understood Acts 2.38 to speak of water baptism in salvific terms.

Trinitarian Pentecostals differed on their interpretations of Acts 2.38, however. And though there is not as much exegetical treatment compared to Oneness periodicals, references to Acts 2.38 are still widely present. In *The Bridal Call* and *The Bridal Call Foursquare*, there are frequent mentions of Acts 2.38 in connection to water baptism. However, these references exclude exegetical and/or theological reflection. While Acts 2.38 is even quoted and used parenthetically at times, these instances lack explanations and fuller treatment.[178] Still, other trinitarian Pentecostals made efforts to expound on its

---

[175] For just a few instances, see *TCO* 3.1 (1925), p. 13; *TCO* (August, 1926), p. 115; *TCO* 4.2 (1926), p. 19.
[176] *TCO* (March 1925), p. 44.
[177] *TCO* (March, 1924), p. 319.
[178] For instances, see *BC* 2.6 (1918), p. 2; *BCF* 11.5 (1927), p. 12.

meaning. Though mentioned previously, G.F. Taylor's comments on Acts 2.38 are worth briefly mentioning again.

According to Taylor, Acts 2.38 'is used by some to teach that water baptism is essential to salvation; by others, to teach that it is essential to the Baptism of the Holy Spirit; by others, to teach that water baptism should be administered in the name of Jesus only. We do not believe that the text teaches any of these things.'[179] Instead, Taylor asserts that 'Peter was preaching to people who had crucified Jesus in the open, and their sin was of such a nature as to demand that they now be baptized in the name of the very one whom they had crucified'.[180] Therefore, the reason baptism in the name of Jesus is mentioned is that to do so would 'be to identify Him with the Son in the baptismal formula, or to make Jesus the Son of God, to give Him His place in the Trinity'.[181] For Taylor, this 'is why they were commanded to be baptized in the name of Jesus, not in the name of Jesus only as some say, but in the name of the Father, and of Jesus (Son), and of the Holy Ghost. When they did this, as many of them as did do it, their sins were forgiven.'[182]

Taylor also argues that 'there is no doubt that Peter referred first to water baptism, but this does not exclude another application of the word … since the word baptism has various shades of meaning'.[183] Taylor then links Acts 2.38 to Rom. 6.3-4, asserting that one can interpret this baptism also to mean 'a baptism of death', which would imply that 'Peter's command to those Jews to be baptized in the name of Jesus carried with it the thought of being crucified with Christ … (and) on these grounds all their sins, both outward and inward, would be taken away'.[184] Within this interpretation, Taylor concludes that 'it cannot be shown that water baptism is required before the Baptism of the Holy Spirit'.[185] Therefore, Taylor seeks to provide an interpretation of Acts 2.38 that is quite different from Oneness interpretations.

---

[179] *PHA* 8.31 (1921), p. 4.
[180] *PHA* 8.31 (1921), p. 4.
[181] *PHA* 8.31 (1921), p. 4.
[182] *PHA* 8.31 (1921), p. 4.
[183] *PHA* 8.31 (1921), p. 4.
[184] *PHA* 8.31 (1921), p. 4.
[185] *PHA* 8.31 (1921), p. 4.

All in all, such a brief sampling shows that Acts 2.38 – fitted within Acts 2.37-40 – was frequently discussed, though interpreted and applied in various ways among early Pentecostals.

D.3.3 The Period of Entrenchment and Adaptation (1929-1967)

Pentecostal scholarship in the second period engaged Acts 2.37-40 irregularly. However, the scholarship available reveals that when consulted, this text was thought to speak of water baptism and/or Spirit baptism.

Myer Pearlman's engagement with Acts 2.38 is limited to the issue of formula. Quoting Acts 2.38, Pearlman states that this verse does 'not represent a baptismal formula' but is 'simply a statement that such persons were baptized' by acknowledging 'Jesus to be Lord and Christ'.[186] For Pearlman, though the *Didache* states that Christian baptism is 'in the name of the Lord Jesus', when 'it comes to describe the rite in detail, the Trinitarian formula is prescribed'.[187] When Acts 2.38 speaks of baptism in the name of Jesus it 'means to commit oneself wholly and eternally to Him as a heaven sent Saviour, and acceptance of His leadership dictates the acceptance of the formula given by Jesus Himself in Matthew 28'.[188] Appealing to 'Thayer's Lexicon', Pearlman states that 'the literal rendering of Acts 2:38 is, "be baptized on the name of Jesus Christ"', which means 'that the Jews were to "repose their hope and confidence in His Messianic authority"'.[189]

Ernest Williams also briefly mentions Acts 2.38 within his treatment of the ordinances. For Williams, Acts 2.38 testifies to the fact that 'Christian baptism signifies our identification with Christ in salvation'.[190] Williams notes that there has 'risen those emphasizing baptism as a saving ordinance, who teach that sinners are to "repent and be baptized for the remission of sins" (Acts 2:38)'.[191] Against such interpretations, Williams instead subscribes to the belief that baptism is an 'outward sign of an inward work'.[192]

---

[186] Pearlman, *Knowing the Doctrines of the Bible*, kindle location 5981.
[187] Pearlman, *Knowing the Doctrines of the Bible*, kindle location 5981.
[188] Pearlman, *Knowing the Doctrines of the Bible*, kindle location 5981.
[189] Pearlman, *Knowing the Doctrines of the Bible*, kindle location 5981.
[190] Williams, *Systematic Theology, Volume III*, p. 150.
[191] Williams, *Systematic Theology, Volume III*, p. 151.
[192] Williams, *Systematic Theology, Volume III*, p. 151.

M.A. Tomlinson, referencing Acts 2.38-39, argues against the notion that water baptism must precede Spirit baptism:

> There are some who would say that water baptism is essential before receiving the Holy Ghost, but this is not true. Peter did say repent and be baptized in the name of Jesus for the remission of sins, and ye shall receive the Holy Ghost, but the incident of Peter's preaching to the household of Cornelius shows that baptism is not necessary before one can receive the Holy Ghost.[193]

Thus, Tomlinson compares Acts 2.38 with Acts 10 to dismantle the idea that one must be baptized before receiving Spirit baptism. Tomlinson also includes Acts 2.38-39 along with Mt. 3.11 and Jn 1.33 to argue for the Pentecostal doctrine of Spirit baptism. He asks his reader, 'Who can receive this blessing?'.[194] In reply, Tomlinson quotes Acts 2.39: 'For the promise is unto you, and to your children, and to all that are afar off, even as many as the Lord our God shall call'.[195] Thus, for Tomlinson, Acts 2.38-39 discusses both water baptism and Spirit baptism, yet it is most constructive in informing our understanding of the latter.

Lastly, in discussing the 'doctrine of church ordinances', James Slay references Acts 2.38 in passing, remarking that Peter spoke of water baptism in Acts 2.38.[196] In Acts 2.38 Slay believes that there is 'conclusive evidence that the writer, Luke, is not speaking of a precise formula used during the rite of baptism, but is reciting the fact that the believers had been or were to be baptized with Jesus as the ground or foundation for their baptism'.[197] Further, we are only 'given the formula ... by our Lord in Matthew 28:19. Elsewhere we are told of what happened and of its significance'.[198] For Slay, then, Acts 2.38 does speak of water baptism, though it does not prescribe a baptismal formula.

D.3.4 The Period of Challenge (1967-1984)

Though there was limited theological publishing forums during the third period, a few significant voices engaged Acts 2.37-40. First, J.

---

[193] Tomlinson, *Basic Bible Beliefs*, p. 22.
[194] Tomlinson, *Basic Bible Beliefs*, p. 28.
[195] Tomlinson, *Basic Bible Beliefs*, p. 28.
[196] Slay, *This We Believe*, p. 101.
[197] Slay, *This We Believe*, p. 101.
[198] Slay, *This We Believe*, p. 101.

Lancaster references Act 2.38 parenthetically several times when discussing water baptism. For Lancaster, 'it is clear that baptism was accepted as the normal, outward responses for those who were converted through the evangelism of the Early Church (Acts 2.38)'.[199] For Lancaster, since Acts 2.38 associates baptism with the profession of faith, this proves the illegitimacy of infant baptism.[200] Also, while Lancaster 'stresses that baptism does not constitute conversion or convey regeneration', he believes 'it would be wrong to minimize its importance as an act required by God'.[201] He too asserts that while Mt. 28.19 shows that baptism is a command of Jesus, Acts 2.38 shows that 'it was required by the Early Church as an important part of the response made by men to the gospel'.[202] Thus for Lancaster, Acts 2.38 speaks to the importance of baptism as an act of repentance and as a response to hearing the gospel.

Guy Duffield and N.M. Van Cleave understand Acts 2.37-40 to give the believer a template for the steps needed to gain the baptism with the Holy Spirit: 'What is necessary before one can receive this marvelous experience? Are there some necessary preliminary steps which must be taken?'[203] In response, the authors suggest a few conditions that must be met.[204] First, looking to Peter's sermon on 'that memorable Day of Pentecost' suggests that 'repentance is the very first step' because 'The Holy Spirit cannot operate where sin holds sway'.[205] The authors, then, suggest that a definite experience of salvation is another important step. Further attention again needs to be drawn to 'Peter's words to those on the Day of Pentecost', specifically Acts 2.37-38, which states that water baptism is essential. According to Duffield and Van Cleave, the order, then, appears to be: 'repentance, regeneration, water baptism, and then the baptism of the Holy Ghost. Each step of obedience opens the way for the next'.[206] And though 'it is not dogmatically claimed that one who has not been baptized in water could never receive the fullness of the Spirit …

---

[199] Lancaster, 'The Ordinances', p. 82.
[200] Lancaster, 'The Ordinances', p. 84.
[201] Lancaster, 'The Ordinances', p. 85.
[202] Lancaster, 'The Ordinances', p. 85.
[203] Duffield and Van Cleave, *Foundations of Pentecostal Theology*, p. 317.
[204] Duffield and Van Cleave, *Foundations of Pentecostal Theology*, p. 317.
[205] Duffield and Van Cleave, *Foundations of Pentecostal Theology*, p. 317.
[206] Duffield and Van Cleave, *Foundations of Pentecostal Theology*, p. 317.

inasmuch as water baptism is a step of obedience, it is necessary'.[207] As a result, Acts 2.38 teaches that the baptism with the Spirit is available to 'newborn babes in Christ'.[208] It also shows that Spirit baptism is not simply for the early church since Peter included both the present generation and subsequent generations in Acts 2.39.[209] Therefore, Acts 2.37-40 speaks to the importance of water baptism while also providing the necessary criteria for receiving Spirit baptism.

D.3.5 The Period of Reformulation (1984-Present)

A review of the current Pentecostal scholarship demonstrates that Pentecostal scholars understand Acts 2.37-40 to be an important scriptural passage on water baptism, though there are some interpretive differences, particularly between trinitarian and Oneness Pentecostal scholars. To summarize the various ways Pentecostal scholars currently approach Acts 2.37-40, I will briefly engage the work of five Pentecostal scholars: Robert Menzies, Frank Macchia, James Shelton, David Bernard, and David Norris.[210]

For Robert Menzies, Acts 2.38 should *not* be understood as proof that 'the gift of the Spirit is the "bearer of salvation", much more than a prophetic endowment'.[211] He argues that 'the promised gift of the Spirit in Acts 2:38 refers to the promise of Joel 3:1'[212] and thus 'it is a promise of prophetic enabling granted to the repentant' which is consistent 'with Lk. 24:49, Acts 1:4 and 2:33'.[213] In fact, for Menzies, the 'collocation of baptism and reception of the Spirit in Acts 2:38 tells us little about the nature of the pneumatic gift. While it may indicate that for Luke the rite of water baptism is normally accompanied by the bestowal of the Spirit, Luke's usage elsewhere suggests

---

[207] Duffield and Van Cleave, *Foundations of Pentecostal Theology*, p. 317.
[208] Duffield and Van Cleave, *Foundations of Pentecostal Theology*, p. 311.
[209] Duffield and Van Cleave, *Foundations of Pentecostal Theology*, p. 315.
[210] While there are certainly others that could be engaged, I am aiming to keep my engagement focused on a few prominent voices within Pentecostal scholarship that speak of and reference Acts 2.47-40 directly. I have chosen five scholars whose engagement with Acts 2.37-40 was prominent. Further, within those five I have intentionally chosen to include two Oneness Pentecostal scholars – Norris and Bernard – since Acts 2.37-41 is a significant scriptural resource for Oneness Pentecostal theology.
[211] Robert P. Menzies, *Empowered for Witness: The Spirit in Luke-Acts* (JPTSup 6; London; New York: T&T Clark, 2004), p. 203.
[212] Here Menzies is using the Hebrew Masoretic chapter/verse numbers, which is Joel 2.28 in English Bibles.
[213] Menzies, *Empowered for Witness*, p. 203.

that even this conclusion may be overstating the case.'[214] Menzies believes that since Luke 'fails to develop a strong link between water baptism and the bestowal of the Spirit elsewhere ... the phrase καὶ λήμψεσθε τὴν δωρεὰν τοῦ ἁγίου πνεύματος ("and you will receive the gift of the Holy Spirit")' should be interpreted as a promise that the Spirit will be 'imparted to those who are already converted and baptized'.[215] The most that can be gleaned from Acts 2.38 is that 'repentance and water baptism are the normal prerequisites for the reception of the Spirit, which is promised to every believer'.[216] In Acts 2.39, Menzies believes 'Luke extends the range of the promise envisioned to include the promise of salvation offered in Joel 3:5 (as well as the promise of the Spirit of prophecy in Joel 3:1) because the audience addressed are not disciples'.[217] Further, 'the promise of Acts 2:39, like the promise of Jesus in Acts 1:8, points beyond "the restoration of the preserved of Israel": salvation is offered (Joel 3:5), but the promise includes the renewal of Israel's prophetic vocation (Joel 3:1)'.[218]

For Frank Macchia, Acts 2.38 exposes that 'the filling of the Spirit is closely connected to repentance, faith, and baptism in Acts'.[219] Acts 2.38 shows that there is even a 'special relationship between water baptism and the baptism in the Holy Spirit'.[220] For Macchia, these elements are related throughout Acts, yet they are 'all connected under what may be termed a complex initiation event'.[221] Still, though they are connected 'one is not entirely certain how'.[222] Macchia believes that to fully understand their relationship, 'one needs help from Paul and other canonical voices to negotiate a broader and more integrated conception of Spirit baptism as an eschatological event that is complex in nature'.[223]

---

[214] Menzies, *Empowered for Witness*, p. 203.
[215] Menzies, *Empowered for Witness*, p. 203.
[216] Menzies, *Empowered for Witness*, pp. 203-204.
[217] Menzies, *Empowered for Witness*, p. 171. Again, Menzies is using the Hebrew Masoretic chapter/verse numbers for Joel, which are respectively Joel 2.32 (for his 3.5) and 2.28 (for his 3.1) in English Bibles.
[218] Menzies, *Empowered for Witness*, p. 171. See previous comments regarding Menzies numbering in Joel.
[219] Thomas and Macchia, *Revelation*, p. 515.
[220] Macchia, *Jesus the Spirit Baptizer*, p. 332
[221] Thomas and Macchia, *Revelation*, p. 551.
[222] Macchia, *Baptized in the Spirit*, p. 15.
[223] Macchia, *Jesus the Spirit Baptizer*, p. 15.

Speaking descriptively, Macchia states that 'the gift of the Spirit is connected with sacramental initiation and Catholic tradition, whereas most Pentecostals (the Oneness Pentecostals being the outstanding exception) would see Spirit baptism as post – initiation'.[224] Yet, 'the challenge posed by the sacramental view of Spirit baptism is based in the observation that Jesus' reception of the Spirit at his baptism was paradigmatic of the connection between baptism and the reception of the Spirit among Christians'.[225] Interestingly, Macchia also cites Acts 2:38 along with other scriptures, to note the scriptural connection between water baptism and Spirit baptism.[226] And while water baptism and Spirit baptism are related, for Macchia, Spirit baptism cannot be contained within the water rite. Macchia advocates for Spirit baptism to follow water baptism.

Further, responding to Peter's command to be baptized in the name of Jesus, Macchia notes that the trinitarian formula found in Matthew 28 does not negate baptism in Jesus' name:

> We are baptized in the name of the Father, who sent the Son and promised the Spirit. We are baptized in the name of the Son, who was sent by the Father and who incorporates us into himself by baptizing us in the Spirit. We are baptized in the name of the Spirit, who bears witness to the Son and shapes us into the image of the Son so that we can hallow the Father's name – on earth as it is in heaven.[227]

Therefore, the command to be baptized in the name of Jesus fits *within* Jesus' command to baptize in the name of the Father, Son, and Spirit in Matthew 28. Macchia also suggests that trinitarians recognize baptism in Jesus' name an 'implicit reference to the Father, the Son, and the Spirit'.[228]

James Shelton believes that 'Luke is probably not averse to associating the Holy Spirit with conversion' which one can 'infer from the conclusion of Peter's sermon' in Acts 2.38.[229] Just like the conversion

---

[224] Macchia, *Baptized in the Spirit*, p. 73.
[225] Macchia, *Baptized in the Spirit*, p. 73.
[226] Macchia, *Baptized in the Spirit*, p. 73. Macchia also notes Acts 19.5-6 and 1 Cor. 12.13.
[227] Macchia, *Jesus the Spirit Baptizer*, p. 332
[228] Macchia, *Baptized in the Spirit*, p. 251.
[229] James Shelton, *Mighty in Word & Deed: The Role of the Holy Spirit in Luke-Acts* (Peabody, MA: Hendrickson Publishers, 1987), p. 129.

of the Samaritans in Acts 8, so Acts 2.38 signals a 'hiatus between repentance-baptism and reception of the Holy Spirit'.[230] Shelton sees this paralleling the 'experience of Jesus in which there appears to be a delay between his baptism' and the descent of the Spirit.[231] He also notes that Acts 2.38 does not make a direct link between the infilling of the Spirit and *glossolalia*: 'While it is apparent that the new converts in Acts 2:38 were empowered for ministry, it cannot be said that it ... resulted in the recipients of the Spirit speaking in tongues. On the contrary, neither context refers to *glossolalia*.'[232] However, Acts 2.38 does demonstrate that the 'Christian rite of baptism also involved repentance and forgiveness of sins'.[233] It also shows the association and relationship between the 'baptism of believers and the reception of the Holy Spirit'.[234] Therefore for Shelton, Acts 2.38 exposes links between water baptism, the forgiveness of sins, and the reception of the Spirit.

In several works, the Oneness theologian David Bernard also discusses Acts 2.37-42 in detail, focusing most intently on Acts 2.38. In discussing the broader context, Bernard states that when the crowd at Pentecost asked Peter, 'What shall we do?' (Acts 2.37), they were asking:

> 'How can we receive forgiveness for our sin? How can we correct the wrong we have done in rejecting Jesus and crucifying Him? How can we now accept Jesus as Lord and Messiah?' The essence of salvation is receiving forgiveness of sins through faith in Christ, so their question simply meant, 'What must we do to be saved?'[235]

Peter's answer in Acts 2.38, then, gives the 'biblical answer to the question of how to be saved'.[236] Bernard concludes by stating that great significance should be attached to this verse. He states that it is for this reason that Acts 2.38 is considered the 'authoritative answer

---

[230] Shelton, *Mighty in Word & Deed*, p. 129.
[231] Shelton, *Mighty in Word & Deed*, p. 129.
[232] Shelton, *Mighty in Word & Deed*, p. 130.
[233] Shelton, *Mighty in Word & Deed*, p. 134.
[234] Shelton, *Mighty in Word & Deed*, p. 11.
[235] David K. Bernard, *The New Birth* (Hazelwood, MO: Word Aflame Press, 1984 Kindle location 498-502.
[236] Bernard, *The New Birth*, Kindle location 502.

of the apostolic church to the question, "What must I do to be saved?"'.[237]

Remission of sins, then, 'of course ... includes water baptism (Acts 2.38)'.[238] Yet, Acts 2.38 is not just about water baptism. This verse gives the 'Bible pattern' of salvation including repentance, water baptism, and Spirit baptism in 'rapid succession'.[239] Therefore, for Bernard, water baptism – along with Spirit baptism – is 'an integral part of receiving Christ ... for it is not a second or third "work of grace", but part of a new life in Christ'.[240]

Acts 2.38 along with other scriptures, such as Mk 16.16, also demonstrate that water baptism and belief are both essential in salvation, so we must not separate baptism and belief in the promise of salvation.[241] Bernard strives to show that this does not mean that scriptures teach baptismal regeneration since the water and the ceremony do *not* hold the power to remit sins. Instead, it is by Christ's work through our faith and being baptized in the power of 'The Name' that remits sin.[242] This also brings up an important point connected to Bernard's articulated theology of water baptism about Acts 2.38: a theology of 'The Name'. Bernard shows that while trinitarians understand the name of Jesus as the name of the second member of the trinity, 'Oneness adherents see it as the redemptive name of God in the New Testament, which carries with it the power and authority needed by the church'.[243] However, one should not understand Jesus' name to be a magical formula for the name is only given power through faith in Jesus.[244] This 'theology of the Name', then, requires a 'Christological baptismal formula'.[245] This implies that baptism should be in the name of Jesus *only,* as demonstrated by Acts 2.38. For Bernard, it is significant that 'in the first sermon of the church, Peter commanded everyone to be baptized in the name of Jesus (Acts

---

[237] Bernard, *The New Birth*, Kindle location 503-504

[238] Bernard, *The New Birth*, Kindle location 1135.

[239] Bernard, *The New Birth*, Kindle location 1430. Again, 'The Bible pattern is to experience all three – repentance, water baptism, and the gift of the Spirit'. See Kindle location 1451-1452.

[240] David K. Bernard, *Essentials of Oneness Theology* (Hazelwood, MO: Word Aflame Press, 1984), kindle location 369.

[241] Bernard, *The New Birth*, kindle location 1885.

[242] Bernard, *The New Birth*, kindle location 1885.

[243] Bernard, *Essentials of Oneness Theology*, kindle location 302.

[244] Bernard, *Essentials of Oneness Theology*, kindle location 302.

[245] Bernard, *Essentials of Oneness Theology*, kindle location 302.

2:38)'[246] and every time the Bible describes the formula used at an actual baptism, it always describes the name Jesus (Acts 2:38; 8:16; 10:48; 19:5; 22:16)'.[247]

Echoing Bernard, Oneness scholar David Norris understands water baptism to be a 'real action of the holy God', thus excluding both 'superstitious and also purely symbolic meanings'.[248] Acts 2.38 shows that the profession of faith, baptism in Jesus' name, and receiving the Spirit (which was accompanied with tongues),[249] are all components of initiation into the covenant.[250] Norris states that he believes James Dunn is correct 'to suggest that the presentation of Luke-Acts is that Peter's pronouncement in Acts 2:38 is meant to be normative for what he calls "conversion-initiation": repent, be baptized in Jesus' name, and receive the gift of the Holy Spirit'.[251] However, Norris wants these components to be situated within a Oneness framework. Speaking descriptively, Norris notes that when interpreting Acts 2.38 as the fulfillment of Mt. 28.19, Oneness Pentecostals focus on 'Jesus as the saving name'.[252] This move leads 'to the second key that the Father, Son, and Holy Spirit in Matthew 28:19 no longer' needs to be understood as 'Persons'.[253] Thus, Acts 2.38 is responsible for 'experience and belief in Oneness Christology'.[254] Finally, Norris states that the promise of 'Acts 2:38 was not merely available to a select few'.[255] Rather, as 'Peter offers in verse 39, "the promise is to you and to your children, and to all who are afar off, as many as the Lord our God will call"'.[256]

D.3.6 Conclusions

In sum, during the period of formulation (1917-1929), Acts 2.37-40 was an important and divisive passage for early Pentecostals. Oneness Pentecostals understood this verse to prove the salvific nature of

---

[246] Bernard, *The New Birth*, kindle location 1834-1835.
[247] Bernard, *Essentials of Oneness Theology*, kindle location 291.
[248] David Norris, *I Am: A Oneness Pentecostal Theology* (Hazelwood, MO: WAP Academic, 2009), p. 191.
[249] Norris, *I Am*, p. 213.
[250] Norris, *I Am*, p. 213.
[251] Norris, *I Am*, kindle location 4024.
[252] Norris, *I Am*, kindle location 4352.
[253] Norris, *I Am*, kindle location 4352.
[254] Norris, *I Am*, kindle location 4586.
[255] Norris, *I Am*, kindle location 7608.
[256] Norris, *I Am*, kindle location 7608.

baptism, along with the necessity of baptizing in Jesus' name. For trinitarians, much time was spent refuting Oneness readings of the passage, though not much on their constructive interpretations. This was also the case in the second period of engagement (1929-1967). Trinitarian Pentecostals engaged Acts 2.38-39 specifically to discuss the issue of formula raised by Oneness Pentecostalism. Trinitarian interpretations of baptism in Jesus' name were also discussed and put forth, along with discussions of how Acts 2.38 proved that baptism signifies the believer's identification with Christ. However, the third period (1967-1984) was marked by trinitarian discussions around baptism as a response to faith and repentance, along with how water baptism prepared the way for Spirit baptism.

Lastly, the current period of Pentecostal scholarship (1984-present) consistently recognizes Acts 2.37-40 to speak of water baptism. However, within this broad consensus, there are differences between contemporary scholars. And since my constructive reading fits within this current body of literature, I will conclude this history of interpretation by putting the five contemporary scholars surveyed into dialogue with one another to show the congruences and incongruences between the five voices.

D.3.7 The Contemporary Dialogue

Robert Menzies emphasizes that while at first glance there seems to be a strong correlation between the reception of the Spirit and water baptism in Acts 2.38, Luke does not consistently show this link elsewhere. The importance, then, should instead be placed upon the relationship between baptism and repentance. For Menzies, Acts 2.38 best expresses that repentance and water baptism are prerequisites for the reception of the Spirit. However, Macchia disagrees. He sees the relationship between the Spirit and water baptism to be consistent and contends that Acts 2.38 exposes a special relationship between water baptism and Spirit baptism. He also sees repentance, faith, baptism, and the reception of the Spirit held together under the Christian initiation complex. James Shelton is similar to Macchia. For Shelton, Acts 2.38 exposes links between water baptism, the forgiveness of sins, and the reception of the Spirit. And though Bernard and Norris agree with Macchia and Shelton on the relationship between water baptism, repentance, faith, and the Spirit, they frame the relationship between these elements quite differently. For both Bernard and

Norris, baptism in Jesus' name grants the repentant believer the remission of sins and enables the believer to receive the fullness of the Spirit, evidenced by *glossolalia*. For Bernard and Norris, water baptism in 'the Name' is salvific. The elements of repentance, remission of sins, water baptism, and Spirit baptism all makeup conversion-initiation, and are available to all believers, as Acts 2.39 signals.

Therefore, while there are variances between contemporary Pentecostal scholars – most notably between Oneness and trinitarians – it is important to note that all understand Acts 2.37-40 to speak of water baptism and its relationship to repentance, the forgiveness of sins, and (in some cases) the reception of the/work of the Spirit. As I move to my constructive reading, I aim to situate my judgments on the passage within this broader context among Pentecostal scholars in dialogue both with Pentecostal and ecumenical voices. Consequently, it is now to this passage that we turn our attention.

D.4 'Brothers, What Should We Do?'

D.4.1 Baptism and Repentance

Following Peter's sermon, many hearers 'were cut to the heart' and in response asked Peter and the apostles, 'what should we do?' (v. 37). In answer, Peter summons them to 'Repent, and be baptized' (v. 38). By appealing to Jesus' words in Mk 1.15 – 'repent and believe in the gospel' – Jaroslav Pelikan notes that repentance 'in the full sense of the word included faith' and such faith was seen as a prerequisite to baptism.[257] In the long ending of Mark, Jesus is recorded saying, 'The one who believes and is baptized will be saved; but the one who does not believe will be condemned' (16.16). Repentance, faith, and baptism, then, are closely related in several prominent places in the New Testament. However, the question remains: *how* are they related?

Thomas Oden reminds us that early Christian exegetes distinguished three types of repentance concerning baptism:

> (First), a repentance for sins committed *before* baptism that call for the decisive once and for all repentance of baptismal faith. But then there is a continuing repentance *after* baptism for the marginal or lighter daily sins, requiring daily repentance after baptism as the medicine of forgiveness. Then there is a solemn third public form of repentance after baptism in the more serious sense of

---

[257] Jaroslav Pelikan, *Acts* (Grand Rapids, MI: Brazos Press, 2005), p. 236.

penitents (*poenitentes*) in the church who are struggling with *grave* sins.[258]

Read through the lens of the Christian tradition, one might consider Acts 2.38 to be referring to repentance for sins committed *before* baptism. This repentance – as Oden states – is decisive repentance of baptismal faith. Daniel Tomberlin rightly points out that repentance and water baptism are themselves 'acts of faith which effect the remission of sins'.[259] Baptism and repentance as acts of faith are so closely connected that 'the possibility of repentance without baptism is *not* considered in the apostolic church'.[260] Therefore, Acts 2.37-40 pushes us towards understanding baptism as the 'normative rite of initiation into the Faith'.[261] Yet, the issue of infant baptism summons Pentecostals to reflect more deeply on the connectedness between faith, repentance, and baptism.

While some Pentecostal scholars, such as French Arrington, would reject the practice of infant baptism because an infant cannot exercise faith,[262] Tomberlin conversely has argued that since water baptism is an act of faith, Pentecostals ought to consider the validity of infant baptism.[263] Appealing to the ecumenical paper on *Baptism, Eucharist, and Ministry*, he notes that 'infant baptism is indeed a believers' baptism, in that it reflects the faith of the believing community'.[264] Though those asking Peter 'what should we do?' (v. 37) were able to exercise decisional faith, Peter reminds them that 'the promise is for you, for your children ... (and) everyone whom the Lord our God calls to him' (v. 39). Jesus also reminds his disciples that the little children should not be stopped from coming to Christ, 'for it is

---

[258] Thomas Oden, *Classic Christianity: A Systematic Theology* (New York: NY: HarperOne, 1992), p. 577. Emphases original. For support, Oden cites Augustine, *Conf. 10* and Ambrose, *Concerning Repentance* 2.2.7-12.

[259] Tomberlin, 'Believers' Baptism in the Pentecostal Tradition', p. 430.

[260] Tomberlin, 'Believers' Baptism in the Pentecostal Tradition', p. 430. My emphasis.

[261] Tomberlin, 'Believers' Baptism in the Pentecostal Tradition', p. 430. My emphasis.

[262] See French L. Arrington, *Christian Doctrine: A Pentecostal Perspective, Volume Three* (Cleveland, TN: Pathway Press, 1994), pp. 208–12.

[263] Tomberlin, 'Believers' Baptism in the Pentecostal Tradition', p. 431.

[264] Tomberlin, 'Believers' Baptism in the Pentecostal Tradition', p. 431. See *Baptism, Eucharist and Ministry, Faith and Order Paper No. 111* (Geneva: WCC Publications, 1982).

to those such as these that the kingdom of God belongs' (Luke 18.16).

Yet, as Clark Pinnock has rightly pointed out, baptizing infants is not without its danger. In his view, the danger of baptizing infants is that the personal faith may be faith lost sight of.[265] Similarly, Moltmann has stated that infant baptism has long been a part of establishing the Christendom-type 'state church' model.[266] Karl Barth and Emil Brunner deplore the fact that baptism has too often become estranged from a living obedience to Christ. At its worst, infant baptism can become 'a rite not of the new birth but of natural birth'.[267] However, believer's baptism is not without its difficulties. Understood merely as an 'experience of conversion' related to 'faith but not to the election of God', believer's baptism becomes stripped of all objective meaning.[268] Thus, one difficulty of believer's baptism is that we can regard 'the human decision so highly that we forget God's enabling grace'.[269] While faith and repentance precede baptism, God's grace precedes faith and repentance. It is God's grace, then, that enables our faithful repentance and response in baptism.

Thus, I want to suggest that 'the two forms of baptism – infant and adult – together express the full meaning of baptism better than each would alone'.[270] While believer's baptism better expresses the relationship between repentance and baptism, this does not exclude the practice of infant baptism since it better expresses God's gracious initiative preceding personal faith and repentance. As Acts 2.37-41 indicates, both God's initiatory action and human response are needed. The 'ecumenical orthodox' theologian Donald Bloesch is helpful here: 'Pedobaptism is a more credible symbolism for the mystery that God's election is prior to human decision. Believer's baptism calls our attention to the biblical truth that God's election is realized through the human decision'.[271] Further, Amos Yong reminds us that

---

[265] Pinnock, *Flame of Love: A Theology of the Holy Spirit* (Downers Grove, IL: InterVarsity Press, 1996), p. 126.

[266] Moltmann, *The Church in the Power of the Spirit*, p. 229.

[267] Donald Bloesch, *The Reform of the Church* (Grand Rapids, MI: Eerdmans, 1970), p. 35.

[268] Bloesch, *The Reform of the Church*, p. 38.

[269] Pinnock, *Flame of Love*, p. 126.

[270] Daniel Migliore, *Faith Seeking Understanding* (Grand Rapids, MI: Eerdmans, 2014), p. 298.

[271] Donald Bloesch, *The Church: Sacraments, Worship, Ministry, Mission* (Downers Grove: IL, InterVarsity Press, 2002), p. 158.

'personal salvation is never merely individualized, insofar as baptism involves the believing community. Yet the individual aspect of salvation cannot be neglected: there are (or should be) identifiable moments in human lives when the awareness of the need for repentance comes to the fore.'[272] This means that in baptism, we must emphasize both 'the electing grace of God and the personal acceptance of our vocation in faith'.[273]

Peter's command to 'repent and be baptized' also shows that 'the world needs to be transformed into the church through a radical break with the past (repentance) and incorporation into the body of Christ (baptism)'.[274] Simon Chan notes that this 'radical break is differently pictured in the New Testament as deliverance from the domain of darkness and transference into the "kingdom of the Son (God) loves" (Col 1.13)'.[275] However, in repentance, the 're-turn' is not so much a 'turn back' as a *'turn to the future'*.[276] By repenting and being baptized, one is pledging devotion to the gospel and lifestyle of Jesus which point to the possibility of a new beginning.[277] The conversion complex – which includes repentance and baptism – is a 'many-sided affair',[278] which is opened up to the believer by the graciousness of God. As Acts 2.37-41 suggests, this turn to the future – repentance – is deeply connected to the work of the Spirit. Repentance is only made possible because the Spirit has come preveniently, and thus, made our response possible. However, since repentance, faith, and baptism happen in the context of hearing the gospel – as seen in Acts 2.37-41 – we must also emphasize the 'importance of

---

[272] Yong, *The Spirit Poured Out on All Flesh*, p. 92.
[273] Bloesch, *The Reform of the Church*, p. 39. Of course, there is a danger here of 'synergism in which the human subject is portrayed as contributing something of his or her own to the unfolding of salvation. God does part of it, and we also do our part'. Yet, we must not neglect also to note that scripture 'does not teach regeneration apart from personal faith'. Therefore, following Bloesch, I want to suggest that 'when we speak of decision, we must have in mind not just our decision for Christ but his decision for us, and we must emphasize the priority of the latter'. See Bloesch, *The Church*, p. 157.
[274] Chan, *Liturgical Theology*, p. 119.
[275] Chan, *Liturgical Theology*, p. 119.
[276] Jürgen Moltmann, *Experiences of God* (Minneapolis, MN: Fortress Press, 1980), p. 2. Emphasis in original, cited in Veli-Matti Kärkkäinen, *Spirit and Salvation* (Grand Rapids, MI: Eerdmans, 2016), p. 266.
[277] Kärkkäinen, *Spirit and Salvation*, p. 266.
[278] Joel Green, *Body, Soul, and Human Life: The Nature of Humanity in the Bible* (Grand Rapids, MI: Baker Academic, 2008), p. 122.

human response to God's doing'.[279] Therefore, we must do justice to the objective reality of baptismal grace and the subjective need for personal surrender and determination.[280]

As Oden has shown, though baptism is a one-time act, there is continuing repentance *after* baptism.[281] Put another way, repentance is a persistent life in 'baptismal grace on the basis of the baptism that has been performed once and for all'.[282] So though we may repent often, we are only baptized once. Any repentance following baptism is a turning towards one's baptism to receive word of who the baptized *have* become and *are* becoming. Though mentioned previously, Robert Jenson's comments are worth noting again: Since baptism is always there as a fact in our past, we can always, 'as Luther said, "creep" back to it and begin anew'.[283]

D.4.2 Baptized in the Name of Jesus

A Pentecostal reading of Acts 2.37-41 will pay special attention to Peter's call to be baptized 'in the name of Jesus' (Acts 2.38), since it has been understood quite differently among Oneness and trinitarian Pentecostals. Notably, a recent study group formed by the Society for Pentecostal Studies that explored key issues of doctrine and practice between trinitarian and Oneness Pentecostals has shed light on potential ways forward. In Frank Macchia's summary of the meetings, he notes that the trinitarian team 'showed an openness to accept the formulaic significance of Jesus' name as it is referenced in baptismal texts of the New Testament', while concurrently 'referencing Acts 22:16 in asking the question as to whether someone who confesses Jesus as Savior or Lord in baptism ... is *implicitly* baptized in Jesus' name, even if the minister performing the rite uses the Trinitarian formula'.[284] As a result, the Oneness Pentecostals 'did not deny this possibility, but neither did they affirm it'.[285] As one involved in the

---

[279] Kärkkäinen, *Hope and Community*, p. 373.
[280] Bloesch, *The Reform of the Church*, p. 42.
[281] Oden, *Classic Christianity*, p. 577.
[282] Moltmann, *The Church in the Power of the Spirit*, p. 228.
[283] Jenson, *A Large Catechism*, p. 50. He also puts it this way: 'Short of the End, the believer never advances beyond his or her baptism but instead falls behind it and must catch up to it'. Robert W. Jenson, *Systematic Theology, Volume 2: The Works of God* (Oxford, Oxford University Press, 1999), p. 297.
[284] Frank D. Macchia, 'The Oneness-Trinitarian Pentecostal Dialogue: Exploring the Diversity of Apostolic Faith', *HTR* 103.3 (2010), pp. 329-49 (342).
[285] Macchia, 'The Oneness-Trinitarian Pentecostal Dialogue', p. 342.

Oneness/trinitarian dialogue, Macchia states that he found this moment to be one of 'genuine breakthrough'.[286] Thus, contemporary Pentecostal scholarship is helping shed light on potential ways forward, which will in turn help shape this reading.

Yet, how might a trinitarian Pentecostal reading of Acts 2.37-40 inform such ways forward? This reading assumes that baptism in Jesus' name specified Christian baptism as distinct from other Jewish immersion rituals.[287] People being baptized in Jesus' name specified whose followers they would be.[288] Another possibility is that baptism in Jesus' name concerned authority, *not* formula. Just as Christ sent out the seventy in the authority of his name to exorcise demons (Lk. 10.17), so Christ has commissioned his church to make disciples of all nations, baptizing them in the name of the triune God, in the authority of Christ. Moreover, though Oneness Pentecostals rightly draw our attention to this crucial text (Acts 2.38) as the beginning of this new ritual, agreeing with Willie James Jennings, 'where they envisage restriction and limitation, it would be more helpful to see expansion and openness'.[289] Still, how might trinitarian Pentecostals show openness while also maintaining hermeneutical honesty?[290]

Some have suggested that trinitarian Pentecostals might affirm baptism in Jesus' name when understood as a '*Trinitarian* act of God in Christ by which the Father anointed the Son with the Spirit to bring about redemption'.[291] Understood within this context, baptism in Jesus' name could be embraced as a legitimate formula, given such qualification. However, trinitarian Pentecostals cannot be too quick to embrace baptism in Jesus' name, even if motivated by the noble desire to participate in the ongoing dialogue/healing between Oneness and trinitarian Pentecostals. While this dialogue is of vast

---

[286] Macchia, 'The Oneness-Trinitarian Pentecostal Dialogue', p. 342.

[287] Keener, *Acts (Volume 1)*, p. 983.

[288] Keener, *Acts (Volume 1)*, p. 983. Further, see 1 Cor. 1.13-15.

[289] Willie James Jennings, *Acts* (Louisville, KY: Westminster John Knox Press, 2017), p. 37.

[290] Perhaps in future conversations between trinitarian and oneness Pentecostals, rather than focusing on issues of baptismal formula, it would be more advantageous to renew conversations on the doctrine of God. Perhaps trinitarian Pentecostals might best converse with oneness Pentecostals by starting with theology proper. By beginning methodologically with the doctrine of God rather than the trinity, conversations with oneness Pentecostals might possibly yield surprising results.

[291] Macchia, *Baptized in the Spirit*, p. 116.

importance among Pentecostals, trinitarian Pentecostals must also consider the ecumenical difficulties of moving away from the trinitarian formula.[292] Further, given the widespread misunderstanding of trinitarian dogma at the lay-level, baptisms performed in Jesus' name within trinitarian Pentecostal churches could have the potential of producing even more confusion among the laity. Thus, I suggest while trinitarian Pentecostals consider the legitimacy of prior baptisms performed in Jesus' name, trinitarian communities retain and continue the practice of baptism in the name of the triune God.

Perhaps a more fruitful way forward is to emphasize the Christological significance of baptism as transference into the life of Jesus. We ought to assert that baptism in Jesus' name should also be understood in light of what Wolfhart Pannenberg terms 'transference': 'Baptism in the name of Jesus ... is an act of transfer. The baptized are no longer their own but God's or Christ's'.[293] Baptism in the name of Jesus links the baptized 'to the Son of the eternal Father' and gives us a 'share in his Spirit'.[294] We then receive a 'new identity ... by being baptized in the "name" of Jesus, which implies his lordship and human commitment and submission'.[295] In baptism, the Christian is claimed by God. Acts 2.37-40 aptly reminds us that by being baptized in the name of Jesus, the early Jewish believers were no longer defined by John's baptism, but now by Christian Baptism with the Spirit. Baptism in the name of Jesus, then, transfers the believer into full identification with Christ.

D.4.3 Baptism and Forgiveness of Sin

At Pentecost, Peter promised that those who would 'repent, and be baptized ... in the name of Jesus Christ' would also receive 'the forgiveness of sins' (Acts 2.38). This relationship between baptism and the forgiveness of sins is echoed in Paul's report of his conversion in Acts 22.16: 'And now why do you delay? Get up, be baptized, and

---

[292] As Josiah Baker has noted, 'The commitments of Trinitarian Pentecostals to Oneness Pentecostals could hinder their involvement in ecumenical contexts that reject Oneness Pentecostals, while their increasing Trinitarian commitments could strain their already tenuous relationship with Oneness Pentecostals'. See Baker, '"One Lord, One Faith, One Baptism?"', p. 95.

[293] Wolfhart Pannenberg, *Systematic Theology: Volume 3* (London: T&T Clark, 2004), p. 239.

[294] Pannenberg, *Systematic Theology, Volume 3*, p. 240.

[295] Kärkkäinen, *Hope and Community*, p. 379.

have your sins washed away, calling on his name.'[296] As the Orthodox Jaroslav Pelikan has noted,[297] while some would 'insist that the sacraments do not convey the forgiveness of sins but only announce it', the language of Acts 2.38 expresses that 'the God who alone can forgive sins has, in sovereign freedom, chosen to attach that forgiveness to the means of grace, and specifically to baptism'.[298] This is further expressed by Paul's Epistle to Titus: 'He saved us, not because of any works of righteousness that we had done, but according to his mercy, through the water of rebirth and renewal by the Holy Spirit' (Titus 3.5). The Reformed Protestant Emil Brunner echoes Pelikan when he states that 'in baptism, it is God, first and sovereign who acts, who forgives sin, who cleanses man and regenerates him'.[299] Yet, Brunner also correctly notes:

> But man too acts in baptism. He allows this cleansing of himself to take place, he lets himself be drawn into the death of Christ, he confesses his faith and his attachment to Christ. Baptism is not merely a gift to man, but also an active receiving and confession on the part of man ... Baptism is not only an act of grace but just as much an act of confession stemming from the act of grace.[300]

Therefore, in baptism, God acts. Yet, our ongoing cooperation in baptismal grace is necessary.

As the Catholic theologian Hans Küng has argued, in baptism the Spirit 'does not operate in a magical, automatic way, but allows free consent'.[301] Therefore, when someone is sincerely baptized in faith we can trust that they are 'born of water and Spirit' and 'become members of his mystical body and receive the forgiveness of sins'.[302] Though some Pentecostals are hesitant to relate baptism too closely to the forgiveness of sins, one might consider that it is not baptism that forgives sin, but God. As Acts 2.38 states, people are baptized in the authority of Christ in the power of the Spirit.

---

[296] Pelikan, *Acts*, p. 239.
[297] Perhaps it is worth noting that Pelikan converted to Orthodoxy towards the end of his life.
[298] Pelikan, *Acts*, p. 239.
[299] Brunner, *The Divine-Human Encounter*, p. 178.
[300] Brunner, *The Divine-Human Encounter*, p. 178.
[301] Hans Küng, *On Being a Christian* (New York: Wallaby, 1968), p. 471.
[302] Pinnock, *Flame of Love*, p. 124.

Even though God has chosen to associate the forgiveness of sins with the water rite this does not mean that forgiveness of sins is not God's doing, nor does it mean that forgiveness of sins is solely contained within the rite. Instead, we might say that the effectiveness is bound up with the Holy Spirit.[303] Early Pentecostals were cognizant of this. Aimee Semple McPherson stated that 'Jesus is our Galilee and the Jordan is the cleansing stream of Calvary which carries our sins far away'.[304] Further, in baptism, we receive 'the forgiveness of sins, not the removal of sin'.[305] Sanctification comes by way of a continual cooperating with God in baptismal grace throughout a lifetime. Luther was acutely mindful of the importance of working out our salvation following baptism:

> But we should note that it is not necessary that all be found in this state of perfection as soon as they are baptized into this kind of death. For they are baptized 'into death,' i.e. toward death; in other words: they have only taken the first steps toward the attainment of this death as their goal.[306]

Even so, the forgiveness of sins in and through baptism is only possible because it is intimately linked with the Holy Spirit.[307]

It is God's Spirit, then, that marks off Christian baptism from John's baptism. Though both baptisms utilize water and a call to repentance, only the latter surely gives forgiveness along with the Spirit in Jesus' name.[308] Those in attendance at Pentecost 'knew only the baptism of John' and were now called 'to be upgraded into the fullness of baptism' with the Spirit in the name of Jesus.[309] This baptism which grants the forgiveness of sins is Jesus' not John's since it is only Jesus who grants forgiveness.[310] Therefore, in baptism, one is not

---

[303] Clark H. Pinnock, 'The Physical Side of Being Spiritual: God's Sacramental Presence' in Anthony R. Cross and Philip E. Thompson (eds.), *Baptist Sacramentalism: Studies in Baptist History and Thought* (Volume 5) (Eugene: OR, Wipf and Stock, 2003), p. 19.
[304] *BCF* 10.7 (1926), p. 26.
[305] Gordon T. Smith, *Transforming Conversion: Rethinking the Language and Contours of Christian Initiation* (Grand Rapids, MI: Baker Academic, 2010), p. 142.
[306] Martin Luther, *Lectures on Romans* (Philadelphia: Westminster, 1961), p. 181.
[307] Smith, *Transforming Conversion*, p.143.
[308] Sarah Hinlicky Wilson, 'Water Baptism and Spirit Baptism in Luke-Acts: Another Reading of the Evidence', *Pneuma* 38.4 (2016), p. 485.
[309] Pelikan, *Acts*, p. 238.
[310] Wilson, 'Water Baptism and Spirit Baptism in Luke-Acts', p. 486.

only identified *with* Christ but forgiven *by* Christ and enabled to share in his life.

D.4.4 Baptism and Reception of the Spirit

In Acts 2.37-40, one witnesses a close relationship between baptism and reception of the Spirit. In fact, Acts 2.38 seems to indicate that the gift of the Spirit is a natural consequence of baptism.[311] Supporting this connection, the overall 'biblical and patristic witnesses both posit an undeniable connection between water and Spirit baptism'.[312] While most Pentecostals have preferred to speak of the Spirit's working in Spirit baptism rather than water baptism, some Pentecostal theologians such as Simon Chan have responded by insisting that 'Christian baptism is unlike John's baptism in that it is Jesus' baptizing with the Spirit' and therefore, 'the water ritual can be understood only concerning the gift of the Spirit'.[313] Amos Yong, too, argues that baptism should be 'understood pneumatically and mystically as an action of the Spirit (e.g., Titus 3:5)'.[314] However, based on Pentecostal experience, one might be left in asking, 'What about a second blessing?'[315]

In following Acts 2.37-40, it seems most beneficial to assert that water baptism is the occasion for sacramental Spirit reception, though one should expect to experience subsequent releases and experience of the Spirit of baptism.[316] Thus, Pentecostals can claim that baptism is the location where God gives the Spirit,[317] while also claiming the necessity of subsequent spiritual breakthroughs following baptism.[318] Theologically, these experiences of the Spirit can be understood as eschatological breakthroughs of the Spirit that remind individuals and communities of the penultimate promises that flow from one's baptism.

In sum, Acts 2.37-40 seems to suggest that the Spirit is received at baptism, though 'the experiential reality enters our consciousness in a variety of ways over time'.[319] Anchoring Spirit reception to water

---

[311] Hans Küng, *The Church* (New York: Image Books, 1976) p. 219.
[312] Yong, *The Spirit Poured Out on Flesh*, p. 157.
[313] Chan, *Liturgical Theology*, p. 119.
[314] Yong, *The Spirit Poured Out on All Flesh*, p. 157.
[315] Pinnock, *Flame of Love*, p. 168.
[316] More on this in Chapter 7.
[317] Pinnock, 'The Physical Side of Being Spiritual', p. 15.
[318] Pinnock, *Flame of Love*, p. 169.
[319] Pinnock notes that Luke sometimes 'describes a second pentecostal event in the lives of the disciples (Acts 4:31). He tells how the Samaritans accepted the

baptism also does not mean that 'the Spirit was absent before', for the Spirit was working preveniently prior.[320] Here Andrew Gabriel is helpful:

> Pentecostals are not alone in observing that the Spirit can fill a place in which the Spirit is already present. While Pentecostals often describe Spirit baptism as a subsequent experience(s) of being filled with the Spirit, it is also clear that all believers, regardless of their understanding of Spirit baptism, have had an experience of Spirit filling that is subsequent to their being filled with the Spirit by virtue of being part of the Spirit-filled creation. One can also discern subsequent experiences of Spirit filling in the church, which, though it already has the Spirit dwelling within it, continues to call for the Spirit to fill her, as well as in Christology, where Jesus Christ was full of the Spirit without measure and yet subsequently received the Spirit from the Father after Jesus' resurrection. In each of these cases, there is a subsequent experience of the Spirit after one is already filled with the Spirit.[321]

Using Gabriel's reasoning, just as the Spirit descended upon Jesus in his baptism and later obtained the Spirit following his resurrection, so we too may have experiences of the Spirit following our baptism. Put another way, we can affirm that 'the Spirit is certainly at work in water baptism ... but the Spirit is not *only* at work in water baptism'.[322]

Yet, the relationship between water baptism and the Spirit must be maintained theologically. As Chris Green notes, Pentecostals must overcome understanding baptism as 'an after-the-fact symbolic re-enactment of an already-accomplished reality'.[323] Instead, following the lead of Acts 2.37-40, we should assert that baptism is sacramental by way of the Spirit's presence and involvement in-and-through the rite. This implies that the 'celebration of baptism as a Christian rite

---

word of God and received the Spirit a few days later (Acts 8:14-15). He shows that Paul's conversion took three days to complete. Such passages, however, do not imply a doctrine of subsequence – their concern is for experience and reality.' See Pinnock, *Flame of Love*, p. 170.

[320] Pinnock, *Flame of Love*, p. 167.
[321] Gabriel, 'The Intensity of the Spirit in a Spirit-Filled World', p. 381.
[322] Wilson, 'Water Baptism and Spirit Baptism in Luke-Acts', p. 498.
[323] Chris E. Green, '"The Body of Christ, the Spirit of Communion": Re-Visioning Pentecostal Ecclesiology in Conversation with Robert Jenson', *JPT* 20 (2011), pp. 15-26 (25).

should include, centrally, the invocation of the Holy Spirit'.[324] And whether one experiences the *charismata* in baptism is not the point. Our assurance of the Spirit's reception in baptism is not based on one's existential experience of baptism but solely based on 'the promise' which is 'for everyone whom the Lord our God calls to him' (Acts 2.39).

D.4.5 Conclusions

In conclusion, what might this reading tell us about what a Pentecostal theology of water baptism might look like? What are the implications for Pentecostal praxis? In short, I want to propose that this reading reveals the need to rework our theology and praxis surrounding baptism and repentance, baptismal formula, and the Spirit's working in the rite.

First, this reading both affirms *and* challenges the traditional Pentecostal insistence upon baptism following repentance. As Acts 2.37-40 demonstrates, baptism is most often a response to repentance and faith. However, this reading also challenges Pentecostals to recall that God's grace precedes faith and repentance. Baptism, then, is not simply our action, but our graced response to God's prior graceful action. Perhaps, then, Pentecostals ought to consider embracing both infant baptism and believers baptism as legitimate, since taken together the two forms express the full meaning of baptism – as God's gracious initiative and our repentant and faith-filled response.[325] Even if Pentecostals retain believers baptism as the norm, Pentecostal churches ought seriously to consider receiving believers baptized as infants into their fellowship, recognizing them as truly baptized Christians.

Second, it suggests a (trinitarian) openness to the formulaic significance of Jesus' name. However, as I have noted, this openness must be met with some firm qualifications and considerations, given ecumenical concerns. Thus, while I suggest Trinitarian Pentecostals consider the legitimacy of baptisms performed in Jesus' name, Trinitarian communities ought to retain and continue the practice of baptism in the name of the triune God. However, these communities should also emphasize the Christological significance of baptism as transference into the life of Jesus.

---

[324] Yong, *The Spirit Poured Out on All Flesh*, p. 158.
[325] Migliore, *Faith Seeking Understanding*, p. 298.

Finally, this reading calls for changes in our pneumatology and sacramentality. I have called for Pentecostals to embrace a sacramental view of water baptism that emphasizes the Spirit's presence in and through the rite. This view does not threaten Pentecostalism's insistence upon subsequent experiences of the Spirit, for Pentecostals already expect the continual filling of the Spirit throughout their lives (Eph. 5.18). However, it should make Pentecostals question if there are more faithful theological readings of the narratives in Acts in relation to the texts surrounding water baptism/Spirit baptism. Given the relationship between water baptism and reception of the Spirit in Acts 2.38 (and Acts as a whole), Pentecostals should affirm the Spirit's working in water baptism. In light of this, Pentecostals ought to consider summoning the Spirit in the waters of baptism, thus bearing witness to 'the promise' of the gift of the Spirit for every new believer (Acts 2.39).

E. Water Baptism in the Church's Scripture: Conclusions

In this chapter, I have attempted to explore what the NT has to say about water baptism by reading what I judged to be relevant texts,[326] though my selection of texts relates to my earlier work of hearing early and contemporary voices (see Chapters 3-5). Romans 6.1-11 and Acts 2.37-40 were frequently referenced by early Pentecostals and subsequently discussed with contemporary Pentecostals in my qualitative, empirical research. Thus, in providing constructive readings of these texts in dialogue with both Pentecostal and ecumenical perspectives, I hope to demonstrate one example of how Pentecostals can read water baptism texts while also providing contours for how a Pentecostal theology of water baptism might take shape. In the following chapter, we will continue with our constructive efforts in defining and articulating a Pentecostal theology of water baptism and its ensuing implications.

---

[326] Green, *Toward a Pentecostal Theology of the Lord's Supper*, p. 239.

7

WASHED IN THE SPIRIT: TOWARD A PENTECOSTAL THEOLOGY OF WATER BAPTISM

> Pentecostal theology must still catch up to Pentecostal experience when it comes to the sacraments of the church. – Frank Macchia[1]
>
> It is said ... that Pentecostals disintegrate the unity of Christian initiation, especially through their lack of understanding of baptism ... this is laid to the account of the subsequence doctrine. – Steven Land[2]
>
> Pentecostal theology has not produced a unique theology of water baptism. – Steve Studebaker[3]

A. Research Context and Focus

At this point in the tradition's theological history, there have been few efforts to formulate a distinctly Pentecostal theology of the sacraments.[4] While recently Pentecostals have begun laying the ground-

---

[1] Macchia, 'Tradition and the *Novum* of the Spirit', p. 46.
[2] Land, *Pentecostal Spirituality*, p. 214.
[3] Studebaker, 'Baptism among Pentecostals', p. 204.
[4] Green, *Toward a Pentecostal Theology of the Lord's Supper*, p. 243. By utilizing the term 'sacrament', I am referring to a repeatable instituted form of the gospel that mediates the mystery and reality of divine encounter. Robert Jenson, *Visible Words: The Interpretation and Practice of Christian Sacraments* (Philadelphia, PA: Fortress Press, 1978), p. 11; Daniel Tomberlin, *Pentecostal Sacraments: Encountering God at the Altar* (Cleveland, TN: Cherohala Press, 2019), p. 2.

work for the developing of a Pentecostal sacramentality that is shaped by Pentecostal concerns and resources,[5] Pentecostal sacramentality, arguably, is still in its infancy.[6] Following the work of Chris E.W. Green and other scholars,[7] this constructive chapter, then, will respond to John Christopher Thomas' call for Pentecostal scholars to 'reclaim and appropriate the sacraments for a tradition that has been a bit uncertain about them and their place in the community's worship'.[8] More specifically, as mentioned previously, this chapter will most directly answer to Green's invitation for scholars to develop a Pentecostal theology of water baptism.[9]

Up until this point, this project has attempted to provide the necessary Pentecostal resourcing. We began with an examination of the current climate on the subject matter (Chapter 1), while giving the rationale for a fresh, integrative Pentecostal methodology that brings together ecumenical, revisioning, and empirical ways of doing theology (Chapter 2). In the body of the study (Chapters 3-5), we engaged three denominations that characterize a cross-section of English-speaking North American Pentecostalism to discern the 'ordinary theology' of *early* denominational Pentecostals, the 'ordinary theology' of *contemporary* Pentecostals in particular denominational churches, and how those resources triangulate with the official denominational statements and scholarly denominational voices that discuss water baptism.[10] The result was a thick description of

---

[5] Green, *Toward a Pentecostal Theology of the Lord's Supper*, p. 244.

[6] Frank Macchia has noted that though Pentecostals have 'experienced baptism and eucharist as occasions for God's redemptive presence through the power of the Spirit', we have 'often regarded them theologically more as acts of repentance or symbolic testimonies than as "sacraments" in the sense of events in which the dynamic presence of Christ through the Spirit is encountered'. See Macchia, 'Is Footwashing the Neglected Sacrament?', p. 241.

[7] For just a few examples, see Archer, 'Nourishment for our Journey', pp. 76-96; Wolfgang Vondey and Chris Green, 'Between This and That: Reality and Sacramentality in the Pentecostal Worldview', *JPT* 19.2 (2010), pp. 243–64; Tomberlin, *Pentecostal Sacraments: Encountering God at the Altar*.

[8] Thomas, 'Pentecostal Theology in the Twenty-First Century', p. 18.

[9] Green, *Toward a Pentecostal Theology of the Lord's Supper*, p. 328. In addition to water baptism, Green also calls for theologies of footwashing and the laying on of hands by anointing oil.

[10] As noted earlier, ordinary theology is defined as 'the theological beliefs and processes of believing that find expression in the God-talk of those believers who have received no scholarly theological education'. See Astley and Francis (eds.), *Exploring Ordinary Theology*, p. 1.

Pentecostal revisioning and empirical resources, put into dialogue with contemporary Pentecostal denominational literature.

While my initial constructive work began by contributing Pentecostal theological readings of two scriptural texts, Rom. 6.1-11 and Acts 2.37-40 (Chapter 6),[11] we have not fully addressed what a distinctly (trinitarian) Pentecostal theology of water baptism might look like.[12] Therefore, now after the compulsory research, we can develop a Pentecostal theology of water baptism in a distinctly Pentecostal way. However, a few remarks about the approach I will employ in this chapter are in order. First, to construct a Pentecostal theology of the water rite, this chapter is resourced and oriented by the Pentecostal resources in prior chapters,[13] while also engaging in critical conversation with dialogue partners selected from the wider Christian tradition – Protestant, Catholic, and Orthodox, historical and contemporary. This suggests that intentional ecumenical dialogue can at times assist Pentecostals in finding fresh ways of addressing the challenges that Pentecostal theology seeks to overcome. Therefore, this constructive chapter – along with my Pentecostal theological readings of scripture (Chapter 6) – will supply the necessary 'ecumenical' resources for the whole of the project, as noted previously (Chapter 2). Second, I will broach the subject matter in three phases: (1) First, I will deal with the relationship between water baptism and the Pentecostal doctrine of Spirit baptism, arguing for a revisionary theology of water baptism that emphasizes its relationship to the coming and indwelling of the Spirit;[14] (2) second, I will put forth a revisionary theology of Spirit baptism that emphasizes the Spirit's releasing and empowering of believers to embody their mission; (3) and lastly, I

---

[11] I chose to engage these scriptural texts since they were frequently referenced by early Pentecostals and subsequently discussed with contemporary Pentecostals in my qualitative (empirical) research.

[12] Though I have engaged both trinitarian and oneness Pentecostal sources, this constructive proposal will be distinctly trinitarian in its construction.

[13] Certainly, it is worth nothing that my construction is also shaped by my Pentecostal experience, not limited to, but including my current local Pentecostal church where I serve as Lead Pastor.

[14] It lies beyond the scope of this study to determine whether or not this is so, but it *may be* that the separation between the holy spirit received at water baptism and/or conversion and the Holy Spirit (as Person), is akin to medieval distinction between created and uncreated grace. Following Barth, Rahner, and others, Pentecostals ought to return to the ancient idea that in grace, God essentially gives himself.

will flesh out what these revisionary accounts imply about the action of God in the ministries of the church and the world.[15]

However, before I begin, a few remarks on the burden of Pentecostal theology and the obligations of Pentecostal theologians are in order.

B. The Role of Pentecostal Theology and the Responsibility of the Pentecostal Theologian

In the editorial of the inaugural issue of the *JPT*, the history of Pentecostal scholarship was discussed in three different phases.[16] In John Christopher Thomas' 1998 SPS Presidential Address, he contends that the last few years have given rise to a new generation of Pentecostal scholarship, marking the fourth phase.[17] Paul Lewis, too, has offered a similar account in a four-period scheme.[18] In Lewis' overview of the four periods that comprise the first hundred years of Pentecostal theology, he concludes his survey by providing several possibilities and projections. He notes a considerable need for constructive theology from a Pentecostal perspective, one which is 'more than a denominational doctrine restatement'.[19] Though Pentecostal theologians have begun answering Lewis' call, no one to date has provided significant reasoning for such a venture. Therefore, within this dialogue surrounding the current state of Pentecostal scholarship, I hope to provide brief and modest suggestions on the role of Pentecostal theology, while also commenting upon the responsibility of the Pentecostal theologian.

---

[15] Thus, while this project will have ecclesiological concerns, it will *also* be concerned with the doctrine of God and eschatology, speaking to the church's vocation, God's agency, and the eschatological nature of baptism.

[16] Rickie D. Moore, John Christopher Thomas, Steven J. Land, 'Editorial', *JPT* 1 (1992), p. 3.

[17] Thomas, 'Pentecostal Theology in the Twenty-First Century', pp. 4-5. Thomas also helpfully provides characteristics of the future of Pentecostal theology and sends up a couple of 'trial balloons' to illustrate potential paradigms.

[18] Lewis, 'Reflections on a Hundred Years of Pentecostal Theology', http://www.pctii.org/cyberj/cyberj12/lewis.html.

[19] Lewis, 'Reflections on a Hundred Years of Pentecostal Theology', http://www.pctii.org/cyberj/cyberj12/lewis.html.

Rowan Williams has suggested a threefold typology of theology styles which he calls *celebratory, communicative,* and *critical.*[20] Celebratory theology seeks to place the doctrinal language of the tradition in its finest light. This type of theology intentionally reveals and demonstrates connections of thought to display the richest possible range of meaning in the language utilized.[21] Communicative theology moves beyond celebratory theology by situating doctrines within new environments and idioms. Thus, it seeks to 'persuade or commend' through illuminating and extending doctrines into different forms of thought.[22] The final style, rather than speaking *for* the tradition, like celebratory and communicative theology, critical/constructive theology seeks to also speak *to* the tradition.

In utilizing Williams' typology – while also admittedly extending its intended limits – I want to suggest that the predominant role of Pentecostal theology is to provide the tradition with various projects that together express all three theological styles. Contemporary Pentecostal theologians have excelled in providing numerous accounts of fresh articulations of Pentecostal doctrine (celebratory theology). These robust descriptive accounts and re-articulations of classical Pentecostal doctrine have helped in the development of Pentecostal scholarship as a legitimate enterprise. Pentecostal scholars have also begun offering postmodern/contextual Pentecostal theologies, which are one example of how Pentecostal scholars are developing communicative theology within the scholarly tradition.

However, the third category – critical theology or constructive theology – as noted earlier by Lewis, is perhaps the most neglected style within Pentecostal scholarship to date.[23] Constructive theology

---

[20] Rowan Williams, *On Christian Theology* (Malden, MA: Blackwell Publishers, 2000), p. xiii.
[21] Williams, *On Christian Theology*, p. xiii.
[22] Williams, *On Christian Theology*, p. xiv.
[23] Lewis, 'Reflections on a Hundred Years of Pentecostal Theology', http://www.pctii.org/cyberj/cyberj12/lewis.html. Certainly there are several reasons for this. Thomas mentions a few reasons this might be: Pentecostal scholars face

> the twin dangers of suspicion and jealousy from those inside the tradition. Several things account for this situation. First, opportunity to study at leading centers for biblical and theological inquiry around the world has been cause for concern on the part of those who have been guardians of the Pentecostal theological tradition. Sometimes this suspicion is the result of anxiety about new methodologies or fears about contamination from 'liberal theology'.

by its very nature seeks to rethink issues to bring clarity, nuance, and strength. Constructive theology, then, aims to move beyond classical formulations – at least as typically understood – and reveals something (re)new(ed). This is a *fundamental* responsibility of the theologian. This implies that Pentecostal theologians are tasked not merely to speak *for* the tradition, but critically *to* it by illustrating how doctrinal language and understandings ought to be at times revised for the strengthening of the tradition. In fact, the constructive theologian aims to do this type of work as an expression of their devotion and affection to/for the tradition.

Moreover, in what follows, I will at times seek to move beyond description and re-articulations of past understandings in a humble effort to bring greater clarity, nuance, and development to the Pentecostal theological tradition. Therefore, as a Pentecostal theologian, I sometimes speak *for* the tradition from within it, both for the sake of those within it and those beyond it. Yet, I also invite others beyond the tradition to speak *to* us, and from within the tradition, I will sometimes join in agreement with those who have spoken from beyond it. As has been expressed, this is an indispensable duty of the theologian. This chapter, then, at times searches for fresh, coherent, and balanced language aimed at bringing Pentecostal theology towards greater maturity and ecumenical potential. While this is perhaps inevitable since 'doctrines ought not and cannot be exact repetitions of

---

> Unfortunately, this fear is compounded by the fact that within certain parts of our movement, the tradition's theological positions have become fossilized so that much more effort is spent rehearsing long held opinions than sharing the work of constructive Pentecostal theology. Efforts to rethink certain issues, even when the rethinking results in stronger, more articulate, and better nuanced understandings of extraordinarily important doctrines, often are simply ignored if not met with criticism for complicating the issue. In addition to suspicion, this and other generations face the danger of jealousy. Part of the problem here results from the competitive spirit that has often been the hallmark not only of Pentecostal educational institutions but also of denominations within the tradition. It is this jealousy that so often makes it difficult to dialogue or support one another for fear of losing one's own place. What has often been absent in these situations is a leadership or, to use more biblical terminology, an eldership that seeks to nurture and empower those whom the Lord is raising up rather than protecting professional and ministerial turf. Sadly, these obstacles combine in ways that result in the loss of many of the tradition's best, brightest, and most dedicated individuals.

Thomas, 'Pentecostal Theology in the Twenty-First Century', p. 6.

past understandings',[24] my construction will be firmly rooted within and informed by the Pentecostal theological tradition, but also in conversation with the wider church.

C. The Spirit of Baptism

C.1 Pentecostalism, Baptism(s), and Acts

As suggested in Chapter 1, one of the reasons Pentecostals have struggled to develop a robust, developed theology of water baptism is its unclear and often confusing relationship with what some consider to be the 'crown jewel' of Pentecostal theology – Spirit baptism.[25] Typically, water baptism is understood to anticipate or foreshadow Spirit baptism. Within this framework, Spirit baptism is often understood to be the deeper reality, tempering water baptism's effect. However, Macchia rightly points out that Pentecostals are beginning to 'reconsider the significance of water baptism for Christian initiation and the gift of the Spirit'.[26] But the relationship has yet to be given a fuller treatment. This point, along with the intensifying pressures some of the older conceptions of Spirit baptism continue to face,[27] makes the need for a revisionary account of the relationship between water baptism and Spirit baptism even more necessary. As I mentioned earlier, this revisioning includes arguing for a theology of

---

[24] Kevin J. Vanhoozer, *The Drama of Doctrine: A Canonical Linguistic Approach to Christian Theology* (Louisville, KY: Westminster John Knox Press, 2005), p. 351. As Jenson puts it, 'precisely to be itself, the gospel cannot be said the same way twice'. See Robert W. Jenson, *Story and Promise: A Brief Theology of the Gospel About Jesus* (Eugene, OR: Wipf and Stock, 2014), p. 11.

[25] One might consider this claim is not supported by the realities of the global movement. Commenting on Spirit baptism and tongues among Pentecostals, David Barrett and Todd Johnson note that 'in practice today only between 5% and 35% of all members have practiced this gift, either initially or as an ongoing experience' (in Stanley M. Burgess (ed.), *NIDPC* [Grand Rapids, MI: Zondervan, 2003], p. 291.) Perhaps Steve Land's emphasis upon a distinctive spirituality is more faithful to this complexity than other projects. Further, Peter Althouse seems to suggest this possibility as well: 'I am not suggesting that Spirit baptism is the only distinctive, nor even the most prominent. Certainly healing, dreams, visions and prophecy are significant Pentecostal distinctives.' See Peter Althouse, 'Towards a Pentecostal Ecclesiology: Participation in the Missional Life of the Triune God', *JPT* 18 (2009), p. 244.

[26] Macchia, *Baptized in the Spirit*, p. 71.

[27] Shane Clifton, 'The Spirit and Doctrinal Development: A Functional Analysis of the Traditional Pentecostal Doctrine of the Baptism in the Holy Spirit', *Pneuma* 29.1 (2007), pp. 5-23 (5).

water baptism that emphasizes its relationship to the coming and indwelling of the Spirit, and a theology of Spirit baptism that emphasizes the Spirit's releasing and empowering of believers to embody their mission.

Most important to this discussion is the fact that Acts is widely considered to be by far the most popular book among Pentecostals and has been called the '*magna carta* of the movement's spirituality'.[28] Pentecostals have tended to appeal almost exclusively to Acts in arguing for Spirit baptism as the subsequent, fulfillment of water baptism. However, G.R. Beasley-Murray has noted that it is because of Acts and Paul's epistles that Christians should assert that 'baptism is the supreme moment of the impartation of the Spirit and the work of the Spirit in the believer'.[29] Thus, considering the number of scriptures that connect the coming of the Spirit with water baptism in Acts, Pentecostals ought to reevaluate the relationship.[30] Further, the separation of the Spirit's coming from water baptism has created an ecumenical stalemate. How might Pentecostals move forward?

Perhaps it is most prudent for Pentecostals to insist upon the primacy of Acts while also considering alternative and ecumenically viable readings. Yet if Pentecostals are to show an openness to alternative readings of Acts, it is sure to open many questions. Macchia is right: 'how one describes the work of the Spirit in conversion, baptism, Spirit baptism, and sanctification opens a hornet's nest of exegetical and theological issues'.[31] Though space will not permit me fully to outline and address all exegetical and theological issues that might arise as a result of such a re-reading of Acts, I aim to approach such a re-reading while remaining true to scripture and the Pentecostal tradition.[32] Such a reading would need to emphasize and draw attention to the various inflections that are of importance to Pentecostals. While I have attempted to provide some outlines for such a reading,[33] the Lutheran scholar Sarah Hinlicky Wilson who has

---

[28] Veli-Matti Kärkkäinen, 'Pentecostal Mission and Encounter with Religions', in Cecil M. Robeck, Jr., Amos Yong (eds.), *CHP* (New York: Cambridge University Press, 2014), p. 306.
[29] G. R. Beasley-Murray, *Baptism in the New Testament* (London: McMillan & Co, 1963), p. 275.
[30] Pinnock, *Flame of Love*, p. 125.
[31] Macchia, 'Tradition and the *Novum* of the Spirit', p. 47.
[32] Green, *Toward a Pentecostal Theology of the Lord's Supper*, p. 245.
[33] See Chapter 6.

234 *Washed in the Spirit*

participated in dialogues between Lutherans and Pentecostals might best provide the needed framework for Pentecostals to move forward.[34] Because Pentecostals understand there to be a relationship between the life of the Spirit and water baptism but are admittedly 'not entirely certain how',[35] Wilson's insights may well provide needed clarity.

C.2 Re-reading the Evidence: Dialoguing with Sarah Hinlicky Wilson

Sarah Hinlicky Wilson began ecumenical work with Pentecostals through the support of the Institute for Ecumenical Research in Strasbourg, France.[36] Significantly for this project, she has noted that perhaps one of the main differences between Lutherans and Pentecostals is their understandings of baptism. As a result, she has devoted space to provide an ecumenical reading of Acts that seeks to 'do justice to both Lutheran and Pentecostal interpretations of Acts and their experiences of baptism and the Spirit'.[37] Her reading, then, is particularly beneficial for our purposes.

In Wilson's reading, she asserts that rather than operating on the assumption that the purpose of Acts is to provide a 'normative template of experience to be repeated in later Christians', the purpose of Luke-Acts is to 'highlight the contrast between John's water baptism without the Spirit and Christian water baptism with the Spirit'.[38]

---

[34] Wilson's essay is just one potential reading that can assist Pentecostals in re-reading Acts from a sacramental perspective. See Wilson, 'Water Baptism and Spirit Baptism in Luke-Acts', pp. 476-501.

[35] Macchia, *Baptized in the Spirit*, p. 15.

[36] Sarah Hinlicky Wilson, *A Guide to Pentecostal Movements for Lutherans* (Eugene, OR: Wipf and Stock, 2016), p. xi.

[37] Wilson, *A Guide to Pentecostal Movements for Lutherans*, p. 35.

[38] Wilson, 'Water Baptism and Spirit Baptism in Luke-Acts', p. 476. Richard Jensen is also helpful here:

> The New Testament phrase 'baptism with the Spirit' needs closer investigation … the term occurs in only two connections throughout the entire New Testament. First, John the Baptist promised that after him would come one who would baptize with water and the Spirit … Secondly, Luke indicates the promise referred to by John was fulfilled on the day of Pentecost when the disciples were 'filled with the Holy Spirit'. The only other reference to 'baptism with the Spirit' is in Acts 11.16 where Peter interprets the Gentile Pentecost which he experienced with Cornelius by referring to John the Baptist's promise and the experience of the disciples at Pentecost … (Thus) what happened to them was unique, and that Christians after the Pentecost experience were baptized with

Therefore, Wilson aims to argue that John's baptism was taken up by Jesus and his disciples and transformed into something new and fresh: 'Luke's purpose is to show where the one baptism ends and the other begins – namely, in the giving of the Holy Spirit and the forgiveness of sins'.[39] Wilson subsequently demonstrates that this begins in Luke's first volume (Luke 3) when there is a critical distinction drawn between John's water baptism and Christian water baptism.[40] This distinction, according to Wilson, is a 'central concern for the Book of Acts and absolutely crucial to its understanding of both baptism and the Holy Spirit'.[41] She further observes:

> Luke goes to great trouble to emphasize the continuity of the water but the discontinuity of the Spirit in the two baptisms. He contrasts John's baptism with the Holy Spirit again and again. He will, however, make it difficult to determine an exact sequence of receiving Christian water baptism and receiving the Holy Spirit.[42]

In some instances, such as the Samaritan story (Acts 8), the Holy Spirit was exceptionally postponed to verify the legitimacy of the Samaritan's place in the church.[43] She notes that this is the only time in Acts that the reader hears of such a delay.[44] Conversely, texts such as Acts 10 expose a tight connection between the Spirit and water baptism. In fact, 'because the Gentiles have received the Holy Spirit, Peter, therefore, commands them to be baptized'.[45] Another contrast between John's baptism and Christian baptism surfaces in Acts 18.24-28 with Apollos, and then again in Acts 19.1-7 with the Ephesian disciples. In the case of the latter, the reader discovers that the purpose of John's baptism was repentance, though it did not bestow the Holy Spirit.[46] In response, Paul taught the Ephesians of the need to distinguish between baptism in Jesus' name and the baptism of

---

water in the name of Jesus for the reception of the Spirit. That is certainly the conclusion of the Pentecost narrative in Acts 2.37-39!

See Richard Jensen, *Touched by the Spirit: One Man's Struggle to Understand His Experience of the Holy Spirit* (Eugene, OR: Wipf and Stock, 2000), p. 36.

[39] Wilson, *A Guide to Pentecostal Movements for Lutherans*, p. 46.
[40] Wilson, *A Guide to Pentecostal Movements for Lutherans*, p. 36.
[41] Wilson, *A Guide to Pentecostal Movements for Lutherans*, p. 36.
[42] Wilson, *A Guide to Pentecostal Movements for Lutherans*, p. 37.
[43] Wilson, *A Guide to Pentecostal Movements for Lutherans*, p. 40.
[44] Wilson, *A Guide to Pentecostal Movements for Lutherans*, p. 40.
[45] Wilson, *A Guide to Pentecostal Movements for Lutherans*, p. 42.
[46] Wilson, *A Guide to Pentecostal Movements for Lutherans*, p. 45.

John.[47] Thus, she concludes that whatever the order, water baptism and the Spirit evidently fit together.[48]

Notably, Wilson's interpretations are similar to Simon Chan's: 'Christian baptism is unlike John's baptism in that it is Jesus' baptizing with the Spirit' and thus, 'the water ritual can be understood only in relation to the gift of the Spirit'.[49] Koo Dong Yun's work which engages ecumenical dialogues between Lutherans and Pentecostals[50] also notes that Lutherans tend to adhere to the Pauline account of baptism while Pentecostals follow the Lukan account in Acts.[51] For Wilson, this means that 'both parties have a valid point, and both have an incomplete one'.[52] Because Lutherans and Pentecostals both hold that Christian theology must be at root biblical, 'neither party profits from a restricted understanding of baptism according to one biblical account but not the others'.[53] The effort, then, is *not* to harmonize Paul and Luke, as Charles Hummel has accused James Dunn of doing,[54] but neither is it to speak of 'the two meanings of baptize in the Spirit', as Hummel himself falls into the trap of doing.[55]

Perhaps an alternative to these approaches reveals itself if we attend to the whole scriptural witness in all its seeming divergence, paying special attention to significant parts that have been mostly overlooked in the Pentecostal discussion. Perhaps the greatest benefit of

---

[47] Geoffrey Wainwright, too, has pointed out that often Pentecostals and 'charismatics' reduce 'Christian water baptism to the baptism of John'. Geoffrey Wainwright, *Doxology: The Praise of God in Worship, Doctrine, and Life* (New York, NY: Oxford University Press, 1980), p. 494 n. 271. Further, Richard Jensen notes that 'The New Testament teaches two baptisms. One is John's baptism. One is Jesus' baptism. One is a pre-Christian baptism with water and is a sign of human repentance. The other is a baptism with water and the Spirit and is a sign of God's presence and activity.' Jensen, *Touched by the Spirit*, p. 33.

[48] Wilson, *A Guide to Pentecostal Movements for Lutherans*, p. 42.

[49] Chan, *Liturgical Theology*, p. 119.

[50] Koo Dong Yun, 'Water Baptism and Spirit Baptism: Pentecostals and Lutherans in Dialogue', *Dialog* 43.4 (2004), pp. 344-51.

[51] Sarah Hinlicky Wilson, 'Spiritless Lutheranism, Fatherless Pentecostalism, and a Proposed Baptismal-Christological Corrective', *Pneuma* 34 (2012), p. 428 n. 29.

[52] Wilson, 'Spiritless Lutheranism, Fatherless Pentecostalism, and a Proposed Baptismal-Christological Corrective', p. 428 n. 29.

[53] Wilson, 'Spiritless Lutheranism, Fatherless Pentecostalism, and a Proposed Baptismal-Christological Corrective', p. 428 n. 29.

[54] Charles Hummel, *Fire in the Fireplace: Charismatic Renewal in the Nineties* (Downers Grove, IL: InterVarsity Press, 1994), p. 262.

[55] Hummel, *Fire in the Fireplace*, p. 182

Wilson's reading for Pentecostal usage is it does exactly that. Wilson's reading rightly focuses attention on Jesus' baptism as paradigmatic, while also giving weight to the importance of Acts within this discussion. While Wilson leads in this direction, she seems to miss an essential insight in support of her argument.

As commonly noted, Acts is divided into two parts. While the first part of the book is marked by a focus on Peter and the Jewish mission, the second half is marked by a focus on Paul and the Gentile mission. This intentional division by Luke might seek to illustrate the overall relational division between Peter and Paul (Acts 15). Yet, this divide is illustrated in other ways, as well. Suggestively for our purposes, Luke records Peter being filled with the Spirit at Pentecost, though Luke never records him being baptized in water. Conversely, Luke records Paul being water baptized, though never filled with the Spirit. The former seems surprising given Peter's commandment to be baptized following his Spirit filling (Acts 2.38), while the latter seems equally startling given Paul's baptism by Ananias following his pronouncement that God had sent him so that Paul may be Spirit-filled (Acts 9.17-18). Taken together, Luke seems to be suggesting that Peter and Paul – in their lives and their teachings – are trying to grasp the fullness of what has happened in Christ, each presenting a fragment of the whole.[56]

Supporting Wilson's overall argument, this general reading of Acts implies that the unity of water and Spirit that is seen in Christ's baptism should be understood as paradigmatic for the Christian. This privileging of Christ's baptism is also quite fitting given that Pentecostal theology is Christocentric. Held together, this overall framework reveals a possible way forward.

C.3 A Forgotten Paradigm: Jesus' Baptism as Archetype

Considerably, both early and contemporary ordinary Pentecostal theology look to Jesus' baptism as *the* overarching scriptural resource on water baptism.[57] The Catholic-charismatic scholars Kilian McDonnell and George T. Montague's landmark historical study of baptism in the Spirit, spiritual gifts, and sacramental initiation in the early church also reveals that if the 'baptism of Jesus in the Jordan was the

---

[56] In a forthcoming article, Chris Green gives a fuller treatment on the divisions between Peter and Paul in Acts.

[57] See especially Chapter 3.

central paradigm for the baptism of Christians, the expectation of spiritual gifts in the life of the Christian continued'.[58] However, at some point in liturgical history, Jesus' baptism was reduced.[59] In McDonnell and Montague's view, the loss of this tradition has been deprivation.[60] The historical study also reveals that as the baptism of Jesus has been overlooked, so was the expectation of the Spirit's power and gifts in the lives of baptized Christians.[61]

Though ordinary Pentecostal theological resources, such as early Pentecostal periodicals and contemporary Pentecostal lay voices, have often engaged Jesus' baptism, Pentecostal scholars and the wider Pentecostal theological tradition have tended to overlook Jesus' baptism as a theological resource for constructing theologies of water baptism.[62] This is especially strange considering how effectively Donald Dayton,[63] Steven Land,[64] and others have shown the Christological nature of Pentecostal theology to be.[65] The exception to this rule, however, is Daniel Tomberlin. He has rightly argued that 'Christian baptism has its precedent in the Jordan baptism of Jesus by John the Baptist'.[66] Perhaps Pentecostal theologians need to follow Tomberlin and early Pentecostals in privileging Jesus' baptism as the principal source for constructing our theologies of water baptism. By doing this, our constructions become more deeply Pentecostal,

---

[58] Wilson, 'Spiritless Lutheranism, Fatherless Pentecostalism, and a Proposed Baptismal-Christological Corrective', p. 427.

[59] Kilian McDonnell and George T. Montague, *Christian Initiation and the Baptism in the Holy Spirit: Evidence from the First Eight Centuries* (Collegeville, MN: Liturgical Press, 1991), p. 352.

[60] McDonnell and Montague, *Christian Initiation and the Baptism in the Holy Spirit*, p. 353.

[61] Wilson, 'Spiritless Lutheranism, Fatherless Pentecostalism, and a Proposed Baptismal-Christological Corrective', p. 427.

[62] As we will see, the major exception to this rule is Pentecostal scholar Dan Tomberlin. Macchia notes the possibility, but does not develop it: 'the challenge posed by the sacramental view of Spirit baptism is based in the observation that Jesus' reception of the Spirit at his baptism was paradigmatic of the connection between baptism and the reception of the Spirit among Christians'. See Macchia, *Baptized in the Spirit*, p. 73.

[63] Donald Dayton, *The Theological Roots of Pentecostalism* (Peabody: MA, Hendrickson Publishers, 1991).

[64] See Land, *Pentecostal Spirituality*.

[65] It is for this reason that John Christopher Thomas has suggested a five-fold paradigm for Pentecostal ecclesiology in general, and the sacraments in particular. See Thomas, 'Pentecostal Theology in the Twenty-First Century', p. 17.

[66] Tomberlin, *Pentecostal Sacraments*, p. 138.

considering the Full Gospel. Thus, Pentecostals need a re-examination of Jesus' baptism as *the* primary theological resource for a Pentecostal theology of water baptism.[67] As we look to Jesus' baptism, the relationship between water baptism and the Holy Spirit becomes much clearer.

According to the Gospel accounts, Jesus' baptism by John is both surprising and scandalous, for 'John preached the coming Christ as a baptizer, not a recipient of baptism'.[68] As John noted, Christ would baptize his people with the Spirit and fire, *not* that he would subject himself to be baptized in water. Yet, Jesus' insistence of being baptized against John's initial refusal signals Christ's subversive, astounding work. As a result, Jesus received the Spirit in power at his baptism.[69] Though Jesus' reception of the Spirit gestured towards his subsequent empowerment and equipping for mission, the result was much more expansive. In his own baptism, Jesus 'permanently united water with the Spirit as the concrete locus of the church's one Baptism'.[70] As G.W.H. Lampe observes, 'in the baptism of Jesus, as we have seen, the preparatory rite administered by John was, so far as the Lord himself was concerned, transformed into the expected Baptism with Holy Spirit'.[71] While in Christian baptism the *epiclesis* of the Spirit consecrates the waters, at the Jordan the Spirit did not consecrate the waters, for Jesus had no need.[72] Pentecostals are right on this point: Jesus is the sanctifier. It was the Spirit-anointed Christ who sanctified the waters. As Gregory Nazianzus has stated: when Jesus is baptized by John, Jesus 'sanctifies the Jordan'.[73]

What, then, does this mean for Christian baptism? It surely means that in Jesus' baptism, he inaugurated water baptism as the place

---

[67] This prioritizing of the Gospel accounts of Jesus' baptism is not at the expense of Acts and Paul's epistles, as my earlier readings of Rom. 6.1-11 and Acts 2.37-40 have shown (Chapter 6), but instead, it is my hope that this prioritization might serve as a bridge between the two and provide a fresh perspective with which to engage.

[68] Frederick Dale Bruner and William Hordern, *The Holy Spirit: Shy Member of the Trinity* (Minneapolis, MN: Augsburg Publishing House, 1984), p. 43.

[69] Pinnock, *Flame of Love*, p. 86.

[70] Bruner and Hordern, *The Holy Spirit*, p. 44

[71] G.W.H Lampe, *The Seal of the Spirit: A Study in the Doctrine of Baptism and Confirmation in the New Testament and the Fathers* (Eugene, OR: Wipf and Stock, 2004), p. 46.

[72] Kilian McDonnell, *The Baptism of Jesus in the Jordan: The Trinitarian and Cosmic Order of Salvation* (Collegeville, MN: The Liturgical Press, 1996), p. 67.

[73] Gregory Nazianzus, *Oration* 39.15.

where his people receive the Spirit.[74] Where Christ 'received the Spirit is where we receive the Spirit: in Baptism, in water'.[75] The One baptized in water and Spirit now baptizes his disciples.[76] Sergius Bulgakov, too, maintains that because 'in the life of the God-man ... baptism signified the descent of the Holy Spirit ... that is what it signifies in every human life'.[77] Since Christ received the Spirit as he was baptized in water, the promise is that we will receive the Spirit through water as he baptizes us.[78] Therefore, Pentecostals need not look farther than the waters of baptism to find the promise of John the Baptist: 'I have baptized you with water, but he will baptize you with the Holy Spirit' (Mk 1.8).

Looking at Jesus' baptism as the archetype for Christian baptism instinctively encourages us to see the relationship between Spirit and water baptism as intimately connected. In fact, one could argue that the connection between water and Spirit is best pictured in the connection between Jesus' divinity and humanity. The synergy between Jesus' humanity and divinity should not only be expressed Christologically, but ecclesiologically and sacramentally too. Like Chan, I find the Eastern Orthodox tradition a helpful dialogue partner on this point.[79] The synergy within Jesus of 'two wills and two operations taking place simultaneously',[80] is reflective of the divine-human synergy that is inherent within his church and his working through the sacraments.[81] While Pentecostals traditionally affirm the divine and human co-operation in the life of Jesus, we too often fail to affirm the communion of the synergy of the divine and human in his church and the sacraments. However, a robust theological understanding of Jesus' baptism beckons us towards this understanding.

By privileging Jesus' baptism, which is in keeping with Pentecostalism's own Christocentricism, it is quite fitting to assert that the Spirit is poured out in baptism.[82] Christian water baptism, established

---

[74] Bruner and Hordern, *The Holy Spirit*, p. 44; Robert W. Jenson, *Systematic Theology, Volume 2: The Works of God* (Oxford, Oxford University Press, 1999), p. 187.
[75] Bruner and Hordern, *The Holy Spirit*, p. 44
[76] Pinnock, *Flame of Love*, p. 119.
[77] Sergius Bulgakov, *The Comforter* (Grand Rapids, MI: Eerdmans, 2004), p. 302.
[78] Pinnock, 'The Physical Side of Being Spiritual', p. 15.
[79] Chan, *Pentecostal Ecclesiology*, pp. 1-144.
[80] Vladimir Lossky, *The Mystical Theology of the Eastern Church* (Crestwood, NY: St Vladimir's Seminary Press, 1976), p. 196.
[81] See also Sections D (The Baptizing God) and E (The Baptized Church).
[82] Chan, *Pentecostal Theology and the Christian Spiritual Tradition*, p. 90.

by Christ, 'moves beyond the water ritual to "Spirit and fire" (Matt 3.11)'.[83] Just as the writer of Genesis records the Spirit's hovering over the watery chaos at creation, the Spirit seeks to work new creation in the newly baptized. Participating in baptism by the Spirit, then, makes us truly human, like Christ. Baptism reinstates a human identity that has been disregarded.[84] Schmemann correctly notes that in baptism, 'the Holy Spirit descends on us and abides in us as the personal gift of Christ from His Father, as the gift of His Life, His Sonship, His communion with His Father'.[85] The bestowal of the Spirit at baptism is for spiritual renewal, rebirth, and making us in Christ. Bonhoeffer, too, rightly reminds us that 'the gift of baptism is the Holy Spirit. But the Holy Spirit is Christ himself dwelling in the hearts of the faithful.'[86] This is what it means to live a Spirit-filled life in Christ. The Holy Spirit is received in water baptism for the sake of the Christian becoming 'in Christ' (Rom. 6.3).

In the end, Pentecostalism suffers from the same mistake that troubles other contemporary Western Christian traditions: separating the indwelling of the Spirit from water baptism and relegating it to a subsequent rite: (1) The rite of confirmation, (2) Pentecostal conceptions of the doctrine of Spirit baptism, unlike the experience and practice, (3) the evangelical conflation of Spirit baptism with conversion and conversion with the moment of confessed belief,[87] all separate the Spirit from water baptism.[88]

---

[83] Hans Urs von Balthasar, *The von Balthasar Reader* (Medard Kehl & Werner Löser [eds.]; New York, NY: The Crossroad Publishing Company, 1982), p. 278.

[84] Rowan Williams, *Being Christian: Baptism, Bible, Eucharist, Prayer* (Grand Rapids, MI: Eerdmans, 2014), p. 11.

[85] Alexander Schmemann, *Of Water and the Spirit: A Liturgical Study of Baptism* (Crestwood, NY: SVS, 2000), p. 79.

[86] Dietrich Bonhoeffer *The Cost of Discipleship* (New York, NY: Simon & Schuster, 1995), p. 233. In support Bonhoeffer cites 2 Cor. 3.17; Rom. 8.9-11, 14; Eph. 3.16.

[87] Richard Jensen rightly asserts that 'conversion is another daily baptismal experience. Conversion could be defined as the daily practice of baptism, a daily death to self.' Jensen, *Touched by the Spirit*, p. 50. Conversion is a process incorporating our past, present, and future.

[88] Alex Mayfield has shown the similarities between the practice of confirmation and the classical Pentecostal understanding of Spirit baptism. He argues that both seek to 'empower believers for future service and to enter into a fuller ecclesial communion'. He also states that both are 'ritual expressions of the transjective experience of the Spirit'. See Alex Mayfield, 'Seal of the Spirit: The Sacrament of Confirmation and Pentecostal Spirit Baptism', *JPT* 25.2 (2016), pp. 222–41 (222).

Let me be clear: This does not imply that before one's baptism, the Spirit has been absent. The Spirit is always working preveniently.[89] Additionally, it is important to affirm that the Spirit is *not* changing, rather the Spirit is changing us in relation to God. Pinnock clarifies it well: 'It is not so much that the Spirit is tied to water as that baptism is part of a conversion complex in which the Spirit is received'.[90] Still, baptism seems to be the occasion when the Spirit comes.[91] In a sense, Oneness Pentecostalism is right to draw a closer relationship between the rite of baptism and the reception of the Spirit. It seems as if Oneness Pentecostals have more readily recognized the spiritual significance of the rite than trinitarian Pentecostals.[92] David Reed who has encouraged trinitarians towards 'theological dialogue' with Oneness Pentecostals on this point especially, states that trinitarians would benefit from 'a careful analysis of OP (Oneness Pentecostalism) *praxis*'.[93] The expectation to meet the Spirit in baptism is exactly right. As our earlier empirical data has shown, trinitarian Pentecostals often come to baptism with an expectation to meet God. Thus, these Pentecostal intuitions, along with Christian tradition and the scriptural witness of Christ's baptism, call us back to reconsider the strong relationship between water baptism and the Spirit.[94]

---

[89] Pinnock, *Flame of Love*, p. 167.
[90] Pinnock, *Flame of Love*, p. 167.
[91] Pinnock, *Flame of Love*, p. 167.
[92] Baker, 'One Lord, One Faith, One Baptism', p. 104.
[93] David A. Reed, 'Oneness Pentecostalism: Problems and Possibilities for Pentecostal Theology', *JPT* 5.11 (1997), p. 93. My emphasis.
[94] Surely some might ask, 'what are we to make of those passages in Acts which speaks of a two-stage initiation?' Michael Green points out two such passages: 'Acts 8 where the Samaritan believers did not receive the Holy Spirit immediately, and Acts 19 where a handful of disciples, who had been followers of John the Baptist declared themselves unaware of the existence of the Holy Spirit, but subsequently received him, spoke with tongues and prophesied'. Green also suggests a potential third – the conversion of Saul of Tarsus. While Green spends time discussing those three instances in detail, he also makes the general point that Luke 'appears quite uninterested in providing a theology of Christian initiation'. Therefore, 'those who have gone to him for tidy theological schemes have been disappointed. Sometimes reception of the Spirit follows baptism (e.g. Acts 2.38ff); sometimes it precedes baptism (e.g. Acts 10:44-48); and sometimes a man is baptized who has no part nor lot in the Christian thing, and whose heart is still fast bound to wickedness (Acts 8:21)'. Green concludes that

> it has often been observed that Paul is more interested in the interior work of the Spirit, assuring believers, transforming their lives, and so on; whereas Luke is more interested in the broader picture of the coming of the Spirit on the Church, his external manifestations in prophecy and tongues, and his direction

In Acts 1.5, Jesus reminds his disciples of John's words, 'for John baptized with water, but before many days you will be baptized with the Holy Spirit' (Mt. 3.11; Mk 1.8; Lk. 3.16; Jn 1.33). The promise at the Jordan was fulfilled 'when the Spirit which has "rested" on Jesus came and "rested" on them, and enabling them to speak in other tongues' at Pentecost.[95] And though the disciples experienced the infilling, Peter instructed the crowds to be baptized in water to receive the Spirit (Acts 2.37-39). The apostle Paul, too, reminds the Corinthian believers of their Spirit reception at baptism (1 Cor. 12.13). Indeed, as Paul exhorted the Romans, 'anyone who does not have the Spirit of Christ does not belong to him' (Rom. 8.9). Jesus' baptism, then, proleptically foreshadows Christian baptism throughout the NT. Baptism with the Holy Spirit, then, is not *only* a subsequent encounter for some Christians but an initiatory reception for all Christians.[96]

Therefore, agreeing with Robert Jenson, I think 'if there is to be any rite that bestows the Spirit, not for special churchly roles but simply for Christian life as such, it must be part of baptism, for that

---

of the Christian mission ... [Thus,] it would be certainly a mistake to try to base a doctrine of theological necessity upon passages in Luke's writing which were designed to describe the various stages which seemed to him significant in the spread of a work for God.

See Michael Green, *I Believe in the Holy Spirit* (Grand Rapids, MI: Eerdmans, 1975), pp. 133-39. As referenced in brief earlier, Sarah Hinlicky Wilson also highlights this point in reference to the Evangelical/Pentecostal debate on Luke-Acts:

In short, what struck me above all about this debate was its fundamental assumption that the purpose of the language about baptism and the Spirit in Luke-Acts is to provide a *template of experience* that is to be appropriated and repeated by subsequent Christians ... To the contrary: the primary concern of Acts is *not* to present a template of Christian experience ... Rather, the dominating intention of Acts is to narrate the ingathering of a sequence of communities from a state of alienation from God to a state of reconciliation to God, as we hear at the outset of the book in 1:8: 'But you will receive power when the Holy Spirit has come upon you, and you will be my witnesses in Jerusalem and in all Judea and Samaria, and to the end of the earth.' The individual or personal experiences – indeed, of power for witness! – are *illustrative* of the larger historical argument that Luke is making about the missionary movement of the good news of Jesus Christ. Illustrative but *not normative*.

See Wilson, 'Water Baptism and Spirit Baptism in Luke-Acts', pp. 477-79. Original Emphasis. For a Pentecostal argument for normativity, see Roger Stronstad, *The Prophethood of All Believers: A Study in Luke's Charismatic Theology* (JPTSup 16; Sheffield: Sheffield Academic Press, 1999).

[95] Green, *I Believe in the Holy Spirit*, p. 140.
[96] Green, *I Believe in the Holy Spirit*, p. 142.

is what baptism is supposed to do'.[97] Jesus' baptism affirms this. By moving such a direction in 'reclaiming the full theological import of the baptism of Jesus' in our practice and theology, Pentecostals can now 'hold together the things that (we) have allowed to fall apart'.[98] Thus, we might consider that the descent of the Spirit is inherent with Christian baptism.[99] Yet, this does *not* imply that Pentecostals should move on from subsequent experiences and releases of the Spirit. Perhaps 'receiving the Spirit in baptism is only the beginning'.[100]

D. Spirit Baptism as the Release of the Spirit of Baptism

D.1 Spirit Baptism: The Conception/Experience Distinction

As I noted earlier (Chapter 1), some Pentecostal scholars have begun reformulating Spirit baptism beyond its classical constructions since the doctrine is coming under growing pressure.[101] In response, Frank Macchia has attempted to expand the boundaries of Spirit baptism to include applications to the whole of the Christian life, looking forward to God's eventual cosmic presence.[102] In this expansion, Macchia asserts that 'the highest description possible of the substance of Spirit Baptism as an eschatological gift is that it functions as an outpouring of divine love. This is the final integration of the soteriological and charismatic. No higher or deeper integration is possible'.[103] For Macchia, Spirit baptism is a metaphor for life in the Spirit that is formed by God's love. And by offering a theology of glossolalia,[104] Macchia seeks to address the difficulties surrounding evidentiary language attached to the doctrine.[105]

---

[97] Jenson, *Visible Words*, p. 163.
[98] Wilson, 'Spiritless Lutheranism, Fatherless Pentecostalism, and a Proposed Baptismal-Christological Corrective', p. 428.
[99] Wilson, 'Spiritless Lutheranism, Fatherless Pentecostalism, and a Proposed Baptismal-Christological Corrective', p. 428.
[100] Pinnock, 'The Physical Side of Being Spiritual', p. 14.
[101] Clifton, 'The Spirit and Doctrinal Development', p. 5.
[102] See Macchia, *Baptized in the Spirit*, pp. 61-85.
[103] Macchia, *Baptized in the Spirit*, pp. 91, 257.
[104] See Frank Macchia, 'Sighs Too Deep for Words: Towards a Theology of Glossolalia', *JPT* 1.1 (1992), pp. 47–73; Frank Macchia, 'Tongues as a Sign: Towards a Sacramental Understanding of Pentecostal Experience', *Pneuma* 15.1 (1993), pp. 61-76.
[105] In another significant work, Aaron Friesen pairs qualitative and quantitative research methods to explore the Pentecostal doctrines of Spirit baptism and initial

Similarly, Simon Chan has suggested a sacramental view of the doctrine, which in his mind 'may be more useful in clarifying the nature of the Pentecostal reality'.[106] Like Macchia, Chan sees the need to revision the theology of Spirit baptism, but for Chan this means understanding Spirit baptism 'as a part of the larger tradition', which will enable Pentecostals to preserve the Spirit baptism experience.[107] In particular, Chan seeks to 'show that *glossolalia* which Pentecostals identify as "the initial evidence" of baptism in the Spirit is a rich theological symbol precisely because it is linked to a reality which is far bigger than the classical Pentecostal conceptualization of it'.[108] Thus, Pentecostals must construct a doctrine that gives weight to the *experience* of Spirit baptism for its long term survival.[109]

---

evidence. He understands a re-examination is necessary given the confusion and dissatisfaction surrounding both doctrines. His approach includes historical and empirical studies of three denominations: Assemblies of God, Open Bible Churches, and the International Church of the Foursquare Gospel. Friesen's findings are worth noting. First, he suggests the history of initial evidence doctrine is not and should never be understood as the whole history of classical Pentecostalism. Second, he suggests that the doctrine of Spirit baptism includes four functions for Pentecostals: it facilitates (a) the group's testimonies as a continuation of the testimonies given in Acts, (b) the group's emphasis upon deep encounters with God, (c) the group's distinct identity from other groups, and (d) the group's making of truth claims and helping guarantee the continuation of the doctrine's effects. Third, he found that despite the divergences over articulations of initial evidence and Spirit baptism, classical Pentecostals are unified in how they convey their experiences of the Spirit. Fourth, he found a correlation between charismatic manifestations and older, less educated ministers who held to initial evidence theory. While these findings might urge some to suggest a safeguarding of the traditional understandings of Spirit baptism and initial evidence, Friesen does not. Instead, he applies these insights to Pentecostal worship, identity, and doctrine, suggesting that classical Pentecostals avoid connecting their spirituality with initial evidence too tightly since Pentecostal spirituality is much broader. He also argues that the doctrine of Spirit baptism should be framed as a metaphor for a fresh life in the Spirit, which allows for further doctrinal reformulation without undercutting identity. In Friesen's mind, without rearticulating Pentecostalism's practice and beliefs surrounding glossolalia and Spirit baptism, the movement will continue to face decline and theological irrelevance. See Aaron T. Friesen, *Norming the Abnormal: The Development and Function of the Doctrine of Initial Evidence in Classical Pentecostalism* (Eugene, OR: Pickwick Publications, 2013), pp. 1-298.

[106] Chan, *Pentecostal Theology and the Christian Spiritual Tradition*, p. 54.
[107] Chan, *Pentecostal Theology and the Christian Spiritual Tradition*, p. 7.
[108] Chan, *Pentecostal Theology and the Christian Spiritual Tradition*, p. 13.
[109] Simon Chan, 'Evidential Glossolalia and the Doctrine of Subsequence', *AJPS* 2.22 (1999), p. 201. This assumes that there is a single, distinct experience of Spirit baptism. There is still much work to be done on whether people's experiences of Spirit baptism refer to a distinct, identical, and repeatable experience for all *or* whether Spirit baptism serves as a metaphor for multiple kinds of mystical and

As David Perry has noted, while scholars such as Macchia and Chan seek to expand Spirit baptism's boundaries, another methodological approach – exemplified by Shane Clifton and Joel Shuman – 'is to engage with the epistemological and methodological issues in an attempt to reframe the methodology employed for the explication of Spirit baptism'.[110] In Perry's work on Spirit baptism, he understands the doctrine to require a reassessment with a view to reflect critically 'on the meaning of the experience and its relevance to Pentecostalism today'.[111] Further, rather than needing more apologetic or biblical assessments of the doctrine, he sees the need for further 'theological reflection on the Pentecostal *experience* of Spirit baptism'.[112] His constructive contribution, then, is to reformulate and refocus the experience of Spirit baptism so that it can become central for Pentecostal spirituality while contending that the doctrines of subsequence, initial evidence, and empowerment for ministry are peripheral rather than core.

In an ecumenical assessment of the doctrine, Veli-Matti Kärkkäinen notes that out of all paradigms that seek to clarify the theological meaning of Spirit baptism in the context of Christian initiation, 'the most novel interpretation is provided by the Pentecostal movement'.[113] He states that within its classical scheme, 'Spirit baptism is a necessary and distinct category in the *ordo salutis* and cannot be removed or replaced by something else'.[114] Commenting further, Kärkkäinen asserts that Pentecostalism's 'separation of Spirit baptism from water baptism is both its strength and its liability'.[115] He sees that 'the benefit of the separation lies in the legitimate reminder to us that there are no necessary biblical nor theological (any more than pastoral) reasons to limit the charismatic breakthrough, even in

---

ecstatic experience of the Spirit. Daniel Castelo's recent work points in the latter direction. See Daniel Castelo, *Pentecostalism as a Christian Mystical Tradition* (Grand Rapids, MI: Eerdmans, 2017).

[110] See Clifton, 'The Spirit and Doctrinal Development', and Joel J. Shuman, 'Toward a Cultural-Linguistic Account of the Pentecostal Doctrine of the Baptism of the Holy Spirit', *Pneuma* 19.2 (1997), pp. 207–23.

[111] David Perry, *Spirit Baptism: The Pentecostal Experience in Theological Focus* (Leiden: Brill, 2017), p. 2.

[112] Perry, *Spirit Baptism*, p. 3. Emphasis original.

[113] Kärkkäinen, *Spirit and Salvation*, p. 395.

[114] Kärkkäinen, *Spirit and Salvation*, p. 395.

[115] Kärkkäinen, *Spirit and Salvation*, p. 399.

its occurrence, to baptism'.[116] Yet, conversely, Kärkkäinen believes that Pentecostals' 'categorically separating it from the wider framework of Christian initiation is also a liability because in the NT, particularly in the book of Acts, water baptism and Spirit baptism are clearly related'.[117]

In response, while Kärkkäinen has rightly noted a benefit to the Pentecostal doctrine, there are others. First, the Pentecostal emphasis upon subsequence naturally draws the believer towards living into the fullness of God throughout their lifetime. It suggests that the life of God is one that takes shape over time in 'a crisis-development dialectic'.[118] The Pentecostal *via salutis* commits one to a life moving towards 'righteousness, purity, witness in the light, love, and power of God'.[119] Further, the Pentecostal separation supports believers in understanding that they are both initiated into the community of God (baptism), and into the mission of God (Spirit baptism). As Kärkkäinen states, when it comes to incorporating the charismatic element in a holistic vision of the faith journey, the 'Pentecostal interpretation does it most robustly'.[120]

Yet, Kärkkäinen is right in noting the difficulty posed by Pentecostalism's separation of Spirit baptism from water baptism, although, it is perhaps more precise to understand it is as a 'limitation' rather than a 'liability'.[121] As Chris Green has pointed out, this separation has also caused some within Pentecostalism to embrace a 'posture of superiority and spiritual privilege'.[122] Amos Yong has also noted that this limitation has sometimes suggested 'that those

---

[116] Kärkkäinen, *Spirit and Salvation*, p. 399.
[117] Kärkkäinen, *Spirit and Salvation*, p. 399; See also Macchia, *Baptized in the Spirit*, p. 62,
[118] Land, *Pentecostal Spirituality*, p. 112.
[119] Land, *Pentecostal Spirituality*, p. 113.
[120] Kärkkäinen, *Spirit and Salvation*, p. 399.
[121] Further, Kärkkäinen's dependence upon the *ordo salutis* exasperates the issue. Kenneth Archer's emphasis upon the *via salutis* as a dynamic Spirit-led faith journey might alleviate *some* of his concerns. See Archer, *Nourishment for our Journey*, pp. 79-96.
[122] Green, 'The Spirit that Makes Us (Number) One', p. 20. For a few examples, Green also cites Frank Macchia, *Baptized in the Spirit*, pp. 27-32, 113-14; Wolfgang Vondey, *Pentecostalism: A Guide for the Perplexed* (London: T&T Clark, 2013), pp. 96-103; and Steven M. Studebaker, *A Pentecostal Political Theology for American Renewal: Spirit of the Kingdom, Citizens of Cities* (New York: Palgrave Macmillan, 2016), pp. 4-5, 224.

without such experiences are second-tier Christians'.[123] In responding to these pastoral issues, as well as Kärkkäinen's ecumenical concern, might there be a way forward that would preserve Pentecostalism's *strength* while minimizing its *limitations* in this regard?

As Perry aptly notes, Pentecostal scholars have used various methodological approaches to reformulate conceptions of the doctrine of Spirit baptism. However, all hold in common the desire to provide a fuller theological reflection on the Pentecostal experience of Spirit baptism. In paving a way forward, this is a move worth following and developing. Yet before proceeding, it is essential to clarify the differences and relationships between the (1) doctrine of Spirit baptism, (2) conceptions of Spirit baptism, and (3) experiences of Spirit baptism.

First, the doctrine of Spirit baptism is best understood to be a broad theological category for various dimensions of new life in the Spirit. Given its widespread nature, classical Pentecostalism also contains many varying conceptions of the doctrine of Spirit baptism that seek further to explain and articulate its meaning. There are also numerous and varying personal experience*s* of Spirit baptism.[124] While all related, these various categories better illuminate how we might best approach further reconsideration of Spirit baptism. Within this framework, I want to suggest that the best way to hold up Spirit

---

[123] Amos Yong, 'From Every Tribe, Language, People, and Nation: Diaspora, Hybridity, and the Coming Reign of God', in Chandler H. Im and Amos Yong (eds.), *Global Diasporas and Mission* (Eugene, OR: Wipf and Stock, 2014), pp. 253-62 (259). Clark Pinnock has stated that such discussion gives 'the impression that some Christians and not others are Spirit-baptized'. See Pinnock, *Flame of Love*, p. 169.

[124] In exploring aspects of Pentecostal experience by means of practical theology, Mark Cartledge has given a useful definition for experience by way of philosopher Caroline Franks Davis: 'An experience ... is a roughly datable mental event which is undergone by a subject and of which the subject is to some extent aware' (Caroline Franks Davis, *The Evidential Force of Religious Experience* [Oxford: Clarendon Press, 1989], p. 19.) Also significant for this project, Cartledge considers a theology of Spirit baptism as mediated through an experiential account. Since experiences do not take place in a vacuum, Cartledge seeks to place a Pentecostal testimony of an experience of Spirit baptism into dialogue with biographical, social, and contextual information. Cartledge concludes that the experience of Spirit baptism documented was not understood within a two or three stage Christian life process. Instead, 'if anything, it appears to be an event in a "punctuated process" rather than the second stage in a set of clearly defined stages'. See Mark J. Cartledge, 'Pentecostal Experience: An Example of Practical-Theological Rescripting', *JEPTA* 28.1 (2008), pp. 21-34.

baptism is to reformulate the conceptions of the doctrine by attending to its experiential reality. Put differently, I am suggesting that our *conceptions* of the *doctrine* need to do justice to our *experiences*. Thus, I am hoping to shift the way the doctrine is conceptualized to accentuate better its experiential existence.

In response, we might say that Pentecostal scholars are right in making a distinction between conceptions of the doctrine of Spirit baptism and experiences of Spirit baptism. As Tan May Ling has stated, 'precisely because this experience is credible, we need to reformulate to make it intelligible'.[125] To help bring clarity to the experience of Spirit baptism, Pentecostals must shape a conception of the doctrine that articulates both God's gifts and ecstasy while also lifting up his freedom and spontaneity. In fact, part of the task of Pentecostal traditioning is to formulate fresh, clarifying language for traditional, dynamic realities.

For our purposes, it is significant that no Pentecostal scholar to date has spent considerable time outlining what Spirit Baptism's reformulation means for water baptism. Since this project seeks to consider water baptism's close relationship to Spirit baptism, in what follows is an outline of a Pentecostal-ecumenical proposal on what this revisioning of water baptism might mean for Pentecostal conceptions of Spirit baptism. More particularly, I aim to explore possibilities emergent within the metaphor of Spirit baptism in relation to the experiences we have identified as Spirit baptism.[126]

---

[125] Tan May Ling, 'A Response to Frank Macchia's "Groans Too Deep for Words: Towards a Theology of Tongues as Initial Evidence"', *AJPS* 1.2 (1998), p. 4.

[126] Paul Fiddes is helpful here:

> The character of theology as a kind of worship should make clear that my appeal to a journey 'from experience to doctrine' must not be taken as meaning that human experience is a mode of access to God outside God's self-disclosure to us … it is not setting experience or nature *against* revelation. Nor is it taking the view that doctrinal concepts are merely a way of expressing some deep and mysterious dimension in human experience alone. Rather, our experiences of ourselves and others must always be understood in the context of a God who is present in the world, offering a self-communication which springs from a boundless love. It is this self-gift of God which already shapes both our experience of being in the world and our language with which we configure our experiences. In taking a path from experience to doctrine we are retracing a journey that God has already taken towards us.

Paul Fiddes, *Participating in God: A Pastoral Doctrine of the Trinity* (Louisville, KY: Westminster John Knox Press, 2000), p. 8. Original emphasis.

D.2 Spirit Baptism: Exploring Terminology

Even before Pentecostal scholars began reformulating Spirit baptism, considering the unique resources of their own spirituality and tradition, Catholic charismatics framed their new experiences of the Spirit in light of the Roman tradition. Speaking in the early 1980s, Pentecostal Russell Spittler noted that 'Roman Catholics, though the latest of the charismatics, have produced a more substantial theological literature in a half-generation than have their Pentecostal forbearers over the past three generations'.[127] Rather than Spirit baptism being an entirely new infilling of the Spirit, the Catholic charismatic interpretation understands it as a revitalization of the sacramental grace received at water baptism.[128] Receiving encouragement from Lutheran, Anglican, Presbyterian, and Baptist circles, this 'sacramental interpretation of Spirit baptism has received the strongest ecumenical support'.[129] However, I wonder if this view is not so much a sacramental interpretation of *Spirit baptism*, but rather a sacramental interpretation of *water baptism*, which emphasizes the Spirit's working in the rite and released experientially beyond it, but in connection to it.

Vondey has identified a 'fruitful theological reinterpretation of the sacramental view' through the work of Catholic theologian Heribert Mühlen, which might appeal to Pentecostals. Especially pertinent to our project, Mühlen identifies 'the baptism of Jesus as a prototype for the baptism in the Spirit'.[130] Vondey notes:

> the importance of his proposal for Pentecostal theology lies in his reformulation of the sacramental and liturgical framework, that is, the integration of Spirit baptism and a revised practice of the church. Mühlen views Pentecost as a historical continuation of Jesus's experience of the Spirit, a corporeal, objective inner occurrence in the life of Jesus, who hears the voice of the Father and sees the Spirit descend on him (see Mt. 3:16 – 17; Lk. 3:21 – 22). Jesus' baptism in the Spirit is the beginning of a personal, public, social, and communal ministry in words and signs (Acts 10:38)

---

[127] Russell P. Spittler, 'Suggested Areas for Further Research in Pentecostal Studies', *Pneuma* 5.2 (1983), p. 41.

[128] H.I. Lederle, *Treasures Old and New: Interpretations of 'Spirit-Baptism' in the Charismatic Renewal Movement* (Peabody, MA: Hendrickson Publishers, 1988), p. 105.

[129] Vondey, *Pentecostal Theology*, p. 94.

[130] Vondey, *Pentecostal Theology*, p. 98.

that also marks the origin of the church. The one who baptizes with the Spirit is himself baptized in the Spirit and releases at Pentecost the Spirit into the history of the church. Jesus himself illustrates with his baptism the proper human response to God's offer of the new covenant, which is continued in the church's celebration of the sacraments. Sacramentality is the human embrace of God's covenant on the inside manifested in outward observable signs that witness to the gospel ... Mühlen describes a renewal of the spirit as a 'charismatic sacrament' in which the 'charismatic graces are sacramentally offered'. The charismatic gifts of the Spirit are not mere external signs of internal experience but corporeal expressions of God's love and ecclesial expressions of grace through the Spirit. The baptism in the Spirit is consequently as much as a personal experience as it is an ecclesial event in which the individual and the churches are renewed from within to become open to all the gifts of the Spirit.[131]

Significantly, Vondey sees Mühlen's capturing of the soteriological dimension of Spirit baptism by developing its 'charismatic, ecclesial, and critical dimensions', and he believes it to resonate with the current Pentecostal reformulations of the doctrine.[132] However, Vondey does not wish for Pentecostals to shift from baptismal language and relate water baptism too closely with Spirit baptism, because he fears that it is unfaithful to Pentecostal theology. But perhaps, that is a mistake. Above all, Pentecostals must be faithful to the way scripture speaks. Shifting from baptismal language, in my view, is quite consistent with the revisioning efforts among Pentecostals scholars and also helps avoid confusion of two Christian baptisms, since the NT knows of only one.[133] Further, as previously

---

[131] Vondey, *Pentecostal Theology*, pp. 98-100

[132] Vondey, *Pentecostal Theology*, p. 100.

[133] In my view, two baptisms can only be spoken of when referring to the pre-Christian baptism of John and the Christian baptism with the Spirit. In reference to the author of Hebrews exhortation of 'his audience to "leave behind the basic teaching about Christ" (Heb 6:1), including, among various doctrinal matters, 'instructions about baptisms' (6:2), Nicholas Perrin is instructive:

> The phrase is curious, not least because it employs a plural as opposed to a singular form ... While it is possible ... that 'baptisms' in Hebrews 6:2 includes the notion of Christian-initiatory baptism, it could hardly have only this non-repeatable rite in view. It is arguable that the phrase 'instructions about baptisms' refers to focused teaching on the differences between Christian baptism

stated, identifying the Spirit with water baptism does not imply a doing away of subsequent experiences of the Spirit. As Kärkkäinen states, both the language and the bifurcation between water baptism and the indwelling of the Spirit are limitations in Pentecostal conceptions of Spirit baptism. To promote Pentecostalism's strengths while overcoming its limitations, we must heed Michael Green's suggestion that Pentecostals pay attention to the reality behind the imprecise description.[134] Put another way, Pentecostals must hold onto the 'genuine experience' behind the 'false linguistics'.[135] Again, I agree with Pinnock: 'the pentecostal reality is much more important than the terminology. It may be best to speak of spiritual breakthroughs as actualizations of our initiation.'[136]

Understanding the Spirit's relationship to baptism also helps Pentecostals stamp out the triumphalist impression 'that some Christians and not others are Spirit-baptized'.[137] Further, speaking of a release of our initiation in the Spirit helps encourage Pentecostals to fan into flame the gift of God that may be lying dormant (2 Tim. 1.6). Though the Spirit falls in baptism, the Spirit is realized in experience throughout a lifetime.[138] This leaves open and even encourages 'moments of renewal and releases of the Spirit'.[139] For surely 'growth is always needed in our relationship with the Spirit, so

---

and Jewish (and perhaps pagan) lustrations. Meanwhile, a minority position holds that 'baptisms' (Heb 6:2) refers to martyrdom (cf. Mark 10.38-39, Luke 12.50) (Lane 1991; 138; Cross 2002). While both options make excellent sense, given the context in which Hebrews was written, the former is preferable. After all, when the *auctor Hebraeos* in short goes to remark that 'it is impossible to restore again to repentance those who have once been enlightened, and have tasted the heavenly gift, and have shared in the Holy Spirit' (Heb 6:4), there are reasons to believe that said 'enlightenment' is Christian baptism (Hartman 1997: 125)'.

See Nicholas Perrin, 'Sacraments and Sacramentality in the New Testament', Hans Boersma and Matthew Levering (eds.), *OHST* (Oxford, U.K.: Oxford University Press, 2015), p. 64.

[134] Green, *I Believe in the Holy Spirit*, p. 146.
[135] Green, *I Believe in the Holy Spirit*, p. 146.
[136] Pinnock, *Flame of Love*, p. 169.
[137] Pinnock, *Flame of Love*, p. 169.
[138] Pinnock, *Flame of Love*, p. 173.
[139] Pinnock, *Flame of Love*, p. 169. This implies that 'earlier encounters with the Spirit call for a fresh infusion in water baptism, and later encounters should be viewed as occasions of release of the potentials of grace bestowed in the sacrament'. See Pinnock, *Flame of Love*, p. 124.

there is always subsequence, always more'.[140] As Chan has stated, Pentecostals need a better articulation of the doctrine and not its abandonment.[141] In many ways, this proposal follows Chan in suggesting that Pentecostals might want to consider having the 'prayer for the Spirit's filling to be carried out during the water baptismal ritual'.[142] This would 'certainly help to correct the mistaken notion that Spirit baptism is some kind of *superadditum*'.[143] By holding water baptism as the place of Spirit reception, Pentecostals might claim baptism to 'be an occasion of charismatic experience',[144] as is evidenced by passages such as Acts 19.5-6. Pinnock is correct in stating that 'the baptized should be led to expect to experience stirrings of the Spirit'.[145]

According to Michael Green, this helps 'make sure that we are not merely immersed in the Spirit' in our water baptism, but also 'in our lives'.[146] This is where Pentecostals excel: 'Pentecostals do validly call the church to the *experience* of Spirit baptism in life'.[147] Consequently, every Pentecostal should continue to expect Spirit breakthroughs throughout one's lifetime. Andrew Gabriel is enlightening in this regard: Just as Jesus was born of the Spirit, later filled with the Spirit at baptism, and 'yet subsequently received the Spirit from the Father after Jesus' resurrection', so the believer can have a subsequent experience of the Spirit after one is already filled with the Spirit'.[148]

D.3 Subsequent Experiences: Loosing the Spirit
In continuity with other Pentecostal scholars seeking to revision Spirit baptism, I am privileging the experience over the conceptions. Put another way, in this regard 'Pentecostal theology must still catch up to Pentecostal experience'.[149] In following this line of thinking, I have argued for a close relationship between the Spirit and water baptism, while also articulating Spirit baptism as a release of the Spirit

---

[140] Clark H. Pinnock, 'A Bridge and Some Points of Growth: A Reply to Cross and Macchia' *JPT* 13 (1998), p. 53.
[141] Chan, *Pentecostal Theology and the Christian Spiritual Tradition*, p. 93.
[142] Chan, *Pentecostal Theology and the Christian Spiritual Tradition*, p. 93.
[143] Chan, *Pentecostal Theology and the Christian Spiritual Tradition*, p. 93.
[144] Pinnock, *Flame of Love*, p. 167.
[145] Pinnock, *Flame of Love*, p. 167.
[146] Green, *I Believe in the Holy Spirit*, p. 147.
[147] Macchia, *Baptized in the Spirit*, p. 74. Original emphasis.
[148] Gabriel, 'The Intensity of the Spirit in a Spirit-Filled World', p. 381.
[149] Macchia, 'Tradition and the *Novum* of the Spirit', p. 46.

given/received in baptism. However, over-and-against other Pentecostal proposals, I have also argued for a revisioning of our language surrounding the latter experience since using baptismal language to refer to the subsequent experience of the Spirit can be confusing.

In seeking a way forward, I am following Daniel Castelo's lead in considering the 'family resemblance between Pentecostalism and Christian mysticism'.[150] For Castelo, what makes 'Pentecostalism a mystical tradition of the church catholic is its persistent, passionate, and widespread emphasis on encounter, which at some level is relatable through the language of union'.[151] Here I believe Castelo has captured the essence of experiences of Pentecostal Spirit Baptism. Castelo's reconstruction of 'Spirit-baptism along the lines of the Christian mystical tradition',[152] presents what he calls a 'scaffolding – a workable structure – with particulars on the table so as to display the kind of efforts that are needed to make the identification all the more secure'.[153] Thus, while Castelo does not provide a fully developed theology of Spirit baptism as a mystical, subsequent encounter with the Spirit, he does provide the outline and necessary direction for such a venture. While a full treatment is beyond the scope of this project, I want to suggest that Castelo's project has great promise for negotiating the relationship between water baptism and Spirit baptism.

Castelo's outline would imply that 'Pentecostals join a host of other Christians who believes in (among other things) exorcisms, miracles, and the active and present work of the Holy Spirit'.[154] Spirit baptism, then, can be expanded to include many ecstatic experiences of the Spirit following water baptism. As Land has pointed out, 'Christian initiation is not generally understood as terminal, and even the critics admit to subsequent sacramental actions and events which, however continuous with the initiation, are nevertheless decisive for ongoing development. Here Pentecostals, still very immature theologically, could learn with the critics in a discussion of the meaning

---

[150] Castelo, *Pentecostalism as a Christian Mystical Tradition*, p. 76.
[151] Castelo, *Pentecostalism as a Christian Mystical Tradition*, p. 80.
[152] Castelo, *Pentecostalism as a Christian Mystical Tradition*, p. 161.
[153] Castelo, *Pentecostalism as a Christian Mystical Tradition*, p. 161.
[154] Castelo, *Pentecostalism as a Christian Mystical Tradition*, p. 77.

and significance' of water baptism, confirmation, and 'Spirit baptism, for example'.[155]

Yet, a subsequent experience or release of the Spirit is not ontological. Since our 'life is hidden with Christ in God' (Col. 3.3), we cannot receive 'more' of the Spirit. Thus, in our lives with God, we are not moving from lack to fullness. Instead, by 'the Spirit' we are being 'transformed into the same image from one degree of glory to another' (2 Cor. 3.18). While the movement of new creation is a movement from nothing to something, the movement from Spirit baptism is a movement from something to something else. We are then moving from 'glory to glory' or put another way, 'fullness to fullness'. Because God is infinite, there is always more fullness in him to journey towards and experience. These subsequent relational/ecstatic/mystical experiences should not be understood as times of *receiving* more of the Spirit, but times of *experiencing* more of the Spirit's fullness. One does not receive the indwelling of the Spirit more than once, but one may be filled with the Spirit many times in terms of consciousness.[156] Following baptism, rather than stifling the Spirit (1 Thess. 1.19), we ought to allow the Spirit to be loosed and re-leased in our lives. In this way, our 'baptism in the Spirit is continually being renewed and realized'.[157]

By emphasizing the freedom of the Spirit's operations, we better underscore the fact that the Spirit blows how/when/where the Spirit chooses (Jn 3.8).[158] Rather than prescribing experiences into tight taxonomies, we ought to affirm the freedom of the Spirit's workings experientially. Consequently, we can be open to subsequent releases throughout one's lifetime. Theologically, this emphasizes God's autonomy, while also acknowledging our frequent temptation to constrain, limit, quench, or stifle the Spirit conceptually and experientially. Going forward, Pentecostals must loose God from our tight

---

[155] Land, *Pentecostal Spirituality*, p. 215.

[156] Pinnock, *Flame of Love*, p. 124. Further, 'We always need a release of the Spirit, a flowering of grace in our experience, new openness to the full range of God's gifts'. Pinnock, 'A Bridge and Some Points of Growth', p. 53.

[157] Pinnock, *Flame of Love*, p. 170.

[158] Since Christian theology's object is God and not human experiences, conceptions of the doctrine that seek to prescribe ordered spiritual encounters of the Spirit must be reconsidered. Might these conceptions imply that God is predictable and repetitive rather than free and spontaneous? Might there be a way to better clarify the relationship between God and our experiences?

dogmatic constraints. Chris Green is right in asserting that we need understandings of God that help us 'be filled, again and again, with the Spirit'.[159] In sum, this move seeks to affirm and clarify Yong's desire to see Spirit baptism understood as 'multiple deepening and intensifying experiences of the Spirit rather than only as "second" or "third" works of grace'.[160]

Castelo's outline assists Pentecostals in providing such a framework. It also does not threaten the distinctiveness of Pentecostal experiences. Castelo rightly suggests that 'if Pentecostalism is to be called a mystical tradition of the church catholic, it needs to be so within its own context and theology'.[161] He recognizes that understanding Pentecostalism as a mystical tradition means that it joins a greater tradition, yet he too argues that it can and should keep its own distinctive spirituality. For our purposes, this is an ecumenically viable option that seeks to minimize current limitations within many conceptions of the doctrine, while concurrently emphasizing its current strengths.

Therefore, now that we have proposed a fresh relationship between water baptism and Spirit baptism, we turn to look at how this revisioning might interact with theology proper, ecclesiology, and eschatology.

E. The Baptizing God (Theology Proper)

As Kärkkäinen has pointed out, 'on the basis of the New Testament data, baptism has both a human and a divine aspect'.[162] Thus, baptism is a 'divine-human act'.[163] In reference to the divine aspect, baptism 'is the visible sign of grace ... and the guarantee and presentation of God's justifying grace proclaimed is given to the believer'.[164] From the human side, it is 'the individual, spiritual and corporeal visible expression of faith',[165] or a 'confession of faith before the

---

[159] Green, 'The Spirit that Makes Us (Number) One', p. 24.
[160] Yong, *The Spirit Poured Out on All Flesh*, p. 119.
[161] Castelo, *Pentecostalism as a Christian Mystical Tradition*, p. 77.
[162] Kärkkäinen, *Hope and Community*, p. 379.
[163] Kärkkäinen, *Hope and Community*, p. 379.
[164] Küng, *The Church*, p. 272.
[165] Küng, *The Church*, p. 272.

community'.¹⁶⁶ Baptism, then, must speak both of the 'the electing grace of God and the personal acceptance of our vocation in faith'.¹⁶⁷

Nevertheless, it is important to qualify such statements, since this kind of speaking can too often lead to a type of synergism in which the human subject is depicted as 'contributing something of his or her own to the unfolding of salvation'.¹⁶⁸ In response, we must assert that God's action is not only always prior to ours, but also that our action is made possible by God's: it is God's gracious choice that enables our own. As Emil Brunner has stated, 'Baptism is not only an act of grace but just as much an act of confession stemming from the act of grace'.¹⁶⁹ History shows, though, that without also emphasizing the human aspect, baptism can become an opportunity for cheap grace.¹⁷⁰ Yet our current position is not any better. Unfortunately, Pentecostals have often associated baptism with subjective, cultural meanings which again prepares the way for cheap grace.¹⁷¹ Thus, when seeking to speak of baptism, we must 'find the means for talking more intelligibly about the interplay of divine and human agency'.¹⁷²

From my vantage point, Pentecostals have most neglected the divine aspect of baptism by avoiding the questions of divine agency. In short, Pentecostals need to address the question of baptismal efficacy by asking not merely what the ritual symbolizes or even what does or does not happen for the baptized, but 'what does God do in/through baptism?' In doing so, we cannot separate God's agency from his identity – or stated differently – we cannot broach the question of what God *does* without also talking about who God *is*. Green is right: Pentecostals 'need to develop adequate accounts of the doctrine of God that deals not only with the second and third articles of the creed and the mission of God, but also with the first article, and the life of God within and without creation'.¹⁷³

---

¹⁶⁶ Kärkkäinen, *Hope and Community*, p. 379.
¹⁶⁷ Bloesch, *The Reform of the Church*, p. 39.
¹⁶⁸ Bloesch, *The Church*, p. 157.
¹⁶⁹ Brunner, *The Divine-Human Encounter*, p. 128.
¹⁷⁰ Bloesch, *The Reform of the Church*, p. 36.
¹⁷¹ Bloesch, *The Reform of the Church*, p. 39.
¹⁷² Chris E.W. Green, 'Let it Be: Predestination, Salvation, and Divine/Human Agency', *JPT* 23.2 (2014), p. 189.
¹⁷³ Chris E.W. Green, 'Fulfilling the Full Gospel: The Promise of the Theology of the Cleveland School'. Paper presented at American Academy of Religion (MWRC session), Denver, Colorado. (Saturday, November 17, 2018).

Gregory of Nyssa rightly reminds us of the limits of such an exercise in our God-talk: 'it is not possible that that which is by nature infinite should be comprehended in any conception expressed by words'.[174] Arguing for the merits of an apophatic approach to realizing God, Green asserts that we are theologically led into this mystery of God-talk mainly through negation.[175] In other words, 'we can know who and what God is only by recognizing who and what he is *not*'.[176] Castelo, too, finds this approach to provide a way forward for Pentecostals.[177] Yet, John Polkinghorne fairly observes that 'the warnings of apophatic theology need to be heeded, but not to the extent of total paralysis of thought'.[178] Perhaps an alternative path between a theology mostly condemned to silence and another marked by overly confident positive statements about the divine nature is one that affirms 'that human talk about God is essentially analogical in character, using terms that are "stretched" in some direction appropriate to the divine infinity, but also in a direction that takes off from an appropriate human starting point'.[179] In my estimation, this overcomes the danger of using 'mystery' as a way of dodging genuine theological contemplation while also moving past the all-to-familiar alternative.[180]

For our purposes here, it is fitting to say that most supremely, 'God is Love'. 'This implies that love is not a "quality" or an "attribute" of God ... Rather, Love – that is, the love of which the Bible

---

[174] Gregory of Nyssa, *Against Eunomius* 3.5

[175] Chris E.W. Green, *Surprised by God: How and Why What We Think about the Divine Matters* (Eugene, OR: Cascade, 2018), p. 14.

[176] Green, *Surprised by God*, p. 14. Original emphasis.

[177] Castelo, *Pentecostalism as a Christian Mystical Tradition*, p. 129; Daniel Castelo, *Theological Theodicy* (Eugene, OR: Cascade Books, 2012).

[178] John Polkinghorne, 'Kenotic Creation and Divine Action', in *The Work of Love: Creation as Kenosis* (Grand Rapids, MI / Cambridge, U.K: Eerdmans/SPCK, 2001), p. 91. Further,

> an apophatic recognition of the ultimate mystery of the divine is an essential component in a faithful theology. Yet, if God has acted to make the divine nature known through the character of creation and revelation within history, as Christians believe to be the case, then kataphatic utterance is also a necessary part of the theological enterprise. Theologians should neither be too rationally over-confident nor totally tongue-tied.

See John Polkinghorne, *Science and the Trinity: The Christian Encounter with Reality* (New Haven, CT: Yale University Press, 2004), p. 90.

[179] John Polkinghorne, *Science and Theology: An Introduction* (Minneapolis, MN: Fortress Press, 1998), pp. 66-67.

[180] Green, 'Let it Be', p. 175 n. 13.

speaks – is the very Nature of God.'[181] In the NT, we find that the mission of Jesus is to reveal God's love.[182] Thus, this self-sufficient love is poured out to creation, revealing God's nature to humanity. As Brunner points out, 'on the basis of this self-revelation of God we have to make statements about His being not only as He is in Himself apart from this created world, but as He is also in relation to the world He has created'.[183] This gets to the heart of the question of God's agency. Perhaps it is best to say that in relation to creation, God has chosen to bind himself together with us and be in a lively relationship with his creation.[184] Certainly, this is because God is 'straightforwardly personal' and desires to *act* in cooperation with his creation, while always remaining sovereign over it and distinct from it.[185]

Within this framework, we can assert that in baptism, God comes to us and invites our coming to him. He has made it possible for us to participate with him through faith by creating such a possibility. Catholic theologian Herbert Vorgrimler reminds us that 'the original connection between faith and sacrament is so close that the question of whether faith is necessary for the carrying out of the sacrament must be utterly bewildering'.[186] However, this does not suggest that the effectiveness of the sacrament is determined by our faith – for our faith does not make the sacrament what it is. Rather, our faith enables us in realizing its effects. As Aquinas states, 'the power of the sacrament is from God alone'.[187] So, it is not as if God *needs* our faith or our prayers to act. Instead, it is more accurate to say that he *desires* them. Here we are in alignment with Augustine: 'God does not need to have our will made known to him – he cannot but know it – but he wishes our desire to be exercised in prayer that we may be able to receive what he is preparing to give'.[188] This kind of framework

---

[181] Emil Brunner, *Christian Doctrine of God: Dogmatics: Volume I* (Philadelphia, PA: Westminster Press, 1950), p. 185.

[182] Brunner, *Christian Doctrine of God,* p. 184.

[183] Brunner, *Christian Doctrine of God,* p. 247.

[184] Pinnock, *Flame of Love,* p. 45.

[185] Robert Jenson, 'Some Platitudes about Prayer', *Dialog,* 9 (1970), p. 64.

[186] Herbert Vorgrimler, *Sacramental Theology* (Collegeville, MN: The Order of Saint Benedict Inc., 1992), p. 83.

[187] Thomas Aquinas, *Summa Theologica, Tertia Pars,* Question 64, Article 2. https://www.newadvent.org/summa/4064.htm

[188] Augustine, *Letters,* Chapter 17.

relieves itself 'from momentary or mechanical conceptions',[189] for a personal and relational one. This is fitting, since 'salvation for Pentecostals is a relational, not a casual category'.[190] God invites our faith into the equation so that we may collaborate with him in realizing and receiving a gift only he can give. The Russian ascetic – Bishop Theophanes – puts it this way: 'the Holy Ghost, acting within us, accomplishes with us our salvation'.[191] Because of God's choosing, 'the relationship between baptism and human response is dynamic' and personal.[192] As I stated earlier, this is why the two forms of baptism – infant and believers' – together express the full meaning of baptism better than each would alone: while infant baptism testifies to God's gracious initiative, believers' baptism testifies to its deep connection with personal repentance and faith. Both forms together witness to baptism as a divine-human act.

Further, Amos Yong encourages Pentecostals to understand baptism as 'a living and transformative act of the Spirit of God' making baptism 'fully sacramental in the sense of enacting the life and grace of God to those who need and receive it by faith'.[193] Macchia, too, argues that divine action should never to be taken for granted since 'sacramental actions received in faith are granted participation by God in the bestowal of grace'.[194] Thus, because the baptizing God is a living and personal God, he desires to act in/through the sacrament in a way that benefits us as we trust in him.

In addressing more specifically what God does in baptism, the ecumenical document *Baptism, Eucharist and Ministry* states the following:

- Participation in Christ's death and resurrection (Rom. 6.3-11; Eph. 2.5-6; Col. 2.13; 3.1)

---

[189] Vorgrimler, *Sacramental Theology*, pp. 85-86.

[190] Clark H. Pinnock, 'Divine Relationality: A Pentecostal Contribution to the Doctrine of God', *JPT* 16 (2000), p. 12. Pinnock's description is well received. Perhaps it is important to note, though, that Pentecostals can develop relational models of God without adopting Pinnock's open theism. Nonetheless, Pentecostals ought to agree that the relationality that is 'implicit in Pentecostal spirituality needs to be made doctrinally explicit' (p. 23).

[191] Cited in Vladimir Lossky, *The Mystical Theology of the Eastern Church* (Crestwood, NY: St Vladimir's Seminary Press, 1976), p. 199.

[192] Kärkkäinen, *Hope and Community*, p. 381.

[193] Yong, *The Spirit Poured Out on All Flesh*, p. 160.

[194] Macchia, *Baptized in the Spirit*, p. 72.

- Conversion, pardoning, and cleansing (Acts 22.16; 1 Cor. 6.11; Heb. 10.22; 1 Pet. 3.21)
- The gift of the Holy Spirit (2 Cor. 1.21-22; Eph. 1.13-14)
- Incorporation into the body of Christ: The New Testament consistently testifies to the pattern of baptism after one becomes a Christian and thereby after one becomes a member of the local community
- Sign of the kingdom of God and of the life of the world to come[195]

God, then, uses baptism to enact his salvific work. Macchia puts it this way: 'the New Testament implies that water baptism is taken up by God so that it participates in the divine agency that incorporates us into Christ'.[196] Surely Pentecostals can assent to this ecumenical consensus by way of the Spirit. For Pentecostals, the efficacy of baptism is bound up with the Spirit.[197] Pentecostals ought to consider baptism to be 'a bath of grace in which the believer is spiritually cleansed in waters upon which the Holy Spirit, the Spirit of grace, is resting'.[198] Because in baptism God is both the giver and the gift, believers often testify to experiencing exorcisms and healings through the bath.[199] Early Pentecostals also found baptism to be an occasion of charismatic experiences.[200] Because the Spirit is active in baptism, we should not be surprised when charisms 'express themselves when the giver of the gifts is present'.[201] Moreover, because of God's self-giving nature, the baptized do not merely encounter God's gifts in baptism, but the baptizing God Himself.

---

[195] BEM-B, ##3-7. I am indebted to Kärkkäinen, *Hope and Community*, p. 379.
[196] Macchia, *Baptized in the Spirit*, p. 72.
[197] Pinnock, 'The Physical Side of Being Spiritual', p. 19. See also Tomberlin, *Pentecostal Sacraments*, p. 150: 'The Spirit resting upon the waters is the effective cause in water baptism'.
[198] Tomberlin, *Pentecostal Sacraments*, p. 138.
[199] Tomberlin, *Pentecostal Sacraments*, p. 151.
[200] See Chapters 3-5.
[201] Pinnock, *Flame of Love*, p. 167.

F. The Baptized Church (Ecclesiology)

From the beginning of the movement, ecclesiology was a central concern for early Pentecostals.[202] Within the last 25 years, Pentecostal scholars have put forth constructive ecclesiologies that have sought to integrate both doctrine and practice.[203] Yet, these proposals are by no means all agreeable. Various models have emerged, some advocating for a free-church model,[204] while others arguing for an episcopal paradigm.[205] From the episcopal wing, Dale Coulter has shown that some early sources offer 'a strong view of the church that approximates Catholic and Orthodox ecclesiologies'.[206] In a similar vein, Simon Chan has sought to construct a 'concept of the church as a spiritual, transcendent, and organic reality (mother church)'.[207] However, others such as Peter Althouse, have accused these projects as being 'overburdened by hierarchical assumptions and a High Church episcopacy that many Pentecostals would find disconcerting'.[208] Instead, Althouse opts for an ecclesiology reflective of the social model of the trinity. Further, Amos Yong has admitted that Pentecostals have at times 'drawn uncritically from the free-church tradition',[209] yet he believes the way forward is to opt for a 'low' church ecclesiology, over-and-against hierarchal models. For our purposes, I

---

[202] Dale M. Coulter, 'The Development of Ecclesiology in the Church of God (Cleveland, TN): A Forgotten Contribution?' *Pneuma* 29.1 (2007), pp. 59-85.

[203] Chris E.W. Green (ed.), *Pentecostal Ecclesiology: A Reader* (Leiden: Brill, 2016).

[204] Veli-Matti Kärkkäinen, *Toward a Pneumatological Theology: Pentecostal and Ecumenical Perspectives on Ecclesiology, Soteriology, and Theology of Mission* (Lanham, MD: University Press of America, 2002), pp. 81-146; Yong, *The Spirit Poured Out on All Flesh*, pp. 121-66; Althouse, 'Towards a Pentecostal Ecclesiology', p. 238.

[205] See Dale M. Coulter, 'Christ, The Spirit, and Vocation: Initial Reflections on a Pentecostal Ecclesiology', *PE* 19.3, pp. 318-39; Chan, *Pentecostal Theology and the Christian Spiritual Tradition*, pp. 15, 101 n. 11; Chan, *Liturgical Theology*, pp. 21-40. When it comes to Pentecostal ecclesiology, the traditional 'Wesleyan' and 'Finished Work' taxonomies are ill-fitting. Perhaps it is better to talk of 'the free-church wing' (Assemblies of God) and the 'episcopal wing' of Pentecostalism (Church of God, Cleveland, TN, and ICFG). Both Dale Coulter and Chris Green's findings seem to point in this direction. See Coulter, 'The Development of Ecclesiology in the Church of God (Cleveland, TN)', pp. 59-85; Coulter, 'Christ, the Spirit, and Vocation', pp. 318-39; Green, *Toward a Pentecostal Theology of the Lord's Supper*, p. 329.

[206] Coulter, 'The Development of Ecclesiology in the Church of God (Cleveland, TN)', p. 82.

[207] Simon Chan, 'Mother Church: Toward a Pentecostal Ecclesiology', *Pneuma* 22.2 (2000), pp. 177, 179.

[208] Althouse, 'Towards a Pentecostal Ecclesiology', p. 238.

[209] Yong, *The Spirit Poured Out on All Flesh*, p. 127.

hope to extrapolate ecclesiological insights from a theology of water baptism within this broad conversation surrounding Pentecostal ecclesiology. I will seek to tease out the inferred ecclesiology that is needed to support the current revisioning efforts. As Schmemann has pointed out, 'it is not "ecclesiology" that gives baptism its true meaning; it is rather in and through baptism that we find the first and fundamental meaning of the Church'.[210]

Baptism or 'incorporation into the body of Christ ... is a communal event' which means that 'baptism and the baptized person cannot be divorced from the community'.[211] While Pentecostals, along with Protestant counterparts, 'tend to think of themselves as making the church (as implied in such expression as "the church is made up of believers") rather than the church making them', this is a grave mistake.[212] This purely sociological understanding of the church has contributed to the symbolic view of baptism that conflicts with Pentecostal spirituality. Robert Jenson has rightly noted that any understanding of baptism is a function of the commentator's understanding of the church.[213] Yet, the inverse is also true: one's interpretation of the church is a function of the interpreter's understanding of baptism. Therefore, revisioning water baptism has natural implications for ecclesiology.

Thus, in following Chan, we must maintain that the 'expression "body of Christ" is not a metaphor for some social dynamics; it is an ontological reality that owes its existence to its inextricable link to Christ as its Head'.[214] This implies that 'the church is God's doing and we are baptized into it and nurtured by it'.[215] Since baptism 'incorporates new members into the body of Christ', the church is inherently communal.[216] Baptism expresses not individualism but an image of communal life.[217] This is perhaps one reason why Pentecostals ought to drop the term 'means of grace', since the term is often aimed at

---

[210] Schmemann, *For the Life of the World*, p. 68.
[211] Kärkkäinen, *Hope and Community*, p. 380.
[212] Chan, 'Mother Church', p. 177.
[213] Jenson, *Visible Words*, p. 136.
[214] Chan, 'Mother Church', pp. 177-78.
[215] Chan, 'Mother Church', p. 178.
[216] Simon Chan, *Spiritual Theology: A Systematic Study of the Christian Life* (Downers Grove, IL: Intervarsity Press, 1998), p. 112.
[217] Chan, *Spiritual Theology*, p. 112.

the individual experience.[218] Baptism, and by extension eucharist – are rites, which imply action. Rites accomplish and do things. Understanding baptism as a rite also gets us away from 'a narrow focus on the physical elements or the invisibility of the elements'.[219] To speak of baptism as a rite, then, implies that baptism is 'performed by a community and [is] embedded in the life of that community'.[220] As the rite of entry into the church, baptism expresses the character of the church – 'that is a community where racial, economic, and sexual divisions are dissolved (1 Cor. 12.12-13; Gal. 3.27-29)'.[221]

Yet, affirming the objective nature of the church should not lead to diminishing all social identity from the church. Just as we must steer from the 'extreme ideas' of baptism as a solely mechanical act, or a solely human act, the divine-human/human-divine nature of baptism must also be applied to the church.[222] This helps steer a revolutionary middle position.[223] Wolfgang Vondey has rightly depicted the church as both 'divine gift and human task'.[224] In much of the same way that baptism is a 'divine gift communicated through the Holy Spirit' and also 'a personal choice that leads to commitment',[225] so the church is an ontological reality that we are baptized into *and then* commissioned to participate in.

This reality is demonstrated by the NT uses of images and metaphors: the church is the 'body of Christ' (1 Cor. 12.27), 'the building of God' (1 Cor. 3.9), 'God's own people' (1 Pet. 2.9), 'the bride of Christ' (Eph. 5.23-32), while also a community called to be 'fishers of people' (Mk 1.17) and 'servants for Jesus' sake' (2 Cor. 4.5). We have been chosen and baptized into the household of God (Eph. 2.19; 1 Cor. 12.13), which requires each part choosing to act according to the Spirit's gifting (1 Cor. 12.14). Because of the Spirit of baptism, a 'revival of sacramentality' in the church makes way for a renewal of 'charismaticality' in the church.[226] Ordained ministers who

---

[218] Schmemann, *Of Water and The Spirit*, p. 143. Further, the term might imply that grace is a 'kind of substance or divine fluid' rather than 'God's gracious coming and dwelling with us'. Fiddes, *Participating in God*, p. 281.
[219] Leithart, *The Baptized Body*, p. 22.
[220] Leithart, *The Baptized Body*, p. 22.
[221] Leithart, *The Baptized Body*, p. 22.
[222] Kärkkäinen, *Hope and Community*, p. 381.
[223] Kärkkäinen, *Hope and Community*, p. 381.
[224] Vondey, *Pentecostal Theology*, p. 243.
[225] Kärkkäinen, *Hope and Community*, p. 381.
[226] Pinnock, 'The Physical Side of Being Spiritual', p. 14.

have received the laying on of hands by church elders (1 Tim. 4.14) must also act with their Spirit-given authority as leaders in the church. As Jenson has noted, 'as baptism is initiation into the believing community, ordination is initiation into a community within the believing community'.[227] This (Spirit) baptized church, then, is one marked both by charism *and* office. There must be 'a dialectic of charism and institution'[228] since the Spirit is offered to all in baptism, yet uniquely to officeholders through their ordination (2 Tim. 1.6-7).

This denotes that the ecclesiality of the church is *not* rooted in historical claims to apostolic succession,[229] but instead depends upon the Spirit's presence in the community of God in/through the Gospel and the sacraments. Both preaching and sacraments 'represent apostolicity as they go back to Jesus and the institution by the apostles'.[230] Luther rightly emphasized this about the church when he stated that 'it is the mother that begets and bears every Christian through the Word of God', and by implication, in relationship with the sacraments.[231] Consequently, baptism makes the church: 'since it is one of the divinely authorized practices by which the church exists as church, baptism is necessary to her existence'.[232] Yet, in the same way, baptism cannot exist without the church. Therefore, baptism must be grounded in the church and the church in it, at the expense of losing the meaning of both.

Ecclesiology is also (in)formed by *who* the church baptizes. As stated before:[233] this project seeks to move toward considering both infant and believer's baptism as parallel and acceptable practices.[234] Ecumenically, we can assert that while infant baptism testifies to God's gracious initiative, believer's baptism testifies to its deep connection with personal repentance and faith. No doubt Pentecostals will benefit from this move, since acknowledging both modes of

---

[227] Jenson, *Visible Words*, p. 188.
[228] Pinnock, *Flame of Love*, p. 140.
[229] The ecumenical document *Baptism, Eucharist and Ministry* provides a way forward: 'The primary manifestation of apostolic succession is to be found in the apostolic tradition of the Church as a whole'. See *BEM* 4.35.
[230] Kärkkäinen, *Hope and Community*, p. 304.
[231] Martin Luther, *The Large Catechism* (Minneapolis, MN: Fortress Press), p. 60.
[232] Peter Leithart, *The Priesthood of the Plebs: A Theology of Baptism* (Eugene: OR: Wipf and Stock, 2003), p. 173.
[233] See Chapter 6.
[234] Pannenberg, *Systematic Theology: Volume 3*, pp. 264-65.

baptism is historically justified and ecumenically beneficial.[235] Yet, from an ecclesiological perspective, some might consider this solution difficult to accept.

Surely strict proponents of infant baptism will not be satisfied. One might argue that if baptism incorporates people into the body of Christ, unbaptized infants are thus considered ecclesial outsiders.[236] Firm supporters of believer's baptism, too, will be displeased by the lack of the personal faith commitment within infant baptism.[237] Yet, implicit within both modes are inherent dangers: The danger of baptizing infants is that at its worst it becomes a 'social convention'.[238] What is regarded as 'important is not the electing grace of God' nor emergence of future faith, but rather 'the naming of the child'.[239] As a result, it becomes 'a rite not of new birth but of natural birth'.[240] However, 'the danger of insisting on believers' baptism, on the other hand, is that we might regard the human decision so highly that we forget God's enabling grace'.[241] Therefore, rather than deciding which 'danger is greater',[242] it is best to embrace both forms. This is consistent with my assertion – following Kärkkäinen

---

[235] See Chapter 4. Further, see Robeck and Sandidge's comments:

> Pentecostal groups that practice both infant and believers' baptism or allow for modes of baptism other than immersion may prove to be particularly useful in interchurch discussions on the subject of baptism. Those that we have identified within this article include the International Pentecostal Holiness Church, the Iglesia Metodista Pentecostal (Chile), the Iglesia Pentecostal de Chili, the Mülheim Association of Christian Fellowships of Germany, and the Yugoslavian Kristova Duhovna Crkva MalokrStenih. These Pentecostal groups appear to have been least affected by 'restorationist' thinking and biblical literalism and may, therefore, serve as primary links between many Pentecostal churches and the historic churches.

See Robeck, and Sandidge, 'The Ecclesiology of *Koinonia* and Baptism', p. 532.

[236] One solution might be to consider Paul's instruction that suggests the child of a baptized parent belongs to the Body of Christ simply by way of their birth (1 Cor. 7.14). See Oscar Cullmann, *Baptism in the New Testament* (Philadelphia, PA: The Westminster Press, 1950), pp. 43-45.

[237] Moltmann has stated that infant baptism has long been a part of establishing the Christendom-type 'state church' model. (Moltmann, *The Church in the Power of the Spirit*, p. 229.)

[238] Bloesch, *The Reform of the Church*, p. 35.

[239] Bloesch, *The Reform of the Church*, p. 35.

[240] Bloesch, *The Reform of the Church*, p. 35.

[241] Pinnock, *Flame of Love*, p. 126. In reference to believers' baptism, Pinnock continues: 'What about the mentally handicapped? Can God not work grace in the young and weak?'

[242] Pinnock, *Flame of Love*, p. 126.

– that baptism is 'divine-human act'.[243] Further, because salvation is a past (Eph. 2.8-9), present (1 Cor. 1.18), and future (Rom. 5.9) reality, allowing multiple forms of baptism speaks to the church's identity as an eschatological community on the salvific journey towards new creation. If allowed, holding to both together can testify to the fact that within any given community, people are in different places within the conversion complex. Perhaps Pentecostals can glean from the insights of Charismatic-Baptist Clark Pinnock:

> As a Baptist, I opt for the dedication of infants and water baptism later, as a practice that can preserve the elements we all wish to protect (anointing, dedication, renunciation, responsibility). On the other hand, infant baptism followed by real confirmation could have the same result … One might think of the Spirit as truly present in infant baptism, with the effectiveness unfolding gradually as the child grows in faith over the years … For all of us, however, baptism points to a lifetime of following Jesus, however performed and whoever the candidates. All the baptized are called to live in newness of life (Rom. 6.4).[244]

Certainly, as argued in the previous chapter, Pentecostals can honor God's working through both infant baptism and believers' baptism. Moreover, if infant baptism is to be practiced, Tomberlin has suggested Pentecostals understand it as prevenient grace.[245] In this way, baptism is 'proleptic, even prophetic'.[246] After all, baptism is prospective for all, 'even for adult converts, and its blessings are realized over a lifetime, not all at once'.[247] Therefore, practicing infant baptism 'with a view towards emergence of future faith' is the best way forward.[248] Though Pentecostals may continue to consider believer's baptism as the theological standard,[249] I urge Pentecostals to see that 'mutual recognition of baptism is … an important sign and means of expressing the baptismal unity given in Christ'.[250] For Pentecostal communities that choose to embrace both types of baptism,

---

[243] Kärkkäinen, *Hope and Community*, p. 379.
[244] Pinnock, *Flame of Love*, p. 126
[245] Tomberlin, *Pentecostal Sacraments*, p. 178.
[246] Tomberlin, *Pentecostal Sacraments*, p. 178.
[247] Pinnock, *Flame of Love*, pp. 167-168.
[248] Kärkkäinen, *Hope and Community*, p. 384.
[249] Kärkkäinen, *Hope and Community*, pp. 382-386.
[250] *One Baptism: Towards Mutual Recognition*, ## 93-95.

I suggest parents in discussion with church leadership should determine the timing.[251] Whatever form one embraces though, 'the relationship between water baptism and Spirit baptism should be kept'.[252]

In consequence, one crucial step in mutual recognition is for Pentecostals to discontinue rebaptisms. Baptism happens once (Eph. 4.5). Not only does the NT know nothing of repetitive baptisms,[253] but also it is ecumenically agreed upon.[254] Over the last few decades, Pentecostal scholars have already begun challenging the practice.[255] Even Karl Barth who (in)famously argued for believers' baptism never called for those baptized as infants to be rebaptized, nor did he seek to be rebaptized himself.[256] At the very least, Pentecostals could follow the suggestion of Cecil Robeck and Jerry Sandidge on accepting persons baptized as infants and *not* require rebaptism but, if desired, offer a service of renewal whereby baptism is understood to be appropriated afresh.[257]

G. The Baptized Cosmos (Eschatology)

As an eschatological gift, God uses baptism to save us (1 Pet. 3.21; Mt. 24.13). Baptism salvifically 'looks back in *mimesis* to the death and resurrection of the incarnate Christ' while also 'simultaneously looks forward in anticipation of the eschatological transformation of all creation'.[258] Therefore, the goal of salvation is cosmic in nature (Rom. 8.18-25). In agreement with Gregory Nazianzus, human beings are 'a second cosmos, a great universe within a little one'.[259] We then cannot think of baptism as merely a gift to humanity, but as a

---

[251] Kärkkäinen, *Hope and Community*, p. 387. For helpful comments on how clergy ought to discern with and prepare parents to fulfill the promises of infant baptism, see Jenson, *Visible Words*, p. 167.

[252] Pinnock, *Flame of Love*, p. 126

[253] As noted earlier, Acts 19.3-5 does not constitute a rebaptism, as these were disciples of John the Baptist had not yet been baptized in the context of Christian faith.

[254] BEM-B, #13.

[255] See Hunter, 'Reflections by a Pentecostalist on Aspects of BEM', p. 333; Robeck and Sandidge, 'The Ecclesiology of *Koinonia* and Baptism', p. 532.

[256] Karl Barth, *Letters, 1961-1968* (eds. J. Fangmeier and H. Stoevesandt; Grand Rapids, MI: Eerdmans, 1981), p. 189.

[257] Robeck and Sandidge, 'The Ecclesiology of Koinonia and Baptism', p. 38

[258] Althouse, 'Towards a Pentecostal Ecclesiology', p. 245.

[259] Grant Gillet and Arthur Peacocke, *Persons and Personality: A Contemporary Enquiry*, vol. 1 (Oxford: Basil Blackwell, 1987), p. 203.

gift to the whole of creation. Schmemann has appropriately remarked that 'baptism by its very form and elements – the water of the baptismal font, the oil of chrismation – refers us inescapably to "matter", to the world, to the cosmos'.[260]

In dying and rising with Christ in baptism (Rom. 6.3-4), we are rescued from the power of darkness, transferred into Christ's kingdom (Col. 1.13), and are brought into a new life in the new creation (2 Cor. 5.17). By way of God's action through materiality, baptism refers us to the eschatological, cosmic defeat of evil. This is well endorsed with the ancient church's baptismal liturgy, which included renunciations and exorcisms. Thus, the baptismal liturgy itself expressed the 'cosmic claim that God's power has vanquished the enemy'.[261] It is a claim 'not on souls alone, but on the totality of life, on the whole world'.[262]

Macchia has also noted that the opening of heaven 'at Jesus' baptism is a typical sign depicting an apocalyptic revelation'.[263] Further, the 'descending of the dove is reminiscent perhaps of the Spirit brooding on the waters of creation and the sign of new creation in the story of Noah'.[264] Jesus' baptism – and our participation in his baptism – then, looks forward to the renewal of all things. While Jesus' Jordan experience, and the biblical witness to it, is the foundation of Christian baptism, there are 'unique eschatological undertones in the complex of events at the Jordan that await fulfillment at the end of salvation history'.[265] This implies that 'the vision of Spirit baptism foretold by John the Baptist and depicted in Jesus' Jordan experience' in some sense, points to the 'final judgment and the final sanctification of the entire creation'.[266]

Macchia also notes that the baptized church can even 'participate in, and bear central witness to, the final sanctification of creation'.[267] Kenneth Archer helpfully describes how baptism allows the church to participate in this eschatological future:

---

[260] Schmemann, *For the Life of the World*, p. 68.
[261] Chan, *Liturgical Theology*, p. 118,
[262] Schmemann, *For the Life of the World*, p. 70.
[263] Macchia, *Baptized in the Spirit*, p. 86.
[264] Macchia, *Baptized in the Spirit*, p. 86.
[265] Macchia, *Baptized in the Spirit*, p. 86.
[266] Macchia, *Baptized in the Spirit*, p. 86.
[267] Macchia, *Baptized in the Spirit*, p. 86.

Water baptism also serves to point us to the ultimate goal of salvation – glorification and the redemption of creation. It is a promise that creates hope and reshapes our identity as we proleptically participate in the redemptive experience. We are the eschatological community of God, and, as this community, we function as a redemptive sacrament for the world – the body of Christ broken for the healing of the nations.[268]

The baptized church, then, receives promise, hope, and identity that propels us deeper into both the church *and* the world. Because the Spirit is uniquely present in the church in a way that the Spirit is not present in the rest of the world,[269] we must allow the Spirit to drive us out into the world, for its sake, as a Spirit-bearing, eschatological community. Peter Althouse helpfully reminds us that we are enabled by the 'Spirit to go into all nations of the world so that the world may be redeemed and gathered into eschatological glory'.[270] The final Pentecost – when the final 'deification of all creation'[271] occurs – is the fulfillment of the Pentecost at the Jordan and in the upper room Pentecost. The descent of the Spirit is always 'directed toward eschatological culminations'.[272] Therefore, one's personal Pentecost, whether experienced in baptism or following baptism, must find its meaning and direction in God's final Pentecost of new creation.

Consequently, part of living out one's baptism is to participate in the mission of God in bringing 'people, nations, and the whole world into the eschatological rain'.[273] This is certainly because the church's nature defines its mission. Since 'the nature of the church's existence is basically characterized by its orientation to the future and the beyond',[274] this makes the church's mission eschatologically focused on bringing renewal to all of God's creation. Therefore, the church's task is not to find out the world's agenda, nor even to set the agenda for the world; rather, 'the church *is* the world's agenda. What the world

---

[268] Archer, 'Nourishment for our Journey', p. 91.
[269] Chan, *'Mother Church'*, p. 198.
[270] Althouse, 'Towards a Pentecostal Ecclesiology', p. 236.
[271] Bulgakov, *The Comforter*, p. 278.
[272] Bulgakov, *The Comforter*, p. 278.
[273] Althouse, 'Towards a Pentecostal Ecclesiology', p. 234.
[274] Chan, *'Mother Church'*, p. 194.

is there to do is to provide the raw materials out of which God creates his church'.²⁷⁵

Just as Green states at the eucharist 'we are invited to participate in Christ's "here" and his "now"',²⁷⁶ so in our baptism, we can experience – whether perceived or not – God's glorious future. Just like the consummation is '*the* moment in which all moments, all events, are drawn not the light of the divine glory where they are truly known and perhaps mercifully remade', so in the sacraments, 'we already experience something of this transfiguration'.²⁷⁷ Therefore, while the future is something that God – and God alone – is bringing to bear *on* time, we are able to experience a foretaste of this transformation *in* time, through our baptism. Thus, baptism is an eschatological foretaste that transforms the church as people that are oriented towards the renewal of all things. Yes, our eschatological vision should focus on evangelism, but not exclusively. For as Green states, our missional *praxis* can also include, 'culture-making, creation care, attending to neglected or abused natural environments, and social-political engagement, seeking justice through peacemaking, creatively resisting and subverting the forces – the "principalities and powers" – that corrupt or destroy the structures of our life together'.²⁷⁸ Eschatological, missional practices must attend humanity *and* creation since God seeks to transform them both. Significantly, the form, element, and subject of baptism all point us in this direction as they testify to the rite's cosmic, eschatological orientation.

H. Conclusion

Though recently Pentecostals have begun laying the groundwork for the developing of a Pentecostal sacramentality that is shaped by Pentecostal concerns and resources, there has been little attempt to construct a Pentecostal theology of water baptism. Therefore, in this

---

[275] See Robert W. Jenson and Carl E. Braaten (eds.), *The Two Cities of God: The Church's Responsibility for the Earthly City* (Grand Rapids, MI: Eerdmans, 1997), p. 4. I am indebted to Simon Chan, 'Mother Church', p. 207.

[276] Chris E.W. Green, 'The Comings of God and the Goings of Time: Refiguring History, Eschatology, and Mission in Conversation with the Letter to the Hebrews', *JPT* 27.1 (2018), p. 44.

[277] Chris E.W. Green, 'In My Flesh I Shall See God: (Re)Imaginging Parousia, Last Judgment, and Visio Dei', *JEPTA* 33.2 (2013), p. 179 n. 17.

[278] Green, '"I am Finished"', p. 17.

constructive chapter, I have sought to do just that. Though resourced and oriented by prior chapters, I have sought to advance the conversation by engaging in critical conversation with ecumenical dialogue partners selected from the wider Christian tradition. In this constructive effort, I first dealt with the relationship between water baptism and the Pentecostal doctrine of Spirit baptism, arguing for a revisionary theology of water baptism that emphasizes its relationship to the coming and indwelling of the Spirit. Second, I put forth a revisionary theology of Spirit baptism that emphasizes the Spirit's releasing and empowering believers to embody their mission. Finally, I fleshed out what these revisionary accounts imply about the action of God in the ministries of the church and the world. The result has been an original contribution to Pentecostal scholarship, generally, and to the theology of the sacraments, more particularly, with the acknowledgment that there is still much left untouched and underdeveloped. In the following chapter, we will conclude our study on this note by spelling out the contributions and practical implications that have emerged from the study, as well as points of entry into areas for further research.

8

Conclusion

I began this study by asking the question: *What might a distinctly Pentecostal theology of water baptism look like?* In seeking to answer this question, I have provided a constructive account that has made use of contemporary ways of doing Pentecostal theology. Therefore, it is now important to review the general flow of the investigation while also outlining the contributions and practical implications that have arisen from the study, as well as points of entry into areas for further research.

A. Contributions

First, chapter 2 offers a fresh and novel methodology that synthesizes and develops contemporary ways of doing theology among Pentecostal scholars. As such, this monograph is the first of its kind in being a work of constructive theology that converges the contributions of early Pentecostal periodicals, contemporary Pentecostal 'field study' perspectives, scholarly ecumenical and Pentecostal voices, denominational statements, and engagement with key biblical texts. As stated prior, this method has made use of the strengths of various strands of Pentecostal scholarship, while avoiding common limitations associated with each. In particular, the ecumenical engagement makes it germane for the wider theological conversation, without becoming detached from its Pentecostal roots through the utilization of resources within the Pentecostal tradition. While the project engages scholarly voices – both Pentecostal and ecumenical – it also makes room for 'ordinary' lay voices – both historical and contemporary. It also avoids the pitfall of becoming overly 'abstract' by including insights from empirical congregational studies. The deliberate engagement with scripture also makes certain that the systematic theological work does not become disconnected from the biblical text. Therefore, this integrative methodology provides a model for constructive Pentecostal theological work.

Second, chapters 3-5 offer engagements of Pentecostal periodical sources, some that have yet to be thoroughly analyzed via a revisioning methodology. My engagement with Oneness sources, especially, adds much to the current conversation surrounding early Pentecostal sacramentality. In the course of my reading, while I discovered that early Oneness Pentecostals held to a sacramental understanding of baptism from the very beginning, I also discovered that, among trinitarians, while explicit statements on the rite's meaning tend to fit within a merely emblematic view of the bath, the majority of testimonies and reflections on baptismal experience disclosed an implicit sacramental understanding of baptism. Therefore, my findings reveal that early Pentecostals were not opposed to using sacramental language to describe their experiences and conceptions of water baptism.

Third, by seeking to discover the 'ordinary theology' of *early* denominational Pentecostals, the 'ordinary theology' of *contemporary* Pentecostals in particular denominational churches and, how these resources triangulate with the official denominational statements and scholarly denominational voices that discuss water baptism, I was able to explore the convergences and divergences between the various resources (chapters 3-5). Among other things, this approach enabled me to uncover a disjunction within trinitarian Pentecostalism's official theology of water baptism and their experiences of water baptism.

Fourth, my utilization of empirical research to resource a constructive project in chapters 3-5 is novel among Pentecostal scholars. As such, this project provides Pentecostal scholars a paradigm for how to place empirical theology into dialogue with systematic theology.

Fifth, chapter 6 provides rationale for a Pentecostal theological reading of scripture built upon and resourced by Pentecostal hermeneutical models. This chapter provides theological readings of two texts that were frequently referenced by early Pentecostals and later discussed with contemporary Pentecostals in my qualitative research. In this way, this project has provided further reasoning for the advancement of Pentecostal theological readings of scripture.

Sixth, chapter 7 explicitly outlined the role and responsibility of the Pentecostal theologian, providing needed justification for constructive theological projects from a Pentecostal perspective. Further, it also provided the most fully developed Pentecostal account of water baptism to date. Resourced and sustained by Pentecostal and ecumenical interchange, chapter 7 offers a distinctly Pentecostal theology of water baptism that is germane to the current ecumenical conversation surrounding sacramentality, in general, and water baptism, in particular.

B. Practical and Ecclesiological Implications

Considering the contributions of this study, what are the implications for Pentecostal spiritual life, ministry, and worship? While space does not permit me adequately to outline all relevant matters, I hope to provide contours of some constructive proposals for Pentecostal practice. Therefore, I want to suggest that this constructive contribution implies needed reformulations of and clarifications on the (1) baptismal practice, (2) baptismal liturgy, and (3) baptismal context.

B.1 Baptismal Practice

As this study has suggested, while pouring and sprinkling are not invalid modes, one might consider that they are deficient in embodying the true character of baptism as death, burial, and resurrection. This is especially pertinent to the discussion given the overall prominence of Rom. 6.1-11 as a scriptural resource among Pentecostals. Hearing early Pentecostal voices and engaging empirical sources also affirm immersion's overall significance and priority. For these reasons, I suggest immersion be the liturgical norm among Pentecostals. As Orthodoxy has shown, this does not exclude baptism of infants. Nonetheless, some Pentecostal churches that choose to embrace both infant and believer's baptism as equal and valid practices might desire another mode in baptizing infants. While I favor immersion, pouring is the best alternative, since it could give attention to the pouring out of the Spirit in baptism.[1]

---

[1] Bloesch, *The Church*, p. 158.

Further, given the trinitarian construction of this project, I recommend a trinitarian formula. Because the bath immerses us into the life of the trinity, a trinitarian structure should be represented. Further, a trinitarian formula also affirms that Christian baptism is a participation 'in Jesus' own experience in the Jordan, in which the Father and the Spirit figured prominently'.[2] A baptism done in the name of Jesus when identified within a trinitarian framework can also be considered useable, given qualification.[3] As I mentioned earlier (Chapter 6), the reason I do not call for a full affirmation of a Jesus' name formula as an equally legitimate formula is for ecumenical and hermeneutical reasons.[4] However, in seeking to honor trinitarian commitments and the continued dialogue with Oneness Pentecostals, trinitarian Pentecostals might consider the best way forward to be including 'Jesus Christ' within the trinitarian formula.[5]

This project has also urged Pentecostals to consider the legitimacy of both forms of baptism. Taken together, baptism of believers and infants express the full meaning of baptism – as God's gracious initiative and our repentant and faith-filled response. Though some Pentecostals may continue to consider believer's baptism as the theological standard,[6] I encourage Pentecostals to see that 'mutual recognition of baptism is ... an important sign and means of expressing the baptismal unity given in Christ'.[7] This also implies that Pentecostal churches ought to receive believer's baptized as infants into their fellowship, recognizing them as truly baptized Christians

---

[2] McDonnell and Montague, *Christian Initiation and Baptism in the Holy Spirit*, p. 19.

[3] As I mentioned earlier (Chapter 6), while trinitarian-Oneness Pentecostal dialogue is of vast importance among Pentecostals, trinitarian Pentecostals must also consider the ecumenical difficulties of moving away from the trinitarian formula. Further, given the widespread misunderstanding of trinitarian dogma at the lay-level, baptisms performed in Jesus' name within trinitarian Pentecostal churches could have the potential of producing even more confusion among the laity.

[4] I maintain that trinitarians rightly assert that references in Acts to baptism in the name of Jesus concern authority *not* formula. Further, it seems to me that in Acts, Luke is seeking to underline the contrast between Jesus' baptism with the Spirit with that of John the Baptist's without the Spirit. Within this reading, baptism in Jesus' name is not referring to formula.

[5] Baker, 'One Lord, One Faith, One Baptism?', p. 107

[6] Kärkkäinen, *Hope and Community*, pp. 382-86.

[7] *One Baptism: Towards Mutual Recognition*, ## 93-95.

and discontinue the practice of rebaptism altogether.[8] Baptism means beginning, and thus it is to be ever remembered but never repeated.[9] Thus, Pentecostals should cease the practice of rebaptism entirely.

Pastoral reasons might warrant some to consider how the church might care for the baptized who wish to express a fresh commitment to Christ and his church. Following the lead of several Pentecostal scholars, then, I suggest the sacramental act of footwashing as a way forward.[10] My recommendation is to recognize footwashing *as* baptismal renewal. Therefore, whereas, 'water baptism is presented as a single, initial event corresponding to the new birth; footwashing is presented as an oft-repeated event corresponding to the believer's need of continual cleansing'.[11] In my view, footwashing as a liturgical act presents untapped possibilities for Pentecostal worship, especially in relation to baptism. Fittingly for this project, Dan Tomberlin gives the following recommendations:

> Footwashing could be scheduled in conjunction with water baptismal services. After all baptismal candidates have been baptized 'for the remission of sins', the pastor could issue a call for repentance and offer an opportunity for penitent sinners to come to the altar, confess their sins, and have their feet washed by the pastor or other congregational leaders.[12]

---

[8] See Hunter, 'Reflections by a Pentecostalist on Aspects of BEM', p. 333; Robeck and Sandidge, 'The Ecclesiology of *Koinonia* and Baptism', p. 532.

[9] Michael Green, *Baptism* (Downers Grove, IL: InterVarsity Press, 1987), p. 120.

[10] The Christian practice of footwashing originates from John 13, where Jesus arises during the meal, takes off his outer garment, pours water into a basin, and washes and dries his disciple's feet (Jn 13.4-5). Peter's hesitation is met with Jesus' statement, 'Unless I wash you, you have no share with me.' (v. 8). Peter's request to then have his head and hands washed as well is met with Jesus' explanation that the 'one who has bathed does not need to wash, except for the feet, but is entirely clean' (v. 10). In response, John Christopher Thomas has convincingly argued that footwashing be understood as a sign of continued forgiveness of post-baptismal sins. Frank Macchia has also intimated that Pentecostals view footwashing as a link between baptism and the Lord's supper. See Vondey, *Pentecostal Theology*, pp. 65-66; Thomas, *Footwashing in John 13 and the Johannine Community*, pp. 148-49; Macchia, 'Is Footwashing the Neglected Sacrament?', p. 248.

[11] Tomberlin, *Pentecostal Sacraments*, p. 225.

[12] Tomberlin, *Pentecostal Sacraments*, p. 242.

Therefore, footwashing can serve as a sacramental act for the 'continual need of spiritual cleansing during the journey to the promise land'.[13]

Footwashing also provides other benefits within this context. As an extension of water baptism, it might further facilitate embodied forgiveness and 'various types of reconciliation' simply because it requires *touching* by 'exposing and contributing to the healing and restoration of the "other"'.[14] Lisa Stephenson rightly notes that the modern dread and disdain for footwashing reveals our current individualism and a lack of intimacy within our ecclesial communities.[15] In this way, footwashing does more than facilitate forgiveness of post-baptismal sin, but it also forms the church into a community marked by 'humility, self-denial, and voluntary poverty'.[16]

Finally, for Pentecostal communities that choose to embrace both types of baptism, I suggest Christian parents in discussion with church leadership should determine the timing.[17] The act of infant dedication can precede believer's baptism, while testimony and spiritual formation[18] – as a Pentecostal alternate to confirmation – can follow infant baptism. Whatever form one embraces though, 'the relationship between water baptism and Spirit baptism should be kept'.[19]

B.2 Baptismal Liturgy

Though Pentecostal worship is often thought to be improvisational and unscripted, Daniel Albrecht has effectively shown that

---

[13] Archer, 'Nourishment for our Journey', p. 92.
[14] Stephenson, 'Getting our Feet Wet', p. 167.
[15] Stephenson, 'Getting our Feet Wet', p. 165. Stephenson is worth quoting in full, here:

> Footwashing is intimate, but intimacy in and of itself is not what makes the rite difficult. Rather, it is the fact that the person washing one's feet or whose feet one is washing is a stranger. Implicitly, then, the absence of footwashing reveals a fundamental problem in the ecclesial communities: individualism. The Church lacks a sense of community in which the body truly considers each other as brothers and sisters. Persons avoid washing other people's feet because they do not want to touch the feet of strangers.

[16] Stephenson, 'Getting our Feet Wet', p. 170.
[17] Kärkkäinen, *Hope and Community*, p. 387. For helpful comments on how clergy ought to discern with and prepare parents to fulfill the promises of infant baptism, see Jenson, *Visible Words*, p. 167.
[18] See Jackie David Johns and Cheryl Bridges Johns, 'Yielding to the Spirit: A Pentecostal Approach to Group Bible Study', *JPT* 1 (1992), pp. 109-34.
[19] Pinnock, *Flame of Love*, p. 126.

Pentecostal worship is already, in some sense, liturgical.[20] Building on this insight, Chris Green has pointed out that 'Pentecostals are not so much anti-liturgical as anti-ritualistic'.[21] The question, then, 'is not whether Pentecostal worship is or should be liturgical, but only *how*'.[22] Because classical Pentecostal denominations have neglected in providing structures/liturgies of initiation for their churches, some scholars within the tradition have responded with their own proposals.[23]

Even so, no scholar has given thorough attention to baptismal liturgy for Pentecostal churches. In failing to provide baptismal liturgies for its churches, Pentecostalism has not provided adequate resources for robust traditioning and theological instruction. As our empirical field-study research has shown, ritual and liturgy shape beliefs and imaginations over time. Further, praxis is 'the fundamental locus of theology, the place where theology occurs'.[24] Ecclesial practices, then, should be viewed as the performance or acting out of one's theology. If we desire people in our churches to become properly (in)formed, we must be intentional about our rituals because of their shaping power. Without a written baptismal liturgy, each church is left to improvise their own way, thus communicating its meaning in conflicting ways. Though contemporary denominational sources neglect providing baptismal liturgies, early sources have indicated that the fathers and mothers of the tradition realized its value.[25]

---

[20] Daniel E. Albrecht, *Rites in the Spirit: A Ritual Approach to Pentecostal/Charismatic Spirituality* (JPTSup 17; Sheffield Academic Press, 1999). In his use of the term, Albrecht is clear that that 'liturgy' is not only a High-Church term. Of course, Pentecostals are not liturgical in the same sense that the Orthodox and Anglo-Catholics are. Yet, Albrecht has shown that Pentecostals have general patterns of worship that can be understood liturgically.

[21] Chris E.W. Green, 'Saving Liturgy: (Re)Imagining Pentecostal Liturgical Theology and Practice' in Mark Cartledge and A.J. Swoboda (eds.), *Scripting Pentecost: A Study of Pentecostals, Worship and Liturgy* (Surrey, England: Ashgate, 2016), p. 108.

[22] Green, 'Saving Liturgy', p. 108. Original emphasis.

[23] For example, see Chan, *Liturgical Theology*, Chapter 5.

[24] Clodovis Boff, *Theology and Praxis: Epistemological Foundations* (Eugene: OR, Wipf and Stock, 2009), p. xxi.

[25] As seen in our study, early Pentecostals often provided written or scripted liturgies for baptism. For instance, the 1911 *Constitution and General Rules of the Pentecostal Holiness Church* contains a baptismal charge to be prayed over baptismal candidates. See 'Constitution and General Rules of the Pentecostal Holiness Church' (1911), p. 22. Another example is from the *Bridal Call Foursquare*. As the periodical records, Aimee Semple McPherson supplied a scripted 'Prayer for Candidates' that was to be prayed over each baptismal candidate:

Therefore, following Chris Green, 'for the sake of conversation, then, let me propose a liturgical structure' for a Pentecostal celebration of water baptism, one that is both resourced by Pentecostal concerns and sensitive to ecumenical currents.[26] First, after inviting the candidate and the candidate's parents (in the case of infant baptism), the clergy would lead the candidate and/or the candidates' parents in the baptismal vows. Following the baptismal vows, the clergy would then speak directly to the candidate and/or the candidates' parents, highlighting that baptism is the moment when the Spirit is imparted, referencing Jesus' baptism. The clergy would then baptize the candidate using the following formula: 'In the name of the Father, the Son, Jesus Christ, and the Holy Spirit'. Immediately following the administration of the water, the clergy would anoint the candidate with oil, place his or her hands on the candidate's head, and invoke the work of the Holy Spirit.[27] Persons nearby, including baptized members of the candidate's family, may join the pastor in this action by extending their hands toward the candidate. Finally, in praying for the candidate, the clergy would be sensitive to the prophetic leading of the Spirit. Perhaps in some instances, the clergy might allow members of the church to speak prophetically over the newly baptized candidate.[28]

> Lord Jesus, bless these new candidates. Many of them are just newborn babes. Many of them gave their hearts to thee just recently yet we do not tremble Lord, for the eunuch was baptized the same hour he was converted and the Philippian jailor the same night. Lord, bless each of these. Even as we baptize them in water, do thou let the old time power fall on them in Pentecostal fullness for thy dear name's sake. Amen.

Further, not only did McPherson pray this over the candidates, but the candidates prayed that they would receive and be filled with the Spirit in water baptism, as seen in the 'Pledge of the Candidates':

> Dear Lord Jesus; I have made thee my Savior. Thou hast made me thy child. Just now I pledge my life – give my all to thee. The old life is buried and a new life begun; lead me by thy hand, dear Lord, and keep me in the center of thy holy will. Fill me with thy Spirit and make me a winner of souls for thy glory. Amen.

See *BCF* 11.1 (1927), p. 15.

[26] Green, *Saving Liturgy*, p. 115.

[27] Following Acts, it would behoove Pentecostals to reunite the coming of the Spirit with the bath and the laying on of hands.

[28] Here I am following Green's structuring of his liturgical proposal. See Green, *Saving Liturgy*, p. 115.

B.3 Baptismal Context

Finally, this constructive contribution has also indicated the need to refine the context of baptism. As this project has argued, the meaning of baptism as it appears in scripture includes several themes, among them being incorporation into the body of Christ (2 Cor. 12.13). Since Paul declares that baptism is membership into the concrete, historical church, we must beg the question: is it fitting for baptism to take place outside of this context? Resourced by this study, we must affirm that baptism should only take place in the church as the community of faith.[29] Since every baptism reaffirms the communities' faith and commitment to God and one another, baptism should always be celebrated and developed in the setting of the body of Christ.[30]

Since baptism is not a rite of personal expression – but a rite of the church – the location of baptism should not be altered for preferential reasons. Put another way, because baptism has objective meaning, it also has an objective location. Emphasizing the objective reality of baptism does not downplay the subjective necessity of personal surrender. Instead, it affirms that the subjective meaning finds its value in the objective reality. Individuals are baptized into the corporate body of Christ and each finds their identity not as a distinct person, but as a part of the whole (Eph. 4.4-6). Also, the role of the church in catechetical and doctrinal instruction also leads in this direction. Because baptism is connected to these ecclesial responsibilities, baptism ought not to be disconnected from the church. The church's responsibilities in baptizing and making disciples (Mt. 28.19) suggests that there is continuity between these assignments.

Therefore, all of this indicates that Christians should resist any effort to locate baptism outside the Christian *ecclesia*. Parachurch organizations and Christian schools/universities operate at their best when they support and not supplant the mission and rituals of the church. Baptism, then, should be the reserved rite of the Christian church.

---

[29] BEM-B, #12.
[30] BEM-B, #12.

C. Suggestions for Further Research

Finally, considering this study, several opportunities present themselves as points of entry for further research.

First, my research indicates that early and contemporary trinitarian Pentecostals often explicitly speak of water baptism in merely symbolic terms, though often implicitly hold to a sacramental understanding of the rite. Why is this so? What historical and theological reasons have aided in this confusion?

Second, Kimberly Alexander's monograph on Pentecostal healing and Larry McQueen's monograph on Pentecostal eschatology demonstrated differences in soteriology between early Wesleyan-Holiness Pentecostals and Finished-Work Pentecostals. Nonetheless, Chris Green's work on the Lord's supper has shown that no significant differences of sacramentality emerged among early Pentecostals. My own work on water baptism supports Chris Green's findings. Yet, my engagement with early Oneness Pentecostals found that Oneness Pentecostals held to a 'sacramental' understanding of water baptism from the very beginning. Yet, still more work needs to be done among early Oneness material to determine how widespread this was.

Third, my field study work among contemporary Pentecostals found great disagreement over the issue of authority to baptize. Not only does this expose confusion around baptism, but it also reveals a lack of clarity surrounding the rite of ordination. What might a Pentecostal theology of ordination look like?

Fourth, following Chris Green's suggestion,[31] it would be worthwhile to develop Pentecostal theologies of other sacramental rites that are significant to Pentecostal communities, such as footwashing and the laying on of hands by anointing with oil.

Fifth, this study has exposed the need for clarifications on baptismal liturgy and traditioning. Further work needs to be done on exploring whether Pentecostals can *tradition* a spirituality marked by high sacramentality and low formality.

Sixth, considering this study's suggestion that trinitarian Pentecostals draw a closer relationship between the Spirit and baptism, what implications might this have upon the current dialogue between Oneness and trinitarian Pentecostals?

---

[31] Green, *Toward a Pentecostal Theology of the Lord's Supper*, p. 328.

Seventh, it would be valuable to engage other Pentecostal fellowships outside of the USA context as well as examining other Pentecostal groups such as the Assemblies of God, Church of God (Cleveland, TN), Church of God in Christ, United Pentecostal Church International, and Open Bible Church.

Eighth, I wonder what other scriptural texts might be taken up to further this study? What might a theological reading of John 3 or 1 Peter 3 (for example) add to the conversation?

Finally, it would be beneficial for Pentecostals to explore other subjects utilizing the approach developed in this study.

BIBLIOGRAPHY

Early Pentecostal Periodicals

The Bridal Call (Echo Park Evangelistic Association, Los Angeles, CA)
The Bridal Foursquare (Echo Park Evangelistic Association, Los Angeles, CA)
The Christian Outlook (The Pentecostal Assemblies of the World, Indianapolis, IN)
The Pentecostal Holiness Advocate (The Pentecostal Holiness Church, Falcon, NC: Franklin Springs, GA)

Other Works Cited

Abraham, W., *Canon and Criterion in Christian Theology: From the Fathers to Feminism* (Oxford and New York: Oxford University Press, 1998).
Adewuya, J.A., *Transformed by Grace: Paul's View of Holiness in Romans 6-8* (Eugene: OR, Cascade Books, 2004).
Albrecht, D., *Rites in the Spirit: A Ritual Approach to Pentecostal/Charismatic Spirituality* (JPTSup 17; Sheffield: Sheffield Academic Press, 1999).
Alexander, D., 'Bishop J.H. King and the Emergence of Holiness Pentecostalism', *Pneuma* 8.1 (1986), pp. 159-83.
Alexander, K., *Pentecostal Healing: Models in Theology and Practice* (JPTSup 29; Blandford Forum, Dorset, UK; Deo, 2006).
Althouse, P., 'Towards a Pentecostal Ecclesiology: Participation in the Missional Life of the Triune God', *JPT* 18.2 (2009), pp. 230-45.
Althouse, P. and Robby Waddell, 'The Pentecostals and Their Scriptures', *Pneuma* 38.1-2 (2016), pp. 115-21.
Anderson, A. and Talmage L. French., *Early Interracial Oneness Pentecostalism: G.T. Haywood and the Pentecostal Assemblies of the World (1901-1931)* (Eugene, OR: Pickwick, 2014).
Aquinas, T., *Summa Theologica*. https://www.newadvent.org/summa/4064.htm
Archer, K., *A Pentecostal Hermeneutic for the Twenty-First Century: Spirit, Scripture and Community* (Cleveland TN: CPT Press, 2nd edn., 2009).
—'A Pentecostal Way of Doing Theology: Method and Manner', *IJST* 9.3 (2007), pp. 301-14.
—'Early Pentecostal Biblical Interpretation', *JPT* 9.1 (2001), pp. 32-70.
—'Nourishment for our Journey: The Pentecostal *Via Salutis* and Sacramental Ordinances', *JPT* 13.1 (2004), pp. 76-96.
Archer, K. and Andrew S. Hamilton., 'Anabaptism-Pietism and Pentecostalism: Scandalous Partners in Protest', *SJT* 63.2 (2010), pp. 185-202.
Archer, M., *'I Was in the Spirit on the Lord's Day': A Pentecostal Engagement with Worship in the Apocalypse* (CPT Press, Cleveland, TN, 2015).
Arrington, F., *Christian Doctrine: A Pentecostal Perspective, Volume Two* (Cleveland, TN: Pathway Press, 1993).
—*Christian Doctrine: A Pentecostal Perspective, Volume Three* (Cleveland, TN: Pathway Press, 1994).

Astley, J. and Leslie J. Francis (eds.), *Exploring Ordinary Theology: Everyday Christian Believing and the Church* (Farnham: Ashgate, 2013).
Augustine, *Against Julian* 1.7.33. https://www.newadvent.org/fathers/15091.htm
Baker, J., '"One Lord, One Faith, One Baptism"?: Between Trinitarian Ecumenism and Onenesss Pentecostals', *JPT* 29.1 (2020), pp. 95-112.
Barth, K., *Letters, 1961-1968* (ed. J. Fangmeier and H. Stoevesandt; Grand Rapids, MI: Eerdmans, 1981).
—*The Epistle to the Romans* (London: Oxford University Press, 1950).
Bauer, K., *Watery Grave: To Die is to Live* (USA: Kyle W. Bauer, 2016).
Beacham, A.D., Jr., *Light for the Journey: A Fresh Focus on Doctrine* (Franklin Springs, GA: LifeSprings Resources, 1998).
Beacham, P., *Primary Catechism: For the Home, Sunday School and Bible Classes* (Board of Publication of Pentecostal Holiness Church, Franklin Springs, GA, nd).
—*Advanced Catechism: For the Home, Sunday School and Bible Classes* (Board of Publication of Pentecostal Holiness Church, Franklin Springs, GA, nd).
Beasley-Murray, G.R., *Baptism in the New Testament* (London: McMillan & Co, 1963).
Bernard, D., *Essentials of Oneness Theology* (Hazelwood, MO: Word Aflame Press, 1984).
—The New Birth (Hazelwood, MO: Word Aflame Press, 1984).
Bonhoeffer, D., *The Cost of Discipleship* (New York, NY: Simon & Schuster, 1995).
Bloesch, D., *The Church: Sacraments, Worship, Ministry Mission* (Downers Grove: IL, InterVarsity Press, 2002).
—*The Reform of the Church* (Grand Rapids, MI: Eerdmans, 1970).
Boellstorff, T., et al., *Ethnography and Virtual World: A Handbook of Methods* (Princeton: Princeton University Press, 2012).
Boff, Clodovis., *Theology and Praxis: Epistemological Foundations* (Eugene: OR, Wipf & Stock, 2009).
Bridges Johns, C., *Pentecostal Formation: A Pedagogy Among the Oppressed* (JPTSup 2; Sheffield: Sheffield Academic Press, 1993).
Brooks, Noel., *The Biblical Basis for Missions* (Franklin Springs, GA: Advocate Press, 1976).
—*Ephesians: Outlined and Unfolded* (Franklin Springs, GA: Advocate Press, 1976).
—*Fingertip Holiness: Studies in Practical Holiness* (Muse Memorial Lectures, Southwestern Christian University, Oklahoma City, OK, 1975).
Bruner, F.D. and William Hordern, *The Holy Spirit: Shy Member of the Trinity*, (Minneapolis, MN: Augsburg Publishing House, 1984).
Brunner, E., *Christian Doctrine of God: Dogmatics, Volume I* (Philadelphia, PA: Westminster Press, 1950).
—*The Divine Human Encounter* (London, S.C.M. Press, 1944).
—*The Letter to the Romans: A Commentary* (Philadelphia, PA: The Westminster Press, 1959).
Bryman, Alan, *Social Research Methods* (Oxford: Oxford University Press, 4th edn., 2004).
Bulgakov, S., *The Comforter* (Grand Rapids, MI: Eerdmans, 2004).
Burgess, S., et al. (eds.), *DPCM* (Grand Rapids, MI, Zondervan, 1988).
Cartledge, M., *Charismatic Glossolalia: An Empirical Theological Study* (Aldershot: Ashgate, 2002).

—*The Mediation of the Spirit: Interventions in Practical Theology* (Grand Rapids, MI: Eerdmans, 2015).
—'Pentecostal Theological Method and Intercultural Theology', *Transformation* 25.2-3 (2008), pp. 92-102.
—'Pentecostal Experience: An Example of Practical-Theological Rescripting', *JEPTA* 28.1 (2008), pp. 21-33
—'Practical Theology: Attending to Pneumatologically-Driven Praxis' in Wolfgang Vondey (ed.), *RHPT* (London/New York: Routledge, 2020), pp. 163-72.
—*Practical Theology: Charismatic and Empirical Perspectives* (Eugene, OR: Wipf & Stock, 2003).
—'Renewal Ecclesiology in Empirical Perspective', *Pneuma* 36.1 (2014), pp. 5-24.
—'The Symbolism of Charismatic Glossolalia', *JET* 12.1 (1999), pp. 37-51.
—*Testimony in the Spirit: Rescripting Ordinary Pentecostal Theology* (Farnham: Ashgate, 2010).
Castelo, D., 'Charisma and Apophasis: A Dialogue with Sarah Coakley's *God, Sexuality, and the Self*', *JPT* 26.1 (2017), pp. 10-15.
—*Pentecostalism as a Christian Mystical Tradition* (Grand Rapids, MI: Eerdmans, 2017).
—*Theological Theodicy* (Eugene, OR: Cascade, 2012).
Chan, S., 'The Church and the Development of Doctrine', *JPT* 13.1 (2004), pp. 57-77.
—'Evidential Glossolalia and the Doctrine of Subsequence', *AJPS* 2.22 (1999), pp. 195-211.
—'Jesus as Spirit-Baptizer: Its Significance for Pentecostal Ecclesiology', in John Christopher Thomas (ed.), *Toward a Pentecostal Ecclesiology: The Church and the Fivefold Gospel* (Cleveland, TN: CPT Press, 2010), pp. 139-56.
—*Liturgical Theology: The Church as Worshiping Community* (Downers Grove, IL: IVP Academic, 2006).
—'Mother Church: Toward a Pentecostal Ecclesiology', *Pneuma* 22.2 (2000), pp. 177-208.
—*Pentecostal Ecclesiology: An Essay on the Development of Doctrine* (Blandford Forum, Deo Publishing, 2011).
—*Pentecostal Theology and the Christian Spiritual Tradition* (Eugene: OR, Wipf and Stock, 2011).
—*Spiritual Theology: A Systematic Study of the Christian Life* (Downers Grove, IL: Intervarsity Press, 1998).
Chaván de Matviuk, M., 'Latin American Pentecostal Growth: Culture, Orality and the Power of Testimonies', *AJPS* 5.2 (2002), pp. 205-22.
Chrysostom, *Homilies on Romans 10* in Gerald Bray (ed.), *Romans* Vol. VI of *Ancient Christian Commentary on Scripture: New Testament* (Downers Grove, IL: InterVarsity Press, 1998), pp. 153-54.
Clifton, S., 'The Spirit and Doctrinal Development: A Functional Analysis of the Traditional Pentecostal Doctrine of the Baptism in the Holy Spirit', *Pneuma* 29.1 (2007), pp. 5-23.
Coakley, S., *God, Sexuality, and the Self: An Essay 'On the Trinity'* (Cambridge, UK: Cambridge University Press, 2013).
—'Response to My Critics in the *Journal of Pentecostal Theology*', *JPT* 26.1 (2017), pp. 23-29.

Coulter, D., 'Christ, 'The Spirit, and Vocation: Initial Reflections on a Pentecostal Ecclesiology', *PE* 19.3, pp. 318-39.
—'The Development of Ecclesiology in the Church of God (Cleveland, TN): A Forgotten Contribution?', *Pneuma* 29.1 (2007), pp. 59-85.
Courey, D., *What Has Wittenberg to Do with Azusa?: Luther's Theology of the Cross and Pentecostal Triumphalism* (New York, NY: Bloomsbury T&T Clark, 2015).
Cullmann, O., *Baptism in the New Testament* (Philadelphia, PA: The Westminster Press, 1950).
Davis, C.F., *The Evidential Force of Religious Experience* (Oxford: Clarendon Press, 1989).
Dayton, D., *The Theological Roots of Pentecostalism* (Peabody: MA, Hendrickson Publishers, 1991).
'Declaration of Faith' (Los Angeles, CA: International Church of the Foursquare Gospel).
Duffield, G. and Nathaniel M. Van Cleave, *Foundations of Pentecostal Theology* (Los Angeles: L.I.F.E. Bible College at Los Angeles, 1983).
Dunn, J.D.G., *Romans 1-8* (Word Biblical Commentary; Dallas: Word Press, 1988).
East, B., 'The Hermeneutics of Theological Interpretation: Holy Scripture, Biblical Scholarship and Historical Criticism', *IJST* 19.1 (2017), pp. 30-52.
Ellington, S., 'The Costly Loss of Testimony', *JPT* 8.16 (2000), pp. 48-59.
Ervin, H., *Spirit Baptism: A Biblical Investigation* (Peabody, MA: Hendrickson, 1987).
Fiddes, P., *Participating in God: A Pastoral Doctrine of the Trinity* (Louisville, KY: Westminster John Knox Press, 2000).
Fowl, S. (ed.), *The Theological Interpretation of Scripture: Classic and Contemporary Readings* (Oxford: Blackwell, 1997).
Friesen, A., *Norming the Abnormal: The Development and Function of the Doctrine of Initial Evidence in Classical Pentecostalism* (Eugene, OR: Pickwick, 2013).
Gabriel, A., 'The Intensity of the Spirit in a Spirit-Filled World: Spirit Baptism, Subsequence, and the Spirit of Creation', *Pneuma* 34.3 (2012), pp. 365-82.
Gillet, G., and Arthur Peacocke, *Persons and Personality: A Contemporary Enquiry*, vol. 1 (Oxford: Basil Blackwell, 1987).
Green, C.E.W. '"The Body of Christ, the Spirit of Communion": Re-Visioning Pentecostal Ecclesiology in Conversation with Robert Jenson', *JPT* 20.1 (2011). pp. 15-26.
—'The Comings of God and the Goings of Time: Refiguring History, Eschatology, and Mission in Conversation with the Letter to the Hebrews', *JPT* 27.1 (2018), pp. 37-52.
—'"Does (Not) Nature Itself Teach You?": Pentecostal Reflections on a Troubled and Troubling Text', *Pneuma* 38.4 (2016), pp. 456-75.
—'Fulfilling the Full Gospel: The Promise of the Theology of the Cleveland School', Paper presented at American Academy of Religion, Denver, Colorado. (Saturday, November 17, 2018).
—'"I am Finished": Christological Reading(s) and Pentecostal Performance(s) of Psalm 88', *Pneuma* 40.1-2 (2018), pp. 150-66.
—'"In My Flesh I Shall See God": (Re)Imagining Parousia, Last Judgment, and Visio Dei', *JEPTA* 33.2 (2013), pp. 176-95.

—'In Word and Spirit: Critical and Constructive Reflections on Theological Method in the Work of Noel Brooks', in Marilyn A. Hudson (ed.), *Mosaic: Papers in Honor of Noel Brooks (1914-2006)* (Norman, OK: Whorl Books, 2012), pp. 3-27.
—'"Let it Be": Predestination, Salvation, and Divine/Human Agency', *JPT* 23.2 (2014), pp. 171-90.
—'The Music of God: Scriptural Interpretation as Aesthetic Performance' in William Oliverio and Kenneth J. Archer (eds.), *Constructive Pneumatological Hermeneutics in Pentecostal Christianity* (London: Palgrave Macmillan, 2017), pp. 103-19.
—*Pentecostal Ecclesiology: A Reader* (Leiden: Brill, 2016).
—'Prayer as Trinitarian and Transformative Event in Sarah Coakley's *God, Sexuality, and the Self*, *JPT* 26.1, pp. 16-22.
—'Provoked to Saving Jealousy: Reading Romans 9–11 as Theological Performance', *Pneuma* 38.1–2 (2016), pp. 180–92.
—*Sanctifying Interpretation: Vocation, Holiness, and Scripture* (Cleveland, TN: CPT Press, 2nd edn., 2020).
—'Saving Liturgy: (Re)Imagining Pentecostal Liturgical Theology and Practice' in Mark Cartledge and A.J. Swoboda (eds.), *Scripting Pentecost: A Study of Pentecostals, Worship and Liturgy* (Surrey, England: Ashgate, 2016), pp. 108-18.
—*Surprised by God: How and Why What We Think about the Divine Matters* (Eugene, OR: Cascade, 2018).
—*Toward a Pentecostal Theology of the Lord's Supper* (Cleveland, TN: CPT Press, 2012).
Green, J., *Body, Soul, and Human Life: The Nature of Humanity in the Bible* (Grand Rapids, MI: Baker Academic, 2008).
—'Commentary' in Kevin J. Vanhoozer (ed.), *DTIB* (Grand Rapids, MI: Baker Academic, 2005).
—*Practicing Theological Interpretation* (Grand Rapids, MI: Baker Academic, 2011).
Green, M., *Baptism* (Downers Grove, IL: InterVarsity Press, 1987).
Greene-McCreight, K., 'Literal Sense' in Kevin J. Vanhoozer (ed.), *DTIB* (Grand Rapids, MI: Baker Academic, 2005), pp. 455-56.
Gregory Nazianzus, *Oration 39*. https://www.newadvent.org/fathers/310239.htm
Gregory of Nyssa, *Against Eunomius*. https://www.newadvent.org/fathers/2901.htm
Hayford, J., 'Baptism' in *Hayford's Bible Handbook* (Nashville: Thomas Nelson Publishers, 1995).
Haywood, G.T., *The Birth of the Spirit: In the Days of the Apostles* (Christ Temple Book Store (Indianapolis, IN, nd).
Hollenweger, W., *The Pentecostals* (Peabody: MA, Hendrickson Publishers, 1988).
Hummel, C., *Fire in the Fireplace: Charismatic Renewal in the Nineties* (Downers Grove, IL: InterVarsity Press, 1994).
Hunter, H., 'Reflections by a Pentecostalist on Aspects of BEM', *JES* 29.3-4 (1992), pp. 317-45.
Jennings, W., *Acts* (Louisville, KY: Westminster John Knox Press, 2017).
Jenson, R., *A Large Catechism* (Delhi, NY: American Lutheran Publicity Bureau, 1999).
—'Some Platitudes about Prayer', *Dialog* 9 (1970), pp. 61-66.

—*Story and Promise: A Brief Theology of the Gospel About Jesus* (Eugene, OR: Wipf & Stock, 2014).
—*Systematic Theology, Volume 2: The Works of God* (Oxford: Oxford University Press, 1999).
—*Visible Words: The Interpretation and Practice of Christian Sacraments* (Philadelphia, PA: Fortress Press, 1978).
—*Touched by the Spirit: One Man's Struggle to Understand His Experience of the Holy Spirit* (Eugene, OR: Wipf & Stock, 2000).
Jenson, R. and Carl E. Braaten (eds.), *The Two Cities of God: The Church's Responsibility for the Earthly City* (Grand Rapids, MI: Eerdmans, 1997).
Johns, J.D. and Cheryl Bridges Johns, 'Yielding to the Spirit: A Pentecostal Approach to Group Bible Study', *JPT* 1 (1992), pp. 109-34.
Johnson, B., 'On Pentecostals and Pentecostal Theology: An Interview with Walter Brueggemann', *Pneuma* 38.1-2 (2016), pp. 123-47.
Johnson, L., *Reading Romans: A Literary and Theological Commentary* (Macon, GA: Smyth & Helwys Publishing, 2001).
Kärkkäinen, V.M., *Hope and Community* (Grand Rapids, MI: Eerdmans, 2017).
—'Pentecostal Mission and Encounter with Religions' in Cecil M. Robeck, Jr. and Amos Yong (eds.), *The Cambridge Handbook to Pentecostalism* (New York: Cambridge University Press, 2014), pp. 294-312.
—*Spirit and Salvation* (Grand Rapids, MI: Eerdmans, 2016).
—*Toward a Pneumatological Theology: Pentecostal and Ecumenical Perspectives on Ecclesiology, Soteriology, and Theology of Mission* (Lanham, MD: University Press of America, 2002).
Kay, W., 'Concluding Reflections' in John Christopher Thomas, (ed.), *Toward a Pentecostal Ecclesiology: The Church and the Fivefold Gospel* (Cleveland, TN: CPT Press, 2010), pp. 283-90.
Keener, C., *Acts, Volume 1: An Exegetical Commentary* (Grand Rapids, MI: Baker Academic, 2012).
—*Romans* (Eugene, OR: Cascade, 2009).
King, J.H., *From Passover to Pentecost* (Franklin Springs, GA: LifeSprings Resources, 2004).
—*Yet Speaketh* (Franklin Springs, GA: The Publishing House of the Pentecostal Holiness Church, 1949)
Kozinets, R., *Netnography: Doing Ethnographic Research Online* (Los Angeles, CA: Sage, 2013).
Küng, Hans., *On Being a Christian* (New York: Wallaby, 1968).
—*The Church* (New York: Image Books, 1976).
Lampe, G.W.H., *The Seal of the Spirit: A Study in the Doctrine of Baptism and Confirmation in the New Testament and the Fathers* (Eugene, OR: Wipf & Stock, 2004).
Lancaster, J., 'The Ordinances', in P.S. Brewster (ed.), *Pentecostal Doctrines* (Cheltenham: Elim, 1976), pp. 79-92.
Land, S., *Pentecostal Spirituality: A Passion for the Kingdom* (JPTSup 1: Sheffield, Sheffield Academic Press, 1993).
Lederle, H.I., *Treasures Old and New: Interpretations of 'Spirit-Baptism' in the Charismatic Renewal Movement* (Peabody, MA: Hendrickson Publishers, 1988).
Leithart, P., *1&2 Kings* (Grand Rapids, MI: Brazos Press, 2006).

—*The Baptized Body* (Moscow, ID: Canon Press, 2007).
—*The Priesthood of the Plebs: A Theology of Baptism* (Eugene: OR: Wipf & Stock, 2003).
Lewis, P., 'Reflections on a Hundred Years of Pentecostal Theology', *CJPCR* 12 (February 2003): http://www.pctii.org/cyberj/cyberj12/lewis.html
Ling, T.M., 'A Response to Frank Macchia's "Groans Too Deep for Words: Towards a Theology of Tongues as Initial Evidence"', *AJPS* 1.2 (1998), pp. 175-83.
Lossky, V., *The Mystical Theology of the Eastern Church* (Crestwood, NY: St Vladimir's Seminary Press, 1976).
Luther, M., *Lectures on Romans* (Philadelphia: Westminster, 1961).
—*The Large Catechism* (Minneapolis, MN: Fortress Press, 1959).
Macchia, F., *Baptized in the Spirit: A Global Pentecostal Theology* (Grand Rapids, MI: Zondervan, 2006).
—'Is Footwashing the Neglected Sacrament? A Theological Response to John Christopher Thomas', *Pneuma* 19.2 (1997), pp. 239-49.
—*Jesus the Spirit Baptizer: Christology in Light of Pentecost* (Grand Rapids, MI: Eerdmans, 2018).
—'The Kingdom and the Power: Spirit Baptism in Ecumenical and Pentecostal Perspective' in Michael Welker (ed.), *The Work of the Spirit* (Grand Rapids, MI: Eerdmans, 2006), pp. 109-25.
—'The Oneness-Trinitarian Pentecostal Dialogue: Exploring the Diversity of Apostolic Faith', *HTR* 103.3 (2010), pp. 329-49.
—'Sighs Too Deep for Words: Towards a Theology of Glossolalia', *JPT* 1.1 (1992), pp. 47–73.
—'Tongues as a Sign: Towards a Sacramental Understanding of Pentecostal Experience', *Pneuma* 15.1 (1993), pp. 61-76.
—'Tradition and the *Novum* of the Spirit: A Review of Clark Pinnock's Flame of Love', *JPT* 6.13 (1998), pp. 31-48.
Ma, Wonsuk., 'Biblical Studies in the Pentecostal Tradition: Yesterday, Today, and Tomorrow', in Murray W. Dempster *et al.* (eds.), *The Globalization of Pentecostalism* (Irvine, CA: Regnum Books, 1999)
Martin, L.R., *The Unheard Voice of God: A Pentecostal Hearing of the Book of Judges* (JPTSup 32; Blandford Forum, Dorset: UK: Deo, 2008).
McQueen, L., *Toward a Pentecostal Eschatology: Discerning the Way Forward* (JPTSup 39; Blandford Forum, Dorset, UK; Deo, 2012).
Martin, F. (ed.), *Acts* (Downers Grove, IL: InterVarsity Press, 2014).
Mayfield, A., 'Seal of the Spirit: The Sacrament of Confirmation and Pentecostal Spirit Baptism', *JPT* 25.2 (2016), pp. 222–41.
McDonnell, K. and George T. Montague, *Christian Initiation and the Baptism in the Holy Spirit: Evidence from the First Eight Centuries* (Collegeville, MN: Liturgical Press, 1991).
McDonnell, K., *The Baptism of Jesus in the Jordan: The Trinitarian and Cosmic Order of Salvation* (Collegeville, MN: The Liturgical Press, 1996).
McKenna, K. and Gwendolyn Seidman, 'You, Me, and We: Interpersonal Processes in Electronic Groups' in Yair Amichai-Hamburger (ed.), *The Social Net: Human Behavior in Cyberspace* (Oxford: Oxford University Press, 2005), pp. 191-217.

Menzies, R., *Empowered for Witness: The Spirit in Luke-Acts* (JPTSUup 6; London; New York: T&T Clark, 2004).
Migliore, D., *Faith Seeking Understanding* (Grand Rapids, MI: Eerdmans, 2014).
Moltmann, J., *Experiences of God* (Minneapolis, MN: Fortress Press, 1980).
—*The Church in the Power of the Spirit* (Minneapolis, MN: Fortress Press, 1993).
Moon, T., *From Plowboy to Pentecostal Bishop: The Life of J.H. King* (Lexington, KY: Emeth Press, 2017).
Moore, R., et al., 'Editorial', *JPT* 1 (1992), pp. 1-2.
Norris, D., *I Am: A Oneness Pentecostal Theology* (Hazelwood, MO: WAP Academic, 2009).
Oden, T., *Classic Christianity: A Systematic Theology* (New York, NY: HarperOne, 1992).
Origen, *Commentary on the Epistle to the Romans: Books 1-5* (USA: Catholic University of America Press, 2001).
Pannenberg, W., *Systematic Theology: Volume 3* (London: T&T Clark, 2004).
Pearlman, M., *Knowing the Doctrines of the Bible* (Springfield, MO: Gospel Publishing House (1937).
Pelikan, J., *Acts* (Grand Rapids, MI: Brazos Press, 2005).
Perrin, N., 'Sacraments and Sacramentality in the New Testament' in Hans Boersma and Matthew Levering (eds.), *OHST* (Oxford, U.K.: Oxford University Press, 2015), pp 52-67.
Perry, D., *Spirit Baptism: The Pentecostal Experience in Theological Focus* (Leiden: Brill, 2017).
Pinnock, C., 'A Bridge and Some Points of Growth: A Reply to Cross and Macchia', *JPT* 13 (1998), pp. 49-54.
—'Divine Relationality: A Pentecostal Contribution to the Doctrine of God', *JPT* 16 (2000), pp. 3-26.
—*Flame of Love: A Theology of the Holy Spirit* (Downers Grove, IL: InterVarsity Press, 1996).
—'The Physical Side of Being Spiritual: God's Sacramental Presence' in Anthony R. Cross and Philip E. Thompson (eds.), *Baptist Sacramentalism: Studies in Baptist History and Thought* (Volume 5) (Eugene: OR, Wipf & Stock, 2003), pp. 8-20.
Polkinghorne, J., 'Kenotic Creation and Divine Action', in *The Work of Love: Creation as Kenosis* (Grand Rapids, MI/ Cambridge, U.K: Eerdmans/SPCK, 2001), pp. 90-106.
—*Science and Theology: An Introduction* (Minneapolis, MN: Fortress Press, 1998).
—*Science and the Trinity: The Christian Encounter with Reality* (New Haven. CT: Yale University Press, 2004).
Porter, S., *The Letter to the Romans: A Linguistic and Literary Commentary* (Sheffield: Sheffield Phoenix Press, 2015).
Ranaghan, K.M., 'Rites of Initiation in Representative Pentecostal Churches in the United States, 1901-1972' (PhD dissertation, University of Notre Dame, 1974).
Reed, D., 'Oneness Pentecostalism' in Stanley M. Burgess, et al. (eds.), *DPCM* (Grand Rapids: Zondervan, 1988), pp. 644-51.
—'Oneness Pentecostalism: Problems and Possibilities for Pentecostal Theology', *JPT* 5.11 (1997), pp. 73-93.

—'Pentecostal Assemblies of the World', in Stanley M. Burgess, et al. (eds.), *DPCM* (Grand Rapids: Zondervan, 1988), pp. 700-701.

Richardson, J., *With Water and Spirit: A History of Black Apostolic Denominations in the U.S.* (Washington, DC: Spirit Press, 1980).

Robeck, C.M. and Jerry L. Sandidge, 'The Ecclesiology of *Koinonia* and Baptism: A Pentecostal Perspective', *JES* 27.3 (1990), pp. 504–34.

Rutledge, F., *Not Ashamed of the Gospel: Sermons from the Paul's Letter to the Romans* (Grand Rapids: MI, Eerdmans, 2007).

Shelton, J., *Mighty in Word & Deed: The Role of the Holy Spirit in Luke-Acts* (Peabody, MA: Hendrickson Publishers, 1987).

Schmemann, A., *For the Life of the World: Sacraments and Orthodoxy* (Crestwood: NY, SVS Press, 1973).

—*Of Water and the Spirit: A Liturgical Study of Baptism* (Crestwood, NY: SVS Press, 2000).

Shuman, J., 'Toward a Cultural-Linguistic Account of the Pentecostal Doctrine of the Baptism of the Holy Spirit', *Pneuma* 19.2 (1997), pp. 207–23.

Slay, J., *This We Believe* (Cleveland, TN: Pathway Press, 1963).

Smith, F.L., *Fundamentals of the Apostolic Faith* (The Department of Publications of the Pentecostal Assemblies of the World, Inc, 1998).

Smith, G., *Transforming Conversion: Rethinking the Language and Contours of Christian Initiation* (Grand Rapids, MI: Baker Academic, 2010).

Spittler, R., 'Suggested Areas for Further Research in Pentecostal Studies', *Pneuma* 5.2 (1983), pp. 39-56.

Stephenson, C., 'Sarah Coakley's Théologie Totale: Starting with the Holy Spirit and/or Starting with Pneumatology?', *JPT* 26.1 (2017), pp. 1-9

Stephenson, L., 'Getting Our Feet Wet: The Politics of Footwashing', *JPT* 23.2 (2014), pp. 154-70.

Stronstad, R., *The Prophethood of All Believers: A Study in Luke's Charismatic Theology* (JPTSup 16; Sheffield: Sheffield Academic Press, 1999).

Studebaker, S., *A Pentecostal Political Theology for American Renewal: Spirit of the Kingdom, Citizens of Cities* (New York: Palgrave Macmillan, 2016).

—'Baptism among Pentecostals' in Gordon L. Heath and James D. Dvorak (eds.), *Baptism: Historical, Theological, and Pastoral Perspectives* (Eugene, OR: Pickwick, 2011), pp. 201-24.

Talbert, C., *Reading Acts: A Literary and Theological Commentary* (Macon, GA: Smyth and Helwys, 2005).

Thomas, J.C. 'The Charismatic Structure of Acts', *JPT* 13.1 (2004), pp. 19-30.

—*Footwashing in John 13 and the Johannine Community* (Cleveland, TN: CPT Press, 2nd edn, 2014).

—'Footwashing Within the Context of the Lord's Supper', in Dale R. Staffer (ed.), *The Lord's Supper: Believers' Church Perspectives* (Scottsdale, PA: Herald Press, 1997), pp. 169-84.

—'Pentecostal Theology in the Twenty-First Century', *Pneuma* 20.1 (1998), pp. 3-19.

—'Reading the Bible From Within Our Traditions: A Pentecostal Hermeneutic as Test Case' in Joel Green and Max Turner (eds.), *Between Two Horizons: Spanning*

New Testament Studies and Systematic Theology (Grand Rapids, MI: Eerdmans, 2000), pp. 108-22.
—*Toward a Pentecostal Ecclesiology: The Church and the Fivefold Gospel* (Cleveland, TN: CPT Press, 2010).
—'Toward A Pentecostal Theology of Anointed Cloths', in Lee Roy Martin (ed.), *Toward a Pentecostal Theology of Worship* (Cleveland, TN: CPT Press, 2016), pp. 89-112.
—'"Where the Spirit Leads" – The Development of Pentecostal Hermeneutics', *JB&V* 30.3 (2009), pp. 289–302.
—'Women, Pentecostals and the Bible', *JPT* 5 (1994), pp. 41-56.
Tomberlin, D., 'Believers' Baptism in the Pentecostal Tradition', *TER* 67.3 (October 2015), pp. 423-35.
—*Pentecostal Sacraments: Encountering God at the Altar* (Cleveland, TN: Cherohala Press, 2019).
Tomlinson, M.A., *Basic Bible Beliefs* (Cleveland, TN: White Wing Publishing House and Press, 1961).
Treier, D., 'Theological Hermeneutics, Contemporary' in Kevin J. Vanhoozer (ed.), *DTIB* (Grand Rapids, MI: Baker Academic, 2005), pp. 787-93.
Van Cleave, N., *The Vine and the Branches: A History of the International Church of the Foursquare Gospel* (Los Angeles: ICFG Press, 1992).
Vanhoozer, K., *The Drama of Doctrine: A Canonical Linguistic Approach to Christian Theology* (Louisville, KY: Westminster John Knox Press, 2005).
Volf, M., *Exclusion and Embrace: A Theological Exploration of Identity, Otherness, and Reconciliation* (Nashville, TN: Abington Press, 1996).
von Balthasar, H.S., *The von Balthasar Reader*, Medard Kehl & Werner Löser (eds.), (New York, NY: The Crossroad Publishing Company, 1982).
Vondey, W., *Pentecostal Theology: Living the Full Gospel* (London; New York, Bloosmbury T&T Clark, 2017).
—*Pentecostalism: A Guide for the Perplexed* (London: T&T Clark, 2013).
Vondey, W. and Chris W. Green, 'Between This and That: Reality and Sacramentality in the Pentecostal Worldview', *JPT* 19.2 (2010), pp. 243–64.
Vorgrimler, H., *Sacramental Theology* (Collegeville, MN: The Order of Saint Benedict Inc., 1992).
Wainwright, G., *Doxology: The Praise of God in Worship, Doctrine, and Life* (New York, NY: Oxford University Press, 1980).
Watson, F., *Text, Church, and World: Biblical Interpretation in Theological Perspective* (Edinburgh: T&T Clark, 1994).
Wenk, M., 'The Church as Sanctified Community' in John Christopher Thomas (ed.), *Toward a Pentecostal Ecclesiology: The Church and the Fivefold Gospel* (Cleveland, TN: CPT Press, 2010), pp. 105-35.
'What We Believe Pamphlet' (Indianapolis, IN: The Department of Publications of the Pentecostal Assemblies of the World, Inc.).
Williams, J.R., *Renewal Theology: Salvation, the Holy Spirit and Christian Living* (Grand Rapids, MI: Academie, 1990).
Williams, A.R., 'Review of *Sanctifying Interpretation: Vocation, Holiness, and Scripture* by Chris E.W. Green', *JEPTA* 38.2 (2018), pp. 184-85.

Williams, A.R., 'Water Baptism in Pentecostal Perspective: A Bibliographic Evaluation', *Spiritus* 4.1 (2019), pp. 69-97.
Williams, E.S., *Systematic Theology, Volume III* (Springfield, MO: Gospel Publishing House, 1953).
Williams, R., *Being Christian: Baptism, Bible, Eucharist, Prayer* (Grand Rapids, MI: Eerdmans, 2014).
—*On Christian Theology* (Malden, MA: Blackwell Publishers, 2000).
Wilson, S.H., *A Guide to Pentecostal Movements for Lutherans* (Eugene, OR: Wipf & Stock, 2016).
—'Spiritless Lutheranism, Fatherless Pentecostalism, and a Proposed Baptismal-Christological Corrective', *Pneuma* 34.3 (2012), pp. 415-29.
—'Water Baptism and Spirit Baptism in Luke-Acts: Another Reading of the Evidence', *Pneuma* 38.4 (2016), pp. 476-501.
Witherington, B., *Paul's Letter to the Romans: A Socio-Rhetorical Commentary* (Grand Rapids, MI: Eerdmans, 2004).
Work, T., *Ain't Too Proud to Beg: Living Through the Lord's Prayer* (Grand Rapids: Eerdmans, 2007).
—*Deuteronomy* (Grand Rapids, MI: Brazos, 2009).
Yong, A., 'From Every Tribe, Language, People, and Nation: Diaspora, Hybridity, and the Coming Reign of God', in Chandler H. Im and Amos Yong (eds.), *Global Diasporas and Mission* (Eugene, OR: Wipf & Stock, 2014), pp. 253-62.
—*Renewing Christian Theology: Systematics for a Global Christianity* (Waco, TX: Baylor University Press, 2014).
—*The Spirit Poured Out on All Flesh: Pentecostalism and the Possibility of Global Theology* (Grand Rapids, MI: Baker Academic, 2005).
Yun, K.D., 'Water Baptism and Spirit Baptism: Pentecostals and Lutherans in Dialogue', *Dialog* 43.4 (2004), pp. 344-51.

Index of Biblical References

Genesis		Mark		1.4	206
1	53	1.8	240, 243	1.5	243
6-9	53	1.9-11	36, 47	1.6-2.47	199
		1.10	150, 194	2.1-47	199
Exodus		1.15	213	2.4	91, 139, 149
14.19-		10.38-39	191, 252	2.14	199
15.22	53	16.9-20	91	2.21	200
		16.16	38, 91, 92,	2.14-40	199
Job			151, 152,	2.33	206
1.1-22	68		165, 210, 213	2.37	200, 209
		16.17	38	2.37-39	235, 243
Psalm				2.37-40	175, 176,
46	157	Luke			198, 199,
88	172	2.22	60		200, 201,
		3	235		203, 205,
Isaiah		3.16	243		206, 211,
42.8	136	3.21-22	36, 47, 250		212, 213,
		7	38		214, 218,
Joel		10.17	218		219, 222,
3.1	206	12.50	91, 94, 96,		223, 224,
3.5	207		252		225, 228, 239
		18.15-17	103	2.37-41	200, 206,
Matthew		18.16	215		215, 216, 217
3.13-17	36, 47	24.25	136	2.37-42	209
3.14	38	24.49	206	2.38	38, 39, 51,
3.15	91				54, 65, 77,
3.11	204, 241, 243	John			78, 79, 91,
3.16	165, 194	1.29-33	36, 47		96, 97, 100,
3.16-17	250	1.33	38, 204, 243		124, 125,
12.40	150	3	78, 151, 283		126, 134,
20.22-23	91, 94	3.5	54, 91, 134,		138, 139,
23.19	38		140, 141,		140, 141,
24.13	268		147, 148,		146, 147,
28	77, 117, 203,		151, 152,		149, 150,
	208		165, 166, 168		159, 165,
28.19	35, 41, 55,	3.3-5	141, 149		166, 168,
	75, 106, 108,	3.3-7	159		197, 199,
	122, 138,	3.8	255		201, 202,
	139, 150,	4.24	136		203, 204,
	204, 205,	10.4	36		205, 206,
	211, 281	13.4-5	277		207, 208,
28.18-20	117				209, 210,
28.19-20	102, 103	Acts			211, 212,

	214, 217,	6.1-3	191	6.8	192, 196
	218, 219,	6.1-4	181, 183,	6.10	196
	220, 222,		186, 187	6.11	182, 196
	225, 237	6.1-5	183, 187	6.12-13	185
2.38-39	204, 212	6.1-7	53	6.15-7.6	177
2.39	204, 206,	6.1-8	180	8.9	243
	207, 213,	6.1-11	162, 175,	8.11	195
	215, 224, 225		176, 177,	8.18-25	268
2.42	91		178, 179,		
2.42-47	197		180, 181,	1 Corinthians	
8	92, 93, 112,		182, 183,	1.14	125
	209, 235		184, 185,	1.18	267
8.16	211		186, 187,	1.13-17	188
8.21	242		188, 189,	2.4	91
8.38-39	150		190, 192,	3.9	264
9	112		200, 225,	6.11	261
9.17-18	238		228, 239	7.14	266
10	112	6.1-14	177	10.1-2	53
10.38	250	6.1-15	159	10.2	91, 92
10.44-48	149, 242	6.2	190	12.13	94, 95, 96,
10.47-48	38	6.2-7	184		141, 142,
10.48	136, 140, 211	6.3	47, 128, 139,		184, 188,
11.16	234		180, 185,		193, 197,
15	171, 237		188, 193,		208, 243, 264
18	91, 92, 93		195, 241	12.12-13	264
19	20, 112, 139,	6.3-4	43, 51, 65,	12.27	264
	140, 242		77, 78, 96,	13.9-12	53
19.1-6	149		106, 124,	15.29	91, 96, 188,
19.1-7	235		125, 142,		191
19.5	94, 136, 140,		165, 168,		
	211		180, 182,	2 Corinthians	
19.5-6	208, 253		187, 202, 269	1.21-22	261
19.6	111	6.4	81, 142, 150,	3.17	241
19.11-12	19		182, 185,	3.18	255
22.16	197, 211,		187, 192,	4.5	264
	217, 219,		194, 267	5.17	196, 269
	220, 261	6.3-5	38, 108,	12.13	281
			117, 186		
Romans		6.3-6	93, 99	Galatians	
5	177	6.3-7	91, 94, 96	2.20	196
5.9	267	6.3-11	260	3.27-29	264
5.12-21	177	6.3-13	142		
5.12-8.39	177	6.5	186, 195	Ephesians	
6	93, 94, 177,	6.6	91, 185, 191	1.13-14	261
	180, 185,	6.6-7	182	2.5-6	260
	188, 190	6.7	192, 196	2.8-9	267

2.19	264	1 Thessalonians		6.2	251, 252
4.4-6	281	1.19	255	6.4	252
4.5	108, 141, 188, 268			7.16	192
		1 Timothy		9.14	192
4.22	56	4.14	265	10.22	261
5.18	225				
5.23-32	264	2 Timothy		1 Peter	
		1.6	252	2.9	264
Colossians		1.6-7	265	3	283
1.13	216, 269	3.15	173	3.20-21	53, 54, 134, 141
1.23	56	3.16	173	3.21	91, 97, 152, 197, 261, 268
2.11-13	186	Titus			
2.12	186, 187, 195	3.5	54, 152, 220, 223		
2.13	260			2 Peter	
2.12-3.11	191			1.4	91
3.1	260	Hebrews			
3.3	193, 256	6.1	251	1 John	
				5.7-8	37

INDEX OF AUTHORS

Abraham, W.J. 172
Adewuya, J.A. 177, 185, 188, 189, 190
Albrecht, D.E. 280
Alexander, K.E. 6, 16, 20, 282
Alexander, P.H. 31, 62, 80, 115, 127, 131, 154, 166,
Althouse, P. 175, 232, 262, 268, 270
Ambrose. 214
Anderson, A.H. 131
Aquinas, T. 259
Archer, K.J. 3, 16, 17, 27, 30, 33, 171, 173, 227, 247, 269, 270, 278
Archer, M.L. 20
Arrington, F.L. 19, 214
Astley, J. 23, 29, 32, 61, 114, 153, 227
Augustine. 36, 137, 191, 214, 259
Baker, J. 169, 219, 242, 276
Barrett, D. 232
Barth, K. 177, 191, 192, 215, 228, 268
Bauer, K.W. 56, 57, 58, 59, 60
Beacham, P.F. 104, 109, 110, 111
Beacham Jr., A.D. 104, 113, 114
Beasley-Murray, G. 233
Bell, E.N. 135, 136
Bernard, D.K. 206, 209, 210, 211, 213
Bloesch, D.G. 215, 216, 217, 257, 266, 275
Boellstorff, T. 29
Boersma, H. 252
Boff, C. 279
Bonhoeffer, D. 241
Braaten, C.E. 271
Childs, B.S. 172
Bridges-Johns, C. 61, 278
Britton, F.M. 88, 92, 93
Brooks, N. 104, 107, 108, 109, 114, 181
Bruner, D.F. 112, 239, 240
Brunner, E. 195, 215, 220, 257, 259
Bryman, A. 29
Bulgakov, S. 15, 240, 271
Davis, C.F. 248

Cartledge, M.J. 4, 5, 6, 9, 10, 11, 16, 20, 21, 22, 23, 24, 25, 27, 28, 61, 62, 63, 64, 65, 66, 67, 68, 70, 71, 82, 114, 115, 116, 117, 118, 119, 153, 154, 155, 156, 158, 160, 193, 248, 279
Castelo, D. 63, 246, 254, 256, 258
Chan, S. 2, 3, 4, 11, 12, 15, 185, 187, 188, 190, 216, 222, 236, 237, 240, 241, 245, 246, 253, 262, 263, 269, 270, 271
Chrysostom. 36, 137, 191
Clifton, S. 2, 233, 244, 246
Coakley, S. 62, 63, 64, 65, 71, 119, 160
Coulter, D.M. 262
Courey, D.J. 192
Cross, A.R. 221
Cyprian. 137
Cyril of Jerusalem. 188
Davis, C.F. 248
Dayton, D.W. 238
Dempster, M. 178
Duffield, G. 19, 55, 56, 57, 184, 185, 205, 206
Dunn, J.D.G. 112, 177, 211, 236
East, B. 174, 175
Ellington, S. 61
Ervin, H. 2
Fiddes, P. 249, 264
Fowl, S.E. 170
Francis, L.J. 23, 29, 32, 61, 114, 153, 227
Friesen, A.T. 244, 245
Gabriel, A.K. 2, 223, 253
Greene-McCreight, K. 173
Green, C.E.W. 4, 5, 6, 10, 11, 20, 24, 25, 26, 27, 57, 63, 109, 111, 170, 171, 172, 173, 174, 176, 185, 197, 199, 223, 225, 226, 227, 228, 233, 237, 247, 256, 257, 258, 262, 271, 279, 280, 282
Green, J.B. 170, 171, 175

Green, M. 242, 243, 252, 253, 277
Gregory of Nyssa. 36, 258
Hunter, H.D. 80, 104, 111, 112, 114, 127, 268, 277
Hayford, J.W. 54, 55, 56, 57
Haywood, G.H. 131, 132, 133, 135, 136, 137, 138, 139, 140, 142, 142, 143, 148, 149, 150, 151, 152, 153, 167, 201
Hollenweger, W.J. 32
Hummel, C.E. 236
Johns, J.D. 278
Jennings, W.J. 218
Jensen, R.J. 234, 235, 236, 241
Jenson, R.W. 4, 12, 15, 26, 194, 217, 224, 227, 233, 240, 243, 244, 259, 263, 265, 268, 271, 278
Jerome. 36
Johnson, D.R. 20
Johnson, L.T. 178, 190, 191, 194, 195,196
Johnson, T. 232
Johnson Jr., B.L. 65
Kärkkäinen, V.M. 197, 216, 217, 219, 233, 246, 247, 248, 252, 256, 257, 260, 261, 262, 263, 264, 265, 266, 267, 268, 276, 278
Kay, W. 8
Keener, C.S. 177, 199, 200, 218
King, J.H. 85, 104, 105, 107, 114, 127, 180
Kozinets, R.V. 29, 154, 155
Küng, H. 220, 222, 256
Lancaster, J. 184, 205
Land, S.J. 1, 10, 61, 197, 226, 229, 232, 238, 247, 254, 255
Leithart, P.J. 191, 196, 264, 265
Lewis, P.W. 178, 180, 200, 229
Ling, T.M. 250
Lossky, V. 240, 260
Luther, M. 192, 194, 217, 221, 265
Macchia, F.D. 1, 2, 3, 18, 83, 185, 186, 187, 190, 192, 193, 197, 206, 207, 208, 212, 217, 218, 226, 227, 232, 233, 234, 238, 244, 245, 246, 247, 249, 253, 260, 261, 269, 277
Martin, F. 1200

Martin, L.R. 18, 25, 171
Mayfield, A.R. 241
McDonnell, K. 12, 237, 238, 239, 276
McGee, G.B. 31, 62, 80, 115, 127, 131, 154, 166
McKenna, K. 154
McPherson, A.S. 31, 33, 34, 35, 37, 38, 39, 40, 43, 44, 45, 46, 48, 50, 51, 52, 80, 221, 279, 280
McQueen, L.R. 6, 16, 20, 32, 282
Menzies, R.P. 206, 207, 212
Migliore, D.L. 215, 224
Moltmann, J. 192, 196, 215, 216, 217, 266
Montague, G.T. 237, 238, 276,
Moon, T.G. 105–6
Moore, R.D. 229
Norris, D.S. 206, 211–13
Oden, T.C. 213, 214, 217
Oliverio Jr., L.W. 173
Origen. 36, 193
Pannenberg, W. 219, 265
Patton, M.Q. 65
Pearce, C. 29
Pearlman, M. 181, 182, 203
Pelikan, J. 213, 220, 221
Perrin, N. 251, 252
Perry, D. 247
Pinnock, C.H. 83, 215, 220, 221, 222, 223, 233, 239, 240, 242, 244, 248, 252, 253, 255, 256, 259, 260, 261, 264, 265, 266, 267, 268, 278
Polkinghorne, J. 258
Porter, S.E. 177, 178, 191, 194, 195
Rahner, K. 228
Reed, D.A. 131, 148, 166, 167, 242
Richardson, J.C. 131
Robeck Jr., C.M. 3, 31, 80, 233, 266, 268, 277
Rutledge, F. 195
Sandidge, J.L. 3, 266, 268, 277
Schmemann, A. 193, 194, 195, 241, 263, 264, 269
Shelton, J.B. 206, 208, 209, 212
Shuman, J.J. 246
Silverberg, J. 118
Slay, J.L. 183, 184, 204

Smith, G.T.   221
Smith, F.L.   149, 152, 153
Stephenson, L.   3, 18, 278
Stephenson, C.A.   63
Stronstad, R.   243
Studebaker, S.M.   4, 226, 247
Swoboda, A.J.   279
Synan, V.   84, 127
Talbert, C.H.   199
Tramel, T.   104, 112
Theophanes.   260
Thomas, J.C.   1, 3, 4, 8, 9, 11, 15, 16, 18, 19, 20, 25, 26, 32, 170, 171, 178, 188, 199, 200, 207, 227, 229, 230, 231, 238, 277
Tomberlin, D.   194, 214, 226, 227, 238, 261, 267, 277
Tomlinson, M.A.   182, 183, 204
Tunstall, F.G.   104, 112, 113, 114
Urshan, T.D.   133, 146, 148

V
Van Cleave, N.M.   19, 55–57, 184, 185, 205, 206

Vanhoozer, K.J.   173, 175, 233
Volf, M.   193, 196
Vondey, W.   6, 30, 227, 247, 250, 251, 264, 277
Vorgrimler, H.   259, 260
von Balthasar, H.U.   241
Waddell, R.   175
Wadholm Jr., R.   20
Wainwright, G.   236
Wenk, M.   185, 188, 190
Wesley, J.   35
Williams, A.R.   172
Williams, J.R.   2
Williams, R.   26, 230, 241
Williams E.S.   182, 203
Wilson, S.H.   221, 223, 233, 234, 235, 236, 237, 238, 243, 244
Witherington III, B.   177, 193
Work, T.   56
Yong, A.   185, 186, 189, 190, 215, 216, 222, 224, 233, 247, 248, 256, 260, 262
Yun, K.D.   236
Zizioulas, J.   12, 15

Made in the USA
Columbia, SC
13 March 2022